THE BUNGALOW

Southern California and Southern England, late 1970s.

What is remarkable is not that urbanism is so different but that it is so similar in all metropolitan centres of the world in spite of significant differences in social policy, cultural tradition, administrative and political arrangements . . . and so on.

David Harvey, *Social Justice and the City*, 1973:278

The forces that put it up are also pulling it down.

(Robert Winter; Author)

THE BUNGALOW

The production of a global culture

Anthony D King

Routledge & Kegan Paul
London, Boston, Melbourne and Henley

First published in 1984
by Routledge & Kegan Paul plc
14 Leicester Square, London WC2H 7PH, England
9 Park Street, Boston, Mass. 02108, USA
464 St Kilda Road, Melbourne,
Victoria 3004, Australia and
Broadway House, Newtown Road,
Henley-on-Thames, Oxon RG9 1EN, England
Set in Linotype Sabon by Columns of Reading
and printed in Great Britain by
Thetford Press Ltd

Library of Congress Cataloging in Publication Data

King, Anthony D.
The bungalow.
Bibliography: p.
Includes index.
1. Bungalows. I. Title.
NA7570.K56 1984   728.3'73   83-13778

ISBN: 0-7100-9538-4

Unlike Major C.S. Jarvis's *Three Deserts* (John Murray, London, 1936) this book is NOT dedicated to

'THE WOMAN WHO GOES EAST – in profound admiration of her selflessness in sharing the lot of the White Man Overseas, softening his hardships, easing his loneliness, and making of his isolated bungalow a place "that is for ever England" '

but

to

Ursula, Frances, Karen, Anna and Nina
and, in memory,
DWK, LRK

v

In the first place, Britain developed as an essential part of a global economy, and more particularly as the centre of that vast formal or informal 'empire' on which its fortunes have so largely rested. To write about this country without also saying something about the West Indies and India, about Argentina and Australia, is unreal

E.J. Hobsbawm, *Industry and Empire*, Penguin Books, Harmondsworth, 1969, p. 20.

much of what is often crucial in explaining local phenomena is extra-local in origin

J. Walton, 'Political economy of world urban systems', in J. Walton and L. Massotti (eds.), *The City in Comparative Perspective*, Wiley, New York, 1976, p. 309.

Contents

List of illustrations

Plates

viii

Figures   *page*

Preface

Few authors have the good (or bad) fortune to have advance publicity in the pages of Britain's satirical paper, *Private Eye*. Yet in April 1977 a notice appeared indicating that 'Anthony King . . . was currently writing a cultural history of the bungalow.' The announcement, culled from the end of a book review and sent in by one of their readers, was in 'Pseud's Corner', and provides a useful place to begin.

In certain circles in Britain, though not in North or South America, continental Europe, Australia, Asia, Africa or anywhere else in the world where the word can be found, the very mention of the term 'bungalow' is sufficient to raise a smile, or better, a smirk. For these essentially middle-class or bourgeois folk, there is something ridiculous, even distasteful about the word, even about the type of dwelling itself. Among a certain generation of architects and planners, or those who write on architecture, the reaction is even stronger, leading to outright condemnation. A recent book on *The Design of Suburbia* describes the square bungalow as 'one of the ugliest dwellings ever designed by man', and in a much acclaimed scholarly study of the architect R. Norman Shaw, his name was dissociated from one of his signed drawings of a 'seaside bungalow' with the comment 'the bungalow has a delightful vulgarity unexampled in Shaw's own buildings' (Saint, 1976:170).

For others, however, the bungalow is proudly displayed as a badge of their proletarian origins, part of an ' "unplanned" struggle of dwellings . . . neither quite "town" nor "country" ' which, located as it was between a working class community and a shiny New Town, created, during childhood, an awareness of town planning and, in later years, led to the development of radical views (Paris, 1982:v). Clearly, therefore, for some people, the word is taboo, fitting precisely the *Oxford Dictionary*'s definition of a shibboleth as a 'test word . . . the use of, or inability to use, betrays one's party, nationality, etc' though in this case, it is probably class.

All this would hardly be worth mentioning were it not for the fact that these attitudes are more likely to be found (though obviously, with very many exceptions) in the architecture and planning profession in Britain. That such views are held by a professional class which, whether in local government or elsewhere, exercises very considerable control over what is built, and where, is obviously of no little importance.

For example, as I drive the seven miles from the suburbs of the large industrial city where I live to friends who live on a farm, I am made very conscious of this. Until the farm is reached, there is hardly a bungalow in sight. The ring road which forms most of the journey is surrounded on both sides by fields. Strategically placed within these are tall blocks of council flats, or tidy estates of council 'semi's'. Even the privately owned houses lining the road leading out of the city are largely uninterrupted by bungalows. Only when I get to the farmer's fields is the edge of the city lined with a bungalow estate. It is a highly controlled, post-1930s *visually* planned landscape resulting from professional decisions; an ordering of buildings and people which is not just physical and spatial, but also political, and social. For the most part, the bungalow has been banned, conspicuous by its absence. The poor are not permitted to build them and if the wealthy elderly want to buy one, they probably migrate to the coast.

It is true that in recent years these professional attitudes to bungalows may have changed. In certain places, bungalows flourish, now often captured only by a wide-angled lens. In some architectural circles suburbia is fashionable and mixed development means that bungalows spring up in the grounds of overlarge Victorian suburban houses or fill in gaps which inter-war developers left behind. Economic or social criteria prevail over visual ones. Nevertheless, it is equally evident that the older attitudes persist, especially among the readers of *Private Eye*. Where do these attitudes come from? Why, amongst a small, yet influential minority, are such strong feelings aroused by what, for the majority of people, is clearly not just a very obvious and practical form of dwelling but one which an increasing number of people prefer? Although only one of this book's eight chapters attempts to answer this question, it is largely because of these attitudes that the wider significance of the bungalow, discussed in the other seven, has been overlooked.

Yet this book is not simply about the bungalow as a particular kind of suburban or country dwelling in Britain. Nor, because it is full of pictures, is it an 'architectural history' or at least not in the usual sense of that term. Rather, in investigating the origins of the bungalow in India, and its later development in Britain, North America, Australia, Africa and Europe, it is about the historical forces – economic, political, social, cultural, ideological – which, in producing the bungalow, have also shaped much of the modern world: colonialism, industrialisation, capitalism and socialism, urbanisation and suburbanisation, and the emergence of a global economy and culture. In doing this, what it attempts is to link up the local with the national, the national with the international. In short, it has three aims: to examine the historical forces producing the bungalow; to explore the meaning of the bungalow for the society where it exists; and to discuss a variety of issues which the investigation of the bungalow suggests, whether these relate to tropical housing, second homes, architectural symbolism, suburbanisation, under-development in the 'third world' or the development of a capitalist world economy and culture.

In a sense then, the book is a bit of a publisher's nightmare in that it is neither 'straight' sociology, architecture, history, geography or urban studies but uses something from them all. What it reflects are my own interests, as a sociologist-historian interested in the built environment: how this is produced, what it 'means', what effect it has on society, and how we should try and understand it. It also represents the interests of the different departments with whom I have worked in the last few years: inter-disciplinary social science, economic and social history, sociology and social anthropology, building, and recently development planning. And though the development studies perspective is not pursued throughout, it informs the chapters on India and Africa, and it is assumptions about development, inter-dependence and the global economy which ultimately provide both the justification and setting for the study.

However, I am conscious that in trying to pursue different interests, there are pitfalls: Indian studies specialists who may be interested in the transformation of domestic life in India (Chapter 1) may not be interested in suburbanisation in the United States (Chapter 4); readers interested in the development of planning in inter-war Britain (Chapter 5) may be less interested in questions of urban development and the transformation of material culture in Africa (Chapter 6). Leisure studies enthusiasts wanting to know about early second homes (Chapters 2 and 3) may be less concerned with the ideology of the 'Arts and Crafts' bungalow in America (Chapter 4) than readers in architectural history. And maybe the 'sociology readers' will be put off by the bits on architecture and some of the 'architecture' ones, by the sociology. Yet, as the chapters are relatively self-contained, perhaps people can pick and choose.

Moreover, books written over a number of years, and using perspectives from different academic disciplines – which themselves have gone through a number of paradigm shifts and sea changes during these years – also present the writer with problems of maintaining consistency, both in argument, style and conceptual framework. The book was begun in a fairly light-hearted fashion, and with a general readership in mind, in 1976, and developed from a couple of papers written some years earlier. It then became a spare-time hobby carried on between other things before, in the late 1970s, becoming a more serious study with the final chapter completed in 1982. Specialist readers will no doubt detect, both in the content and references, the influence of different schools of thought. For those brave enough to read through the whole, I can only apologise for the inconsistencies in argument which might remain. The first seven chapters contain the main 'story', which hopefully may be of interest to the general reader. The later part of the Introduction and the concluding chapter deal with the more specialist or academic issues, though not to any great depth. Some of these, and the theoretical approaches behind the book itself, have been further developed since it was finished (King, 1983b,c,d, 1984b) and some minor modifications in this text have been possible at proof stage (1983) to incorporate recently published work. One main aim of the book is to raise issues for further research.

Some chapters are heavily documented with plenty of 'proof' and most of the sources are indicated in the Bibliography. The illustrations are also included as 'evidence', yet they are also misleading in that they do not 'illustrate' the themes of the book. On the whole, they are best regarded as extra punctuation.

Other chapters, especially the last, are more in the way of speculation. I believe some of the issues raised here could be proven by studies which already exist though including further discussion would make a long book even longer. For example, Walton, writing on cities and the world economic system, has drawn attention to the interdependence between cities of the advanced capitalist states and third world markets, as well as between third world cities and production for export to metropolitan centres. Yet where this latter fact has become a central concern in research on the underdevelopment of third world societies and cities, the reverse is not true (1979:14). In short, much research on modern 'Western' cities, and historical research in particular, has too often assumed that they developed independently of a global economy. For a century or more, for people in today's 'third world cities', the urban environment has been a daily reminder of their connection to advanced economies in 'the West' (King, 1976). Yet only in recent decades have people in these 'Western' cities become aware, through the transnationalisation of labour ('immigration' and 'guest workers') of the same fact.

Other questions raised could only be clarified by further research. My object here, however, has been to suggest some ideas and approaches, especially for more comparative studies, whether undertaken over time or contemporarily, between different cultures and societies with different forms of political economy. Comparing social arrangements in Britain or the USA with those, for example, in contemporary Sweden, India, Mali, Brazil, China or the Soviet Union, suggest that people live in many different ways.

More importantly, however (and the amount of material on the bungalow itself has prohibited the requisite attention being given to this aspect here), the speculations arise from a conviction that studies of the urban environment, and no doubt many other topics, whether of a historical or contemporary nature, need pursuing from a global perspective. With the increased transnationalisation of labour and capital, there needs to be a transnationalisation of education and knowledge.

Acknowledgments

This book could never have been written without the help of many friends, both in Britain and abroad. In the first place, I owe a great debt of gratitude to my colleague at Brunel, John Burnett, and also to Colin Rosser, of the Development Planning Unit, University College, London both of whom read an earlier version of the manuscript. Their comments have been greatly appreciated.

My interest in the bungalow arose from research on colonial urban development in India. The idea of writing a specifically historical study, however, occurred only after my attention was drawn to what turned out to be the first bungalows to actually carry the name built in Britain, and probably in the Western hemisphere. For this, and innumerable other helpful items of information since, I am greatly indebted to Robert Thorne.

The chapter on North America would have been impossible without the help of Clay Lancaster of Kentucky and Bob Winter of Occidental College, California, the experts on the American bungalow. Both have very patiently answered correspondence on many occasions, generously permitted me to read the manuscripts of their books prior to publication, sent illustrations and, by commenting on my draft chapter, eliminated various howlers. My thanks are also due to sociologist, Dave Popenoe, at Rutgers University whose comments on this chapter I have also appreciated. On Australia, I am indebted to Bob Freestone (Macquarie University) and Don Johnson (Flinders University) who have helped initiate me into an understanding of Australian urban and architectural development, written detailed responses to my queries and sent photocopies and photographs of key evidence. Their comments on the Australian chapter have been of great use. That my interpretation of the facts differs from the accounts of these different scholars in no way detracts from my indebtedness to them.

Many others have given generously of both their time and expertise. I am especially grateful to friends who have read and commented on particular chapters or sections, especially Chris Bayly, Cambridge (India), Jerry Eades, Kent and Meg Peil, Birmingham (Africa) and Alison Ravetz, Leeds, on part of the English material. For other advice and information on different parts of the world, I am indebted to Kirti Chaudhuri of SOAS, Arvin Shah of Delhi, and Ranajit Guha of Sussex (India), Bob Fogelson, MIT, Pierce Lewis, Pennsylvania (North America), David Saunders and Jennifer Taylor, Sydney, Peter Newell (Australia), Tony Hopkins, Birmingham and Tony Kirk-Greene, Oxford (Africa). In many papers and fruitful conversations, Deryck Holdsworth of Toronto, Canada, provided more ideas, illustrations and information concerning Canada than I have been able to use and Roy Wolfe, also from Toronto, exchanged many papers and letters. I have also received assistance and comments from Robert Aitken, George Atkinson, Martin Banham, Gilles Barbey, Ron Brunskill, Alan Crawford, the late Jim Dyos, Jay Edwards, Adrian Forty, Herbert Hambidge, Gilbert Herbert, Phil and Jo Heywood, Vere Hole, R.S. Holmes, Alan Jackson, Rosie Llewellyn-Jones, Peter Keating, Otto Koenigsberger, Ron Lewcock, John Myerscough, Hugh Prince, Amos Rapoport, Colin Ward, John K. Walton, Tony Warnes, John Whyman, the late Clough Williams-Ellis and others, though not mentioned, to whom I am very grateful.

The Aga Khan Program for Islamic Architecture at Harvard/MIT provided an invaluable opportunity to air some of the issues raised in the last chapter with various faculty members and students in architecture, urban studies and planning at MIT; both to the organisers and especially to Rafique Keshavjee, I owe my thanks. Many of the issues I have discussed with Mike Safier, of the Development Planning Unit, University College, London and David Page who, as always, has helped in ways too numerous to mention; to both of these I am particularly grateful. More indirectly, I have benefited from the meetings and perspectives of the Research Committee on Urban and Regional Development of the International Sociological Association, the Planning History Group, Development Studies Association and, more recently, the Sociology and Environment Study Group of the British Sociological Association. Many insights have been picked up from Indian friends, both in Britain and India, and I can only apologise for grossly oversimplifying some of the issues discussed.

Any research develops in a particular historical and intellectual context. The promotion of inter-disciplinary studies was largely associated with educational expansion in the 1960s when I had the opportunity to spend five years in an inter-disciplinary social science department at the Indian Institute of Technology, Delhi. The chance to apply these approaches to the study of the built environment arose with the development of a course in sociology throughout a new, 4-year degree in building at Brunel University. That professionals responsible for actually constructing the built environment should have an understanding of what it is for, and of the social processes both affecting, and affected by, building seems obvious enough, though courses in this area only rarely give these issues any attention. Likewise, sociologists rarely have the opportunity to think about buildings as social products or the many intriguing theoretical and empirical questions concerning the relationship between the built environment and society. I am therefore very grateful to Syd Urry, erstwhile Head of the department whose imagination and enthusiasm created the degree course, for providing the academic space in which to explore new avenues of research.

The help of Mildred Archer, previously of the India Office Library, was indispensable in researching the drawings, paintings and photographs of the Western Drawings Collection there. I would also like to thank Judith Parkinson for her patience, efficiency and co-operation in typing the manuscript.

It is always a pleasure to record the help and professional skills of library staff. Here, special mention should be made of that of the University of Cambridge, where much of the empirical data was gathered, and also the Reading Room of the British Library (Lending Division), Boston Spa, where more general works were consulted, for their excellent and friendly service. In addition, I am grateful to the library staff of Brunel University, Leeds University, the Royal Institute of British Architects, the India Office, the British Library, London, the London School of Hygiene and Tropical Medicine, Australia House, the Church Missionary Society, the Royal Commonwealth Society, Liverpool Reference Library, Kent County Library, Ramsgate, Leeds City Library, Croydon Public Library and Avon County Library.

To all of the above, I owe my thanks and appreciation; needless to say, the responsibility for what follows is entirely my own.

I would also like to acknowledge the help of those institutions and individuals whose names are listed by the illustrations for their permission to reproduce them.

At Routledge & Kegan Paul, I am again indebted to Brent Curless for his patience and co-operation, as well as his professional expertise, in the design of this book and to Julia Warner for her sympathetic sub-editing. I have indicated in the Preface (p. xvi) some of the 'work contexts' in which this book was produced. Equally, if not more important, has been the domestic context of time spent at home with our growing-up daughters, all under ten when the research was begun in the early 1970s. To have lived with jokes, songs and comments about bungalows for most of one's life is an experience which everyone will be relieved to see come to an end. It is, therefore, to Frances, Karen, Anna anad Nina that this book is dedicated, with love, for their infinite patience and help. And above all, to Ursula, without whom it really would not have been produced.

The study developed from two preliminary articles in the *Architectural Association Quarterly* 1973; parts of Chapter 1 were published in two articles in *Art and Archaeology Research Papers*, 1977 and some of the ideas in Chapter 5 were initially explored at the International Sociology Association Conference, Uppsala, 1978 and subsequently published in the *International Journal of Urban and Regional Research*, 1980. Some passages of Chapters 2 and 3 were previously published in an essay on 'the social production of the vacation house' in *Buildings and Society* (1980). The details of these are given in the Bibliography. Presenting these in this more comprehensive framework will, I hope, be sufficient reason for re-publishing, in a revised version, what some readers may already have read before.

Introduction

To choose a particular dwelling form or rather, one distinguished by a particular name, as the subject for a book is, in one sense, accidental. The attraction of the bungalow is that it provides an excellent opportunity to investigate a large number of questions concerning our understanding of the built environment and the relation of that environment to society. Hence, the study has two dimensions: a 'cultural history of the bungalow' including the conditions that produced it and a discussion of various issues which the investigation of that history suggests. Readers primarily interested in the first but not the second aspect are probably best advised to skip or skim through this Introduction and start with the chapter summaries on page 9.

For the purpose of this book, a bungalow is defined as a dwelling form known by the term 'bungalow'. If this seems a Humpty Dumpty sort of definition where 'a word means just what I choose it to mean', it is because, in the three hundred years of its known history, 'bungalow' has been defined according to varying criteria. In the earliest known, seventeenth-century use of the term in India, these were explicitly geographical and cultural, and implicitly economic: the bungalow (or 'banggolo', with various spellings) was the peasant's hut of rural Bengal. Subsequently, when it came to mean a house for Europeans in India, the criteria were explicitly racial and cultural, and implicitly political. When the term and idea were transferred from India to England in the second half of the nineteenth century, the bungalow was defined in different ways. The notion that generally prevails today, that the term refers to a separate house of one storey, is far too simple. When the bungalow was first introduced, it was distinguished by its function, as a purpose-built leisure or holiday house or, at other times, by its manner of construction (prefabricated, or simply built) and sometimes by its design or structure (of one storey). On certain occasions, combining some or all of these features, or on others, utilising none of them, it was defined according to its location and use in the country, at the sea or riverside: it was a house for a particular place. Transferred to Africa, the bungalow became a house-type 'suitable for European residence in the tropics', a definition which again relies on racial or cultural and geographical criteria. In the early years of this century, as can be seen from some of the illustrations, 'bungalow' could equally describe a shack at the beach or a substantial, architect-designed, two-storey country house, though one in a particular style. In short, it expressed an idea, 'getting away from it all' and at the turn of the century, this might apply equally to the 'Bungalow Hotel' on the seafront at Weston-super-Mare in England or the 'Villa Bungalow' in the wooded outskirts of Anneberg, near Solberg in Sweden. Today in France, a bungalow can be a tent-like fibre-glass shelter for long-term vacationers; in Germany, a luxury one-storey suburban house; in Italy, a lightly built structure in the grounds of a hotel, accommodating the overflow of guests, and in Mexico or the Caribbean, a place where a 'first world' bourgeoisie spend their vacation. On other occasions, in England or the United States, it might simply refer to a style or appearance, a meaning which it can retain today. Thus, apart from such criteria as location, age and site, how is a single-storey cottage or lodge to be distinguished from a bungalow?

Such detailed questions might be regarded as trivial, until we think about the images associated with terms for dwellings and the care with which people refer to different types of house. What meanings do such terms and images have? None of the criteria suggested above indicate the variety of social meanings attached to the word 'bungalow', either in the past or even today. An American President was once described as 'bungalow-minded'; an Indian friend tells me that in Lucknow, one could once ask (in Hindi) for a 'bungalow haircut' (i.e. like that of a British sahib). It might be added that in Swansea (Wales), so I am told, 'Dai Bungalow' is the fellow 'with nothing upstairs'.

Notions that 'a cottage is a little house in the country but a bungalow is a little country house' (England, 1891) or that a bungalow is 'a house that looks as though it was built for less money than it actually cost' (United States, 1911) are not included in dictionaries. It is because of these images that this study pays as much attention to the term 'bungalow' and the meanings attached to it as to the reality it describes. Although more attention might have been devoted to exploring the 'functional', social and geographical predecessors of the bungalow in, for example, the idea of the mass, purpose-built vacation house, 'tropical houses' for Europeans, specialised accommodation (and locations) for the elderly, second homes and so on, it has not been the intention, for obvious reasons, to discuss the 'architectural' predecessors in the form of single-storey dwellings.

To give a simple definition indicating what the term 'means', therefore, is not easy. In practice, in Europe and North America until the advent of the 'semi-detached' bungalow, the term referred to a separate or detached dwelling, sometimes with a verandah, generally occupied by one household or family and located on its own plot. Only from the early twentieth century, and outside Asia and Africa, has the term usually been restricted to dwellings principally on one storey.

It is, however, the various themes suggested by these meanings with which this study is concerned: the social and political symbolism of building and architecture, the influence of economy and culture on dwelling form and of dwelling form on economy and culture, the role of housing, whether seen as shelter or property, in the transformation of economic life and material culture in India and Africa, and others discussed in more detail below.

Yet apart from these more academic issues, there are at least three reasons which justify a study of the bungalow in its own right. Firstly, it is a dwelling type – possibly the only one – which, both in form and name, can almost certainly be found in every continent of the world.* Where every language has its own set of terms to describe different forms of dwelling, 'bungalow' has been accepted into the principal world languages and also many more. It has been used, sometimes much more in the past than it is today, throughout the English-speaking world (the United States, Canada, Australasia, the United Kingdom, South Africa) as well as in ex-colonial or Commonwealth countries. Listed in standard dictionaries as a word of foreign origin, it has been incorporated into French, German, Arabic, Spanish, Portuguese, Italian, Turkish, Dutch, Swedish, Norwegian, Danish, Japanese, Polish, Rumanian, Czech, Thai – even in Serbo-Croat – and possibly other languages.

Its existence in these societies, either in the past or today, to describe a particular type of dwelling (usually of one storey), used temporarily for leisure or vacation purposes or for permanent suburban living, is an example of a trend best described by David Harvey: 'what is remarkable is not that urbanism is so different but that it is so similar in all metropolitan centres of the world in spite of significant differences in social policy, cultural tradition,

---

* The name and form of 'villa' is also found in many European languages but is probably less widespread, and hardly exists in India.

administrative and political arrangements, institutions and laws, and so on.' Why this is so, according to Harvey, is that the conditions in the economic base of capitalist society, together with the technology which it has produced, put 'an unmistakable stamp upon the qualitative attributes of urbanism in all economically advanced capitalist nations' (1973:278).

One of the main tasks of this study, therefore, is to try to explain how both the term and the phenomenon came to exist on a global scale and to assess what the meaning and significance of this is. This will be taken up later in the Introduction.

The second reason results from the significance of the bungalow as a distinctive form of dwelling and property. Whilst there are literally dozens of terms for dwellings in Britain, each describing a distinctive kind of building (from the single-fronted detached house and mews cottage to the through terrace and mansion flat), accommodation is conventionally divided – by the Building Societies Association, for example – into six basic categories: bungalows, detached, semi-detached and terraced houses, and purpose-built or converted flats. Official government statistics also distinguish 'maisonettes'.

Other countries obviously have different dwelling types with different names to describe them, and identifying the criteria, whether physical, social, cultural or other, by which dwellings are known provides interesting insights into their society and culture. For example, why, and with what social significance, is a dwelling called a 'single family house (or home)' in the United States but a 'detached house' in Britain, or a 'duplex', a 'semi'? Why do Germans refer to a 'Mehrfamilienhaus' ('multi-family house') rather than a 'block of flats'? Most modern industrial societies, whether capitalist or socialist, have multi-household forms of accommodation, built in a number of storeys, whether described as flats, apartments, Etagenwohnungen or something else; or, if in a continuous line, as terrace or row housing; or, if in twos, as a semi-detached, duplex, Doppelhaus; or, if a villa, single family house, or whatever. And this is without mentioning the myriad types of physically 'collective' house forms in 'non-Western' societies, if that ethnocentric term can be excused (see also King, 1982a).

In this context, therefore, the significance of the bungalow, understood as a separate, single-storey, single-household dwelling is that, in contrast to these multi-household forms, it is a form of dwelling, usually owned by its inhabitants, with no one living above, at the side or below. It is also a 'modern' form of dwelling for a 'Western type' nuclear family, or in some cases only one generation of it, in contrast to the more 'traditional' dwelling forms associated with the extended or joint family.

All this may seem very obvious. Yet whilst much has been written, both in Britain and other free market societies, about changes in different types of tenure over the years, and many people are aware that, in England, owner-occupiers have increased from under 10 to 59 per cent since 1914, whilst 'private' renters have decreased from almost 90 to 12 per cent, there has been much less discussion on the changing distribution of households over time between different *types* of dwelling (terrace, semi-detached, bungalow, flats, etc.), although some interesting studies have been recently published (Agnew, 1981; N. Duncan, 1981; Kemeny, 1981). The economic, social, political and not least, land-use significance of these trends can be seen especially in comparison to both Australian and American experience discussed in this book. The question is explored in the final chapter.

Finally, despite the fact that the bungalow is known in many parts of the world and, in Britain, is one of the most popular dwelling types whose numbers are constantly increasing, there is no comprehensive history of its development. Only in North America and Australia, does it attract increasing attention (Chase, 1981; Downing and Flemming, 1981; Downing,

1982; Flemming, 1981; Johnson, 1980; Lancaster, 1958; Ricci, 1979; Winter, 1980, Harmon, 1983; Holdsworth, 1981, 1982; Wright, 1981).

The reasons for its neglect as a topic of research would seem to stem directly from the attitudes suggested in the Preface, and prompt a number of questions (King, 1980a:7). Who undertakes research into particular topics and what values and parameters govern both the choice of that research and the way it is carried out?

To take only the British experience, it would, for example, be possible to list a large number of books on urbanisation, housing, architecture or planning where some discussion of the bungalow as a separate and socially significant form of dwelling might be expected: yet for whatever reasons, there is little or no mention of it. For example, in studies of the housing system (Murie, Niner and Watson, 1976), building in Britain between the wars (Richardson and Aldcroft, 1968), the development of pre-fabrication (Herbert, 1978), 'Arts and Crafts' architecture (Davey, 1980), Pevsner's surveys of the buildings of England, suburban development (Oliver, Davis and Bentley, 1981; Thompson, 1982), there is practically no reference to the bungalow. Its role in the historical development of mass vacation or second homes, or in the emergence of specialised housing for the elderly, has also been neglected. In the official statistics of the General Household Survey, no distinction is generally made (except for local authority housing), between bungalows and other detached housing (*Social Trends*, 1981). Only in urban geography and social policy studies does the existence of the bungalow seem to have been acknowledged (Carter, 1981; Karn, 1977).

The most plausible explanation for what is apparently a conscious decision either to ignore or, if recognising, to disparage it, would seem to be in the class attitudes towards the bungalow developed in Britain between the wars and which have persisted since then.

Over the last decade or so, the attitudes described above have changed. In this context, some of the arguments stated here, first explored some ten years ago (King, 1973), are now dated. The suburban experience, the anathema of inter- and post-war architects and planners, has been reassessed, largely as a result of a public revolt against professional control. Peter Willmott has drawn attention to his own defence of the suburb in the 1950s and 1960s (1982:13) and other architectural writers have taken a specifically proselytising stance in favour of suburban housing (Cowburn, 1966; Oliver et al., 1981). From the early 1970s, an increasing number of studies in urban and housing history have adopted an objective rather than normative approach to these issues (e.g. Burnett, 1978, Jackson, 1973).

Equally important have been changes in attitudes to housing and architectural standards in Britain not unconnected with developments in the 'third world'. Terms such as 'self-build' have been introduced into the British housing vocabulary, legitimising alternative solutions to housing problems, previously impeded by the rigid application of professional criteria. Here, the writings of John Turner, Colin Ward and others have been important. Yet even acknowledging these changes, the persecution of the bungalow persists (*The Times*, 24.10.1981:7) (p. 178).

The framework

Although a lengthy discussion of the 'intellectual genealogy' of the study is hardly warranted, some comments on the theoretical background might be made. These are offered simply as an indication of 'influences' rather than as any contribution to a serious debate. Basically, the book draws on three sets of literature: the study of buildings and house forms as products of society and culture, the political economy of urbanisation, and studies of urbanisation and the world economy.

In recent years, a number of books have appeared which, focussing on specific types of building or environment, have aimed to demonstrate what might be called the 'social production of the built environment', investigating the way in which particular kinds of economy, or modes of production, and the ideologies with which they are associated, first give rise to distinctive institutions and activities which, in turn, become embodied in urban and architectural forms (Evans, 1982; King, ed. 1980a; Hayden, 1976, 1981; Mellossi and Pavarini, 1982). Without arguing for a kind of architectural determinism, how far these forms then help to maintain social and cultural forms, whether by structuring people's perceptions and images and suggesting, for example, what type of housing they might choose or what treatment might be appropriate for society's deviants (whether law-breakers or the mentally ill), or in other ways, is a continuing source of controversy. Does the existence of the actual prison or asylum predispose people to use it? Does the existence of particular types and styles of housing suggest to people what they would like to have, or how they would like to invest their surplus wealth? Many people would say a qualified 'yes' to both these questions. Despite statements to the contrary (Pahl, 1975:188), it seems likely that buildings, and the social meaning attached to them, do have effects on people's behaviour, especially when seen in a long-term historical perspective. They are part of a process of social reproduction.

Other scholars, perhaps paying less attention to the social relations and processes in themselves, have none the less demonstrated the relationship between economy, social organisation and the actual buildings and environments which result. In Britain, as one example of the development of a modern, industrial, capitalist society, there are studies of the prison, hospital, factory, asylum, workhouse as well as distinctive forms of accommodation such as working, middle and upper class housing, the semi-detached and terraced house, multi-storey flats and housing estates. In general, these studies differ in respect to the amount of attention each devotes to the economic, political and social phenomena on one hand – the institutions, productive forces, activities, values, beliefs, ideologies – and the resulting physical, spatial and architectural forms on the other. In addition, there is a substantial body of literature relating the forms of towns and cities to the economy and society which produced them (e.g. Abrams and Wrigley, 1978).

The comparisons which are made in these studies are often of an economic and social kind, within one geographically defined society differentiated according to income, class and region: thus, we have studies of 'working', 'middle' and 'upper class' housing in England, Scotland or Wales.

In recent years, many people have become interested in two other dimensions of comparison, the 'cultural' understood in the 'anthropological' sense (and represented, for example, by the work of Amos Rapoport) and the form of political economy, whether capitalist, socialist, colonial, 'mixed economy' and so on (for example, the work of Manuel Castells, David Harvey and the 'new urban studies'). For example, grossly to oversimplify, whilst the British observer may be interested in knowing what distinguishes the average 'middle' from the average 'working class' house in industrialised England (ignoring regional and other variations) at any one time, the one from France or Italy may be more interested in knowing, firstly, what is common to *all* English housing forms and also, how such housing differs (whether in physical form or tenure, and with what consequences) both in general and at particular social levels from housing in her or his own society.

Moreover, though French culture and experience may be different from that of England, both societies share a common European and Christian-Judaic tradition and have a more or less comparable industrial and free market economy. How would one go about explaining English forms of housing when compared, for example, to those of a Hindu village cultivator in India, a Hausa chief in Benin or a Yemeni Arab nomad?

Secondly, were our observer from Cuba, East Germany or the Soviet Union, it is also obvious (as it was to Engels, visiting Manchester in 1845) that cities, as well as the houses and buildings they contain, result not just from 'industrialisation' and a particular English cultural tradition, but also from specific class relations and economic processes in the historical development of capitalism.

Much of recent work in the study of urbanism has been concerned with questions related to these, even though it has often been pursued in different academic 'camps', with some scholars concentrating on the economic, social and ideological issues and others, on the more visible, tangible form that cities and buildings take. Yet explaining the built environment, even of otherwise comparable 'industrial' societies primarily by reference to either 'culture' or 'political economy' is also too simple. For example, the notion that the preference for physically separate, single-family houses in the United States results primarily, or solely, from some 'cultural ideal' of privacy, family-centredness or the like is seen as naive. Such an explanation 'not only fails to deal with supply factors, it misrepresents the basis of demand' and obscures the social, ideological, political and economic factors which underly demand (N. Duncan, 1981:102).

Similarly, explanations of the shape and form of cities and buildings simply in general terms as resulting from 'the mode of production' or the 'logic of capitalism' are equally vague (ibid.:103). None the less, one of the major outcomes of the 'new urban studies' of the 1970s has been well stated by M.P. Smith. In much of the earlier writing on urban society, he writes,

> urbanisation is often confused with capitalism. The effects of capitalist economic development are often mistaken for effects of urbanisation. . . . The concentration of the working population in large cities is itself a consequence of the economic necessities of capitalism at a particular point in its historical development (1980:235).

Contemporary programmes of socialist village development in Tanzania, or studies of urbanisation and planning in the Soviet Union, obviously bring out the relevance of these comments. The reasons for the difference between modern Soviet cities where planners have 'in all cases' had a preference for multi-family, and state-owned, apartment houses (Jensen, 1976:34; White, 1980) and the privately owned, separate family dwelling houses of the United States are fairly obvious. Hence, it is with reference to some of the insights of these new 'political economy' approaches that this book is written.

The main characteristics of the 'new urban studies' were usefully summarised some years ago. Though subsequently re-examined (e.g. Walton, 1979; Saunders, 1981), they included

  (i) examining the larger social, economic, political context of cities;
 (ii) using an historical perspective to study urban problems and phenomena, meaning a strong emphasis on the process of social change over time in urban sytems; and
(iii) exploring the critical role of the economic system in shaping the nature of urban systems.

More specifically, a fundamental assumption underlying these approaches is that 'a given element of an urban system cannot be properly isolated as a separate object of study, meaning it cannot appropriately be removed from the economic, social and historical context of which it is inextricably a part' (Aiken and Castells, 1977:7).

Although these comments apply particularly to 'cities as a whole', they are equally applicable to elements in them, including distinctive forms of housing and the social and economic forms they represent and contain. It is perhaps of more than incidental interest that one of the most well-known analyses of the ecological zones of the city, produced by Chicago sociologist, E.W. Burgess, in 1925, included in the 'Commuters Zone' a 'Bungalow Section'.

By tracing the development of the bungalow in the very different historical contexts of pre-capitalist, pre-industrial India, of capitalist, industrial England, and of the United States and Australia in the twentieth century, and by examining the economic and political conditions in which it was introduced into West Africa, with its own peasant economy and forms of shelter and settlement, the study aims to be both explicitly and implicitly comparative, and in this way, to cast some light on the issues discussed above.

Urbanisation on a global scale

As earlier suggested, the most significant fact about the bungalow is that the term, the ideology it represents and the reality in which that ideology is expressed can be found in many quarters of the globe. It is a physical, but also an economic, social and cultural phenomenon.

A context, or framework is therefore needed to understand this fact and here, perhaps the most suggestive is offered by the writings of Wallerstein and others on the 'world system' (Wallerstein, 1974; 1979; Brockway, 1979). Though the theory and ideas of these have not been systematically used, they provide a useful perspective.

Wallerstein defines the world economy as 'a single division of labour within which are located multiple cultures' (1979:159). His major task has been to trace the development of the capitalist world economy since the sixteenth century when its elements were first established in Europe. What he makes clear is that the present global economy emerged not simply from 'the expansion of Europe' but from 'the expansion of the capitalist mode of production' (1976:30).

Although the scale and nature of world urbanisation has frequently been recognised, the way in which its specific patterns and forms (including the migration and transportation of peoples) have been affected by this emerging capitalist system are now being increasingly explored (Walton, 1976). Other studies have, for example, drawn attention to the links between industrial urbanisation in Britain and urban and regional underdevelopment in Latin America (Roberts, 1978; Browning and Roberts, 1980), between West African urbanisation and industrialisation in Europe (Mabogunje, 1980), the role of specifically colonial cities in the development of global urbanisation (Ross and Telkamp, 1984; also Harvey, 1973:228) and the internationalisation of labour and capital (Walton and Portes, 1981). However, where much of this work has concentrated on political and economic processes, the material and cultural expression of these has only occasionally been mentioned.

Some of the deeper insights have been suggested by Hobsbawm who, for example, notes that the term 'world economy' was already in use in 1880 when the phenomena it described were making for 'an international standardisation which goes beyond the purely economic and technological.'

The railroads, telegraphs and ships of 1870 were not less recognizable as international 'models' wherever they occurred than the automobiles and airports of 1970. What hardly occurred then was the international, and interlinguistic standardisation of culture which distributes, with at best a slight time-lag, the same films, popular music styles, television programmes and indeed styles of living across the world. . . . The 'models' of the developed world were copied by the more backward in the handful of dominant versions – the English throughout the Empire, in the United States and to a much smaller extent, on the European continent, the French in Latin America. . . . A certain common visual style . . . could be discerned (1975:65).

The setting for this 'common culture' was the transfer of a physical and spatial environment, the forms and images of dwellings and cities in which everyday life was to be increasingly contained. Some attention has been paid to the transplantation of these forms in earlier work and, especially, the role of urban planning in this process (King, 1976, 1980c); the way in which planning ideas and mechanisms were diffused throughout Europe and North America has also been explored (Sutcliffe, 1981). Yet in addition to the ideas and images, people, capital, material, technology and institutions were also moved around, to create the cosmopolitan urbanism of today. It might seem an obtuse example on which to conclude, but the abandonment by middle class couples of depressed industrial cities in Britain to bungalow resorts on the coast, partly 'to escape' from what are euphemistically called 'ethnic minorities' (Law and Warnes, 1980), are facts to be understood within a global, not local or national framework.

The book, therefore, is not simply a study of 'diffusion', implying the spread of a phenomenon from one continent to another, but an exploratory attempt – the full investigation of which would require data of a much more comprehensive kind – to suggest the emergence of an ever-expanding capitalist world economy in which a particular type of individual, and consumer-oriented urban development, represented by the bungalow, has developed.

A note on organisation

As hinted in the preface, the book began as a popular social history. Chapters 1-3, drafted in 1976, are therefore mainly descriptive with more attention being given to explanation in the later part of the book. The important questions of 'Westernisation' or 'bourgeoisification' of Indian urban life with which the first chapter concludes are, therefore, only hinted at, though I return to this problem in Chapter 6 on Africa. Obviously, such large issues can hardly be treated seriously in a book of this nature; none the less, they should prompt some further research.

The seven main chapters are ordered geographically, and chronologically, roughly according to the development and appearance of the bungalow in different regions of the world. Although each chapter pursues particular themes, described below, the major issues on which the study focusses are these:

(1) large-scale suburbanisation, both historical and contemporary;
(2) the phenomenon of 'dual residence' or the 'second home', whether conceived geographically as 'seasonal suburbanisation' or economically, in terms of property ownership and the accumulation of capital; this also relates to resort development;

(3) the relationship between capitalism, as an economic and political system, property ownership and the expression of this in the built environment as particular dwelling and settlement types;

(4) the global scale of economic, social, political and cultural processes affecting urban and residential forms.

The choice of themes pursued has to a considerable extent been influenced by the type of material available and in some cases, issues raised in one chapter could equally be pursued in others; similarly, explanations for the development of the bungalow in one country could also apply to others. Though each chapter can be read separately, in putting them all together there is a hope that the whole will be seen as larger than the sum of the parts.

Chapters: themes and content

A summary of the themes and content is given at the beginning of each chapter. For readers only wanting to read some, all the summaries are given below.

Chapter 1: India 1600–1980
European expansion in Asia was a major stage in the development of capitalism on a global scale. Against this background, the chapter discusses evidence relating to a Bengali peasant dwelling known as a 'banggolo' and the way in which this was adapted and adopted by the European community in India. In doing so, it focusses on the relation between economy, culture, social organisation and dwelling form.

Related to this is the second theme, of how economic and political change gives rise to distinctive building and urban forms. With the growth of industry and capitalism in Britain, and the exploitation of colonies abroad, the bungalow – and the architecture in which it is expressed – becomes a symbol of the new imperial power.

Finally, the chapter explores the way in which architecture and urban form not only result from social change but also help to bring it about. It examines the process by which traditional Indian culture and the dwellings in which it was contained were influenced and transformed by an international market economy and the influence of European lifestyles and ideas.

Chapter 2: Britain, 1750–1890
The contribution of mercantile profits from India to the genesis of the Industrial Revolution in Britain provides the background for tracing the introduction of the bungalow, as a purpose-built leisure or holiday dwelling, into England. The first theme of this chapter concerns the connection between industrialisation, the accumulation of surplus capital and the specialisation of building form.

The second theme is an exploration of the way in which the values, beliefs and activities of a society, as well as its social structure, are reproduced in the built environment. The first bungalows and their urban setting were the products of a society increasingly divided, both socially and spatially, according to class.

Chapter 3: Britain, 1890–1914
In this period, the bungalow was developed as a specialised dwelling form for country and

outer suburban use. Its introduction at this time suggests the first theme: the changing use of rural land, from one of production (for agriculture) to that of consumption (for recreation) as it became subject to the influence of the world economy and an increasingly international division of labour.

The second theme, touched on in Chapter 1, concerns the symbolic meaning of architecture. As the bungalow was, by definition, simply constructed, of one storey, and physically distanced from city and town, it acted as a metaphor for various social and intellectual trends at the turn of the century – the revolt against convention and a search for alternative lifestyles by a growing bourgeoisie.

Finally in this period, whether in Britain, Australia or the United States, the bungalow became a prototype for the modern concept of the mass vacation or holiday house. Inherent in this development were technological changes, both in transport and the prefabrication of building, which encouraged this social and environmental change.

Chapter 4: North America 1880–1980

The chapter examines the introduction of the bungalow into North America, first as a vacation house (and apparently linked to the fluctuations of investment in the Atlantic economy) and then, in the form of the 'California bungalow', as a purpose-built dwelling produced by, and helping to produce, large-scale suburbanisation. In both these contexts, the first theme is the relation of ideology to architecture: how do social and intellectual beliefs mould the dwellings and landscapes in which people live? The second theme explores the relation between dwelling and settlement forms, and particularly, the 'suburban sprawl' which technology, cheap energy and the free play of market forces brought about.

The final theme considered is the role of the bungalow in America in the emergence of modern architectural design.

Chapter 5: Britain, 1918–1980

As world developments in agriculture brought depressed land and farm prices in Britain, now an industrial nation largely dependent on overseas food, rapid urbanisation occurred in rural areas. With extensive growth in home and car ownership, and a parallel fall in household size, the bungalow was a prominent feature in this 'urbanisation of the countryside', which traditional class interests attempted to control.

In this chapter, the main themes are the influence of economic, technological and especially demographic change on the built environment and the way in which changes in that environment give rise to new institutions and ideas. It explores the question of control over the aesthetic quality of that environment, highlighting the conflict of interest between people with different ideas and the power to carry them out.

Chapter 6: Africa 1880–1980

The changing position of Britain in the late nineteenth-century world economy, vis-à-vis other industrialising powers, caused her to turn her attention to 'under-developed' areas of the world both as sources of raw materials and as providing new markets for her goods.

The bungalow, defined in this chapter as a dwelling suitable for European occupation, was introduced into Africa in the last years of the nineteenth century as part of the new colonial urban and residential forms as a basically peasant economy was incorporated into the metropolitan, and world capitalist economy. The main theme of this chapter, then, is the transfer of norms, standards and domestic lifestyles from Europe to Africa, as part of the colonial process, and the relevance of this for present day economic and social development.

A second theme, only partly explored, is the history of 'tropical architecture' for Europeans and its significance for understanding social and cultural change.

Chapter 7: Australia 1788–1980

The case of Australia is useful as a 'control group' to test some of the propositions advanced earlier. As Australia was, for much of its history, a dependent economy and society, bound by political, economic and cultural ties to Britain, it provides a useful context to examine the various influences, whether social, cultural or of the larger political economy, on housing and urban form and in turn, of these on society. Departing from the criteria used to define the bungalow in earlier parts of the study, this chapter attempts to explain why the typical Australian dwelling has, from the nation's beginning in 1788, generally been a 'bungalow' in form (i.e. single-family, single-storey, detached house on its own plot) if not in name. Also discussed are the various influences on, and explanations for the so-called 'tropical bungalow' in Queensland. Some of the forces affecting early Australian dwelling forms are also considered, as also the introduction of the named bungalow into the continent.

Finally, the chapter looks at two imported 'design ideologies' which helped to transform Australian cities and increase the value of suburban land in the early decades of the twentieth century: 'town planning' and 'garden city' ideas from Britain and the 'California bungalow' from the United States.

Chapter 8: Speculations

This final chapter speculates on a number of issues which the investigation has suggested, for example, about the way in which different societies, whether capitalist, socialist, 'mixed-economy' or others, have responded to the phenomenon of 'urbanism'. In some ways connected to this is the relationship between different types of dwelling and different kinds of tenure: does socialism mean that city people live in state-owned apartment houses, and capitalism that they live in privately owned houses or bungalows in sprawling suburbs? Is it only the difference in the availability of land which has made the twentieth-century suburban experience of Britain so different from that of Australia or the United States? This question raises the issue of professional and class control over urban development and planning.

Over the last century, the idea of the 'second home' has gradually taken root. With increases in leisure, 'time-sharing' and international tourism, the importance of this phenomenon for future urbanisation is explored. The bungalow as 'tropical house' focusses attention on the way in which urban standards and institutions of 'the West' help to incorporate developing nations into the international market economy. Finally, the chapter explores the larger meaning of the bungalow for understanding urbanisation and development, whether at the local or global scale.

A note on sources and fieldwork

The Bibliography indicates the more important secondary sources on which I have drawn as well as many, though not all, of the primary ones. For the early history in India, information comes from travel literature, historical ethnographies, accounts of British social life and some official government publications. By far the greatest source of information has been the collection of paintings, drawings and photographs from the Western Drawings Collection of the India Office Library, London. For much of the remainder of the study, building, architecture and planning material has been consulted, supplemented, in the case of the United States and Australia, by the writings of Clay Lancaster, Robert Winter, Don Johnson and others indicated in the Bibliography. Fairly lengthy correspondence has been exchanged with these and other scholars and this is referred to in the acknowledgments and notes to the chapters.

According to Robert Winter, there were hundreds of bungalow books published in the United States in the earlier decades of this century, many of them consisting of designs and plans. In Britain, there were certainly a few dozen, irrespective of the annual Daily Mail *Book of Bungalows*. As these titles are far too many to list, I have only included in the bibliography those from which I have quoted, and only the important sources of information are referenced.

Novels, poems and popular songs have also been very useful and, like other researchers, I have discovered the value of picture postcards. On a subject like the bungalow, however, material is picked up from newspapers, TV and radio almost every week.

Any research on the built environment depends on fieldwork. This has been undertaken in a fairly painless way, and in both a systematic and haphazard fashion. Much of it is absorbed as part of everyday experience determined, as sociologists would say, by the stage in one's lifecycle.

We lived in India for five years in what my Indian friends called a bungalow (though this was usually spelt 'banglow' which, in an initial ethnocentricism which I shudder to recollect, I used to maintain was 'wrongly spelt'). It was a brand-new, two-storey, flat-roofed house on a campus – but it was detached. The significance of this may be realised at the end of the first chapter. But these years also included first-hand acquaintance with the older variety of bungalow in its various settings – civil lines, hill station, cantonment, as well as the capital of New Delhi and innumerable Public Works Department and dak bungalows, as well, of course, as more indigenous Indian dwellings in towns, cities and villages.

Subsequently, living in London and later, in Cambridge and Leeds, like many other parents with young children in Britain (though perhaps with some extra motivation), our experience included visits to friends and the seaside on the south, east and west coasts: Sussex, Hampshire, Kent, Yorkshire, Lincolnshire, Norfolk, Suffolk, Essex, Lancashire, as well as in Scotland and Wales and considerable car mileage in countryside areas in between. En route to France, or at other times, visits have been made to Birchington and Westgate in Kent (about 30 minutes drive from the Hovercraft Port at Ramsgate) and Dorman's Park, Surrey, the sites of the earliest bungalow settlements in England (and Europe). Travelling in Germany, France or Switzerland, other information has been picked up, supplemented by friends met at conferences. In North America, generous and tolerant hosts have driven me miles round older inner, as well as new outer suburbs: Lindy Biggs, in Cambridge, Mass., Deryck Holdsworth, in Toronto, Canada and Clay Lancaster, in Lexington and other Kentucky towns.

Living in the suburbs of a large industrial city with three-quarters of a million inhabitants has provided the opportunity to notice, if not to explore, the bungalow phenomenon both in the early electric tram and automobile phases of suburban expansion as well as in contemporary developments. Finally, commuting by train, occasionally by car, between Yorkshire and London for some years, and on the underground between King's Cross and Brunel University at Uxbridge (near Heathrow), has provided me – almost subconsciously – with additional insights into the urban morphology of London and the role of the bungalow within the larger 'urban field'.

Since this manuscript was completed, our six-person household has moved one mile further into the inner suburbs of the city from our previous house to The Bungalow on plate 50 – eight minutes from the station and motorway and, like the first bungalows to be built in Britain, about two hours by train from London.* The move was prompted by various factors which, surprisingly, had little to do with this book: one of them is the 23-foot billiard room which makes a useful 'enterprise zone'.

---

* and in regard to other places mentioned in the text, 9 hours by air from Los Angeles, 11 from Lagos and about 12 from Lahore.

Chapter 1

India 1600-1980*

There should be a bangla – magical, spacious, beautiful –
  Where the whole family stays.
House of gold and railing of sandalwood,
  Very beautiful and close to my heart.
So high, it is like a star in the sky,
  So our son could swing on a rainbow.
The blessings of the Goddess of Wealth, Lakshmi,
  That all their wishes may be fulfilled.

K.S. Saigal, 'Ek Bangla Bane Nyara' Hindi popular song (India)
Mid twentieth century (translated, Anu Kapur)

Introduction

The bungalow, both in name and form, originated in India, a fact more easily recognised since the creation of *Bangladesh*. Yet though the name was given by India – from the Hindi or Mahratti *Bangla*, meaning 'of or belonging to Bengal' (H-J)* – the dwelling it came to describe was primarily European. In the first period of its development, the era of mercantile capitalism of the seventeenth century, the bungalow was a product of cultures in contact, an indigenous mode of shelter adopted and adapted for Europeans living in India.

In tracing these and later developments, this chapter pursues three themes. The first concerns the influence of economy, or mode of production, and social organisation on building form: it shows how the simple hut of the Bengal peasant was transformed to meet the requirements of a European commercial and governing class. The Anglo-Indian bungalow which resulted was a product of the cultural and social expectations of its new inhabitants.

The second theme, related to the first, shows how economic and political change gives rise to distinctive buildings and urban forms. With the growth of industry and capitalism in nineteenth-century Britain and the exploitation of colonies abroad, the bungalow in India became a symbol of new imperial power.

Finally, the chapter looks at the way in which architecture and urban form not only result from social and cultural change but also help to bring it about. It examines the process by which traditional Indian ways of life and the dwellings in which they were contained, were transformed by an international market economy and the influence of European lifestyles and ideas.

---

* H-J Hobson-Jobson (H. Yule and A.C. Burnell, *Hobson-Jobson. A Glossary of Colloquial Anglo-Indian Words and Phrases*, Murray, London, 1903, under 'bungalow'. The glossary gives some twenty sources of the term between the seventeenth and nineteenth centuries.

14

Bengal origins, 1600-1757

The context: European settlement in India

The arrival of Vasco da Gama on the southwest coast of India in 1498 marked the beginning of a century-long Portuguese monopoly of the spice trade, the pursuit of which was the stimulus for European interest in Asia. The rise of this trade was to give a whole new dimension to economic activities on a global scale: as Chaudhuri points out, European trade with Asia was part of a much larger movement of expansion, responsible for forging entirely new forms of economic ties between Europe and the areas peripheral to it. It was also part of the steady growth in commercial capitalism which was to have repercussions on a world scale. The products of Indian land and labour, raw cotton converted into cloth, ended up on the slave plantations of America and the West Indies, producing tobacco and sugar for Europe, just as the silver reales from the mints of Mexico City found their way into the major trading towns of India and China (Chaudhuri, 1978:7-10).

These economic changes were to bring cultural changes, also on a world scale. Though these were only to occur at a mass level with industrialisation, colonialism and the maturing of the world economy from the late nineteenth century, it is the beginnings of this system with which we start.

The Portuguese monopoly was broken at the end of the sixteenth century by the Dutch and, subsequently, by the British, Danes, Swedes and French, all of whom were to establish trading posts in India. The earliest architectural manifestations of this trade were the so-called 'factories', a term used to describe both the trading settlement itself as well as the building (factory-house) in which its activities were pursued. The grounds of a factory, situated on an enclave of land granted as a concession from the local ruler, formed a 'compound', an enclosed and generally fortified place of territory.

Dutch commercial interests were focussed less on India than elsewhere in the East Indies. Yet because of their superior sea and military power, the English, whose East India Company had been founded in 1600, were obliged to accept a minor role in the East Indies and settled on India as 'second best' (Spear, 1965:66).

The earliest of the Company's factories was established at Masulipatam, north of present-day Madras, in 1611. The following year, a second was set up at Surat, north of what later became Bombay. Here, in the reign of James I, simultaneously with the founding of New Amsterdam (later, New York) by the Dutch and with the Emperor Jahangir on the Moghul throne at Delhi, the main English trading centre was to develop. Subordinate agencies in the north of India were soon to follow as well as a third major factory, and the building of Fort St George, at Madras in 1639.

The extension of operations to Bengal probably arose as a result of widespread famine in Western India in 1630-2. Yet though the Company obtained permission from the Moghul court to trade there about this time, it was only in 1651 that a factory was established at the Moghul town of Hugli on the main tributary of the Ganges. By then, there were some twenty-three English factories in India with about ninety English employees. The establishment of other major factories at Patna and Qasimbazaar (Bengal) was soon to follow.

The picture of these and other European settlements which emerges from descriptions is of enclaves containing storehouses, barracks, a director's house and other accommodation lying within a walled and possibly defensible compound or, as at Madras, or after 1700, Calcutta, a newly constructed fort. However, at the English factory at Surat, itself a large Moghul town, some twenty-five merchants lived a 'collegiate' existence in an indigenous house in the town

(Woodruff, 1965:53). In *A New Account of the East Indies and Persia, 1672-81*, Fryer writes:

> Before President Andrews time, they always lived in tents, but since, wooden houses tiled
> with pantiles have been raised in an enclosure allotted by the Governor, in which
> compound are included warehouses, stables and other out-houses, with as good a garden
> as this sandy soil will allow (1909:119).

Figure 1.1   Steps towards a global economy, 1: Factory of the East India Company, Surat, India.
17th Century. Italian, source unknown.
1 Church   2 House   3 Magazine
This is evidently a later factory than that described by Fryer (See also Plate 1.) (*BBC Hulton Picture Library*)

The 'factory-house' was installed in an existing Muslim building in the city, and consisted of a
two-storey, flat-roofed, courtyard-type building with an upstairs balcony and a garden in the
centre. The ground floor was used for trading purposes, general stores and 'godowns' or
warehouses; the upper storey was used for living accommodation, council and entertainment
rooms and a bathing room. Similarly, in the Moghul capital of Agra, the Company officials
adopted much from the Indian way of life, living in a house in the city, 'the rooms in general
covered with carpets and great high cushions' on which to lean (Woodruff, 1965:54). In
Calcutta, founded in 1690, Fort William had been constructed as

an irregular Tetraon (sic) of brick and mortar called *Puckah* which is a composition of Brick dust, Lime Molasses and cut Hemp and is as hard and tougher than firm Stone and Brick and the Town was built without order as the Builders thought most convenient for their own Affairs, everyone taking in what ground most pleased them for Gardening so that in most houses you must pass through a Garden into the House, the English building near the River's Side and the Natives within Land. . . . About fifty yards from Fort William stands the Church built by the Pious Charity of Merchants residing there. . . . The Governor's house in the Fort is the most regular piece of architecture that I ever saw in India. And there are many convenient lodgings for Factors and Writers within the Fort and some storehouses for the Company's Goods and the Magazine for their Ammunition. The Company has a pretty good hospital at Calcutta . . . also a pretty good garden that furnishes the Governor's table with Herbage and Fruit (Spear, 1963:3).

In 1689, Bombay consisted of a fort situated on an island which a contemporary thought was 'beautified with several elegant Dwellings of the English and neat apartments of the Portuguese'. Between seven and eight hundred English lived in the fort at this time.
Somewhat later (1710), Madras was said to present

a great variety of fine Buildings that gracefully overlook its walls, with straight and wide, paved streets, the walls of the fort penetrated with five gates. The public buildings included a Town Hall, St Mary's Church, The College, New House and Hospital with the Governor's lodgings in the inner Fort (Ibid:4).

With their main factories on the coast and smaller ones inland, the various European companies despatched agents, generally travelling by river, into the interior. In the unstable conditions of India, with fighting frequent between local rulers, such traders were constantly at risk. Responsible for negotiating with Indian merchants, they led uncertain lives 'up country', depending on the 'safe conduct' of the Moghul ruler whose authority was frequently not recognised. It is from one of these agents, Edmund Foster, that the earliest – albeit scanty – information on the bungalow derives.

In 1659, Foster was in Qasimbazaar, one of the Company's main Bengal factories. Whilst skirmishes between rival armies continued in the region, Foster was arranging the transport of saltpetre down the Ganges, from Patna to Hugli. The invading army, under Mir Jumla, set up camp in the vicinity. 'They have begun to make bunguloues and some houses within nine course (*kos* – a Moghul unit of measurement) of this place, by a great tank called Sheck Tank,' wrote Foster to his Company colleague (Foster, 1921:290–1).

This first reference clearly distinguishes between 'bunguloues' and 'houses' and, as in an account of three decades before, suggests some form of quickly built and temporary shelter. In that case, a party of French merchants had been trading, in 1633, in the region of Satganaur, north of Patna on the Ganges; according to a contemporary account, they had established themselves close to the town, famous for its silks, and 'under the pretence that a building was necessary for their transactions in buying and selling . . . erected several houses in the Bengali style' (H-J).

In trading along the tributaries of the Ganges, the European merchants were probably accompanied by members of the local Bengali community. Staying for a few days or even longer, it is likely that, between towns and villages, when not sleeping in the large, barge-like boats or *budgerows* in which they travelled, they set up camp and were accommodated either in tents or in quickly built shelters, made from material at hand and constructed by local peasants. In 1676, Streynsham Master, the East India Company's agent at Madras, travelled up from there to Bengal to inspect the warehouse and buildings at Hugli and to supervise trading activities. He arrived late in November. 'There being a plott of ground, part of the Compound of the Company's Factory', he wrote in his diary,

> which lies conveniently neare the river side, it was thought fitt to repaire and enclose it, and to set up Bungales or Hovells for a habitation for all such English in the Company's service as belong to their sloopes and vessells . . . and those that now live out in houses of their owne, by degrees, to be brought within that Compound, and all others that shall come hereafter to live within the same, and to be allowed to build such accommodation as they shall desire, if they be marryed; and all persons soe living to be under the inspection of the purse marine and to live under such orders as they shall receive from time to time from the Chiefs and Councell. . . . No Englishman was to be permitted to reside or buy or build houses in India except in Factors or those places where we have a garrison (Temple, 1911, 2:209-10).

This more detailed passage confirms the makeshift nature of the shelters; it also suggests the 'territorial' nature of early trading settlements with the incoming English being limited to living within the enclosed area of the compound.

These assumptions are confirmed by the Comte du Modave, travelling in India in the mid eighteenth century. 'A *bangla* is a pavilion of bamboo covered . . . with thatch or leaves from trees which one constructs for some special occasion, like a marriage, a big fête, a meeting place during the hunt or simply a meeting place.' Where the Frenchman preferred the local term, the Dutch slightly adapted it, noting on one of their navigation charts of the Hugli estuary, 'Bangaelaer op Speelhuys', apparently referring to a place for rest or recreation (H-J). According to a later authority, the local *seerky* grass from which these shelters were made, 'being remarkably light', when doubled or trebled was completely waterproof and enabled itinerant Bengali peasants to construct 'a very comfortable cabin in a few minutes'. Similarly, Bishop Heber, travelling in the early nineteenth century, describes how temporary huts were put up for his party 'made of frames of bamboo, each something like a hurdle in shape and size, well thatched and light and easily carried from place to place and supported on props when they were wanted'.

The indigenous banggolo

The 'bangla' was also used more permanently. In the later nineteenth century, the term described the common hut of the Bengal peasant, which had 'a sloping roof on two sides and two gable ends' (H-J). It is probably this type of dwelling which is described at greater length by Francis Buchanan in 1810 (1838, 2:922-4):

> The style of private ediface that is proper and peculiar to Bengal, consists of a hut with a pent roof constructed of two sloping sides which meet in a ridge forming the segment of a circle so that it has a resemblance to a boat when overturned. . . . This kind of hut, it is said, from being peculiar to Bengal, is called by the native Banggolo. . . . Among the natives, the poor man has one hut for himself and cattle, the richer men increase the number without altering the plan of the building.

A wealthy Hindu family had a group of ten such huts, for various purposes and family members, the average size of each being about ten by eight cubits;* a 'common labourer', with a wife and two children, had only one, eight by six cubits.

Where the materials admit, the walls of the hut are made of mud and the floor is always raised a foot or two above the level of the plain, but not always so high as to be above water in the rainy season; so that a platform of bamboos is then constructed at one end of the hut and upon this the family sit and sleep while they must wade through the mud to reach the door.

Where the soil was too loose for making walls, the sides of the hut were formed of hurdles made of straw grass or reeds confined between sticks or split bamboos, tied together. In the better kind of houses, in place of straw, hurdles made of mats were used, or those of straw were plastered with cow dung and clay. The frame of the house consisted entirely of bamboos tied together. Only in the houses of the very wealthy were wood posts and beams used and these were neither polished nor painted, nor were they fastened with nails. The door to the hut was usually the only aperture, 'crevices excepted', and was usually shut by a hurdle (*jhangp*), tied to the upper part of the door which fell down, like a valve, to close. Wooden doors which folded from the side were used only by the very wealthy. Very few houses had any window openings to admit air or light.

If the house was intended for a shop, one side of the roof was extended four or five feet beyond the wall and was supported by a row of bamboos to form a gallery.

The number of huts depended on the size and social standing of each family. At the top of Buchanan's scale, the ten huts of the 'Hindu family of high rank and station' consisting of a man, wife and child, a married dependent relative, another male dependent relative and four servants (ten persons in all) included a small brick house, 14 by 7 cubits (the following dimensions are all in cubits), with wooden doors and small, shuttered windows, where the man, wife and child slept; a hut (8 by 6), of bamboo posts and walls of clay or hurdle, where the male relative and his wife slept; a hut similar to this for a servant and store room; three more huts of similar size, one for a temple, the other for accommodating friends or religious mendicants; a larger hut (12 by 8), the *baitokkhana*, was for receiving company, with wooden door and windows shut by jhangp. Here, the male relative slept with his servants; a further hut (8 by 6) was for cattle. The tenth hut (10 by 7), for the watchman, also formed the entrance to the 'compound' which was surrounded by a mud wall or fence.

Buchanan implies that very few people occupied such extensive accommodation. Possibly more representative of the wealthier inhabitants of Dinajpur was the family 'of some consideration' of eight people occupying eight structures: a clay-walled house (15 by 8), a kitchen, where the cook slept, and other huts for a store house, cattle, a temple, baitokkhana, and the watchman.

The material wealth of such a group at this time is suggested by their furniture and equipment, as well too as their ornaments, clothing, food and number of servants which Buchanan also lists. Durable furniture for the temple included three copper cups, a plate, a brass salver, tripod, pot and plate, conch shell, stone for grinding sandalwood, grass mat for prayer, a bell metal plate for ringing, brass lamp and wooden throne for the gods. For household use, eleven various water vessels of brass, betel salvers and two pairs of betel nut cutters, four plates, six cups, two lamp stands, two rice pots, all of brass; one pot for boiling milk and frying, ladle and hook, iron rod for cleaning the *hungka* (pipe for smoking tobacco); hoe, hatchet, bill-hook, two sickles, two kitchen knives, scissors, three plates and two cups of

---

* Cubit: 'Ancient measures of length, 18-22 inches (45-55 cms). From Latin, cubitus, elbow, length of forearm' (OED).

stone, stone for rubbing curry, two bedsteads for the master and mistress, one large and one small wooden chest, bamboo trunk, six wooden stools, wooden mortar, instrument for beating rice, four rattan stools, two wooden plates for cakes, two pairs of wooden shoes. Less-durable furniture included, for the bed, two pairs of cotton curtains, two cotton-filled mattresses, two quilts, five pillows, four sheets, two blankets; for the floor, two cotton carpets, two woollen carpets, two split-reed mats, and one umbrella.

At the lower end of the scale, the family of an 'artist' (artisan?), a man, wife and two children, owned two huts, one for sleeping (7 by 5) and another shared between the cow and for cooking purposes. Finally, for a 'common labourer', his wife and two children, the dwelling consisted of one hut (8 by 6) with very little furniture or possessions: two stone plates, a sickle, one metal plate, earthern or bamboo pots for drinking water and one hungka. Perishable goods included three pieces of sackcloth for bedding, three rugs and some few mats and straw pillows.

In other regions of India, single households are frequently accommodated in single dwellings, separated into rooms or spaces according to function, the status of family members or other social and cultural criteria. Whether the multiplication of the single, simple hut in the Bengal peasant household resulted from structural limitations of bamboo building materials or other cultural factors is not clear.

Building material and techniques

These comments on Bengali huts and the relation of household structure to their number and utilisation are supplemented by Captain Thomas Williamson, writing about the same time (1810, 1:488-518). As an engineer, Williamson was primarily interested in building materials and techniques. Though not identifying the location described, his account is interesting for its detail and the sympathy he manifests for indigenous building methods. Moreover, at a time when industrialisation had not yet affected building methods and materials in the remoter parts of rural England, his comparative comments are more easily understood.

The walls of permanent buildings were usually constructed of mud laid in strata of 18-20 inches in depth, each stratum being allowed to dry before the next was added. Walls were between 26 to 30 inches thick at the base, tapering to about three-quarters of this breadth at the top. Williamson reports seeing some 'native bungalows' with mud walls which, after being chipped down to a uniform thickness, were then plastered with a mixture of fine sand and chaff.

On top of the mud wall of the hut, a stout piece of timber was laid to which rafters were fastened, each by one or more nails; rafters projected at least a foot beyond the exterior in order to sustain the thatch which hung over the edge of the wall to throw off heavy rains. Thatches were made of *kuss* or common wild grass. The manner of making these, especially for larger huts, Williamson found particularly intriguing. The side of the building to be covered was first measured. This measurement was then represented on level ground by means of four cords fastened to four stakes. Each side of a quadrangular or other building was marked out in this way. Then, large bamboos or bundles of smaller ones were laid down, in parallel lines, about one foot apart, at right angles to the base line. These were then crossed, at 5- or 6-inch intervals, by battens of split bamboos which were tied on with fine grass (*moonje*). This frame was then lifted by the joint efforts of fifty or sixty men, by hand and with forked poles, on to the ready-laid rafters on the walls. When the frames had been placed on each roof slope, they were tied down and a scaffolding fixed under the eaves to enable the thatchers to begin. When the thatching was complete, the angles of the roof and the ridge, sometimes the whole roof, were overlaid with layers of fine seerky grass, a technique which Williamson reports seeing gipsies use in Essex.

The wooden doors were made of a few vertical planks held together by horizontal battens; fastenings were by staples and hooks in which strong wooden bars slipped. Where windows existed, they were not more than 2 feet square and closed by wooden shutters with a jhangp outside made of bamboo battens and mats; these were suspended at their upper borders by hooks or rings fastened into the wall and could be raised to any elevation and kept there by bamboo stilts. They also kept sun and rain off the doors and, when lowered close to the wall, kept out rain and dust. Windows were high up, 'scarcely allowing a person to look in'. Chimneys were 'utterly unknown among the natives' though sometimes an aperture was left for the escape of smoke. However, food was generally cooked outside or, more usually, in a small shed.

The outside of the wall was preserved rough so that the large cakes of cow dung, used for fuel, could more easily be stuck on to dry in the sun. Interior walls were smoothed for some 3 feet from the floor and smeared with cow dung, as was the floor, made from rammed clay. In some instances, a slight kind of flooring of rough planks or bamboo laths was installed. Joists of rough wood were occasionally placed from the top of one wall to the other. On here, brushwood, bamboo poles, nets, mats or utensils might be kept; occasionally, it also provided sleeping accommodation. Whatever the flooring, it was always smeared with cow dung which 'certainly gives a freshness and may probably tend to salubrity; nor is it so devoid of neatness as a European would imagine'. Some people ornamented both the interior and exterior of their house by dipping the palms of their hands into solutions of red ochre and then imprinting the walls with their coloured hands. According to Williamson, this was 'to typify the infinite power of the Creator whose hands are supposed to be innumerable and perpetually in action'.

It was usual for a separate building to be set apart for the female members of the family; cattle were generally kept outside during good weather but during the great heat or rains, they had their own separate sheds, where also any *dooly* or other vehicle was kept. Such dwellings had few possessions. Instead of candles, simple oil lamps were placed in niches in the walls; although *charpoys* or small cots were in use among all classes, most people slept on mats; the whole contents of a sleeping room included a red *durmah* mat, a small cotton carpet, a sheet to wrap round the body (*chudder*), a pillow (*tuckeah*), a quilt (*goodry*), and a spitting pot (*peek-daun*), for use when chewing betel nut.*

Graphic and photographic evidence

Many of these details are confirmed by three drawings made by the English artist, George Chinnery, travelling in the Barrackpore region outside Calcutta in 1813. These suggest banggolos of the poorer peasant with walls of matting and of mud. A few metal vessels can be seen, as also an up-ended charpoy. The extension of the roof structure for a 'shop', mentioned by Buchanan, is also visible. Hungkas, umbrellas, the thatch framework and jhangp can also be seen (Figures 1.2, 1.3).

Three basic roof-types can be seen in these drawings. That with a curved ridge, discussed in more detail below, is described by Nilsson (1969:186) as the 'curvilinear hut':

a rectangular building with a special roof structure; wooden ribs are bent and jointed

---

* A more detailed discussion of this account is in King, 1977b.

Figure 1.2 Peasant dwelling: sketches of the indigenous 'banggolo', 1813. Bengal, George Chinnery (see also Figure 1.3) (*India Office Library*)

together to form a grid which is then covered with straw. This roof protrudes over the walls and forms curves resembling a crescent moon on its sides. At the front, the protruding part of the roof may be supported by wooden poles, thus forming a gallery.

This very striking type of Bengali hut is well illustrated in a painting of 1786 (Plate 2) and even more so, in a photograph taken by Samuel Bourne in the later 1860s (Plate 3). This also illustrates the 'upturned boat' analogy of Buchanan of some sixty years before.

Muslim architecture and the Bengali hut

If these accounts and illustrations reveal a fascination for the bamboo technology and forms of Bengal peasant housing, it is a reaction which had earlier precedents. Long before the Moghuls ruled in Bengal, other Muslim overlords had settled there, adapting in their own brick and stone buildings the characteristic forms of the simple peasant's hut.

Dani somewhat oversimplifies the variety in these dwellings in suggesting that the bamboo huts with curved roofs and long-drawn eaves basically take two shapes, the *chauchala* type, having four sides, and the *dochala* type, having two sides with gable ends and a central curved ridge (do two; chau four). The chauchala roof has a covering on four sides which are 'more or less curved, in some domical, in others, flatter, but they never make a straight pyramid; secondly, the coverings have eaves drawn out lower down to a point at each corner, thus making the roof-base curved like the segment of a circle'. This form was copied in brick to cover a rectangular space. Dani refers to examples of Muslim building, dating from the mid fifteenth century where this occurred. Subsequently, the curvilinear form was spread throughout northern India by the Moghuls and, in the eighteenth century, was adopted from them and used in Rajput buildings too.

The dochala hut, Dani refers to as the 'bungalow roof'. This

has coverings on two sides, which are joined at the top thus making a curved ridge with gable ends. The eaves are curved as before and the ridge is generally crowned with finials in imitation of the knots found in the original roof.

The adaptation of this particular constructional form was first made during the Moghul period, an early example being the mausoleum of Fath Kahn (d. 1657) at Gaur (Dani, 1961:12-13, 181) (plate 4).

These Muslim buildings confirm the existence of the curved thatched roof hut in Bengal at least in the fifteenth century and, in all probability, for many centuries before. With Gaur within miles of the early English factory at Englishbazaar ('Angrezabad'), this region may be seen as one of the 'cultural cross-roads' of Asia. From here, the cultural influence of a modified simple Bengali hut was to be diffused, via India and Europe, throughout the world.

The adaptation and use of the many forms of the Bengali hut – still the same today – by Bengalis building under European supervision in rural areas continued well into the twentieth century (plates 5 and 6).

The growth of colonial power, 1757-1857

The background

The dearth of evidence about the Anglo-Indian bungalow in the early years contrasts with its abundance later on. The explanation lies not simply in the growing number of Europeans in India but in their changed political position.

The death of the Emperor Aurungzeb in 1707 began the gradual decline of Moghul power in India. Throughout the empire, the provinces successively established their independence. Increasing rivalry for the spoils between the English and French came to a head in a series of conflicts. The defeat of the Nawab of Bengal and his French allies at Plassey in 1757 is usually taken as the symbolic beginning of the British Empire in India (Cohn, 1971). Where the operations of the East India Company in the seventeenth century had been those of trade, though increasingly armed trade at that, after Plassey, they rapidly turned to plunder. According to the *Parliamentary Report on the East India Company* (1813), 'the importance of that immense Empire to this country is rather to be established by the great annual addition it makes to the wealth and capital of the kingdom, than by any eminent advantage which the manufacturers of the country can derive from the consumption of the natives of India' (Frank, 1978:88). The accumulation of capital, whether through plunder or Company fraud (Kemp, 1978:138) was, as will be seen in the following chapter, to be behind the first Indian influences on architecture, and early hints of the bungalow's development, in England.

In the sixty years after Plassey, a series of wars against the Indian states brought the entire sub-continent under British military, administrative and diplomatic control. By 1818, the effective conquest of India was complete. It is against this background that the bungalow, to become the rural, and subsequently suburban, 'model dwelling' of the next political rulers of India, was developed. The opportunity was provided by the installation of the two principal instruments of the new 'proto-imperial power', the army and its system of civil and juridical administration.

In the first half of the eighteenth century, the interior of India had been largely closed to Europeans. The exceptions were occasional embassies, some few soldiers taking service with local rulers and the agents of chartered companies. With the rise of the East India Company's power, the number of Europeans in the interior or '*mofussil*' settlements now rapidly increased.

The basis of Company rule was military strength. The first permanent military camps or cantonments were established outside Patna (Bankipur) and Calcutta (Dinapur, Berhampur and Baraset) in 1772 (Ghosh, 1970:108). Here Indian and European troops were housed in 'hutted lines', tents or barracks; their European officers, in a rapidly evolving version of the bungalow.

Administrative developments ran parallel to military control. In 1765, the East India Company was granted the management of the Bengal revenues, a further opportunity for accumulating capital. The task of collecting these, as well as administering justice in the newly created districts, previously undertaken by local Indian officials for the Moghul Empire, was now handed to the Company. With the establishment of the suitably named office of Collector (1772), British administration began. By the end of the century, a network of officials had been created as the British took over responsibility for their new possessions. With the introduction of the office of District Judge and then that of Commissioner, the juridical and administrative system was extended to the Company's territory in Madras.

The emergence of the bungalow as a culturally distinctive house form is inseparable from these developments. The 'officer's bungalow' on the cantonment, like the 'magistrate's', 'collector's', or 'commissioner's bungalow' in the districts, was the workplace and residence of the representatives of the new ruling power.

At first, the scope as well as area of this authority was limited, the number of its officials few; in the mid eighteenth century, less than 700 Europeans were in Bengal and only a third of them in 'up-country' factories: 'tiny knots of Englishmen . . . barely noticeable on the fabric of Bengal society' (Ghosh, 1970:110). As the Company's power and numbers grew, however, so the extent of its control increased. The effect on building developments and the growing inland towns became increasingly more marked. When the responsibility for ruling India was transferred in 1858, from the Company regulated by Parliament, to the British government itself, the control and influence over the environment became even more apparent. Where a few European travellers had adapted themselves to Indian forms of shelter in the seventeenth century, the representatives of an imperial political and cultural power brought an extensive adaptation of Indian forms two centuries later.

It was also during these years (c. 1770-1830) that the most detailed evidence on the bungalow is produced. It shows, on the one hand, its widespread acceptance as the typical, 'up-country' dwelling for English officials; on the other, the phenomenon becomes of sufficient interest 'at home' for extensive descriptions to be made.

Theories of origin

According to Buchanan, the real banggolo described above was not the true prototype for the 'European' or 'Anglo-Indian' bungalow.

> Another kind of hut called a *Chauyari* (literally, 'four sides') has been introduced and this is the form which Europeans have adopted in their cottages (sic) when they use a thatched roof. It [presumably the roof] consists of four plain sides which, if the building is square, are triangular and meet in one point; but, if the cottage is long, the two ends of the roof

only are triangular and the two sides (which are triangular truncated at the apex), form a straight ridge. Europeans have made great improvements in this kind of building, have surrounded it with a gallery to exclude the heat, have introduced windows, have divided it into convenient apartments and have suspended cloth ceilings to free them from the vermin that occupy the thatch. These luxuries seem unknown to the natives of the district (Dinajpur). Their *chauyaris* are built of the same materials with their *Banggolos*; but

Figure 1.3   Peasant dwelling: materials and form. Chinnery's sketches show two or three types of hut, one or more of which accommodated a household (*India Office Library*)

being used chiefly among the rich, have usually wooden posts and many of them have garrets that are inhabited and have openings by way of windows.

Buchanan's suggestion that the gallery round the house was a European addition can be questioned. Other sources indicate that houses having a 'gallery' were already indigenous to Bengal. According to a later authority, 'native houses to this day are divided into *ath-chala*, *chau-chala* and *Bengali*, or common huts' (H-J). The ath-chala implies that the roof had four sides, with four more projections so as to cover a verandah all round the house, which is square. Nilsson (1968:186) refers to this type as the 'double-roofed house' and believes it to be the true prototype of the European bungalow. The basic difference here is that the upper and lower (or verandah) roofs are separate.

A third alternative prototype, combining the roof structure of the chauyari with the pillared gallery of what Buchanan sees as the 'true banggolo', is described by Grant in 1849. In the ground plan of a native's bungalow,

the centre square consists of either one or two apartments, according to the circumstances or wants of the individual, whilst the thatched roof, extending

Figure 1.4 Colonial influence: the indigenous dwelling transformed. Grant (*Anglo-Indian Domestic Life*, 1849) shows two types of hut, the 'chauyari' and the curvilinear-roofed 'banggolo', both on a raised mud plinth and with a verandah

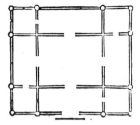

Figure 1.5   According to Grant, Europeans adapted the former, partially or totally
enclosing the verandah and partitioning the corners to form separate rooms,
usually used for bathing or sleeping

considerably over all sides, is supported at the extreme edges upon bamboo or wooden
pillars, thus forming a verandah round the building (Figure 1.4).

By featuring the pyramidal roof of the chauyari alongside the curvilinear structure of the
banggolo, Grant appears to be deliberately excluding the latter as the true prototype.

The European resident, improving upon this, encloses the verandah by erecting either a
mat or brick wall, and in like way, throwing partitions across the corners, converts the
verandah into little rooms for the convenience of himself or visitor friends. The roof
being carried beyond these as before, would complete nearly all which exists in the
European's bungalow of the present day (Figure 1.5).

This last account accords most closely with the earliest detailed description of an Anglo-
Indian bungalow dating from 1783 and the earliest known drawing (not illustrated here),
both referring to Lucknow, of three years later.

Bungalows are buildings in India, generally raised on a base of brick, one, two or three feet from the ground, and consist of only one storey; the plan of them usually is a large room in the centre for an eating and sleeping room, and rooms at each corner for sleeping; the whole is covered with one general thatch, which comes low to each side; the spaces between the angle rooms are *viranders* or open porticos to sit in during the evenings; the center hall is lighted from the sides with windows and a large door in the center. Sometimes the center *viranders* at each end are converted into rooms (Hodges, 1793:146).

This description, as well as Grant's ground plan, are confirmed by a German traveller writing in 1890, with the exception that the bedrooms are placed at the side of the bungalow and the bathing rooms in the corners. This was the more usual arrangement (Figure 1.6).

Not all of these early European bungalows had verandahs. In 1803, a young army officer, Henry Roberdeau, wrote:

The Englishmen live in what are really stationary tents which have run aground on low brick platforms. They are 'Bungalows', a word I know not how to render unless by a Cottage. These are always thatched with straw on the roof and the walls are sometimes of bricks and often of mats. Some have glass windows besides the Venetians but this is not very common. . . . To hide the sloping roof we put up a kind of artificial ceiling made of white cloth. . . . There are curtains over the doorway to keep out the wind. . . . I have two Bungalows near to each other, in one I sleep and dress and in the other, sit and eat (Nilsson, 1969:186).

The fourth suggestion comes from John Lockwood Kipling, father of Rudyard and founder of the Bombay School of Art.

Our early residents in India, engaged in military, administrative or trading duties, lived a nomadic life for the greater part of the year in tents, and since there was nothing in the indigenous buildings of Bengal suited to their requirements, their first dwelling houses, designed by themselves and built of materials at site, are naturally planned on the model of the Indian service tents to which they were accustomed, i.e. a large and lofty room surrounded by double walls of canvas enclosing space between them, with partitions at two or more corners for bath or store rooms. It is probable, indeed, that in the beginning the tent itself was occasionally covered with the sun-proof thatch or 'bangla'. The name and the thatch were all we took (Kipling, 1911) (plate 7).

Some credence to this theory is lent by Roberdeau's description and by the affinity of the structural components and enclosed areas of the tent and bungalow. It would also be supported by present-day Indian army practice whereby the sides of semi-permanent tents are often reinforced by brick walls.

Kipling also suggests that the 'double-roofed' bungalow with a 'clerestorey' was a later, mid-nineteenth-century development of the earlier version where 'the roof covers both living rooms and verandah, as an extinguisher covers a candle, and which admits light through the doors only.'

Whilst Kipling's suggestions are credible, the true origins of the bungalow would seem to lie more in the explanations of Buchanan and Grant. The main characteristics of the developed Anglo-Indian bungalow in the late eighteenth century – its free-standing and single-storey structure, the plinth, the pitched, thatched roof and the verandah – are all characteristic features of the indigenous Bengal hut, whatever additions came from the Europeans.

Moreover, consideration of the labour and expertise responsible for the construction of these early bungalows would seem to confirm this.

The early visitors to India were travellers and traders not settlers. In North America, Australia or South Africa, early emigrants had, in general, built their dwellings with their own hands and according to the cultural models in their heads. In India, however, Europeans were merchants, officers or diplomats rather than settlers. The social relations of production were such that manual labour, then as later, was carried out by the appropriate Indian castes with local materials and technology. If Europeans wanted work undertaken, it was carried out by 'native labour' under European supervision. Even the European common soldier had 'native

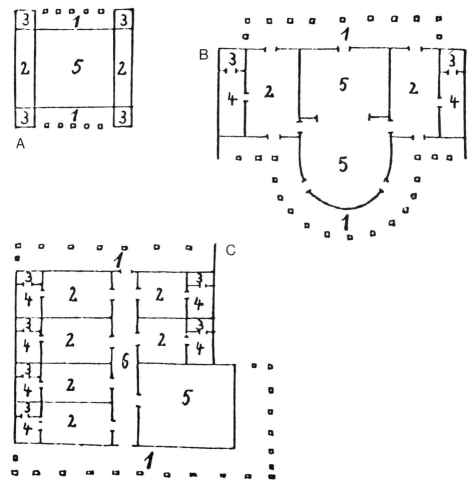

Figure 1.6   Domestic space: evolution of ground plans
A Basic form   B & C Developed form
1 Verandah   2 Bedroom   3 Bath   4 Dressing room   5 Living room   6 Hall
(K.Pfeil, *Die Indische Stadt*, 1935. *India Office Library*)

coolies' and servants to undertake manual tasks. Whilst European officials in rural districts might have had their own idea of the sort of dwelling they wanted, as it was not they but the local population who actually built it, the end result was more of a native product. The persistence of Indian 'housing models' over those of the European patrons for whom they were built was a frequent source of amusement (Figure 1.7).

The Anglo-Indian bungalow; 1810: structure, materials and form
By the last quarter of the eighteenth century, therefore, a new form of dwelling had been produced, based on a Bengal prototype but used only by Europeans. For Williamson, first in India in 1778, there was no doubt about the main characteristics of the bungalow which distinguished it from the substantial, and often architect-designed, city houses of Europeans in Calcutta.

Thatched, on one (ground) floor, and not envisaged for long-term or permanent use, it was of *cutcha* not *pukka* construction, that is, built with sun-dried bricks and plastered with either mud or mortar: 'such (of these *cutcha*) houses as are so built for the sake of cheapness, being, almost without exception, intended for thatches, and thus becoming what we term *bungalows*.' Moreover, 'with respect to *bungalows*, or any other building coming under the designation "temporary", their foundations are usually very shallow . . . and as their inner walls are well secured by *verandas* . . . very shallow foundations are deemed sufficient.'

> Most of the *bungalows* built by Europeans are run up with sun-dried bricks; usually of a large size, eight of them making a cubic foot; each being a foot long, six inches broad, and three inches thick. . . Bricks are generally made in wooden moulds, which, being laid on some level spot, previously swept . . . are filled with mud; the surface is then levelled, with the hand, or with a strike, when the mould is raised, by means of handles, and washed in a large pan of water, and then placed on a fresh spot. . . An expert labourer will, if duly supplied with mud and water, make from 2000 to 2500 bricks daily . . . one labourer mix[es] the soil, one suppl[ies] the water and two hand-barrow men keep one brick-maker in constant work; the whole expense may be about sixteen to eighteen pence; the same quantity of work done in England would cost full as many shillings' (Williamson, 1810, 1:514-16).

Around the bungalow was a verandah (italicised throughout Williamson's account), a term and feature of tropical building which had probably been brought to Asia from Portugal in the fifteenth century (see Appendix A). Its base was incorporated into the foundations, a feature adapted from the indigenous banggolo.

> With respect to *bungalows* . . . their foundations are usually very shallow . . . for the most part, raised a foot or two from the surrounding level; and, as their inner walls, that often run from sixteen to twenty feet in height, are well secured by the *verandas*, which likewise preserves the precinct for full twelve or fourteen feet from being softened by the rains, very shallow foundations are deemed sufficient. The surrounding parapet which limits, while it raises the *veranda*, is usually of burnt brick, cemented with good mortar, and plastered over with the same. . . . The *verandas* of *bungalows* are sustained either by strong wooden posts, or by pillars of masonry (1810, 2:34-8).

Verandahs were frequently used for sleeping. They were also

> generally allotted to the accommodation of servants . . . and . . . serve for the home of

whatever . . . bearers may be employed. These have each their mat, on which they sleep, forming a pillow of any bundle of cloaths and covering themselves with their quilts. . . . When a gentleman has company, the side-board is usually set out in the *veranda*, where also the several guests' *hookahs* are prepared; and, in rainy weather, their water cooled.

Although most bungalows had 'an abundance of out-offices', few people allowed their palanquins or gigs to be kept there as 'they would be subject to various unpleasant purposes whereby their interior especially would be often soiled'. Hence, the gig and palanquin were also kept within the verandah, the form requiring a ramp up which it was drawn. The inside woodwork was generally of mango wood, a cheap and not particularly durable timber; alternatively, the rafters of such cheaply made bungalows were bamboo, an all-purpose material found everywhere in India. The ceilings 'were rendered inconceivably neat', not by plaster but,

by means of a double sheet . . . of very coarse cotton cloth called *guzzy* of which tents are usually constructed. These sheets are fitting to the several apartments . . . bound with strong tape around and have . . . various tapes forming an union cross of eight limbs, or rays, all meeting in the centre. As the cornices commonly project near a foot, abundance of space is left for lacing the sheet (called a *chandny*) to battens, nailed to pegs built in the wall; these battens . . . admit the sheet to be strained very tight, so as to bag very little, if at all, in the centre. Some white-wash their *chandnies*, and take so much pains in establishing a firm appearance, as to render them very similar to well-made ceilings. Without this last mode of preparation, music has no effect in a *bungalow*; indeed . . . the most powerful instrument is heard under great disadvantages, owing to the number of apertures . . . mats, couch and table covers . . . all of which deaden the tone considerably (1810, 2:51-2).

Because of white ants, warping and the noise of footsteps where 'menials . . . are ever moving about in various parts of the house', boarded floors were 'almost unknown in India'. Instead, they were made according to local tradition by coating the brick base with a solution of cow dung and mud.

One of the chief merits of such a bungalow, constructed with local labour, technology and materials, was its cheapness and flexibility.

In almost every part of India, an excellent *bungalow* may be built for about five thousand rupees, completely fitted with glass doors, and windows, and with all the necessary out-offices duly tiled, or thatched, according to their purposes; while a house suited to the accommodation of the same family, in Calcutta, could not be finished for less than ten times that sum.

Williamson has little to say on the internal lay-out or dimensions of the bungalow though, in most cases, this probably followed the simple structural arrangement suggested by Hodges in 1783: one central room or hall, occasionally sub-divided, with additional sleeping or bathing rooms in the verandah.

Some insight into the dimensions can be obtained from other sources. Descriptions of two bungalows from about 1830-40 in the Punjab suggest an overall plinth area of over 7,000 square feet (84 by 84). Verandahs on either side of 15 feet each, and one at the rear of 10 feet reduced the 'core area' to 54 feet wide by 74 feet deep. This was divided into a narrow

THE NEW HOUSE

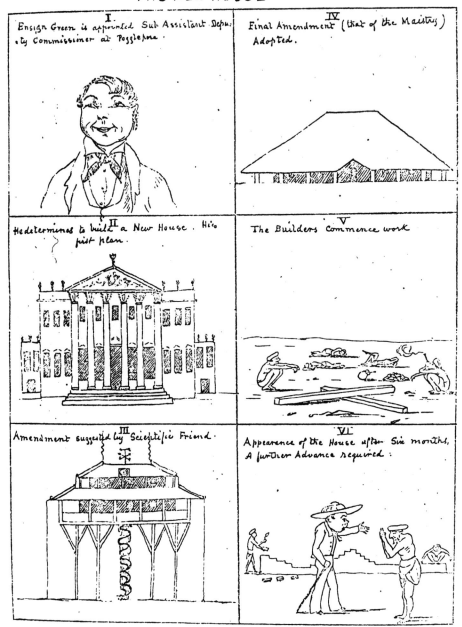

Figure 1.7   The bungalow as a political and cultural product, 1853
Apart from the joke and indifferent quality of reproduction, this cartoon also demonstrates
the cultural division of labour responsible for the production of the Anglo-Indian bungalow.
      The patron (Ensign Green) is the representative of European colonialism whose own idea
of a dwelling is determined by models of a land-owning aristocracy in an emergent industrial-
capitalist state. Alternative models of the 'scientific friend' embody the concern with health

THE NEW HOUSE

VII Ensign Green's Enjoyment of his New House during the Hot Season.

X Honest Pride of the Maistry, Disgust of the Scientific Friend, Resignation of the Proprietor.

VIII Putting on the Roof.

XI The House in the Rains

IX The House Complete.

XII The House After the Rains.

and comfort required by Europeans in the tropics.

Labour, however, is Indian, as also is its supervision (the maistry) whose conception of an appropriate dwelling (a bungalow) stems from an earlier, pre-industrial phase of British settlement in India. The unsuccessful outcome might be read as resulting from the application of an inappropriate technology to a culturally unfamiliar design (*Delhi Sketch Book*, 1853. *India Office Library*)

entrance hall on either side of which was a dressing room and servant's room; at the rear were a drawing and dining room. The four corner rooms followed the traditional pattern: two for bathing to the front and two for stores at the rear. Fanny Parkes describes the dining room of her Kanpur bungalow in the 1820s as of 40 by 28 feet and the swimming bath, 30 by 21 feet. The 'fine garden' round the house contained two wells, coach house, stables, cow house and servants' accommodation. For this they paid 150 rupees a month, or about 150 guineas a year, 'a heavy rent for an up-country house'. (1850:137)

One way of keeping out the excessive heat was first to thatch the roof and then to cover this with tiles, a practice which Bishop Heber noticed at Kanpur. The main method of controlling the thermal environment, however, was to modify behaviour rather than the building: when the inside got too hot, the occupants moved on to the verandah. Technology was adopted from the local inhabitants. *Chicks*, a type of roller blind, were made of split, thin, bamboo canes, from four to six feet long, loosely strung together and bound at the edge with tape. Rolled up and tied with a cord when not in use, these were fixed to the lintels of windows or the door plate and lowered to reduce the glare. In the gaps between the pillars of the verandah, *jangps*, adopted from the Bengali peasant hut, were heavy wooden screens, secured at the top of the verandah roof and raised or lowered with the aid of a pole. For other means of thermal control, the Anglo-Indian bungalow depended on labour-intensive technology. *Tatties*, screens made of the fibrous roots of sweet-smelling grass (*khas*), were fitted to doors and windows. During hot periods, these were splashed with water by servants to cool the hot breezes blowing through the house. The *punkah*, hung from the ceiling, was a heavy cloth fixed to a wooden beam and pulled to and fro by a rope to stir the air. The punkah was known in Moghul India and had been first adopted in a modified version by Europeans in Bengal in the 1780s. Both with tatties and punkah, the comfort of the occupants depended on local manpower. Indeed, the total environment of the bungalow and compound as well, of course, as its construction, depended on colonial ability to employ cheap native labour (plates 10 and 11).

Williamson's description is confirmed by contemporary pictures. What is probably the earliest drawing of an Anglo-Indian bungalow named as such (1820) clearly shows the raised plinth, mud walls, pyramidal thatched roof, and verandah (plate 12). What Williamson does not mention, however, was both the site and location of the bungalow without which neither its form nor function could have been developed.

The bungalow was invariably situated in a large compound, an area of marked territory which, in turn, was located at a distance from other buildings or places of settlement. The compound, as the description of Streynsham Master suggests, was an enclosed space either leased, bought or appropriated by representatives of an incoming, 'invading' society from the indigenous inhabitants of the land. The development of the bungalow as a culturally distinctive form of dwelling depended, first and foremost, on the secure possession of territory in which cultural choices could be expressed in an environment over which there was considerable, if not total, control.

The spacious compound, of 2, 10 or even 20 acres, was a prerequisite for the bungalow's development. Being of only one storey, and with an extensive thatch covering the whole, the dwelling depended on the space around for ventilation and light. In fact, the compound was simply an extension of the bungalow's internal space, an outdoor room, fulfilling a variety of social, political, cultural and psychological needs (King, 1976). Thus, the bungalow was in direct contrast to the courtyard house in the 'native city': here, a central courtyard allowed the penetration of light and air; as the houses were three or four storeys high and there were closely clustered, cellular-structured buildings all around, the lower rooms were dark and cool. Activity in this courtyard house was centripetal: movement was inwards, towards the courtyard. In the bungalow, it was centrifugal, outward, on to the verandah, and further into the compound.

The location of the bungalow-in-its-compound, away from places of Indian settlement, expressed the political and social relationship between the occupants of both. Spatial distance reflected social distance. The closely clustered houses of the Indian town or village were functional not just in terms of climate or existing technology and transport; they also expressed the basic social and economic relationship of their inhabitants. The occupants of the courtyard house were members of a larger joint family; the inner court provided a place of exercise and relaxation for those female members whose religious customs restricted their free movement outside; the blank, windowless outer walls giving onto the narrow street ensured privacy for the occupants inside. The people of a crowded *mohulla* (neighbourhood) of a city, or the grouped banggolos of the Bengali peasant village, might share kinship, caste or religion; the overall physical pattern of the town or village reflected the social structure and relationship of the people it contained.

The European occupants of the bungalow, however, had neither social nor religious ties with the inhabitants of the Indian town. Their relationship was one of 'ruler and the ruled': the spatial separation of the district officer or army subaltern from the Indian town expressed a social and political divide. It was also explained on cultural grounds, European beliefs leading them to perceive the 'native city' as a source of illness and disease.

By the end of the eighteenth century, therefore, the idea of the Indian banggolo had undergone a basic change. On one hand, many items of structure, technology and materials were comparable to the Bengali dwellings. On the other, the political and cultural needs of its British inhabitants had radically transformed its setting and site. Social changes were to increasingly modify its form.

The bungalow in use

In the eighteenth and early nineteenth century the bungalow was put to a variety of uses. Though primarily a rural, 'up-country' dwelling, in the growing suburbs of Calcutta it often served as annexe or temporary house. In some cases, one, two or more bungalows were built in the grounds of a substantial mansion. Here, at a time when the idea of the hotel was still a novelty in England, and hardly known in India, the bungalow provided accommodation for guests, storage space or acted as a 'summer house' (plate 8). The first reference to appear in an English dictionary or encyclopaedia (1788) referred to 'an Indian term for a thatched house with walls of mud or matting' and, giving an indication of its function, added, 'a cottage or warehouse'. Thus, the *India Gazette* advertised in 1780 'to be sold or let, a Commodious Bungalo and out houses' in Calcutta; four years later, in the *Calcutta Gazette*, 'a large and commodious house' was advertised in Chinsurah, 20 miles north of Calcutta, 'the outbuildings (including) a warehouse, . . . six store-rooms, a cook room, and a garden with a bungalow near the house' (H-J). Bishop Heber, visiting Calcutta in 1824, noted that Lord Amherst's house at Barrackpore 'barely accommodates (his) own family; and his aides-de-camp and visitors sleep in bungalows built at some little distance from it in the park.'

At this date, most Anglo-Indian bungalows were probably in cantonments. Though references are occasionally found to 'collector's' and 'judge's' bungalows, most civilian officials still relied on tents for accommodation. Heber describes the collector of a district near Bareilly, 'settling with the Zemindars with their taxes' in the early 1820s, and inspecting irrigation work, with 'an establishment of tents' which was 'extremely large and handsome'. He lived in 'a very spacious tent with glass doors, a stove and a canvas enclosure at one end which in Calcutta would have passed for a small compound'. However, judges on circuit were already provided at this date with a bungalow for a 'circuit house' in each of the minor stations.

Where there was no circuit house, judges 'make their circuits during the travelling months of the year, generally pitching their tents near towns and holding their courts under trees.' It was a practice which had arisen from the recognition that alien European surroundings could seriously inhibit Indian behaviour.

> one of the judges said [that] . . . an Indian of the humbler class is really always under constraint and fear in a house, particularly if furnished in the European manner, and can neither attend to what is told him nor tell his own story as well as in the open air and amidst those objects from which all his own objects are drawn (Heber, 1828, 1:187).

A further use of the bungalow was for temporary summer accommodation in the newly created 'hill stations' developed in the lower Himalaya and Nilgiri Hills since 1815 (plate 15). The relatively late development of the hill station bungalow meant that architectural ideas from 'home' influenced its form. On the conquest of Almorah (1817),

> Government very liberally built a number of small bungalows in airy situations around it, for the accommodation, gratis, of any of their civil or military servants who might come here for their health. They are small, with slated roofs, and looking extremely like the sea-bathing cottages on the Welsh coast, having thick walls, small windows, low rooms and other peculiarities (most different from the generality of Anglo-Indian houses) which suit a boisterous and cold climate. The bungalows are also built low because of the danger from earthquakes (ibid:272).

Reference to the bungalow in the mid eighteenth century generally refers to 'up-country', rural areas in Bengal. Gradually, however, as British influence spread throughout the country, mention is found in Lucknow (1783), Bombay (1793), and South India (1809); by 1810, according to Williamson, it seems to have been in use wherever the British were settled in India.

Compared with the evolution of dwelling forms in other colonial societies, two factors deserve comment. First, at no time in the history of the Anglo-Indian bungalow was consideration given to questions of defence. Though cantonment bungalows were, after 1857, increasingly tiled rather than thatched as a precaution against incendiarism, the bungalow was never fortified; the security of its occupants was provided by the cantonment, never very far away.

Moreover, unlike dwellings of early emigrants elsewhere, the bungalow was never a farm, accommodating animals, stored crops or tools. Nor was the surrounding compound ever meant for cultivation or pasture. The Anglo-Indian bungalow was for living in; alternatively, it combined the functions of residence and work, the work being that of administration or managing native labour. In the later colonial bungalows, this function of political economy was reflected in the 'office', an institution in the plan which remained long after colonial rule. It is the office which, for Marxists, would symbolise the appropriation of surplus value.

Growth and change, 1800-1857

Whilst a comprehensive picture of the bungalow at this time can be constructed, two developments make the analysis more complex: there are changes in the materials and form, and also in the use of the term.

The first can be described as a gradual 'Westernisation'. Already in the later eighteenth century, architectural ideas were being introduced by the Company's engineering officers to transform the design. Related to this change there occurred a different use of the name. To understand the social changes, this needs looking at in detail.

In the seventeenth century, 'bangla' (with various spellings) was an Indian term used both by Europeans and Indians to describe an Indian structure. As this was adapted and Europeanised in the eighteenth century, so also was the term: bungelow, bungelo (1711), bangallaa (1747), bungalo (1780), with the modern English spelling of 'bungalow' first recorded in 1784 (H-J). After 1820, spellings other than this are rare.

By the late eighteenth century, 'bangla' or 'bungalo' was used in three different ways: it referred to the native Bengali hut, to the Anglo-Indian dwelling adapted from this and, finally, it was beginning to be indiscriminately applied to any kind of small European house in India. When the term is first recorded in print in England, the second meaning was most common; it was recognised as 'an Indian term' and, according to the earliest dictionary definition in English (1788), decribed 'a thatched house with walls of mud or matting'. Such definitions, in terms of the bungalow's structural characteristics, continued till the middle of the nineteenth century. Thus, two early encyclopaedia appearances (1832, 1838) confirm that it is 'an Indian term for a house with a thatched roof'.

By the mid nineteenth century, the anglicised form of the term seems to have been fully accepted into the English language. It is no longer described as 'an Indian term' but is given in anglicised form with its etymology acknowledged as being 'from the Indian word "bangla" '. In 1850, for example, the *Imperial Dictionary* recognises two distinct phenomena. The bungalow was 'in India, a house or villa of a single floor'. There were two types: 'native bungalows are generally built of wood, bamboo, etc. but those erected by Europeans are generally of sun-dried bricks and thatched or tiled'. Here again, however, both are defined according to their structural attributes.

By the early twentieth century, and probably earlier, changes in the form of the bungalow, together with a less specific use of the term, had subtly changed its meaning. A 'bungalow' was 'the most usual class of house occupied by Europeans in the interior of India'. Though this was usually 'of one storey, with a pyramidal thatched roof' it is important for future developments to notice that the major criteria of definition are not related to what it *is* but rather, who it is *for* – which is, of course, the way in which the term originated: 'bangla', 'of, or belonging to Bengal'. Significantly, however, as a result of the colonial process, the ownership of the term has been transferred.

Indeed, even in 1824 there already existed the idea that the bungalow was a house type the use of which was limited to a particular ethnic or racial group: the cantonment at Barrackpore had bungalows, according to Heber, 'for the European officers and other white inhabitants'. In the early twentieth century, 'bungalow' was already widely used in South Asia generally to describe the type of house 'most frequently used by Europeans', whether of one or two storeys, but always detached and located outside the city in the suburbs. Yet the earlier meaning still remains 'with reference to the style of the house', the term being 'sometimes employed in contradistinction to the "usually more pretentious" *pukka* house; by which latter term is implied a masonry house with a terraced roof' (H-J). This is confirmed by Fanny Parkes (1850): 'If a house has a flat roof covered with flag-stones and mortar, it is called a pukka house; if the roof be raised and it be thatched, it is called a bungalow.'

The development of such 'pretentious houses', adopting features from the classical architecture of Europe for the single storey bungalow in India was already in evidence early in the nineteenth century. In the vast mansions and 'garden houses' of East India Company nabobs in Calcutta, Madras and their suburbs (Archer, 1964, 1966) there were plenty of precedents. Contemporary illustrations confirm, however, the two distinct forms of single-storey 'bungalow', one based on the English 'classical' tradition, the other, on the development of the indigenous Bengali hut (plates 18 and 19). Both Williamson and Buchanan comment on these influences: Williamson, comparing 'the first European builders in India' with 'the moderns', suggests, in 1810, that 'more attention is being given to the exterior', with Europeans adopting the Indian idea of the flat, beaten clay roof: 'Many gentlemen have adopted the plan, some wholly, some partially, in their *bungalows*', a practice that was to be widely followed. He regretted that, 'of late years, the European architects have been rather prone to sacrifice comfort to appearance.'

Similarly, Buchanan, concluding his discussion on the origins of the term, indicated that 'the name has been somewhat altered by Europeans and applied by them to all their buildings in the cottage style although none of them have the proper shape and many of them are excellent brick structures adorned with the forms of Grecian architecture'. Heber (1828) confirms this. 'Bungalow . . . is the general name in this country for any structure in the cottage style and only of one floor.' However, he goes on to suggest that it is still primarily applied to the 'genuine' Anglo-Indian bungalow:

> Some of these are spacious and comfortable dwellings, generally with high thatched roofs, surrounded with a verandah and containing three or four good apartments with bathrooms and dressing rooms enclosed from the eastern, western or northern verandahs. The south is always left open (1824, 1:34).

In the first half of the nineteenth century, therefore, two parallel developments took place. On the cantonments and in *mofussil*, 'up-country' stations, the 'original' Anglo-Indian bungalow continued to be built. In many of these, the verandah was supported by brick-built, plastered columns. Many of such dwellings, frequently caricatured, still survive. They 'look nearly all roof without and contain only one storey within' (Blanchard, 1867:33) and appear 'like exaggerated beehives perched upon milestones, a judicious combination of mud, whitewash and thatch' (Atkinson, 1859:2) (plates 16 and 17).

Alongside this was the independent growth of the more substantially built, flat-roofed 'classical' bungalow used particularly to house the officials, first of the Company and after 1858, of the Crown: the district officer, judge, civil surgeon, superintendant of police, as well as army officers on the cantonment. Here the form was increasingly influenced by metropolitan pattern-books of 'cottage architecture' familiar to the engineering officers who supervised their building. With the establishment of the Public Works Department (PWD) in 1854, an 'engineering vernacular', known more widely as the 'Military Board' style, became the standard form for official Government of India buildings (plates 19, 30 and 31).

G.F. Atkinson,
Curry & Rice, 1859

Delhi Sketch Book, 1853

THE DESERTED BUNGALOW

There stands on the isle of Seringapatam,
    By the Cauvery, eddying fast,
        A bungalow lonely,
        And tenanted only
    By memories of the past.
It has stood, as though under a curse or spell,
Untouched since the year that Tippoo fell.

The garden about it is tangled and wild,
    Sad trees sigh close to its eaves,
        And the dark lithe shapes
        Of chattering apes
    Swing in and out of the leaves;
And when night's dank vapours rise grey and foul,
The silence is rent by the shrill screech-owl.

The windows are shuttered, the doors are shut,
    And the odour and stain of decay
        Is on plaster and beam,
        And the stone steps seem
    To be ooze-corroding away;
And the air all around is as tinged with the breath
of the felt, though invisible, presence of Death.

'T was a pleasant abode, no doubt, in its prime;
    Two storeyed, facing the tide;
        A verandah deep,
        And a broad stone sweep
    Of steps to the riverside,
And a boat-house, close to the water's edge,
Flanking the stairs, on a rocky ledge.

The stream flows by in a low-banked curve,
    And higher up, to the right,
        Are the battlements grey
        That could not stay
    The rush of old England's might;
And, higher up still, the world-famed breach –
A lesson we to posterity teach.

Stirring times were those times, forsooth,
    And bold the hearts of our men,
        Who plunged through water,
        And rocks and slaughter,
    And carried the tiger's den.

Heroic the onset and crushing the blow
That was struck near this lonely bungalow.

When the siege was over a Colonel dwelt
    With his wife and daughters here,
        In command of the fort
        Where the bloody sport
    Has cost Mysore so dear.
I can fancy the girls with their prattle light,
And the house all trim, and the garden bright;

I think I can see the early morn
    The horses held at the door,
        And the girls riding out
        With the Colonel stout
    To visit the breach once more,
Or gaze at the gate where Tippoo fell,
Stabbed to death in the fierce pell-mell.

And then the breakfast after the ride,
    Under the shadowy trees,
        Mamma in her chair,
        And the homely fare,
    And the Colonel at his ease,
Conning the sheets of the night-brought post,
Between attacks on the tea and toast.

And, after, the long yet happy day
    In the cuscus-tattied gloom,
        The cheery tiffin,
        And giggling griffin
    'Sconced in the drawing-room;
And the voice of the grand piano, half
Hushing the man's and the maiden's laugh.

And hushed they were; for one dreadful eve
    The Cholera tapped at the door;
        Nor knocked in vain,
        For mother and twain
    Answered the summons sore.
When dawn broke over the house next day,
The mother and daughters had passed away.

The Colonel buried his loved ones three,
    Then fled from the house of woe.
        And ne'er since then
        Have the feet of men

Trod in that bungalow,
Save feet of the traveller, passing near,
Who turns to see it, and drops a tear.

The mouldering rooms are now as they stood
Near eighty years ago:
The piano is there,
And table and chair,
And the carpet, rotting slow,
And the beds whereon the corpses lay,
And the curtains half time-mawed away.

A type of gloom and decay and death,
And happiness overcast,
Is this bungalow lonely,
And tenanted only
By memories of the past.
Peace to the shades of the three who died
In that lonely house by the Cauvery's tide!

from Aliph Cheem, *Lays of Ind*. Thacker & Spink, Calcutta, 1883.

Colonial house type, 1857-1947

The background

The revolt of 1857 combined with other developments to bring a marked change in British views of India. As the economic transition from an agrarian to an industrial base proceeded in Britain, so India was seen in a different light. With the expansion of the cotton industry in Lancashire, the sub-continent became a vast market for cheap textiles coming from the factories of new industrial towns. As Kemp puts it, mercantile capital had to face the challenge of industrial capital, which saw India as a market and as a source of raw materials and was therefore hostile to the East India Company's monopolistic position (1978:138). The Company operated with the help of a comprador class of Indian merchants; the continued development of trade opened up further opportunities inside India for the enrichment of a merchant class.

The changes after 1857 were to reflect these developments. In the process they were to have a drastic effect on British residential settlement in India. In the fifty years following the transfer of authority from the Company to the Crown, British numbers rapidly increased. Colonial rule required a strong state: in the army and police, 450,000 troops were commanded by British officers. The growing purchasing power in Britain and the increasing international division of labour brought plantations and the development of cash crops: the tea gardens of Assam, worked by Indian coolies, were run by British managers. By 1913, nine-tenths of the total trade in Calcutta passed through European hands: 'non-official' British in planting, commerce and the professions numbered more than 50,000 (Fuller, 1913:197-205, 269-76, 297-8). In the railways, jute mills and larger retailing stores, the managers, like the capital, were from Britain. There were also British engineers, lawyers, newspaper editors, as well as missionaries and teachers.

In 1869, the Suez Canal opened. With this, Asia was brought some 4,000 miles closer to Europe: the voyage from Bombay to Britain was cut to just over 6,000 miles (Latham, 1978:27).

As the economy was increasingly orientated towards British interests, government services grew. To ensure that India remained a market for British goods and a producer of raw materials, the state provided an infrastructure of roads, bridges, railways, telegraphs, irrigation works, administrative centres and army camps, the construction of which was supervised by the PWD. In the second half of the century, forest, agriculture, engineering, education and medical services were established or organised on different lines. At the peak of the system was the 'steel frame' of the Indian Civil Service. Here, the highest administrative and political offices in a country of 244 million people (1913) were held by just over 1 thousand British officials. The 250 administrative districts, each ranging in size from 2,000 to 10,000 square miles and with a population from $\frac{1}{2}$ to 4 million people, were still controlled, depending on the region or province, by the collector and magistrate or deputy commissioner. Excluding British troops and their dependants, there were some 120,000 Europeans in India (Fuller, 1913:197-205, 269-76, 297-8).

The most visible sign of this presence was the expanding 'European quarter' of the towns. Calcutta, Madras and Bombay had originated as European settlements. Hence, the Europeanised architecture and spatial pattern which had emerged was an urban form to which the residential needs of Indian newcomers had had to adapt.

Outside these major centres, however, European areas had grown up round the civil stations and cantonments. These, for obvious reasons, had been placed next to, but usually 2 or 3 miles removed from, existing Indian towns. Alternatively, where a cantonment had been established in virgin territory, a 'native town' had often grown alongside. In these provincial towns, therefore, there had developed two separate and unequal urban settlements, one 'European', the other, the 'native city'. Here, in the civil station and cantonment, the typical dwelling was the bungalow-in-its-compound, a scattering of them taking up a vast area just outside the indigenous town. It was the 'classical' Anglo-Indian bungalow of civil station and cantonment which became, in these years, the symbol of the new European political and cultural presence in India.

The setting: cantonment and civil station
How European contemporaries saw the 'station' and 'native city' can be seen by the following.

> An Indian station consists of two parts: the cantonments of the Europeans and the native city and bazaar. The west and east are far apart, separated by a waste common, fields or gardens. . . There is no bond of union between the two, in language, faith or nationality. The west rules, collects taxes, gives balls, drives carriages, attends races, goes to church, builds its theatres . . . and drinks its pale ale. . . . The east pays, takes in the shape of what it eats grown on taxed land . . . sits in decaying temples, haunts its rotting shrines, washes in failing tanks, and drinks its semi-putrid water. Between the two is a great gulf; to bridge it over is the work reserved for him who shall come to stabilitate our empire in the East. . . .

The European station is laid out in large rectangles formed by wide roads. The native city is an aggregate of houses perforated by tortuous paths. . . . The Europeans live in detached houses, each surrounded by walls enclosing large gardens, lawns, out-offices. The natives live packed up in squeezed-up tenements, kept from falling to pieces by mutual pressure. The handful of Europeans occupy four times the space of the city which contains tens of thousands of Hindoos and Mussulmen.

The cantonment of Kanpur (Cawnpore) was typical of its kind.

The cantonments lay along the bank of the river, over a tract extending six miles . . . for, wheresoever in Hindostan Englishmen make their homes, no regard is had to economy of space. Each residence stands in a separate 'compound' . . . of some three or four acres, surrounded by an uneven crumbling mound and ditch, with here and there a ragged hedge of prickly pear. For all over India fences appear to exist rather for the purpose of marking boundaries than for protection against intruders. The house consists of a single storey, built of brick, coated with white plaster; the whole premises, if the owner be a bachelor or subaltern, in a most shabby and tumbledown condition. A flight of half a dozen steps leads up to a verandah which runs round three sides of the building.

The principal door leads . . . into the sitting room, a spacious, ill-kept, comfortless apartment; the most conspicuous article being a huge, oblong frame of wood and canvas suspended across the ceiling. . . . The furniture . . . is in the last stage of dilapidation. Every article in an Anglo-Indian household bears witness to the fact that Englishmen regard themselves but as sojourners in the locality. . . . A large, rickety table . . . eight or ten chairs . . . a couch with broken springs . . . a Japanese cabinet . . . and an easy chair of colossal dimensions, the arms of which are prolonged and flattened, so as to accommodate the occupant with a resting place for his feet. . .

The centre apartment is flanked on either side by a smaller chamber, both of which are employed as bedrooms, if . . . our young friend is keeping house with some . . . chum. The door into the Sahib's bedroom stands open, like every other door in British India; the multitude of servants, and the necessity of coolness, forbidding the very idea of privacy. There stands a bedstead of wood . . . inclosed in all sides with mosquito curtains of white gauze. . . Little of ornament or convenience is seen around save a capacious brass basin on an iron stand, a half a dozen trunks. . . . An inner door affords a view into the bathroom, paved with rough bricks; the bath consisting of a space surrounded by a parapet six inches high, in which the bather stands while his servant sluices him with cold water from a succession of jars. . . .

Such are the quarters of a British subaltern. The home of a married pair may be somewhat more comfortable . . . the lady must have her drawing room, where she can display her wedding presents. . . . The Commissioner, his sanctum where he can wallow in papers.

At Kanpur, there was also a church, 'meeting houses of diverse Protestant persuasions, a Roman Catholic chapel, a mission for the Society for the Propagation of the Gospel . . . a race-course, as there is in every spot in the East where a handful of our countrymen have got together; a theatre . . . a freemason's lodge . . . a racket court . . . library and newsrooms, and billiard rooms . . . the . . . band-stand (Trevelyan, 1894:2-11, 40).

The quarters of the Indian troops consisted of long rows of huts built of mud on a framework of bamboos and thatched with straw. Every soldier had his own cabin in which 'he kept an inconceivable quantity of relations. . . . There he rules supreme, for no Sahib, be he ever so enthusiastic on the subject of sanitation and drainage, would care to intrude upon the mysteries of the sepoy household.' Each regiment had a bazaar: at Kanpur, it contained two-thirds of the native city's 60,000 inhabitants. Some sixty years later, a similar cantonment at Bangalore was described by a young cavalry officer, Winston Churchill, in *My Early Life* (1937):

> All round the cavalry mess lies a suburb of roomy, one-storeyed bungalows standing in their own walled grounds and gardens. . . . We three . . . took a palatial bungalow, all pink and white, with heavy tiled roof and deep verandahs sustained by white plaster columns, wreathed in purple bougainvillia. It stood in a compound of perhaps two acres . . . we took over from the late occupant about a hundred and fifty splendid standard roses. . . Our three butlers formed a triumvirate in which no internal dissensions ever appeared . . . and thus freed from mundane cares, devoted ourselves to the serious purpose of life.
>   This was expressed in one word – Polo.

As the cantonments bore a remarkable similarity to each other, so also did the civil stations. The comments of visitors over a century, irrespective of date, are striking in their similarity.

> The approach to Kishnagur, which is exceedingly pretty and woody, early indicates proximity to European city or town – a beautiful avenue of Teak trees, shaded a remarkably smooth [and] well-kept road. We fairly entered Kishnagur, and I, for the first time in my life, a civil station.
>   A civil station . . . is so called in contradistinction to a military one; and contains those courts and offices of Government with their functionaries, that are distributed over the land to administer its laws, civil and criminal, and regulate its revenue affairs.
>   Kishnagur is, indeed, a delightful place, and for salubrity bears the highest reputation. The only fault I can find with it is that, as a station, it is so very straggling. There is a handsome little church . . . a Government College . . . a park, a truly beautiful English-like place. The centre is a race course, whilst plantations of magnificent Teak trees, cultivated by order of Government . . . everywhere meet the eye. . . .
>   I must not omit to notice the little Dak bungalow which is here found – the first of those staging conveniences . . . we have met in this mofussil trip (Grant, 1859).

The dak and inspection bungalow

The straggling handful of bungalows provided a private cultural environment for both 'official' and 'unofficial' Europeans. Between such stations, the major cities and 'the hills', smaller areas of 'cultural territory' were needed if the traveller was to feel 'at home'. The 'dak' system, by which mail was carried by relays of runners, had been taken over from the Moghuls, and from the early nineteenth century the British had built 'dak bungalows', not only where relays changed but where officials might stop overnight. Offering solitude and familiar surroundings, the dak bungalow was preferred to the unfamiliarity of the *dharmsala* in the Indian town.

With the expansion of the government's activities, 'inspection', 'forest', 'canal' and 'irrigation' bungalows were added. Like the dak bungalows, these were private cultural enclaves, which, though spartan in their furnishing, were permanently staffed by two or three Indian servants. According to *The Times* correspondent, W.H. Russell, in 1859,

> though varying greatly in actual comfort, all are on the same plan. A quadrangular building of masonry, one storey high with a high-pitched roof of thatch or tiles, projecting to form porticoes and verandahs. The house divided into 'suits' of two, three or four rooms, provided more or less imperfectly with charpoys (cots), deal tables, and deteriorating chairs. . . . Off each room, however, is that universal bathroom and the earthern jars of cool water. . . . The bungalow generally stands at a distance of twenty to thirty yards from the road, in an enclosure, which contains the kitchen and sleeping places of the *khitmatgar* (caretaker) and servants. . . These buildings, though in theory open to all, are in practice and reality, almost exclusively used for Europeans. I have never yet met a native gentleman stopping in one (1860, 1:141-3).

Later dak bungalows followed the basic pattern of 'PWD vernacular'. The central room, with its flat roof, was higher than the verandah and to ensure ventilation and a cool breeze at ceiling level, windows were high up in the 15- or 20-feet high walls. Already common by 1850, the type remains at the present day (plate 23).

The architecture of empire

In Britain, growing interest in India combined with the increasing self-consciousness of the architectural profession to bring this 'engineering vernacular' under fire. The first official architect to the government of India was appointed in 1858. In 1865, the leading architectural journal spoke out.

> The revival of architectural taste which has sprung up in England within the last twenty years is slowly but gradually spreading to India; and within the last few years . . . public buildings [have] been erected which would do no discredit to any European capital. This improvement has not come before it was wanted. Until lately, we did not shine in designing public or private buildings at home . . . but we certainly surpassed ourselves in India, and succeeded in inventing a style (irreverently known as the Military Board style) which for ugliness beat everything that was ever constructed by man.

The Principal of Thomason College, Roorkee, in the Punjab, where engineering officers received some little architectural training, was equally conscious of 'the sense of desolation that comes over one at first sight of our Indian cantonments . . . the straight and dusty roads, the rows of glaring white barracks, and the barn-like church'. The reasons for this lack of architectural merit in government buildings were put down to the exigencies of climate and the over-riding need for economy.

It was also felt, however, that 'the true principles of architectural construction for buildings in the East, which are to be used by men habituated to an entirely different climate, have not yet been discovered' (*The Builder*, 1865:441). Another reason was that earlier British residents had hardly seen themselves staying for long. After praising the fine buildings of the Hindus and Muslims, one army officer wrote in the early nineteenth century,

> All colonisation being discountenanced, no buildings but such as are intended for immediate comfort or security, are ever thought of, either by Government or individuals. . . . When half a century shall have elapsed, after the cessation of our dominion in Hindustan, there will not perhaps be a stone left to point out where dwelt

any portion of the 40,000 islanders who so long held in subjection 100 millions of people (Blakiston, 1829, 2:107-8).

With the formal creation of Empire, things were to change. The challenge was taken up by a leading metropolitan architect. In probably the earliest paper on what later became 'tropical architecture' given to the Royal Institute of British Architects in 1868, T. Roger Smith spelt out some of his Indian experiences (1868-9:197-208).

Smith was only concerned with buildings for the use and occupation of Europeans; his comments represent an accurate account and 'rationalisation' for the evolution of the bungalow's form over the previous hundred years.

For Smith, the main determinants were climatic – the intense light, heat, seasonal and torrential rains, and the wind, dust and thunder storms. Hence, the main walls had to be screened from heat and rain, windows and doors should admit every breeze, and walls be as thick as possible: 'a screen called a verandah is essential and it becomes, in fact . . . the leading feature of buildings in the tropics.' This was usually about 10 feet wide with the roof running over it in a continuous line. The rooms provided by the verandah served as work places for 'native people', or were used by the occupants for 'lounging, smoking, walking and even

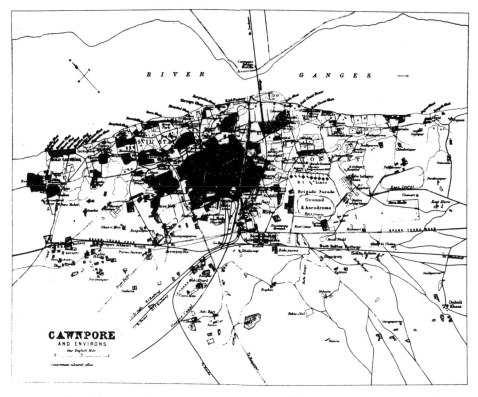

Figure 1.8   Colonial space: civil station, cantonment and city, 1931.
In many places, this tripartite division was to provide the setting for modern suburban development (*Imperial Gazetteer of India*, 26, Atlas, 1931)

1 Steps towards a global economy, 2: Dutch East India Company factory, Hugli, Bengal. 1665. Painting by
   Hendrik van Schuylenburgh.
   The enclosed 'territorial' nature of separate development, later to characterise European settlement in
   India, is already apparent. Transport was largely by river, hence the location by the River Hugli. For
   temporary accommodation or storage outside the compound, tents were used and also the indigenous
   'banggolo' or 'bangelaer' as it was referred to in Dutch (*Rijksmuseum, Amsterdam*)

2 'Banggolo' as accommodation for servants: 'House of a Hindu', Calcutta, 1786. Painting by O. Humphry. Travelling in Bengal about this time, the French Comte du Modave wrote of the larger houses of Hindu families having 'cabins' around them in which lived the servants of the household (*British Library*)

3 The indigenous 'banggolo' of the peasant economy of rural Bengal, 1860s. Photograph by Samuel Bourne.
Traditional skills and bamboo technology combined to produce the characteristic curvilinear roof line. Used for centuries, it influenced the more formal architecture of India, both Muslim (as below) and Hindu (*India Office Library*)

4 Mausoleum of Fath Khan (d. 1657), Gaur, Bengal (A. H. Dani, *Muslim Architecture of Bengal*, 1961)

THE SCHOOLMASTER'S DWELLING.

5 Appropriation of culture:
Mulnath, Bengal, 1859.
The indigenous 'banggolo',
built with local labour and
materials but adapted for
European use (original
caption) (C. Grant, *Rural Life
in Bengal*, 1859)

6 Appropriation of culture: Ranaghat, Bengal, 1914.
European use of Bengali building forms continued into the present century: the building is Indian, the
institution it contains – a missionary Women's Hospital – European (*Church Missionary Society*)

7 Bungalow origins: alternative theory.
According to J. Lockwood Kipling, the bungalow may have evolved from the British army service tent,
shown here in a painting of the 1820s (*India Office Library*)

8 Bungalow functions: accommodation for guests, Orissa, c. 1825. The two bungalows to the right form annexes to the main house (*India Office Library*)

9 Bungalow functions: opium godown and bungalow, Bihar, c.1825.
Opium production in India was part of the triangular system of trade promoted by a mercantilist political economy. England imported tea from China, sent finished cotton goods to India and maintained the trade balance by exporting raw cotton and opium from India to China.

In Bihar and Bengal, peasants cultivated the plant under contract to the E.I.Company and, later, the opium agencies of the Raj. Agents at Patna and Benares supervised the processing and packing of the opium for sending to Calcutta. The bungalow here was occupied by Company agent, Charles D'Oyly, who also made the drawing (*India Office Library*)

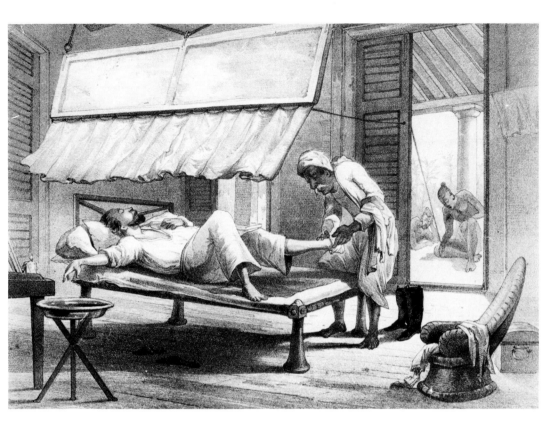

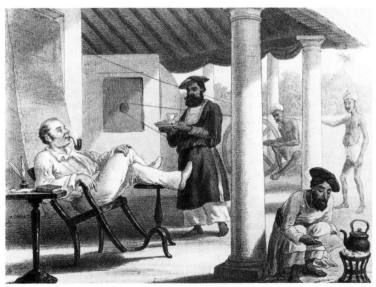

10, 11 Colonial technology: the
punkah.
Different cultural
expectations about comfort
standards led to the
development of local
technology. Thermal
control was a labour-
intensive activity: one
servant operated the
punkah; another, the
thermantidote which blew
cool air into the interior (G.
F. Atkinson, *Curry and
Rice*, 1859)

12, 13 Bungalow functions: studying the local culture.
Like that at the Jagannath Temple, Orissa (above), the travellers' bungalow at Surseya Ghat, Kanpur,
provided separate accommodation away from the indigenous town for Europeans visiting the local
sights. The Jagannath painting, dated 1820, is one of the earliest identified records of a bungalow
named as such (13 from C.R.Forrest, *A Picturesque Tour along the River Ganges and Jumna*, London,
1824. Both illustrations, *India Office Library*)

14 Bungalow functions: colonial dwelling on the plains, Punjab, 1860s.
The characteristic compound and bungalow form, with corners enclosed for bathing rooms. Separate kitchen and servants' quarters are at the rear (right); the well, located behind the tree in the foreground (*Photograph, Samuel Bourne*) (*India Office Library*)

15 Bungalow functions: second home in the hills, Himalayas, 1836.
The piano (the sheet music of which can just be discerned through the open door) helped hill station visitors reproduce the cultural life of 'the plains' which they abandoned during the summer (*India Office Library*)

Coffee-planter's bungalow

Rev. J. F. Cole's bungalow, Taljan

16, 17   Economy and society: Ceylon and Bengal, late 19th century.
          Bungalows were symbols of the colonial political economy, in this case, the plantation and, as part of
          the process of cultural change, the church (*Church Missionary Society*)

18 Bungalow functions: military control. The 'Public Works Department' or 'Military Board' style, 1860s. Increasing professional knowledge in the military engineering service resulted in the development of ideas about 'tropical architecture' (i.e. architecture for Europeans in 'the tropics'). The raised central hall, with windows at ceiling height, was one result (*India Office Library*)

19 Military cantonment: officers' bungalows, c.1860s.
The masonry 'pukka house' in the foreground contrasts with the 'cutcha' pyramid-roofed bungalows to the rear (*India Office Library*)

20, 21 Bungalow functions: administrative control. The typical 'Magistrate's' or 'Commissioner's Bungalow' of the later nineteenth century. Photographs by Samuel Bourne.
The horizontal development of living space partly resulted from the command over local resources and the location of the occupants away from the indigenous town. The porch to the left (above) provided shelter for waiting carriages or callers not invited indoors. After the conflict of 1857, tiles gradually replaced thatch as a precaution against incendiarism (*India Office Library*)

Colonel Chapman's bungalow - Peshawur -

22 Separate development: cantonment and 'native city', Peshawar, late 19th century.
Despite the poor quality of the print, the contrast – social, cultural, political, economic and, not least,
spatial and architectural – between 'Colonel Chapman's bungalow' and the 'native city' is precisely
captured on this single page of a photograph album (*India Office Library*)

23 Moving territory: the dak bungalow, Grand Trunk Road, Haryana. Photograph, 1970.
Like the 'canal' or 'forest bungalow', the dak bungalow provided private cultural territory for European officials travelling around their domain (*Author*)

Hawkers on verandah at East Parade Bungalow.

24 Semi-private space: the verandah (*India Office Library*)

25 The verandah had social as well as climatic functions, providing space for those not invited indoors. Its height gave added status to occupants, especially when greeting visiting guests (*India Office Library*)

26 Servicing the bungalow: the political economy of space, 1860s.
As with thermal control, running day to day life in the bungalow was made possible only by command over local labour, in this case, some nineteen staff. The *jhangp*, an item of technology adopted from the indigenous hut (see Figure 1.3) could be raised or lowered, controlling shade and temperature in the verandah and modifying its use as public or private space (*India Office Library*)

27 Transformation of culture: Calcutta, 1850s. Photograph by F. Fiebig.
The economic and political penetration of India was accompanied by cultural change; in cases, the latter was a pre-requisite of the former. Commenting on the comprador merchant class of Calcutta in 1823, Bishop Heber wrote: 'their progress in the imitation of our habits is very apparent, though still the difference is great. None of them adopt our dress. But their houses are adorned with verandahs and Corinthian pillars' (*India Office Library*)

28 'Westernisation' and the local economy: 'Sakar Bag. Small Banglow' (original caption).
By the late 19th century, 'bungalow' had come to mean the type of house occupied by Europeans in India, that is, detached and in its own grounds. Its adoption by Indian princes, either for their own use or for that of guests, as well as by 'landed gentry' and merchant families, was part of what Bayly (1983:429) has called a 'colonisation of taste'. With the new buildings and architecture came changes in clothes and domestic property, all of which were to exercise a formative influence on the economy (*India Office Library*)

29 Drawing room, palace of an Indian prince, early 20th century (*India Office Library*)

30 Bureaucracy: the bungalow as symbol of rank, New Delhi, 1940.
The original caption on the reverse reads 'Gazetted Officer's bungalow, Class "C"' (*India Office Library*)

31 Colonial legacy: Civil Lines bungalow, Delhi, 1970 (*Author*)

32 Nabob's return: hints of the Bengal
connection, 1803 (cf. plates 2–6)
Indian cultural influences in Britain
came in with East India Company
wealth: some of the cultural brokers
were Company officials, one of whom
built a country seat at Sezincote,
Gloucestershire. The cottage was
located nearby (*Author, 1973*)

33 The image transferred, 1800.
With the move to capitalist agriculture,
land increasingly came onto the market.
The new landlords 'improved' their estates,
often adding 'ornamental cottages' for
which architects produced the designs, in
this case, 'with a viranda in the manner of
an Indian bungalow' (J. Plaw, *Sketches for
Country Houses, Villas, etc.* 1800. *Royal
Institute of British Architects*)

dining and sleeping in', Indian life, 'being much *al fresco*, and privacy little studied compared with comfort' (plate 24).

The bungalow ought to be oriented to catch the prevailing breeze, with rooms arranged *en suite* from side to side, with doors and windows opposite each other so that a breeze blows throughout. This necessity of a through draught and a thoroughfare all round the building (the verandah) had combined to exclude corridors almost entirely from dwelling-houses; 'your life in an Indian bungalow (or house) is public to a degree that would here seem strange'. The general plan of the bungalow should be kept simple, at once both compact and roomy. It was important for his middle class audience to know that 'all servants reside apart' and the few stores in the house were kept in the verandah which 'swelled the bulk of the building extraordinarily'. Over this simple mass a roof was thrown which, if not a terrace, had a flat pitch with the eaves overhanging so as to give most shadow and throw the heavy tropical rain away from the foot of the walls.

As stairs were 'a serious fatigue in a hot climate', buildings of many storeys were not common. The ordinary height of a storey was about 18 to 20 feet, supplying 'all the air we can get'. The single storey was also safer during earthquakes. Smith's rationalisation of the single-storey structure was, if nothing else, naive. In a continent not known for earthquakes, and with a centuries-old, multi-storey tradition, the real explanation passed him by: the political economy of colonialism where the economics of land and labour were rarely considered (King, 1976).

The absence of water-borne sewage arrangements combined with local caste practices to ensure that all sanitation activities were located along the external walls. To each bedroom, a 'bathroom' was attached in which the shallow ledged platform was filled by a water-bearer from a skin. The water was either carried inside or poured through a pipe leading in from an outside wall. As the system of water conservancy was not established in India, 'in or adjoining each dressing room is a convenience taking the place of a water closet'. The 'removal of faecal matter was done twice daily, and the persons whose business it is to do this work (termed sweepers), must not, both on account of the offensive nature of their work, and their lowness of caste, come into the building so as to risk their contact with higher caste servants.' A sweeper's staircase was therefore necessary, with access along the verandahs to the external wall of each dressing room. Here, a small doorway through the wall gave access to each convenience.

> This necessity for a dressing room to each bedroom, and for a secluded and external
> access to each dressing room for the water carrier and sweeper, makes no inconsiderable
> demand on the ingenuity of the architect.

Another peculiarity of 'tropical life' (not, it might be noted, 'colonial life'), was that every European who could afford it rode to his business or pleasure, and thus every building required a carriage porch. Each house also needed stabling and coach houses. The compound was, 'a compromise between a meadow, an orchard and a garden'. Within this nestled a cluster of huts where the servants and their families lived, household work was done, and a kitchen stood. 'The number of attendants required is very great. As a rule in tropical countries' (read 'colonial') 'native labour is cheap and plentiful; each individual does not do much and the subdivision of labour is carried out to a perplexing extent.' Stabling and servants' dwellings should be located to the windward of the main building, particularly as the smell from burning the dried dung cakes used for fuel was 'particularly offensive in a hot climate'.

After discussing climatic factors, as well as the 'taken-for-granted', social, cultural and administrative requirements of 'buildings for European occupation', Smith comes to 'the question of aesthetics'.

> There still remains the ultimate question, and perhaps the most purely architectural question of all. What aspects, as works of art, shall we, as artists, strive to impress upon the buildings . . . for the art of any building is undoubtedly the one element . . . which concerns us architects peculiarly and most exclusively.

As many 'unprofessional men' were required to comprehend the arrangement of buildings and the organisation of works 'it is our special honour . . . to render (those works) not merely serviceable as structures but impressive as monuments; that of us is expected, indeed, not merely a work of skill but a work of art'.

This then was the expression of the growing consciousness of a professional, architectural role; there was, however, an added political role which the new, empire-conscious architect had to fulfil. The solution to the question of style lay 'in the adoption of a type essentially European', though blending with it admissible features as are found in the best styles of architecture developed in tropical climates. The difficulty lay, however, in the lack of a distinctive 'modern English style'. Had that existed, 'we ought . . . to use it as the Roman did in his colonies'. In Smith's view,

> as our administration exhibits European justice, order, love of law, energy and honour, so our buildings ought to hold up a high standard of European art. . . . [Such buildings] ought to be European, both as a rallying point for ourselves, and as raising a distinctive mark of our presence, always to be upheld, by the natives of the country.

Although such views had existed for decades, they had rarely been so clearly articulated. In recognising that architecture provided 'a rallying point', Smith touched on one of the most important symbolic functions of colonial architecture, that of providing the European community with a visible assurance of their own cultural identity. As a 'distinctive mark of our presence', such architecture fulfilled its major function: the affirmation of authority by the dominant cultural and political power.

The dwelling which Smith describes had evolved over more than a hundred years; it was to continue almost unchanged for many years to come (plate 31). In comparison to the buildings of those who were ruled, it had roots in a different tradition. For an economic and political elite, there were few constraints on the use of land, or governing the selection of sites. In making such decisions, it was the exercise of a cultural choice by a group who had political control which determined locations in respect to the indigenous town.

The bungalows were nothing if not spacious. In Bengal in the early twentieth century, accommodation for officials was provided in four categories. In the third (next to the most senior), for officers drawing £960 to £1,600, the cost was not to exceed £2,800. The accommodation comprised (in feet):

Dining room	18 by 22	2 Dressing rooms	19 by 22
Drawing room	23 by 22	6 Bathrooms	10 by 10
4 Bedrooms	18 by 18	1 Store room	12 by 10
Study	25 by 12	1 Lamp room	9 by 10

A verandah 14 feet wide fronted the bungalow, one 10 feet wide ran along the rear, and the verandahs on the other two sides formed the bathrooms. The cost of Indian labour varied, but was between 2d and 4d a man per day (Colonial Office, 1909:Appendix).

In influencing the form and size, political and cultural considerations were likewise paramount. Command over economic resources enabled travel by carriage or later, car. It also provided for the occupants between ten and thirty servants to undertake the tasks which English middle class lifestyle required. The excess of leisure time, combined with plentiful Indian labour, encouraged entertaining. Servants were cheap: *malis* to tend the garden, a *chowkidar* to guard the gate, a *syce* to care for horses, the *bheesti* to carry water in a skin, *dhobis* to do the laundry, a *darzi* to manufacture European clothes, a *jamadar* to clean the scattered areas of the dwelling, substituting their labour for mechanical systems of sanitation, a cook to shop in a bazaar unfamiliar – or distasteful – to the bungalow's inhabitants, *chokras* to assist in the preparation of meals, *bearers* to wait on table when entertaining was a pasttime for all, craftsmen to make furniture and reproduce an expanded version of a middle class environment 'at home' (plate 26).

The nature of Anglo-Indian society and the activities of its members were instrumental in the evolution of the bungalow and its distinctive location, appearance and form. As imperial rule extended, it spread throughout the land, embodying a single, cultural and political meaning, a type of dwelling which contrasted, everywhere it was found, with the regional types of Indian house. From Bangalore to Bombay, though frequently differing in style, the plan and structure of the bungalow was more or less the same. For the official and his family who used it, moving at the end of each 'tour', it provided continuity through the progress of a colonial career.

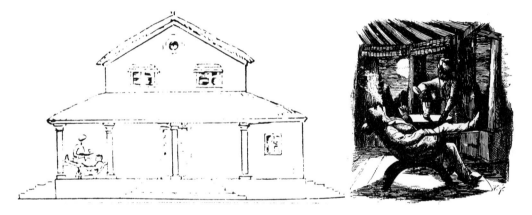

Figure 1.9   Semi-private area: uses for the verandah; (J.L. Kipling, 'Origins of the Bungalow', *Indoors and Out*, 1911) (A. Cheem, *Lays of Ind*, 1869)

In the first half of the twentieth century, the 'classical bungalow' though by no means the only form of residence for Europeans in India, was none the less the most typical, and most favoured for official and non-official elite. Of equal importance, it was increasingly being adopted by the growing Indian middle class.

Indian inheritance, 1900-1980

Traditionally, Indians ate their meals sitting on the floor. The food was served either on leaves or on metal . . . plates. Among the upper castes, and especially among Brahmins, eating was a religious act. The food had to be cooked while the women were in a ritually pure state, since it was offered first to the domestic deities before being served to members of the family. . . . At the end of the meal the dining leaves became impure and were thrown out. The places where the leaves had rested were purified with a solution of cowdung.

Now, in the larger towns and cities, the educated and Westernised groups increasingly prefer to eat at tables. The most obvious feature of the change is the new technology – chairs and table, stainless steel utensils, spoons – but it also has other implications . . . the new mode of eating contributes to an increase in secularisation as the table is not likely to be purified with cowdung solution after meals, and the ritual acts traditionally performed before and after meals tend to be dropped (Srinivas, 1976:53).

The process which Srinivas describes, namely, the 'Westernisation' of Indian domestic material culture, has so far been little explored. To put it briefly: just when, where, how, and for what reasons did members of a rising middle class abandon traditional behaviour, stop sitting cross-legged on the floor, eating with their fingers, sleeping on roll-away mattresses, living in traditionally designed houses in the ancient cities and villages and move into Western-style 'bungalows', adopting, in the process, the chairs, dining tables, cutlery, tableware, bedroom suites and 'sofa sets' with which the houses of contemporary middle and upper class Indians are filled? Such a sweeping generalisation obviously needs qualifying: much 'traditional' behaviour persists and the vast majority of so-called 'Westernised' Indians vary their behaviour to suit situation and circumstances. More important, to label 'Western' what is clearly international, 'modern' or simply 'bourgeois' is both ethnocentric and simplistic. What is here referred to as 'Westernisation' was only one of many influences on Indian architecture and social life and material culture which have included borrowings from foreign rulers in earlier times – Afghans, Turks, Persians and, in some parts, even the Chinese. Moreover, 'Western' or even 'European' is far too crude a term in that it makes no distinction between Portuguese, Dutch, French and British influences which had made themselves felt in Western India from the fifteenth century. Even British influence was differentiated, not least over the two centuries during which it was felt; and none of these reservations refers to the much more basic question concerning the transformations brought about by changes in the mode of production and the development of a world-wide economy with which this chapter began (King, 1983b). Yet for the sake of convenience rather than accuracy, Srinivas's term will be used. The discussion in this section, on a theme deserving a full length book in itself, is therefore no more than exploratory. A more detailed discussion of the issues, though relating to Africa, is taken up in Chapter 6.

'Westernisation' and the built environment

Urbanisation is usually seen as an economic and social process, the creation of a labour force for new kinds of production, and also consumption, the investment of capital and the development of new forms of social organisation and behaviour. It is also, obviously, a physical and spatial process, one that creates new buildings and environments in which the variety of everyday life is acted out. New types of behaviour, the 'sit in', strike or international athletics contest, are acted out in particular buildings and environments. And these new buildings and environments, the way they are perceived, and what they encourage or suggest, have effects on people's behaviour.

In the Indian context, what effects have the distinctive planning, building and architectural developments of the last century, or even the last decades, had on the way people have seen (or presented) themselves and others? How have government housing projects helped to modify traditional caste structures or generate new social formations? How have 'Westernised' dwelling-types modified, if at all, family forms and behaviour? How has new technology — electricity, sanitary equipment, prepared foods — affected caste practices and beliefs, and what effects have new technologies had on a traditional occupational and caste structure? The questions are endless.

Srinivas uses the term 'Westernisation' to refer to 'the changes brought about in Indian society and culture as a result of 150 years of British rule, and the term subsumes changes occurring at different levels – technology, institutions, ideology, values'. Here, the notion of 'Westernisation of domestic architecture' implies three inter-related changes which have both affected urban house forms in India as well as the larger urban setting in which these forms are located. Though the processes are of a physical, including 'architectural', and spatial nature, they obviously result from larger social, economic, technological and cultural processes.

1 A change in house plan, form and structure, and the addition of an enclosed compound or garden. Whilst regional differences are recognised, this typically means a change, especially in Northern India, from a one-, two- or more-storeyed, courtyard-type dwelling, with rooms giving inwards onto the courtyard, and structurally joined to similar houses on one or more sides, to a free-standing, 'courtyard-less', 'outward-facing', one- or two-storeyed 'European-style' bungalow. It also implies a change in the number, size and arrangement of rooms.

2 As such bungalows are, by definition, detached and free-standing, the change in house form also involves a change in location. This, therefore, involves a move away from the traditional, indigenous city to a suburb, in many cases, a move to those suburban areas, at first exclusively European, generally known as the 'civil lines' or 'civil station'.

Such a change is not to deny the existence, prior to European settlement in India, of free-standing, detached dwellings, outside the traditional town, occupied by ruling nawabs or wealthy Hindu families.

3 The adoption of Western domestic equipment, especially cutlery, tableware, cooking and serving utensils, furniture and sanitary equipment (either 'Indian' or 'Western style' closets), wash basins, shower equipment and (very rarely) bath tubs. A distinction might be made between those items of equipment which bring no apparent benefits (i.e. eating from a table and sitting on a chair is no more 'efficient' than sitting and eating on the floor) even though the possession of such equipment has important social functions, and other equipment such as electric stoves or refrigerators which obviously bring increased efficiency as well as the saving of time and labour. This latter type of equipment (of relatively recent introduction, i.e. post-1950) is not implied in the notion of 'Westernisation'.

Obviously, there is a chain of relationships by which the adoption of one 'Western' item leads to the adoption of others. Cutlery and tableware have to be stored, hence, a 'sideboard'; its use requires a table and dining chairs which require a place to be used, hence, a 'dining room'. Rooms then take on specialised functions, defined in terms of use and equipment ('sitting room', 'dining room', 'bedroom'). Other social functions are used to define rooms in traditional Indian houses; with sleeping equipment that can be put away in wall cupboards, rooms have multiple, rather than single functions. The addition of a compound which, like the house itself, becomes an expression of land-holding and property-ownership, leads to what has been called a 'compound mentality'.

Three tentative assumptions might be made. The 'Westernisation' or 'bourgeoisification' of domestic life in India began 'at the top', so to speak, with the 'nobility'; it advanced most rapidly in urban centres, particularly those with large and influential European populations; thirdly, its progress was affected by regional, religious, political and, as far as domestic buildings were concerned, local architectural factors. A useful distinction may also be made between two types of city: those major metropolises which were effectively European settlements (Calcutta, Madras, Bombay), where the dominant urban pattern was European and indigenous inhabitants were arguably more likely to be exposed to the dominant culture of the emerging market economy. On the other hand, there were those long-established Indian cities (Varanasi, Lahore, Delhi, Bangalore), where European settlement took place outside and away from the indigenous settlement.

'Westernisation' and the Indian elite

The mutual architectural influences between European and Indian elites in the early period of European settlement have been well documented (Archer and Archer, 1955). British fashions in household furnishing had been adopted as early as the 1770s: the nawabs of Lucknow imported 'all sorts of European manufactures', including mirrors, lustres, framed European prints and Worcestershire china. Lord Valentia, visiting Lucknow in 1803, noticed that the palace was equipped with English chairs, tables, a service of plate, knives, forks and spoons, wine-glasses and decanters (ibid:56-7, 74-8). Apart from this attachment to Western furnishings, many Indian princes built new palaces, modelled on the 'classical' residences and public buildings of the colonial community.

'Middle class' houses: changes in style and form

The operations of the East India Company in Calcutta had created a comprador class of Indian merchants. As early as the eighteenth century, these had commissioned houses in a mixture of Hindu, Muslim and British styles, an architecture – to use Sinha's phrase – of 'comprador syncretism' (1978:17). Holt Mackenzie, commenting on the new class behaviour in Calcutta in 1832 referred to 'the marked tendency among the natives to indulge in European luxuries; they have well-furnished houses and . . . are fond of carriages . . . and drink wines (Misra, 1961:154).

It was Macaulay's Minute of 1835, however, which opened the way for the growth of a Westernised middle class. This famous decision had launched English education and knowledge into India. The object of the Minute, imparting 'to the Native population knowledge of English literature and science through the medium of the English language' was 'to form a class who may be interpreters between us and the millions whom we govern; a class of persons, Indian in blood and colour, but English in taste, opinions, in morals and intellect' who would help govern in the interests of the British (Edwardes, 1967:241; Spear, 1965:126-7). Engaged in government offices or commerce, they would emulate Europeans in the development of India's resources and increase the demand for the consumption of British goods.

To appreciate these stylistic changes, some consideration must be given to traditional urban house-types, with their many regional variations. In northern India in the eighteenth century, wealthier urban families lived in brick houses, of two, three or even five floors, with flat roofs. Two-storey houses were also common in parts of Bengal, but in the Purneah district the houses of the rich middle class were a collection of huts called *baris* or *havelis*, fenced all round. In Varanasi 'rich Hindus preferred to live in detached houses with open courts surrounded by high walls'. In the south, however, there was a greater frequency of one-storey dwellings with a courtyard plan and a gallery inside the courtyard. 'The bungalow, a single-family residential dwelling of mixed European style . . . was not popular with any section of Indian society till the end of our period,' i.e. the early nineteenth century (Raghuvanshi, 1969:232-6).

The early stylistic influences on these two- and three-storey house-forms occurred with the eclectic adoption of 'classical' elements. Thus, Bishop Heber, writing about wealthy Indians in Calcutta in 1823, commented 'their progress in the imitation of our habits is very apparent, though still the difference is great. None of them adopt our dress. But their houses are adorned with verandahs and Corinthian pillars. . . .' (quoted in Misra, 1961:153) (plate 27).

About Delhi in 1835, the *Tourists Guide from Delhi to Kurrachee* reported:

> In no other part of our Eastern possessions do the natives show so earnest a desire to imitate European fashions . . . the houses are of various styles of architecture, partaking occasionally of the prevailing fashions of the West. Grecian piazzas, porticos and pediments are not infrequently found fronting the dwellings of Moslems or Hindoos . . . shops are crowded with European products and manufactures and many display signboards on which names and occupations are emblazoned in Roman characters.

Stylistic change was one thing: however, change in form and location was another.

'Middle class' dwellings: the 'Westernisation' and changing function of the house
Even for comparable socio-economic groups, urban houses varied greatly throughout different regions of India. None the less, at the end of the nineteenth century, the Reverend J.E. Padfield believed that there were some main principles which pervaded all Hindu domestic architecture. As much of his description still holds good for traditional urban areas, his comments on 'an ordinary house of the fairly well-to-do Hindu in the town' are worth quoting at length (1896:16-24). Though sympathetic to his hosts, they also betray the assumptions of a European bourgeois taste, already oriented to a consumer economy.

> The chief feature in the building is that it must be in the form of a square, with an opening to the sky in the centre. The roof slopes outward and inward, and the inner sides all converge around a rectangular open space. . . . In large houses, this . . . space will form a regular courtyard, whilst in smaller buildings . . . it is only a few inches square. . . . The origin of this is not very clear . . . some say it is in order that the sun's rays may shine into the house . . . others say . . . for the rain to fall into the house in order to secure happiness . . . there are few windows, if any at all, looking out upon the street . . . often there is nothing presented to the public road but a blank wall with a more or less imposing doorway. . . .
> On entering the front door [one may] step into the open space or court . . . or there may be a passage from the door with rooms on either side leading into it . . . around [the court] there is a kind of verandah upon which open out the rooms of the dwelling. The four points of the compass are strictly considered in arranging the rooms. The kitchen should always be on the south side and it runs the whole width of the building. This is the most sacred part of the whole house and persons of a lower caste than the household are never allowed to enter it. . . . I have been inside many native houses but I have never been

allowed to cast even a glance into this sacred room . . . except in the Presidency cities, and other large towns, houses have, as a rule, no upper storey at all. . . . The rooms opening out on to the inner verandah are the bedrooms and other private rooms, as well as the store-room, and any other necessary rooms and offices. All the arrangement of rooms is regularly fixed in the [two books of the *Vastu Shastram* – the science of domestic architecture] and great blessings are promised where these rules are complied with . . . one portion of the verandah is apportioned off as a kind of office, or study, in which writing work and the like is done. . . .

If we look at the furniture of a house we are at once struck by its extreme simplicity. Taste and wealth are not manifested in grand furniture and costly hangings, or any other of the things that go to make up a luxurious home in Europe. . . . The furniture . . . is very little. . . . In the houses of the more modern and more advanced, there are occasionally a few chairs, and a table or two; and a chair is usually produced for a European visitor; but as a rule even among the better classes, there is a complete absence of most of the domestic conveniences which even the poorest Europeans consider indispensible. In the kitchen-dining room there are no tables or chairs, no knives, forks or spoons, no plates, or dishes. . . . A few metal or earthenware pots and pans and a simple fireplace suffice for the culinary operations, and the large leaf of the lotus or plantain, or a few smaller leaves cleverly stitched together, form the dinner plate. . . . One needs to live amongst such people to learn how very few, after all, are the real necessities of life, if we only rid ourselves of notions formed by habit and custom. . . . In the office place . . . there may be a low kind of table serving as a seat by day and a couch by night . . . a rug or two . . . a few cushions . . . a few simple pictures representing scenes from the life of Krishna . . . being paintings on glass. . . . Occasionally a print or two may be seen, perhaps a cutting from some illustrated English paper. . . .

The bedroom furniture too, would not strike an English lady as having that air of snugness and comfort which is the charm of the European bed-chamber. There may be a native cot . . . a box or cupboard for the . . . more expensive cloths and jewels . . . a shelf, and in the wall, a few niches for the little native lamps . . . a few native pictures on the wall representing scenes from the *Ramayana* . . . a brass, mug-shaped vessel serving [for washing], a few square inches of looking glass. . . . The water from the brass vessel is poured from the left hand into the right . . . and applied to the face. . . . The complete bath, in the absence of a river, or tanks or other means of immersion, is taken by pouring water over the person from the same brass vessel . . . for both men and women, it is generally done in the back-yard or some such suitable place as may be convenient. . . . In passing along the streets in the early morning, one often sees the ordinary citizen, brass pot in hand, performing his morning ablutions, seated on the edge of his front verandah. . . .

There is no 'going to bed' in the sense understood by the European. . . . The men . . . seem to lie down anywhere, in the inner verandah or along the narrow verandah seat that usually runs along the front wall next to the street. . . . The long, sheet-like cloth is unwound from the body, or some sheet or blanket which is kept for the purpose is used and with this the person is covered, head and all. . . . In the . . . better off class or the aged, and generally by the master of the house, a cot is used for sleeping upon [and] . . . shifted about from place to place to suit convenience. . . . It is easy to see how little difficulty there is in providing for visitors . . . there is plenty of room for the men to lie down . . . and the females lie down with those of the household. . . .

It is . . . the absence of comfort which (to the European) seems most conspicuous in a Hindu home. Of this the idea, or sense, or whatever it may be called, does not seem to exist in the Aryan inner consciousness, and hence there can be no manifest development of it.

Unfortunately Padfield did not say anything of the homes 'of the modern Europeanised Hindu . . . the hybrid civilisation which we see presenting itself'.

For Muslims, a different interpretation of the courtyard house in the mid-nineteenth century is given by A.H. Sharar writing about Lucknow (1974):

There is no necessity for courtyards in Europe because women are not confined to their homes and go out as men do. In contrast it is necessary for houses in India to have courtyards so that women may be able to enjoy fresh air within the perimeter of their own homes. . . . There has always been a distinct difference between Hindu and Muslim houses and this exists to this day. In Hindu houses the courtyards are small and the building is constructed without regard to whether or not air and light will get in. In contrast to this, Muslims like bright, open houses. . . .

As Padfield and others suggest, it is safe to assume that the abandonment of this traditional dwelling for a bungalow in the suburbs was more prevalent in the major cities and other mainly British settlements. Yet given the ambiguous use of the term 'bungalow' in the nineteenth century, gradually replacing the term 'house' (at least, in the English language), it is not always certain just what building type later nineteenth-century commentators are referring to. Nevertheless, 'bungalow' usually implies a free-standing, ex-urban dwelling, usually, in the nineteenth century, of one storey, though increasingly in India in the twentieth, of two or more. More particularly, it would be a dwelling conforming more to a colonial 'Indo-European' than traditional Indian model.

If 'bungalow' does suggest 'Westernisation', then Heber's comment on Mirzapoor in 1824 implies an early development. The town 'had greatly increased since the arrival of the English'; 'numerous and elegant bungalows' had arisen in the outskirts, 'partly in European style but obviously inhabited by natives'. At Ahmedabad in the 1840s, wealthy merchants were likewise adopting Western habits and building houses 'in the English style'. Other merchants built bungalows outside the city. According to Lord Napier, writing in 1878, 'the moment a native of this country becomes educated and rich, he abandons the arts of his forefathers and imitates the arts of strangers whom in this respect, he might be competent to teach.' Domestic architecture ought to be the expression of social institutions and the necessities of climate, both of which were expressed in the 'old-fashioned Indian dwelling', with its interior courtyards: this was 'the feature which the Indian house-builder should never forsake [yet] it is just the feature which he is giving up'. Napier had just visited a 'native nobleman' in his 'country residence' where he had built a small palace to entertain his European guests. 'Every trace of native style had disappeared from this more recent example of native building, and a handsome European villa, of spotless chunam, had risen among the grey pagodas' (*The Builder*, 1870:680-2) (plates 28 and 29).

Though these developments were relatively rare before 1857, they gradually became more common. To understand the change, however, would require a thorough analysis of the many factors behind the creation of the 'middle classes' themselves, including the transition to a commercial capitalist economy. Here, a few comments must suffice.

In England, the middle class developed largely as a result of economic and technological change and was mainly engaged in trade and industry. In India, however, it emerged more from changes in public administration and law than in economic development and belonged to the learned professions. This basic difference had far-reaching implications for the process of 'Westernisation'. It meant that in government service or, after 1918, commissioned ranks in the army, acceptance into the higher echelons was conditional upon a lesser or greater degree of 'Westernisation': not merely the acquisition of language, dress, behaviour and lifestyle but also, a willingness to adapt to Westernised environments and equipment. Thus, the rules for 'The Occupation of Public Works Inspection Bungalows' in one province include 'Asiatic officials are eligible to occupy these bungalows if they have adopted European customs'. Much of the controversy regarding the question of opening up club membership to Indians also revolved round these issues (see King, 1976).

The growth of government services resulted in increasing numbers of Indians being accepted into government occupations. With the creation of Indian universities after 1857, the Indian professions grew. Between 1857 and 1901, the number of Indian government servants rose from less than 3,000 to some 25,000. The Indian Civil Service, long the preserve of Europeans, slowly began to admit Indians and by 1913, some 50 of its 1,000 or so members were Indian. Police services expanded, with 7,000 Indian members in 1901 and getting on for 20,000 by the end of colonial rule. Whilst science and technology were slow to develop, extensive irrigation, railway and public works developed in the late nineteenth and early twentieth centuries and though senior posts were, till 1921, monopolised mainly by Europeans and Anglo-Indians, many Indians were employed as contractors. After 1918, the process of Indianisation proceeded among the commissioned ranks of the Indian army.

The real growth in the Indian middle classes, therefore, was a twentieth-century phenomenon, even though, for medical doctors, the Calcutta Medical College had been established in 1835. In the world of business, the rise of a middle class was particularly associated with the expansion of the joint stock company, especially in banking, planting and trading (Misra, 1961; see also Bayly, 1983).

This growth in the professions and the number of Indians in government service coincides with a steady increase in urbanisation after 1900 and the faster growth of individual cities. It implies an increasing exposure to European lifestyles, not only 'on the ground' but through the media of photography, the press and books. To meet the demand which had been created for Western consumer goods, European department stores were established in Calcutta (Furedy, 1979).

The effect of these developments on the residential behaviour of the middle class, on the architecture of their houses and the growth of 'Western-style' suburbs as places for the investment of growing surplus wealth after 1900, however, are subjects still to be researched. Some insights can be gained from case histories of individual cities and autobiographies. Of these, Allahabad was typical, with a quarter of its professional families, Indian and British, and most of the major Indian lawyers living in the cantonment and Civil Lines in 1891 (Bayly, 1975:53-6). Motilal Nehru, already an eminent lawyer, was soon to follow.

He moved from the densely populated city of Allahabad to a bungalow, 9 Elgin Road, in the spacious and exclusive 'civil lines', where European and Eurasian families lived in solitary splendour. . . . It signified a desire on his part to live in healthier surroundings with greater quiet and privacy. . . . It was also a sign of the transformation that was taking place in his life: the rise in the standard of living was accompanied by increasing Westernisation . . . having a lively curiosity and zest for living he made a point of ordering the latest gadgets and improvements. Anand Bhavan (1, Church Road where he subsequently [1900] had moved to) was the first house in Allahabad to have a swimming pool and it was also the first to have electricity and water laid on (Nanda, 1965:30-1).

About the same time (1896), Padfield referred to the homes of the 'modern Europeanised Hindu' which, however, were 'comparatively few in number and chiefly confined to the large towns and cities'. Departures from traditional lifestyles were only beginning 'in the Presidency cities and other seats of light and learning'. In 1900, Indian industrialist J.N. Tata began building about 100 one-storey bungalows in European ('Queen Anne') style and designed by a British architect, in the Bombay suburb of Bandora (*Building News*, 1900:114). The most detailed description of the process, however, comes from a member of India's post-independence business elite. Prakash Tandon describes how the social, architectural and administrative environment of British rule in Lahore influenced his father's style of life.

On retirement from government service, he built himself a house in 'Model Town', a suburb south of the Civil Lines six miles out of Lahore. Model Town was

almost entirely populated by retired government officials . . . somebody had conceived the idea in 1925 of acquiring a big tract of wasteland . . . and dividing it into plots. The plan of the town was completely geometrical. It had a series of concentric circular roads, crossed by four main roads at right angles, and smaller roads in between. . . . The roads had no name but the blocks were alphabetically numbered so that our address was 12G while the house opposite was 12F. . . .

One after the other, old engineers and army doctors, retired civilians and sessions judges arrived and started laying their foundations. The results of their efforts were all curiously alike, because they were all patterned on the government bungalows which had been their homes, and the dak bungalows which had been the scenes of so much of their activity. Each house was divided into two parts by a huge vestibule in the middle. On one side, were dining and drawing rooms and an office room; on the other, the bedrooms, with dressing rooms and bathrooms (Tandon, 1961:236-9).

The lay-out of the bungalows was similarly based on PWD tradition, now being applied in the new imperial capital at Delhi. The 1935 map of Lahore shows four very distinct types of spatial pattern in the built-up area of the city, which it is tempting to associate with different kinds of values, social relations and behaviour. The old walled city with its intricate, meandering network of streets and tightly packed houses, suggests a traditional society and culture; the 'civil lines' area to the south with its spacious bungalows, wide metalled roads and sparse development intimates the 'ruralised', middle class values and leisured lifestyle of the European governing elite; the rectangular grid system of the military cantonment implies the formal social organisation of the army; the more relaxed, yet still geometrical, lay-out of Model Town suggests the social life of the retired official whom Tandon describes.

Bangalore was another centre of cultural change in the early twentieth century. The Indians who moved into Western-style suburbs from 1920 were in senior government positions, and were 'foreign-returned', Western-educated engineers or army officers or – like the military contractor – in roles mediating between the local and the colonial society. The change was in the first decades of this century: into their bungalows were imported German chandeliers, Czech crystal doorknobs and Western sanitary fittings. Their new-style habitat provided the setting for such Westernised habits as 'drinks', 'afternoon tea' and 'cricket'. Cultural attitudes to colour also changed: 'people didn't think so much about interior decoration (sic) then as they do now.' Not everything 'matched' or conformed to a 'colour scheme' (Pott, 1977:50-71). As Western influence grew strong, the 'dwelling had changed from a house in which one put things' to an object of conspicuous consumption and social display.

Begum Shaista Ikramullah describes a similar process in Lilloah, a suburb of Calcutta. In 1915, the family had been living in a traditional Muslim town house. Four years later, the Begum's father, the second Indian Muslim doctor to take an FRCS qualification in London and one of the first Indians to do so, entered the East India Railway as District Medical Officer and took a government bungalow in the 'civil lines' area.

> We had a very nice house and a really lovely garden. . . . This was the stage when Indians went in for extreme Westernisation in every way, particularly those who joined the Service, which so far had been reserved for the English. They felt it was their incumbent duty to prove to Englishmen that they could emulate him to perfection. . . . Our house, therefore, was furnished to look exactly like an English house. In the drawing room there were heavy sofas . . . lace curtains, gleaming brass and silver . . . and knicknacks displayed in cabinets. The dining room had a fairly massive sideboard . . . displaying a love of heavy silver. The hall and study were furnished in the typical English style of the

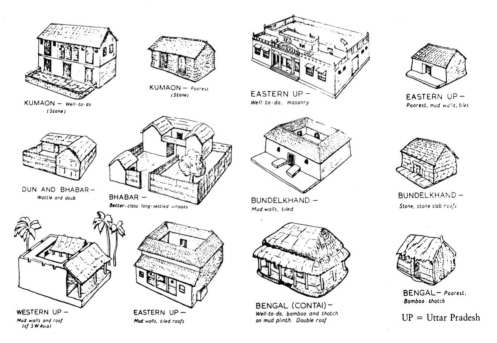

Figure 1.10   Indigenous dwelling forms: Northern India, 20th Century.
The variety of north Indian dwelling forms shows the distinctiveness of the Bengali house in comparison to those of other regions. Its use by Europeans possibly arose from two circumstances, the fact of their initial settlement being principally in Bengal and the congruence between the 'banggolo' (as opposed to less familiar courtyard house forms) and their own cultural expectations about what a dwelling should be. In modern Indian suburban developments, the detached bungalow takes priority over alternative courtyard forms (O.H.Spate and A.T.A.Learmonth, *India and Pakistan*, Methuen, 1965)

times. . . . We had afternoon tea with hot buttered toast and even at other meals we ate what was called 'English' food which I now realise was a mixture of English, French, Portuguese and Indian culinary efforts.

This was also the period of the building of New Delhi, based on the planning and architecture assumptions and values of British colonial power. The Delhi 'civil lines' area, with less than thirty bungalows in 1871, expanded rapidly, and after 1920 had been developed as a colonially modified, 'Indo-European' style suburb, with some 150 bungalows, many soon to be occupied by Indian families as their inhabitants moved to New Delhi (plate 30). Here, each bungalow was located in a compound of 1 to 5 acres, creating – in a city sprawled over 30 square miles – densities of less than ten people to the acre (plate 31). In Old Delhi, 2 or 3 miles to the north, were half a million people living within a walled town of 2½ square miles, at densities eighty times as great (King, 1976).

Conclusion

The aim of this chapter has been to present some preliminary descriptive data on a topic where there has been little previous research. To suggest in a few pages 'conclusions' would be grossly to oversimplify the complexity of the issues involved; these are of at least two kinds: the first, relating to policy and practice; the second, of a more academic kind.

In a study of this nature, any discussion of the policy implications is neither possible nor appropriate. Some of these have been discussed elsewhere (King, 1976, 1980) and others are taken up in Chapter 6. Most obviously, such issues concern the implications of 'the bungalow', as symbolic of colonial housing and urban development, for urban planning, the question of developing appropriate standards, or the radical modification of inequalities which colonial developments left behind. The bungalow and the segregated environment in which it existed was, however, not just a physical and spatial form but was also an attitude of mind, institutionalised in Public Works Departments and lasting long after colonial rule. Following the creation of Pakistan, for example, it was continued in the lay-out of new settlements, and in Islamabad, as at Chandigarh some years before, the bungalow formed the basis of 'Western-style' developments, manifesting in style and scale, the ranking and status of its occupants. If the direction of urban planning has now drastically changed, remnants of colonial environments still remain, though each year made decreasingly significant by urban development all around.

The second set of issues are more theoretical, yet are still of practical concern. What is the relationship between economic, social and environmental change? What insights does the history of the bungalow in India provide? A physical move from the old to the new part of the city, even to a European-style bungalow, might represent a change of attitudes, values and behaviour; it need not imply, however, a change in family structure or relationships and may even extend opportunities for traditional ways of owning property. As Shah suggests, the notion of the multi-membered 'joint-family' in India as it relates to household membership and residential behaviour is a stereotype not bearing close analysis (1974). Although urban households of eight or more may exist, those of four to five people are more common.

It would be difficult to believe, however, that 'bungalow-type' colonial urban development prior to 1947, as well as government housing programmes since, with tens of thousands of flats and houses laid out in strict 'PWD' style, have not influenced the size, structure and

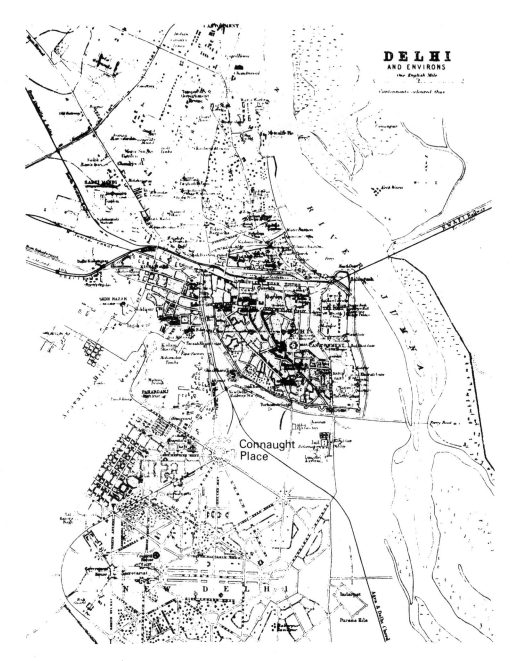

Figure 1.11   Bungalow planning: Old and New Delhi, 1931
The dots along the avenues of New Delhi, south of the old city, are colonial-type bungalows
(see Plate 30). Since Independence (1947), this central area has been partly re-developed and
reduced in scale by extensive urbanisation in and around New Delhi (*Imperial Gazetteer of
India*, 26, Atlas, 1931)

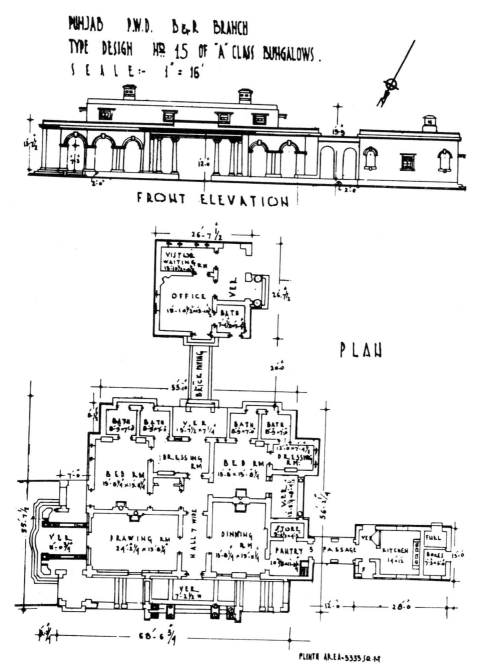

Figure 1.12 Colonial legacy: government housing designs, West Pakistan, 1956
(Government of W.Pakistan, Punjab Works Department, Buildings and Roads Branch.
Designs of 'A' class bungalows and houses for satellite towns, 2nd edition. Lahore,
Superintendent of Government Printing, 1956)

Figure 1.13 Imperial expansion: the bungalow in South East Asia, Penang, Malay Straits, 1853.
'The . . . bungalows are erected here in the same manner, and with similar materials, as they
are near Madras . . . They are surrounded with gardens, and each has its verandah'
(J.Wathen, *Journal of a Voyage*, etc. 1814)

Penang became a key entrepôt port of the mercantile colonial trading system between India
and China in the 19th and 20th centuries, the leading port of what is now Malaysia. It was
founded as Georgetown by Captain Francis Light of the E.I. Company in 1786 whose son,
Colonel William Light, was to lay out Adelaide in South Australia some fifty years later.
The influence of military engineers on the planning, administration and design of this single
colonial urban system is a subject yet to be explored (C.W.Kinluch, *Rambles in Java and the
Straits*, etc. *Robert Aiken*)

relationships of Indian families or other aspects of society as a whole. As to the relation of
suburban development to the massive expansion of a speculative market in land and housing,
this would need another book.

As for the introduction of 'Western' furniture and equipment, there is no doubt, as Srinivas
suggests, that this has not only resulted from economic and cultural change but has also
helped to bring such change about. Both the planning of modern Indian housing as well as the
introduction of equipment is bound up with changes in beliefs and actual behaviour,
particularly relating to cooking, eating, hygiene, the serving of meals, relaxation and defaeca-
tion. Alexander Kira, for example, has shown in *The Bathroom* (1976) how religious and
social beliefs relate to body postures and sanitation practices and these govern the way people
bathe. Unlike the British, people in India do not lie in their own dirty water. Yet while bath
tubs are rare in modern Indian houses, Western-style closets are less so. As any orthodox
Brahmin will confirm, the arrangement of rooms in modern Indian government housing,

particularly regarding the location of kitchen and bathroom (i.e. where access for low caste sweepers to clean WCs is possible only through the kitchen or past the main dining room) creates conflict in regard to orthodox Hindu beliefs.

The scope of these issues is huge and needs more detailed research, particularly regarding the relation of urbanisation to increasing consumption. Recent research has shown how, from the 1860s, landowners founded urban establishments, constructing stone-built houses and, with new merchant and professional families, making a big impact on the local economy. With these new buildings came new tastes in clothes and personal property: foreign cloth replaced homespun, leather replaced cloth bags, and kerosene lamps the traditional flames of vegetable oil. The growth of 'colonial style' consumption created retail shops and general stores (Bayly, 1983: 430, 448). In the 1870s, 'wandering minstrels' composed *kirtans* (songs) protesting at the importation of European industrial goods: glass chandeliers, wall shades and 'Horrocks long cloth'. These 'industrial ballad singers' reprimanded fellow Indians for buying 'umbrellas, walking sticks, Guernsey frocks, waistcoats with green and red buttons, double coats, watches and chains . . . pouring out the crucible of wealth to fill up the houses of foreigners' (*The Builder*, 1880:494).

Other studies have investigated the emergence of land markets, the development of retailing in consumer goods and of changes in taste brought about by 'Western' criteria of design (Neild, 1979; Furedy, 1979; Tarapor, 1981): all were instrumental in incorporating India into the global market economy of today. To understand the role urbanisation played in this process, more needs to be known about the transformation of indigenous building, the introduction of new technology, journals and 'Western' architectural forms as well as urban legislation (bye-laws, building regulations) and the rise of the architecture and planning professions in India. The role of modern transport and market forces in developing bungalow suburbs also needs research. As elsewhere in the world, the city in India has become part of a global system of production and consumption.

From *Dawn* (Karachi), 11 November 1983

A TALE OF EAST AND WEST

Silent and still the bungalow
  As the fire-flies gleam around;
Silent and still the bungalow,
  Save for the murmuring sound
Of the night winds rustling through the gloom
Of each dark, decaying, deserted room.

The English planter was debonair
  As he mounted his horse to ride
Out in the vigorous Eastern air
  On the tea-clad mountain side,
As he rose he thought of a word of love,
And his heart was bright as the skies above.

The Eastern maiden was fair to see
  (The story is shortly told),
The Eastern maiden was fair, and he
  Was youthful, was strong, was bold.
He beguiled the Eastern heart away
On the mountain side in the Eastern day.

An English bride to the Eastward came,
  To the home which the planter made;
She had taken the English planter's name –
  Trustful, of nought afraid.
And the Eastern girl on the hill-side wept, –
Maiden no more, as the darkness crept.

The English planter sat in his chair, –
  Placid his evening rest;
His blood bespattered the evening air,
  Bespattered his wife's fair breast.
And peace fell over an Eastern mind,
Her honour avenged before her kind.

Silent and still the bungalow
  As the fire-flies gleam around;
Silent and still the bungalow,
  Save for the murmuring sound
Of the night wind rustling through the gloom
Of each dark, decaying, deserted room.

from Philip Randell, *Bungalow Ballads, Echoes from the East*, Simpkin Marshall, London, 1910

Chapter 2

Britain 1750-1890

'I find everybody charmed with my Bungalow . . . if there were many
Bungalows, there would be many buyers.'
Sir Erasmus Wilson, eminent physician, to the architect, on
occupying the first to be built in England.

H. Mayhew, *Birchington and its Bungalows*, Canterbury, 1881:16

Introduction

The first bungalow to be built and named as such in Britain – and almost certainly in the
Western hemisphere – appeared on the north Kent coast, some two hours train journey from
London, in 1869. In the next four years, six more were built close by (see p. 269). What were
they? What function did they serve? Why this particular time, location and place? Who built
them and for whom? Not least, what was their connection to India?

In answering these questions, this chapter first considers the 'invention' of the bungalow – a
purpose-built leisure or holiday dwelling – as a case study in the specialisation of building
form. It suggests that the accumulation of surplus capital which industrialisation brought in
its wake led, on the one hand, to an increasingly differentiated urban environment and, on the
other, to the creation of specialised building types. The new leisure environment of the mid-
Victorian seaside resort resulted from surplus capital, railway developments and an increase
in leisure and material consumption, all of which had been brought about by the Industrial
Revolution. The bungalow was a further, and logical, extension of these developments. Yet
basic to this revolution was the growth of a global market economy and this was also to
provide the context for the introduction of the bungalow image and name.

The second theme has been touched on in Chapter 1. How are the values, beliefs and
activities of a society – as well as its social structure – reflected in its buildings and physical
environment? The bungalow as introduced into Britain was a product of prevailing ideas
about property, but also about health, behaviour and the divisions of a society, increasingly
divided, both socially and spatially, according to class.

International context

The international economy and its effects
By the middle of the eighteenth century, the trade between Europe and Asia with which the
previous chapter began was rapidly expanding into a system of capitalist production working
on a global scale. Though the Industrial Revolution was totally to transform the economy and
society of Britain, leading to immensely increased productivity and wealth, behind it lay the

colonial and 'under-developed' markets overseas. As Hobsbawm points out, exports provided the leading sector of demand in the genesis of Britain's industrialisation, along with the growing home market. Infant industries were helped, sometimes created, by accelerating overseas trade. In Europe, this rested on the rise of an everyday market for overseas products (like sugar) and overseas, on the creation of systems for producing such goods (such as the slave-operated plantations), and the conquest of colonies. 'Our industrial economy grew out of our commerce, and especially commerce with the under-developed world . . . the exchange of overseas primary products was to be the foundation of our international economy' (1969:54; Barrat Brown, 1978:78-85). After 1750, this was to grow rapidly and have both direct and indirect effects on urban and architectural developments in Britain (Gubler, 1980), not least on the emerging seaside resorts.

Just as the profits of the West India sugar plantations had provided their owners with country seats such as Fonthill or Harewood (Williams, 1944:87-94), so the wealth of the East India trade had a similar impact on the landscape at home. In between Plassey (1757) and Waterloo (1815), the total wealth (or plunder) flowing from India has been put at £1 million to £16 million a year (Alavi, 1980:387-91) and a total of £1,000 million by Frank (1978:88). Some of this financed the country (and Parliamentary) seats of the Anglo-Indian 'nabobs' returning with fortunes from the East. Between 1760 and 1785, fifty of the more prominent of these were established (Holzman, 1926), one of the more exotic being at Sezincote in Gloucestershire. Here, making use of wealth accumulated during service with the East India Company, Sir Charles Cockerell, assisted by his architect brother, Samuel, built an elaborate farm and country house in 'Oriental' or 'Indian' style (Archer, 1960; Connor, 1979:120-4). Apart from providing the inspiration for the Prince Regent's Pavilion at Brighton, the façade of the house, built in 1803, and the nearby cottage, in adopting the distinctive curvilinear form of the thatched-roof 'banggolo', were to anticipate the arrival of other bungalow images from the East (plate 32).

The foundations of Britain's industrial economy were laid in the first half of the nineteenth century, with India playing a considerable part in the process. As the early steps towards a world division of labour took place, Britain's manufactured cotton exports were to help transform India into 'the agricultural farm of England'. Giving evidence to a Parliamentary inquiry in 1840, the President of the Manchester Chamber of Commerce wrote

> In India there is an immense extent of territory, and the population of it would consume British manufactures to a most enormous extent. The whole question with respect to our Indian trade is whether they can pay us, by the products of their soil, for what we are prepared to send out as manufactures (quoted in Barrat Brown, 1978:118).

India provided some of the essential raw materials, hides, oil, dyes, jute and cotton, required for the Industrial Revolution, and at the same time, afforded a growing market for English manufactures of iron and cotton. Economic surpluses from India were invested in British railways and, from the 1860s, India was Britain's main supplier of cotton, tea and jute and one of the main suppliers of rice and wheat imports. In return, by the end of the century, India and the empire were taking 35 per cent of Britain's exports and over 40 per cent of those in textiles, iron and steel (Barrat Brown, 1978: 105, 118, 136; also Bayly, 1983; Woodruff, 1978).

The second phase of capitalist industrialisation, however, had begun about mid century, and was based on coal, iron, steel and the railways. By then, a situation had already developed where an annual capital surplus of £60 million was crying out for investment. In 1850, the 'great boom' started, leading Hobsbawm to label the next twenty-five years 'the Age of

Capital' (1969:112; 1975). The two developments which were increasingly to absorb and ultimately create more wealth in this era were extensive investment in railways and the massive geographical expansion of the economy, as a result of the railway, steamship and telegraph, with the subsequent huge growth in markets for industrial products. The major theme of these years, then, is the extension of the capitalist economy round the world (Hobsbawm, 1975:xiii).

If railways supplied one major field for investment, another was provided by urban developments linked to them, especially the new seaside resorts, which grew remarkably in the third quarter of the nineteenth century. 'By the mid 1860s, a middle class holiday boom was already transforming parts of the British coastline with seafront promenades, piers and other establishments, enabling landed proprietors to draw unsuspected profits from hitherto uneconomic stretches of cliffs and beaches' (ibid:204). It is in the context of this railway and resort development, and the emergence of an international system not only of economy but also of linguistic and cultural exchange, that the introduction of the bungalow into Europe, was to take place. Yet before it arrived 'in the flesh' so to speak, the word and image had to be known.

The word and image

English merchants and travellers in India were quick to adopt aspects of its language and culture and by the early seventeenth century many terms had entered their vocabulary. Some, like *bazaar*, *godown* or *serai* (market, warehouse and accommodation for travellers), described the places where they worked; others, like *hookah*, *cheroots*, *mangos*, *curry* and *punch*, were items of local culture which they adopted. At first, such terms only belonged to the small speech community of the European in India, though possibly shared with Company officials back home.

Until the mid eighteenth century 'bunglo' was such a term; it had restricted circulation and this, in speech more than writing. Unlike *chintz*, *jute* or *calico*, words for goods actually carried to the West, written in bills of lading and attached, as it were, to the materials when they arrived, the term 'bunglo', like the object it described, stayed for long in India. When written, it was in manuscript rather than print: in correspondence, diaries, navigation charts or documents, all with restricted circulation (Subha Rao, 1969; H-J). Before the middle of the eighteenth century, the term and concept were virtually unknown outside the restricted culture of Anglo-India.

About that time, however, India came to the front of the English political scene. In 1756, the Nawab of Bengal, Suraj-ud-Daula, attacked and captured the British factory at Fort William, now re-built as an 'octagon' fort with escarpments. Some occupants fled: others were imprisoned in what became known as the infamous 'Black Hole'. The East India Company's military commander, Robert Clive, moved up from Madras, rapidly gathered his troops and re-took Calcutta. In the ensuing battle at Plassey, the Nawab's troops (allied with the French) were routed. The Nawab was displaced and Clive's nominee, Mir Jaffa, whose 'firman' or 'permission to trade' was immediately obtained, was put in his place. The British were the masters of Bengal.

With the India lobby in London avidly interested in the wealth which now seemed likely to flow, the event found expression on the London stage. A Murphy's farce, *The Upholsterer*, or *What News?* (1758) celebrated the victory in India. In the play, full of references to current events, 'Quidnunc' makes what might well be the first public reference to the 'bunglo' in England.

I bring you joy – the Nabob's demolished . . . Suraja Dowla is no more . . . our men diverted themselves with killing bullocks and camels till they dislodged the enemy from the octagon, the counterscarp and the bunglo – the new nabob, Jaffir Ally Cawn has acceded to a treaty and the English company have got all their rights in the phirman.

As British power was established, the traffic in ideas, as well as goods, increased. Knowledge of India as well as the Anglo-Indian community filtered back to England. In India, printing presses were set up and newspapers published (*The India Gazette, Calcutta Gazette, Bombay Courier*), copies of which soon began to reach the metropolis. Here, curious readers might have seen 'bungalos' advertised as part of large Calcutta estates. The 'nabobs', also the subject of a play of the same name by Foote (1768), became important cultural brokers between India and the West.

It was another political event, however, which re-focussed attention on Anglo-Indian life: the impeachment of Warren Hastings, ex-Governor-General of Bengal, for alleged misgovernment. For the large public interested in the proceedings, the need for background information was met by publications such as John Stockdale's *Indian vocabulary: to which is prefixed the Forms of Impeachment* (1788). Here, people were told about Hastings's vast Calcutta estate including 'a convenient bungalow containing two rooms and a verandah all round' (Nilsson, 1968:123).

Yet knowledge of Indian culture, and particularly, its topography, peoples and architecture, was still virtually absent in late-eighteenth-century England. If familiary with what it looked like began to improve at this time, it was through the activities of a handful of artists, especially the brothers William and Thomas Daniell, and William Hodges who, as official draughtsman, had accompanied Captain Cook to the South Seas. Under the patronage of Warren Hastings, Hodges had gone to India in 1788 where he produced a series of sketches and paintings before returning home six years later.

Hodges published his *Select Views in India* in 1786 and *Travels in India, 1780-3* in 1793. As he wrote in his Preface, it was 'a matter of surprise that, of a country so nearly allied to us, so little should be known'. Particularly interested in architecture, his descriptions of India's cities and European buildings were, in 1793, the most detailed and perceptive up to that time. Hodges travelled from Calcutta, up the Ganges to Benares, Allahabad and Lucknow. Here, in 1781, he stayed in the 'large bungelow' of a senior Company Officer. His exact description of the plan, structure and materials were not to be equalled for another sixty years (see Chapter 1, p. 28).

The end of the eighteenth century saw an increasing commercialisation of agriculture as landlords enclosed common land, either to follow modern farming methods or create, where previously tenants had farmed, 'Arcadian' prospects on their estates. As part of the process, architects produced books of designs for 'picturesque' cottages, the object of which was to enhance the view of the estate and in the process, as Williams points out, convert its function from one of production to consumption (1973:294). In one of these collections, *Sketches for Country Houses, Villas and Rural Dwellings* (1800), John Plaw included a cottage design 'with a viranda, in the manner of an Indian Bungalow'. Though still described as a cottage, here was a close approximation of the pyramidal, thatched roof form (plate 33). The innovation here, however, was not the bungalow itself but the 'viranda', a term and feature which, from this time on (possibly the first record of its use in Britain), became gradually more common. As Plaw, Hodges and the Daniells all seemed to have exhibited at the Royal Academy in the 1790s, they could well have been in contact (Connor, 1979:114).

As more travellers undertook the long, yet now less hazardous, journey to India, travelling in the interior, staying in up-country stations and returning to publish their travel accounts back home, the idea of the bungalow became increasingly familiar. Such travelogues were supplemented by the memoirs of Company officials, both civil and military; of these, the most detailed accounts of European bungalows appeared in the books of Williamson and Buchanan between 1810 and 1820 (see pages 18-34), and these accounts often included glossaries of unfamiliar Indian terms. Thus, Maria Graham's popular *Journal of a Residence in India* (1813) described the 'bungalo' as 'a garden house or cottage' and included a distant sketch of a temporary version 'built of bamboos, covered with cotton cloth and decorated with leaves, flowers and coconut' encountered in Ceylon.

The term seems to have been adopted as English rather than Anglo-Indian around the 1830s. About ten years prior to this, for example, an 'old India hand' seems to have built a farm between Newmarket and Cambridge. No doubt with nostalgic memories of days in South India, he named 'Bangalore Barn' about 1825. Unfamiliar to local ears, 'Bangalore' had, by 1838, been changed to what was then a more familiar 'Bungalow Farm', one, if not the earliest, use of the word as a place name in England.

As the mails improved and more middle class women accompanied their husbands to India, they felt obliged to describe domestic life for their sisters back home. Thus, in 1847 Mrs Graham writes that bungalows were 'for the most part built of unbaked bricks and covered with thatch, having in the centre a hall . . . the whole being encompasssed by an open verandah' (H-J). Letters helped to fill information gaps. 'I hope you will send the sketches of the country, the natives, of yourself, your Bungalow', Mrs Lewin wrote to her soldier son in 1826 (Lewin, 1909:214). Similar sympathies inspired Colesworthy Grant to send home 'Sketches of Anglo-Indian Domestic Life' to his sisters, later to be published with their detailed drawings in 1859. For a few people with connections in India there were occasional paintings and, in 1825, the lithographs of Charles D'Oyly, who, as Opium Agent, had spent a number of years in Patna (plate 9). Anglo-Indian life was now a topical subject for humour, as expressed for example in George Atkinson's *Curry and Rice (on forty plates) or The Ingredients of Social Life at 'Our' Station* (1859).

By the mid nineteenth century, therefore, 'bungalow' was simply one of many Indian words and ideas familiar to the educated English public. For example, Thackeray sprinkled his novels (particularly *The Newcomes*, 1854) with words like backsheesh, cashmere, juggernaut, Nizam, purda, bungalow. In *Our Street* (1848), Captain Bragg, retired Commander of the *Ram Chunder* East Indiaman, comes home to settle in the 'splendid new white-stuccoed, Doric-porticoed genteel Pocklington quarter of the borough of Lathanplaster'. Here, he built 'Bungalow Lodge', though, as he lived on 'the first floor', this was somewhat of a misnomer.

In the fictional Captain Bragg, Thackeray was parodying the many Anglo-Indians by then returning to England. Captain Bamford, however, was real. Returning from India in 1859 to the sylvan suburb of Norwood in South London he built himself a lodge-like house, calling it 'The Bungalow'. In later years it gave its name to Bungalow Road, not far from the Crystal Palace.

It was the massive uprising of 1857, however, which brought India once more to the centre of events. Apart from his weekly reports in *The Times*, W.H. Russell's *My Diary in India in the Year 1858-9*, with its detailed descriptions of dak and hill-station bungalows and bungalow life on the plain, circulated widely during these years. By the time E. Sullivan's *Bungalow and Tent (Travels in Ceylon)* appeared in 1859 there was little need to describe or define the phenomenon. Since the 1850s, photography had brought images to the descriptions; by then, the word was fully naturalised, incorporated into English speech in England and illustrated in the *Imperial Dictionary* of 1851.

More important than a mere acquaintance with the term, however, were the images now attached to the bungalow style of life. In the 1860s and 1870s, life in the country or hill-station bungalow was seen as a positive experience, far from the madding crowd and waited on hand and foot. Like other facets of Indian and Anglo-Indian life, it seemed to represent something which had been lost in England, increasingly industrialised and urban, and offering an opportunity to escape from social changes which some people were beginning to deplore (Hutchins, 1967). Without the discomforts of actually going to India then, here, in the single-storey simple bungalow, was an institution which, with profit, could be modified and adopted back home.

National development: economy and society

The development of leisure resorts[1]

As introduced into England, the bungalow was a new type of dwelling, designed for a particular function. It was the prototype of a purpose-built 'leisure' or holiday house built not at the request of a particular client, but speculatively, for a growing middle class market with surplus money to spend. As the buyer of the first one wrote to the architect, 'if there were many bungalows, there would be many buyers'. The ultimate development of the bungalow as a holiday house for the mass or, in the present century, as a 'second home' provides a good example of the tendency to segmentation and specialisation – in this case, of building types – which industrial capitalism has brought about (King, 1980b).

When viewed in the long history of urban and architectural development in Britain, the purpose-built bungalow was part of the emergence of a new form of urban settlement, the recreational or leisure town which, in England, was typically the seaside resort. To explain the 'invention' of the bungalow, therefore, we must look briefly at the development of the resort. Although the Romans had reputedly patronised leisure resorts on the Adriatic (Turner and Ash, 1975), the development of the modern phenomenon from the mid eighteenth century in Britain is very much a product of capitalist industrialisation and the consequent growth of large urban populations. The major outcome of industrialisation was the creation of material wealth. It represented a rise in *per capita* production which, in comparison with the agricultural economy it first complemented and eventually displaced, resulted in the accumulation and then circulation of surplus capital.

The surplus was not just of material wealth; it was also, for a sizeable minority, a surplus of time. The application of new forms of energy and the mechanisation of industry meant that more goods were produced with less time and effort. While the development of factory production in the early nineteenth century meant, for the new urban working class, longer working hours and, in comparison to their agricultural forebears, a loss of traditional rural holidays, for the growing minority of employers and rentiers it meant a substantial increase of leisure. As industrialisation and the size of the surplus increased, as markets expanded and workers gained more control over their conditions of labour from the 1860s, increased prosperity and leisure became available to a larger proportion of the population – at first, the middle class and then, towards the end of the century, with increasing dependence on the empire for food and markets, a fair proportion of the skilled working class.

The most obvious environmental expression of these developments – surplus capital and surplus time – was in the new purpose-built leisure environments of the nineteenth century, the seaside resorts. These had developed from the earlier aristocratic and upper class practice of visiting inland spas and had grown especially from the mid eighteenth century. By the first decades of the nineteenth, they were the main location for leisure for the aristocracy and upper middle class. With the rapid expansion of bourgeois society and developments in railways between the 1840s and 1860s, the seaside resorts were to provide an important source for the investment and circulation of surplus capital (Harvey, 1977).

The most recent studies suggest that, in the majority of south eastern resorts, the direct investment came from London (J.K. Walton, personal communication, 1982), though just how much of this ultimately derived from overseas profits would only be found out with further research. What it is reasonable to assume is that without the vast expansion of foreign trade and imperialism during these years, the rapid development of the 'leisure resorts' is unlikely to have taken place: urbanisation in Britain was essentially the product of capitalist development and expansion and this process was one that occurred world wide (Roberts, 1978:11).

Industrialisation was also to have immense effects on society and lead to new forms of stratification. The vast increase in the size of the surplus and its uneven distribution created greater inequalities: new industrial and scientific techniques generated a host of new occupations, each with its particular status; and a vast growth in material goods (especially in housing and material consumption) allowed this stratification to be expressed in different ways. Thus, in comparison with the relatively simple divisions of the 'ranks' and 'orders' of pre-industrial Europe, the new class structure of the industrial society was based on wealth, its differentiated rungs frequently expressed in the dwellings produced for members of the various classes.

These developments were part of an overall spatial division of labour which took the form of spatial specialisation according to economic sector: thus, some areas produced only ships and heavy engineering whilst others produced coal and woollens, or iron and steel (Massey, 1979:235). London was the principal investment centre and the emerging resorts, the specialised environments for leisure. In a gradually evolving international division of labour, surpluses extracted from one part of the world were increasingly consumed in another.

Within the towns, further differentiation occurred. With changes in the manner in which goods were produced, and in the social relations of production, the place of work was separated from the place of residence; and as suggested above, increased leisure and consumption were accommodated in the specialised environment of the resort.

Such a spatial differentiation was accompanied by, and expressed in, a parallel specialisation of building types. As technological processes became diversified, new, purpose-built building types emerged: the textile mill and foundry for production; the bungalow for consumption. In the new industrial towns, the stratification of society was expressed in various ways: the location of various classes in different sections of the town; the allotted space for, and size of, each house; the form, name and quality of the dwelling itself: the labourer's cottage, working class tenement, gentleman's villa, and mansion flats, and the location where they were found: suburban residence or country seat. On the one hand, therefore, the seaside bungalow was evidence of the increasing tendency towards functional specialisation in building form: on the other, it was simply another way in which social stratification was expressed in the built environment.

In the nineteenth century, the seaside resorts seem to have developed in three phases, each influenced, among other factors, by the operations of the capital market and the available means of transport, especially its carrying capacity and speed. The earliest (e.g. Brighton or Worthing) were accessible only by horse-drawn coach, with its small carrying capacity and infrequency of trips. Dependent on the patronage of royalty and upper class, they were located close to the metropolis. The second phase, from about 1815 to the 1840s, relied on steam-powered, sea-borne transport (the hoy and steam packet) with its faster speed and much increased passenger capacity. By then, patronage was drawn from a much wider social clientele, though still largely from London, and the resorts, such as Margate and Ramsgate, were a greater distance away. From the mid 1840s, however, the development of the railway brought a form of transport which, in terms of speed, frequency, the number of passengers carried and at relatively little cost, was unrivalled. It led, from the middle of the century, to the development of resorts within easy reach of large populations in the towns (Pimlott, 1976).

During the first phase, some nine 'seaside watering places' were established on the Channel coast, four in Sussex and five in Kent. In 1841, of the thirty-six 'principal sea-bathing places' in England, two-thirds of them lay south-east of a line drawn from the Wash to the Bristol Channel: a quarter were in the two coastal counties closest to London, Sussex and Kent. Ten years later, when the census takers decided for the first time to distinguish between 'seaside towns' and 'inland watering places', five of the largest resorts were in these two counties (Margate, Ramsgate, Dover, Brighton and Worthing) (Whyman, 1970), that is, closest to their patrons and the finances which had largely developed them.

The growth of these resorts (as also the inland spas) was as phenomenal as that of the commercial and industrial towns. In the fifty years after 1801, the population of eleven 'resort towns' and four 'inland watering places' increased by over 250 per cent, a higher rate than that of some fifty manufacturing towns (224 per cent) and the metropolis itself (146 per cent) – evidence enough that institutionalised leisure was a product both of industrial growth and the capital which this, and expanding markets overseas, had generated (Pimlott, 1976:96-8). By 1851, when the population of the leading resort (Brighton), overtook that of Bath, as the most eminent of the inland spas, the seaside had become society's principal location for leisure.

Fundamental to these developments was the same form of energy which had sparked off the Industrial Revolution itself – steam power, applied to transport both at sea and on land. Though the first railway to Kent was established in 1830, the opening of the London, Chatham and Dover line to Ramsgate and Margate in 1863 was to double the number of daily visitors between 1861 and 1881 and Margate's resident population of 10,000 also practically doubled. In the thirty years before 1870, the journey time between London and Margate was cut from three to two hours.

Masses and classes: segregation at the resorts

The development of Westgate and Birchington, the location of the first English bungalows, was an outcome of the 'great Victorian boom' which occurred between 1850 and 1873 (Church, 1975).

From the 1850s, an increasing level of investment occurred in building construction and urbanisation, rising to a peak in the mid 1870s. Between 1860 and 1873, when the first bungalows were built, the London building cycle was at a peak, even though the national one was in decline. At nearby Ramsgate, the London-based British Land Company were largely responsible for the building boom at this time (Cooney, 1949; Thomas, 1973).

At Westgate, capital was apparently supplied from Coutts Bank of London, long connected to the East India Company (Morrison, 1905; Robinson, 1929). As in other realms in the market economy, both the resort and the type of residential buildings it contained were carefully to exploit, and reinforce, existing social divisions.

The earliest seaside 'watering places' had developed primarily as places for the rich. Yet as their size and number increased, the divisions of the larger society were reflected in the newer resorts round the coast (Walvin, 1977:37, 125). Where Brighton and Weymouth had been patronised by royalty and the elite, the resorts of Kent became associated with the new middle class. By 1841, London supplied most of Margate's visitors, the vast majority people of 'independent means', merchants, manufacturers and members of the professions, but few titled aristocracy (Whyman, 1970). In the middle of the century, the common practice was for the entire family to come down from London for some weeks, dependent on income, during the two- or three-month season. After a week, the head of the family would return to his business activities.

By 1870, however, Margate and Ramsgate had become increasingly favoured by the lower end of this middle class market. They were, in the words of a visiting London architect, 'somewhat plebean watering places'. Wealthier people were already moving out to nearby Cliftonville, or, from the mid 1870s, to the rapidly rising town of Westgate.

In the 1860s, the site of Westgate had contained little but a farmhouse and coastguard station. After the opening of the railway in 1870, however, it grew rapidly and by 1881, was a 'populous town with a semi-circular promenade, terraces, squares and shops, a fashionable hotel and a railway station' (Mayhew, 1881:6). The transformation had been effected by a local capitalist in combination with Coutts Bank. A London architect was employed to lay out the town and strict covenants governed the type of property built. All the roads were private and only detached houses were to be allowed (plate 34).

By the late 1870s, Westgate-on-Sea had become, with Cromer, one of the most fashionable and exclusive metropolitan resorts, the first town in the country to test out electric lighting in its streets. The town was

> next door to Margate . . . yet had nothing in common with it but the finest stretch of open sea on the coast of England. . . . One may walk its whole length . . . without being reminded, even by an advertisement or a signboard, of such things as we wish to forget when we leave cities and come to the sea. . . . There is no regulation line of flat, white lodging houses to overshadow the sea itself. . . . There is no obtrusive hotel with a stucco face and a style of architecture too well known as Anglo-Marine. Indeed, there is no stucco at Westgate at all. . . .

Westgate, 'where there was nothing conventional, not even a pier' was reserved for the well-to-do. It was 'a seaside corner, practically close to London, with none of the seaside discomforts and vexations'. It was not a place

> such as the energetic excursionist would choose for his peculiar purpose. . . . Westgate does not want him and will do nothing to attract him . . . for its own convenience it uses the express train which . . . without stop or change, turns its seventy miles from London in distance into about an hour and a half in time; but the excursion train never comes at all. A great number of the houses belong to residents who either live there all the year round or make it their autumn quarters. So far as society is concerned . . . Westgate is somewhat rigidly exclusive in its tastes and strongly aristocratic in its feelings and ambitions – a sort of Mayfair by the sea (*Granville Illustrated News*, 25 October 1879).

The test of these aspirations rested with the people it was able to attract. In this it was apparently successful rivalling 'other upstart watering places in Normandy' in attracting 'persons of refinement and artistic sympathies', numbering a nationally eminent physician, the editor of *Nineteenth Century*, the MP for Boston and an eminent painter, Sir W.Q. Orchardson. Both in the 1870s and later, it was a place where metropolitan wealth paid metropolitan architects to develop a resort for the benefit of a metropolitan clientele. Westgate's appeal remained for some twenty years; in 1893 it still prided itself 'on its exclusiveness . . . laudably careful in appearances; in its public manner, not a little prudish'. During twenty years it was, according to a local guide (1903) 'prominent among the most aristocratic resorts in the South of England' and both local and London interests benefited from the property boom which it sparked off.

Three miles down the coast was the village of Birchington, an adjunct to these developments. Close to the sea, 'with quiet nooks for bathing', the ancient village was rapidly incorporated into the metropolitan 'leisure zone' with the opening of the railway station in 1864; building operations were begun, the church re-decorated and the local tavern re-furbished. In these two places, the first bungalows were to be built.

Local setting

Bungalow developments: phase one
It will be clear from the following account that the first English bungalows were designed for a particular purpose; they incorporated many new features and were especially adapted to the social and behavioural needs of their potential clientele. Less than two hours' rail journey from London and five minutes' carriage ride from the train, they were constructed by a local contractor, but the developer, architect, agent and future occupants were all from London. The innovations which they incorporated were not just technical (building materials and techniques) but also social and architectural. Stylistically, they hinted at developments to come. By combining these elements with the positive and increasingly familiar image of the one-storey Indian bungalow, the architect 'invented' a new form: the specialised recreational house by the sea.

The first two bungalows were part of a small development of four houses on the seafront at Westgate, formerly 'the nucleus of the town'. Having built these between 1869-70, the architect – no doubt looking for a better site for his idea – moved up the coast to Birchington. Here, between 1870 and 1873, the first bungalow settlement was established.[2]

If the economic basis was supplied by London's surplus capital, the site and design of the bungalows were determined by the beliefs and social behaviour of its upper middle class. These were ideas about health, aesthetics and the type of social setting which, in the last third of the nineteenth century, were being increasingly preferred. In comparison with those of earlier times, these ideas had changed considerably.

The built environment of the early resorts had resulted from a combination of factors – economic, social, ideological and health. Of the latter, beliefs in the beneficial effects of sea water, both for drinking and for bathing, had become increasingly widespread since Russell's famous *Dissertation on the Use of Sea Water* had been published in 1752. Every resort had its resident physician and 'dipping ladies' to help visitors to bathe (Howell, 1974:185; Walvin, 1977:185).

The logical consequence of these ideas was that building developments took place close to the sea and, as these had to be protected from the storms, sea walls were constructed and the residential terraces were built along the 'sea front'. Previously, coastal settlements such as fishing villages and ports had been built somewhat inland, their simple houses huddled together for protection, their backs generally turned towards the sea. For the population of these small villages, the sea was there for fishing, a source of livelihood which was otherwise to be feared.

For the patrons of the purpose-built resort, however, the sea had a new-found aesthetic and emotional appeal, as well as curative effects. As part of changed attitudes to Nature, central to Romantic ideas of the time, the sea, like the mountains, had become a phenomenon to be admired. 'Grand, vast and terrifying', it was a perfect example of the 'sublime'. It was there to look at as well as a place to bathe. These ideological factors were reflected in the early-nineteenth-century resorts, with building development running parallel to the coast and 'marine villas' sited to ensure 'sea views', strung along the sea front. A road, soon developed for use as a 'promenade', separated the building line from the beach and sea. For people wishing to bathe, prevailing norms of privacy required that bathing machines (first seen at Scarborough in the 1730s) were hired, used to disrobe and change, and were then drawn by horses into the sea where the occupants could be easily immersed. For those too irresolute or old, salt-water bathing establishments were built (as at Brighton or Margate in the 1760s) where the waters could be enjoyed more calmly.

Yet apart from hoping to benefit their health and indulge their romantic ideas, people also visited resorts for recreational and social reasons, to relax, meet and gossip, and these activities were both accommodated in, and reflected by, buildings and urban form.

The early and mid nineteenth-century resort was essentially a social and public place, characteristics most obviously expressed in the institutions which it contained: the assembly rooms, pump room, theatre, bathing establishments, promenades, parades, card rooms, public gardens and library – the latter, a place as much for exchanging gossip as books. These institutions, many of which had been transplanted from the inland spas, provided for collective forms of leisure, encouraging social encounters and the opportunity for personal display (practices transferred to Indian hill stations, King, 1976: 160-2). Bathing, often at regulated hours, was very much a social routine. This 'social characteristic' of the resort was also reflected in the type of residential accommodation provided.

The earliest patrons of places like Brighton had simply hired lodgings in local cottages, but soon other purpose-built provision had been made. Typically, this was the boarding house and hotel, with public arrangements for eating. (In Kent, the first reference to a 'hotel' is in 1759; to a 'boarding house', in 1775) (Whyman, 1970). Gardens, where they existed, were shared between visiting guests. As an urban form, the early and mid Victorian resort was compact, keeping its inhabitants together. The prevailing type of housing, the terrace, and its generally carefully planned lay-out as street, square, crescent or place, encouraged a concentration rather than dispersal of inhabitants. Accommodation was primarily for middle and upper middle class visitors and tended to be similar to that in the towns from which they had come. Only slight concessions – most often on terraced housing or 'marine villas' facing the sea – were made to the specifically health, recreational and ideological functions of the seaside. Balconies, for example, were occasionally built on windows, and verandahs (an early-nineteenth-century innovation) permitted occupants to smell, listen to or gaze at the sea (as well as passers-by), in addition to providing variety. 'No decoration has so successfully varied the dull sameness of modern structures in the metropolis as the verandah' wrote architect J.B. Papworth in *Rural Residences* (1818). If the informality of their function was expressed in architectural design, it was in a more decorative use of cast-iron, on railings, stairs or balconies. By and large, however, the terraces and villas of mid-nineteenth-century Brighton or Scarborough could equally well have been found inland, at the spas, or in the more fashionable parts of London. In brief, although the 'seaside watering place' was a purpose-built leisure resort, and specialised built types such as assembly rooms and piers had been provided for public recreational use, private *residential* provision was still generally similar to that prevailing in inland towns.

By the later 1860s, however, although similar aesthetic ideas prevailed, medical and social views had changed. Where late-eighteenth-century opinion had stressed the curative qualities of salt-water, that of the mid and later nineteenth century increasingly emphasised the importance of 'bracing sea air' (Pimlott, 1976:106; Walvin, 1977:66-7). And with changes in both the nature of work and the permanent, year-round environment of people coming to resorts, their social function and character had also altered.

In *Health Resorts of Britain and How to Profit by Them* (1860), Dr Spencer Thompson, like other contemporary physicians, had recognised that people visited resorts for 'relaxation, freedom from business cares and exercise'. His principal concern, however, was to stress the beneficial effects of the sea air. A change of air was 'especially important for the man who has been shut up, day after day, in the unventilated office or workshop'. Going to the sea or hills was where 'the ozone is most abundant'. Ozone ('the oxygen gas of the atmosphere in a peculiar condition') was greater at the seashore and in mountains and less pure in cities. Such emphasis on the atmosphere rather than the water recurs throughout mid and late nineteenth-century literature on the seaside; to a large extent, it reflected the understandable obsession with pulmonary complaints and particularly, tuberculosis, which made ravages among city-dwellers irrespective of social class (Walvin, 1977). According to the *Dictionary of Daily Wants* (1859:14)

> Air, vitiated by the different processes of respiration, combustion and putrefaction, or
> which is suffered to stagnate, becomes prejudicial to the human frame; hence, large cities,
> public assemblies, hospitals, burial grounds, etc., are injurious to the health and often
> productive of contagious diseases.

The quality of the air was 'greatly influenced by local causes'. Because of these beliefs, sea air was seen to have particularly healthful properties:

> Sea air is well known to be beneficial and invigorating [because of] its constant agitation
> by the winds and tides and also, the absence of many deteriorating causes to which land is
> subject.

Different types of air were suitable for different ailments: for 'relaxation and debility', 'dry and bracing' air was needed; for the tendency to 'fever and inflammatory action', a 'soft and humid climate was to be preferred'.

As social places, the later-nineteenth-century resorts were different in two distinct ways. As suggested above, they had become increasingly differentiated according to social class. And, as part of this process, a type of small, upper middle class 'seaside watering place' had emerged where collective, public forms of amusement were deliberately kept out. Even in 1841, Granville had complained that the 'upper and wealthier classes of society' had been 'driven away from every point on the coast by the facilities offered to the "everybody" and the "anybody" of congregating in shoals at the same watering place, creating bustle, noise, confusion and vulgarity.' This 'congregating in shoals' had been helped by the 'interminable terraces, parades, paragons and parabolas of houses of every sort and size' which speculators had run up (Sloane, 1978:80). It was a sentiment increasingly expressed as the resorts grew in size and number, to be repeated again in the early 1880s.

> Who is not sick . . . of the interminable terraces and places, crescents and squares, of most of our seaside resorts? . . . Do we not know the painful and reiterated experience of those long rows of bricks, whose very similitude to each other depresses one the very moment the excitement of leaving home and the subsequent journey are over? (ibid.:380).

What the patrons of the later Victorian resort wanted was social exclusiveness and individuality, expressed both spatially and architecturally. These were the reasons why Westgate (and subsequently, the bungalows) had such an appeal. The town stood 'behind the green edge of the white cliffs' and

> apart from the one row of no longer visible shops, it consists of handsome houses, mostly detached and of infinite variety in style. Each house seems to say 'I am a house and a home and not merely four walls to lodge in'. To this regularity of irregularity the special character of Westgate is largely due (*GIN*:14)* (plate 34).

In these newer resorts, therefore, natural qualities were stressed: climate, scenery, antiquities and shore. Such resorts were appreciated for their social exclusiveness, their absence of noise and commerce, and for the opportunity they offered for private, not public, forms of recreation. Here, away from the social bustle of the town, in detached houses bordering the sea, visitors indulged in family-centred activities. The early-nineteenth-century resort had been an essentially adult place but, with the 'discovery' of children and their distinctive needs in mid Victorian Britain, a new type of environment (and accommodation) was required. The large middle and upper middle class family seeking holidays by the sea preferred to 'do it themselves', walking on the sands, collecting shells and seaweed, relaxing in the company of friends 'far from the madding crowd'.

Birchington was typical of these developments. Its attraction was in the absence, not the presence, of public amusements. Even ten years after its development as a resort

> the jaded professional man in search of ease may pass his well-earned holiday in the most invigorating tranquillity, for the perfect repose of the place is unruffled by the noisy seaside attractions. There are no German bands . . . no distressing niggers on the shore, and no revolting donkey-drivers in the roads. Shorn of these excitements, the cheap excursionists shun the spot . . . Birchington on Sea, without a jetty, or an 'Assembly Rooms', or a 'Tivoli', or a 'Ranelagh', offers absolutely nothing – not even a solitary tea-garden – to lure Cockaigne from Margate. [It was simply] an uncontaminated play-ground for large families and a secluded sanatorium for invalids (Mayhew, 1881:7).

Patrons of the earlier resorts had sought a change in both their physical and social environments. At Brighton or Scarborough, they had found not only different air but also different people. By the later 1860s, patrons of this newer type of resort were less interested in meeting different people than in meeting no people at all. The aspiration, typical of a later urban age, of wanting to get away from others in a crowded city was becoming increasingly common. Earlier, it had been confined to a wealthy few. Now, increasing prosperity and the

* *GIN Granville Illustrated News*, 1879.

railways made it attractive to the bourgeois population in the town.

The writer who was to describe the new bungalows at Birchington as 'rural-looking and isolated' was therefore assigning them positive, not negative, qualities. The city had always been the centre of culture and civilisation, but now for the totally urbanised inhabitant, 'rural-looking' was an attribute which obviously had an appeal. And social and physical isolation, to be increasingly sought in the 'isolated country cottages' in the decades to come, was a sign, on the one hand, of the taken-for-granted human contact in the city; on the other, of the development of means of communication (telegraph, telephone, motor car and press) by which, when need be, the state of isolation could be rapidly exchanged for the reassuring company of the town.

In this context, it was fitting that the detached and socially separate form of the bungalow, imposed from 'outside' on the outskirts of an existing community, should carry a suitably exogenous name which, unlike the cottage of the cottager, expressed no social relationship to the village.

The design and siting of the bungalows embodied these new medical and social criteria. Medical views on the benefits of sea air, as well as separation from 'public assemblies', coincided with preferences for isolation from one's fellow men. This meant that the

Figure 2.1 Bungalow development, phase two: 1870-3 (*Building News*, 15 August, 1873)

34 Capital transforms the seaside: Westgate, Kent, 1870s

Some of the profits accumulated from Britain's mid-nineteenth century position as 'workshop of the world', articulated through London, were reinvested in the resorts, helping to finance new types of consumer-oriented leisure building, not least of which was the bungalow.

Partly financed by a London bank, Westgate became an exclusive resort for the metropolitan bourgeoisie. The conditions of development required that all houses be detached. The first two bungalows to be built and named as such in Britain (1869-70) were part of the separate development just left of centre (*Granville Illustrated News*, October 1879)

35 Bungalow development, phase two: Birchington, Kent, 1870.

   The ideology behind the bungalows included changing social attitudes to resorts, positive associations
   with life in Indian hill stations and a characteristic concern with health. In 1875, one was advertised in
   The Times (7 August) as 'a complete seaside sanatorium for a family'.

   At the date of this photograph (1973), when it was unoccupied, this was the earliest 'named'
   bungalow surviving in England, if not in the Western world (*Author*)

36 Social location and site:
    'nothing between it and the
    sea' (*Author*)

37 Space for leisure: private
access to the beach (*Author*)

38 Tunnels provided direct access to the bungalows. Changing land values over the last century are evident in
the new housing on the right built on one of the original bungalow sites. The artist's studio in the cliff can
be seen just right of centre (*Author*)

39 Space for leisure: the croquet lawn.
Though 'bungalow' generally meant a one-storey dwelling, the architect also applied it to this
two-storey house 'under one span of roof' and of 'the most simple construction' (*Author*, 1973)

40 The imperial connection.
Contemporaries described the bungalows as 'modified Indian country houses' and 'a capital reproduction
of a cool, spacious, Indian-like hill dwelling'.
Lower land prices at a time of metropolitan investment in resorts combined with the convenience of
single-storey living seem to have provided part of the logic for the design (*Author*)

41 Industrial prototype: the first prefabricated timber bungalow.
Beach (later Rossetti) Avenue, Birchington, Kent. Photograph, c.1952 (See also Figures 2.3 and 2.6)
Industrialised building methods, rail transport and investment in the resorts were the pre-requisites for the
innovation, built 1877 and demolished about 1952. Here, the ailing artist D. G. Rossetti came early in
1882 at the invitation of one of the two architects associated with the development. He found the
environment healthy, the bungalow 'in all respects commodious' but nevertheless died there some weeks
later (*Benefield and Cornford*)

42 System building: The Bungalow Hotel, Birchington, Kent. 1973.
Similar prefabrication methods were used to construct the hotel about 1878 (*Author*)

43, 44, 45 Metropolitan culture: lodge decorations at the Tower Bungalows, Birchington, 1882. Photograph, 1973.
The 'Age of Capital' which generated the bungalow also gave a boost to the arts. The London artist and sculptor, George Frampton, later to provide Calcutta with a statue of Queen Victoria, was brought to the bungalows to add to their already arty reputation (*Alan Crawford*)

Royal Bungalow Snettisham Beach.

46, 47 Royal bungalows: England and India, 1908-10.
Despite the bungalow's dubious connotations, Queen Alexandra had a hand-crafted, rubble stone model put up on Snettisham beach, near the Sandringham estate in Norfolk. A year or two later, one of a more formal kind was being built for the visit of the Prince of Wales to Delhi (*India Office Library*)

48, 49, 50 Suburban innovation, 1890-1900 (see also Figure 3.7)

The shift, from the vertical two- or three-storey Victorian villa, often semi-detached, with cellar and attic (above, built 1879) to the horizontal Edwardian bungalow, with some bedrooms in the roofspace, appropriate to the more spacious outer suburbs of the times, was a radical innovation. The Bungalow (1900-1), in the Roundhay area of Leeds, is one of the earliest architect-designed examples in a suburban (rather than country or seaside) location. The gable over the recess is likely to have contained the billiard or smoking room; the end elevation shows the single-storey construction; the roof has dormer windows at the rear, which originally incorporated a verandah. Though designed as a whole with The Bungalow, the double gabled house (right) forms a separate dwelling.

As here, the bungalow was also an architectural style: both the concept and various features were apparently taken from *Bungalows and Country Residences* (1891) by Arts and Crafts architect, R. A. Briggs (see also plate 65) (*Author*)

RAILWAY CARRIAGE CROSSING RIVER "ADUR" AT SHOREHAM BY SEA FOR BUNGALOWS.

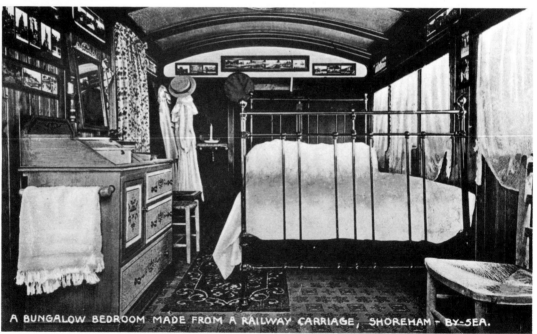

A BUNGALOW BEDROOM MADE FROM A RAILWAY CARRIAGE, SHOREHAM-BY-SEA.

51, 52 Setting up the simple life: railway carriage bungalows, Bungalow Town, Shoreham, Sussex, c.1910 (original captions).

At the turn of the century, increased living standards, helped by cheap food imported from both formal and informal empires, combined with increased leisure to boost working class trips to the seaside (*Marlpins Museum*)

53, 54, 55 Informal settlement:
the railway carriage
beach bungalow,
Lancing, Sussex, c.
1910.
Prior to the
introduction of
planning laws, the
beach provided a
relatively unrestricted
site for local or self-built
bungalow
developments

56, 57, 58 Free and easy retreat: views of Bungalow Town, Shoreham, Sussex, 1912-14. Bungalow Town quickly acquired a reputation: for H. G. Wells, living at nearby Sandgate, it was 'a queer village of careless sensuality'. In the 1980s, myths persist about film-stars in the 1930s 'going down there for the weekend'

High Tide, W. Parade, Bognor

E.46382. SCARBOROUGH: BUNGALOWS, N.SANDS.

Bungalows, Felpham, near Bognor

59, 60, 61 Changing behaviour on the beach, c.1905 - 10. Relaxation of the stricter Victorian codes governing behaviour on the beach was one of a number of factors gradually replacing horse-drawn bathing machines with bungalows; moreover, the latter didn't mess up the beach. At Felpham, near Bognor in Sussex, mass-produced cast and corrugated iron bungalows, possibly surplus to export requirements to the colonies, were being sold for £125

62, 63, 64 Bohemian bungalows: the riverside simple life, 1910 - 15.
According to *The Bungalow* magazine (1900) a Bohemian was 'one who lives a simple life where he can be in close communion with nature . . . unfettered by the tyranny of convention'. The views are of the Thames at Thames Ditton, Kingston and Walton.

DR. EMERSON'S BUNGALOW AT SOUTHBOURNE
Designed by C. H. B. Quennell. From the architect. [Plate 64]

65, 66, 67 Word as symbol: bungalow = 'free and easy . . . away from the over-bearing etiquette of town' ('Home Counties', 1905; Bungalow Hotel, Weston-super-Mare, 1907: Hightown Bunglows (sic), near Liverpool, 1912)

HIGHTOWN BUNGLOWS

Other interiors on pages 110, 133; exterior on page 98
Large cobblestones have been used in this fireplace facing and scattered through the cement hearth. The hob, constructed of one large projecting stone, is noteworthy. The door at the left harmonizes particularly well with the rough battened walls

68, 69 Ideology and environment: the Craftsman bungalow in the USA. For 'The Craftsman', the bungalow was a socialist response to capitalism and the excesses of urban-industrial life. It was simple, 'craftsmanlike' and literally 'close to nature', bound to the earth by the cobble stone fireplace (H.Saylor, *Bungalows*, 1911)

bungalows, fully detached, and each in an acre of ground, should be as close as possible to the sea and as far as possible from older places of settlement. Sited well apart from the village, they were perched on the edge of a 50-foot cliff and had no other houses around. The site 'had

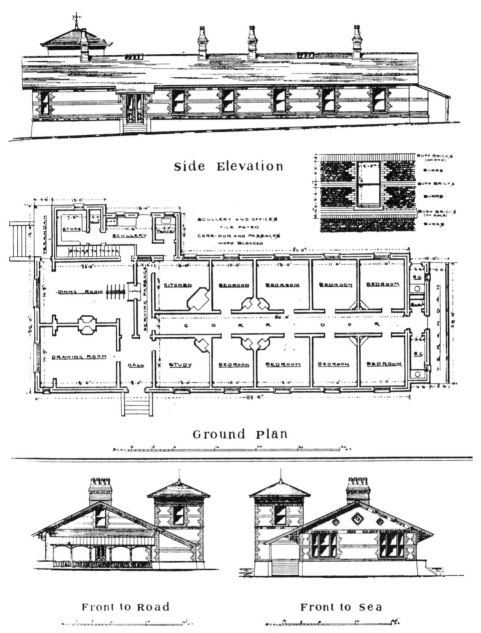

Figure 2.2 Bungalow development, phase two: 1870-3 (*Building News*, 4 August, 1905) (also plates 35, 39)

nothing but sea between it and the North Pole.' It was 'as bracing a spot as our island can supply' (*BN*, 1870:200).* Health considerations meant that the bungalows had 'many novel sanitary appliances' and were praised for 'the airiness of their verandahs'. Bathing facilities were equally important, though in comparison to earlier times, the mode of bathing was now different (plates 35 and 36).

In the early 'seaside watering places', bathing had been a restricted, almost medical, practice, with various arrangements, such as the bathing machine and the segregation of sexes, to safeguard public morals. By the 1860s, however, swimming, rather than mere immersion, was being recommended as a health-giving and pleasurable activity for both women and men. In 1875, the Channel was swum for the first time between Dover and Calais and this had done much to enhance the popularity of the sport. Though men had often swum naked in the 1850s, twenty years later convention required that costumes had to be worn (Thompson, 1860:36; Walvin, 1977:86).

These activities and conventions had been assumed in the siting of the bungalows. Located at the edge of the cliffs, each had a private tunnel which led from an entrance in the garden via a 'private dressing room' at the foot of the cliffs right to the edge of the sea, thus ensuring total privacy (plates 37 and 38).

The occupants of the bungalows were not, of course, completely isolated. There were, after all, a group of five in the initial development (1870-3). Still, in 1879 they were said to be 'cut off by deserts of mud and mire from all chance of Christian intercourse'. 'Perfect privacy' was assured as there was no public way along the cliff.

The main functions of the bungalow were those of recreation and health. As the location had been chosen because of the absence of public amusements, private leisure facilities had to be available on site. Hence, gardens were amply laid out, with the front, sea-facing lawn laid out for the new game of croquet, introduced in the late 1850s and increasingly fashionable in the next decades. At the other end, the conservatory and south garden afforded 'a pleasant retreat'. The dimensions of the plots were some 70 by 300 feet (plate 40).

The location gave endless opportunity for inhaling bracing sea air, gazing at passing boats and appreciating the restless waves. A contemporary had noted that 'people at the seaside are, for the most part, intent on doing nothing, and the object is to do this in as great a variety of ways as possible. The only pursuit of men and women is looking at one another, and at the sea' (Walvin, 1977:72). These ideas no doubt accounted for the low belvedere tower in each bungalow where, in the privacy of the single bedroom-study, one could steal away and read, or enjoy, in private, more distant views of the sea. Strung along the cliff edge and with no communicating links between them, the bungalow lay-out deliberately rejected any notion of 'community'.

Inside, the bungalows were spacious, 'cool, commodious cottages by the sea'.

The dining room (23' × 15') and saloon (15' × 18') both looked seawards; the saloon had been arranged 'to admit a billiard table capable of removal into the bay window and forming therein a buffet when required'.

The bungalows were designed for the typical Victorian middle class family, with five or six children, and servants. Apart from the bedroom in the tower, all accommodation was on one floor. In the larger version there were nine bedrooms (each approximately 11 by 12), two of which were for servants. The rooms were planned 'to require the least amount of household work' with a serving hatch from kitchen to dining room 'to economise the labour of service'.

---

* *BN Building News*.

Service arrangements included a butler's pantry, store room, larder, scullery, tradesman's entrance, kitchen yard, wash-house, stables and coach house. As the bungalows were separated from the main town, sewerage could only be provided by cesspit. This was perhaps the least satisfactory aspect as the two earth closets, located at the end of the corridor, meant that 'the smell . . . was always complained about as most objectionable'. The total plinth area was some 4,400 square feet.

An extensive basement was sunk into the chalk below. This had a large dairy, wine and beer cellars, and a separate garden entrance. A deep shaft was also sunk in the chalk into which larder shelves were suspended, by balance weights. Here, butter was kept in air 'so cold that no fly will remain in it'. The bungalows also contained partial central heating with the saloon, conservatory and garden pits warmed by hot pipes.

The emphasis on sea air, sea views and bathing which determined the cliff-edge site nevertheless brought technical problems. If the major object was to provide a healthy house, it was essential to keep out the damp. In the mid and later nineteenth century, this was a constant middle class worry, posing problems which, as yet, were little understood.

> In hundreds of instances . . . the interiors of rooms, even in houses occupied by persons of means and intelligence, are as moist as some caves. The paper peels off the walls, the plaster cracks and falls to pieces, the covers of books become mouldy and have a fusty smell. . . . These, and other evils, are as nothing in comparison with the ill effects produced on our health.

In the interior of the Birchington bungalows, however, 'none of these unpleasant phenomena are present'. The architect (reputedly the inventor of the damp-proof course), had introduced various devices to combat 'descending, ascending and drifting wet', including self-locking tiles on the roof and intricately built, damp-proof walls. In these, the outer and inner faces of the wall were separated by slates which overlapped both horizontally and vertically. Outer walls were of locally quarried flint, and the string courses, as well as quoins and reveals, were of special bricks. Severe tests had proved that 'the most penetrating rains and salt sea spray' would not penetrate the walls. The roof was of the simplest construction, with large (7" by 1½") common rafters replacing the usual roof truss. Ceiled beneath, this was then covered with asphalted felt, and topped with the architect's patented tiles.

Inside, the floors were covered with Indian matting. The furniture, specially designed by the architect, was prefabricated and built on a modular system. Chairs, used singly or bolted together, could be made up into settees, sideboards, dressing tables and bedsteads.

The bungalows were a speculative venture, the freehold price (including furniture and fittings) for the smaller 7-roomed version was £1,000; for the 11-roomed bungalow, £1,800. At a time when clerks received between £100 and £200 a year, and 75 per cent of the working class between £25 and £100, it seems that they were probably meant for an upper middle class of professionals, businessmen or rentiers with at least £500 or more per year (Best, 1973:100; Burnett, 1978:196).

The importance of beliefs about health in promoting the idea of the bungalow can be seen in their first owner, an eminent physician and antiquary who, apart from other claims to fame, paid £10,000 to bring Cleopatra's Needle to London. Sir Erasmus Wilson bought the first bungalow at Westgate in 1869 and, later, two others at Birchington to let to his clients. Professor of Dermatology at the Royal College of Surgeons, Wilson was the greatest authority on skin diseases of the century. According to the *Dictionary of National Biography* it is to him that 'we owe in great measure the use of the bath, so conspicuous a feature of our national life'. His book, *Healthy Skin*, reaching eight editions between 1845 and 1876, was dedicated to the great drain brain of the nineteenth century, Edwin Chadwick. In it, the author's recommendations for sea-bathing were based on both physical and psychological grounds. The sea apparently had

> a stimulating and penetrating power . . . it opens the pores and reinvigorates the whole nervous system . . . its great healing power in case of diseases is most agreeable in preserving health. Moreover the noble, grand and indescribable prospect of the sea . . . has an effect capable of bracing up the nervous system and producing a beneficial exhalation of the whole frame . . . the physical effects of sea-bathing must be greatly increased by this impression on the mind and that a hypochondriac or nervous person may be half cured by residing on the sea coast and enjoying a view of the grand scenes of nature which there present themselves, such as the rising and setting of the sun over the blue expanse of the water, and the awful majesty of the waves during a storm.

Wilson was particularly pleased with his bungalow, flying a red flag above it whenever he was in residence. He wrote to the architect,

> I find everybody charmed with my Bungalow and I believe if there were many Bungalows, there would be many buyers. The house is a novelty, very convenient and fitted for a single family and easy as to price. . . . They are novel, quaint, pretty and perfect as to sanitary qualities. The best sanitary home for a family is a Bungalow (Mayhew, 1881:6).

Another was bought by a wealthy and eccentric woman from London who lived there with a menagerie of animals; yet another by a London merchant. According to the architect, the others had been sold to 'gentlemen of position'.

All, however, were generally unoccupied for much of the year, being let furnished (through the agent and *The Times*) at between 7 and 15 guineas a week, depending on the month. In the season, Birchington could accommodate, at the most, forty or fifty families at a time, 'many of them belonging to the world of fashion with a pretty large sprinkling of carriage people among them' ('An Old Bohemian', 1881:258).

Bungalow developments: phase two

As new, purpose-built 'sanitary' and recreational dwellings, the first five bungalows had obviously met with success. After trying the same building methods on a 'bungalow' of two storeys, though still under one roof span, the architect turned to pre-fabrication. By this time, about 1877, the initial site had been completed and the new model was constructed further inland.

Pre-fabricated timber building was already a sophisticated industry; in the early nineteenth century, timber cottages had been made and exported round the world and barracks, hospitals and stores had been sent for use in the Crimean War (Herbert, 1978). This, however, was apparently the first example of a 'pre-fab' bungalow, a phenomenon which was to assume immense significance in the years to come. In this new style, though foundations and extensive basement were as before, the walls were of weatherboarding outside and matchboarding within. Between them, wheaten straw was packed for insulation. For the roof, the same simple structure was used as before.

Built on a three-quarter-acre site, the bungalow was on an equally spacious scale with ten bedrooms, large drawing room (30' by 20'), dining room (27' by 16'), with overhead lighting, study, conservatory and verandah running along the front. Attached were extensive offices

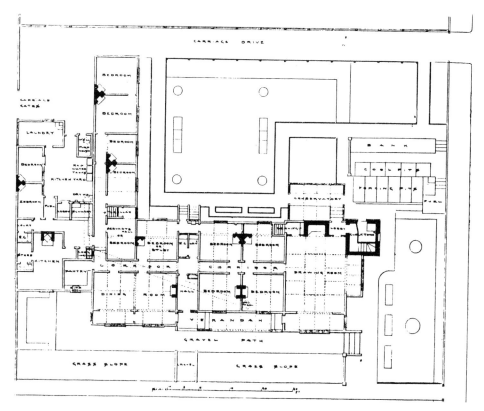

Figure 2.3   Large family home: portable timber bungalow, with 12 bedrooms, 1877. Plan
(*Building News*, 1 September, 1905) (See also plate 41)

including kitchen, scullery, pantry, laundry, two bedrooms and yards. In a basically L-shaped plan, the main corridor, 60 feet long, joined to a lesser one, giving a total length of 100 feet. 'This afforded ample space for exercise under cover if the weather was un-favourable for walking outside.' Though simply constructed, a special feature was made of the fireplace, with 'red brickwork in the chimney breast picked out with gold leaf'. Here, the architect lived for some time, designing his system-built furniture 'to export to any country not a mere shell of a house but a complete bungalow residence, furnished with appropriate chair furniture.' Using the same pre-fabricated methods, the Bungalow Hotel was built nearby about the same time (1877-9) (plates 41 and 42).

By 1880, the bungalow idea had become fully established. Benefiting from the pioneering efforts of ten years before, between 1881-2 four more bungalows were erected along the cliff top. These, without the special materials of the originals, none the less followed the same general plan, with bedrooms on both sides of the corridor and dining and drawing rooms overlooking the sea. Larger than the originals, these incorporated an additional billiard room at the end and, to give extra room in the tower, the staircase was built at the side.

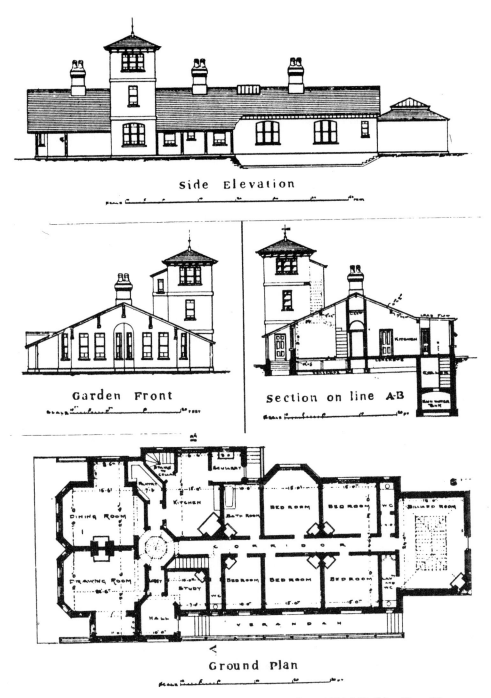

side Elevation

Garden Front

Section on line A-B

Ground Plan

Figure 2.4   Bungalow development, phase three: Tower Bungalows, 1881-2 (*Building News*, 20 October, 1905)

Contemporary response

Comments provoked by the bungalows suggest that they satisfied not only prevailing health and social requirements but also, emerging aesthetic tastes. These were increasingly moving towards the simple, the 'countrified' and away from ostentatious display. From the mid 1880s they were to emerge, in the 'Arts and Crafts' movement, as a definite style.

They combined 'real comfort . . . with pleasing rusticity'. They were not only 'cosy, isolated and rural-looking . . . but novel and quaint.' The Indian associations were both recognised and acclaimed: the architect 'must be awarded the credit of the introduction of these modified Indian country-houses into England'. In one particularly, 'he has given a capital reproduction of a cool, spacious, Indian-like hill-dwelling' (Mayhew, 1881:21).

Preference for the individual, the unique, for simplicity and the desire to be distinguished from what was increasingly perceived as a standardised 'resort architecture' can also be recognised. The development was commended for

> rescuing this class of building from the commonplace character invariably given them by speculating builders who . . . make the most of every foot of frontage and carry up their houses to the same regulation heights and to the same dreadful regulation patterns in town and country.

The architect's intention had been 'to create novelty by attention to extreme simplicity and adaptibility'. The bungalows were 'tasteful as well as useful . . . without the addition of anything that could be considered in the way of ornament'. These qualities had resulted in 'the greatest comfort with the least amount of household work', giving 'simplicity and freedom from care in use' to produce 'a perfect summer abode'.

These aesthetic ideas, a reaction against the formalism and clutter of the times, characterised other developments at Westgate, particularly Beach House, a hotel decorated according to avant garde London taste and financed by Coutts, the bankers. Nowhere, according to a contemporary, was there a hotel

> so comfortable . . . and so artistic . . . thoroughly and exquisitely homely. No hideous wall-papers hit the eye with their glaring hues, but the decorative patterns showing the hand of Walter Crane, Christopher Dresser or Lewis Day cover the rooms and corridors with their sober cheerfulness. Gillows' most artistic and comfortable furniture makes you feel that this is a place to stop in (*GIN*, 1879:15).

These aesthetic fashions added to Westgate's reputation, attracting patrons from theatre and the arts and giving Birchington and its bungalows a certain Bohemian image and appeal.

> All is pretty at Westgate and prettiness is a quality more to my liking than the Beautiful or the Sublime. When I marry . . . she will not be one of your classic tragedy queens . . . but a laughing little gipsy . . . and we will go to live in one of those brown, red-roofed bungalows beyond the smooth lawns and enamelled flower beds of this hotel (ibid:14).

With thinly-veiled irony, 'An Old Bohemian' described, in a London magazine, Birchington's 'rural simplicity' and 'enchanting primitive ways'. The bungalows were sufficiently novel to be pictured on contemporary souvenirs.

The idea of simplicity, to become a major characteristic of bungalows in future, and have a powerful influence on architecture, was not just an aesthetic fad. When Birchington was developed, the 'servant problem' was already being felt as new work opportunities were opening up for women. The single-storey plan with the absence of a real upstairs, the simple

Figure 2.5   Bungalow souvenir: view on a letter opener, late 19th century (*A. Stevenson*)

furnishing, serving hatch between kitchen and dining room with sideboard underneath (an early example of this device), overall planning and the emphasis on 'the least amount of household work' were portents which would explain the bungalow's future success.

Architects and innovators

The man who identified these social, medical and aesthetic values and translated them into the bungalow was a metropolitan architect, John Taylor, working with, or perhaps employed by, another more well-known member of the profession, John Seddon.

The development at Birchington arose from some astute land speculation. In the late 1860s, Seddon, like others profiting from railway expansion, had been involved with various professional activities in Kent. Pursuing his interests in the *Ancient Domestic Architecture* of Kent (1872) and combining business with pleasure, he had bought a piece of seafront land on which the bungalows were later to be built. Possibly because of his involvement in the building of an orphanage near Broadstairs, the initial responsibility for developing the Birchington land was handed over to his colleague. Though Seddon retained ownership of the estate, Taylor, who thought up the idea, was responsible for designing the first seven bungalows, though the subsequent 'Tower Bungalows' were designed and built by Seddon, between 1881-2. Also in Seddon's office between 1874 and 9 was an impressionable young man in his late teens, Charles F.A. Voysey (Gebhard, 1975:9) on whom the bungalow idea was not to be lost.

Seddon's connections with London's artistic circles and his more 'arty' tastes resulted in a departure from his colleague's original adherence to simplicity. A grid of roads was laid out on the small estate. To the two earlier and modestly named 'Cliff Road' and 'Beach Avenue' he added suitable literary and artistic names (Shakespeare, Spenser, Constable, Gainsborough, Wilkie, Leslie, Nasmyth), or those of natural scientists (Darwin, Lyell, Berkeley and Herschel) appealing to future patrons from the metropolis. A young sculptor, George Frampton, later to make his reputation with statues of Peter Pan and Nurse Edith Cavell in London and Queen Victoria in Calcutta, and to become a leading designer of the 'Arts and Crafts' movement, was brought from London in 1882 to decorate the outside of the coach house and domestic offices of the 'Tower Bungalows' (plate 43). In the chalk cliff under one of these, a large studio was carved out with a window overlooking the sea, sufficiently appealing to the Victorian painter, Solomon J. Solomon, who subsequently lived there. Other London artists were to visit – J. Stevens, Raffles Davison and Alfred Gilbert, the sculptor. In the last few months of his life, shortened by addiction to chloral, Dante Gabriel Rossetti, an old friend of Seddon, was brought to this exclusive and 'artistic' haven of Birchington. At Seddon's suggestion he was installed in Taylor's large, prefabricated bungalow. According to his brother, it was 'a good-looking wooden erection, without being a beautiful one'. Its interior was conveniently laid out for an invalid with 'a long corridor and rooms on either side. At the further end was a drawing room, running the width of the house.' It stood conveniently near to the railway station, yet not so close 'as to interfere with habits of retirement' (Rossetti, 1895, 1:390) (Figures 2.3, 2.6; plate 41). In February 1882, he wrote to his sister:

> There is a large garden belonging to the house, which is in all respects commodious. The journey by train is very easy; two hours to Westgate and a quarter of an hour by chaise to come here (Rossetti, 1906:1945).

Despite the sea air, and the suitably healthy bungalow, Rossetti lasted only a few weeks. He died on 10 April 1882, to be buried in the churchyard and leaving only his name to the avenue where he had spent his last days.

Like many other innovatory ideas, the bungalows built by Taylor were a synthesis of the old and new. The patented building materials and methods, and the prefabricated units were his, but the plan of the most successful of Taylor's three basic bungalow types was borrowed from a popular book of designs by John Weale (1857) (*BN*, 1895:541). The idea came from another cultural context increasingly familiar and attractive to a potential clientele in the previous years. Taylor's contribution was to combine these elements into a whole and, more importantly, do so at a time of economic expansion.

Just what he meant by using the term 'bungalow' is not immediately clear. On one occasion he applied it to 'one and two storey buildings under one span of roof of the most primitive and simple construction', though in fact all but one of his bungalows were of one storey. It was left to others increasingly to associate the term with what, in fact, Taylor had created: single-storey, purpose-built and 'simple' holiday houses by the sea. In the circumstances of the time, the innovation is easy to comprehend. Yet one enigma remains. From where did John Taylor get the immediate inspiration for the bungalow?

For someone who had probably not been to India, there are two plausible explanations. In the year before beginning at Birchington, Taylor could well have been at the Royal Institute of British Architects, of which he was a member, listening to what was probably the Institute's first lecture on tropical building. Here, T.R. Smith had discussed the design of bungalows in India (see above, p. 46). Alternatively, as an architect interested in 'portable buildings', he

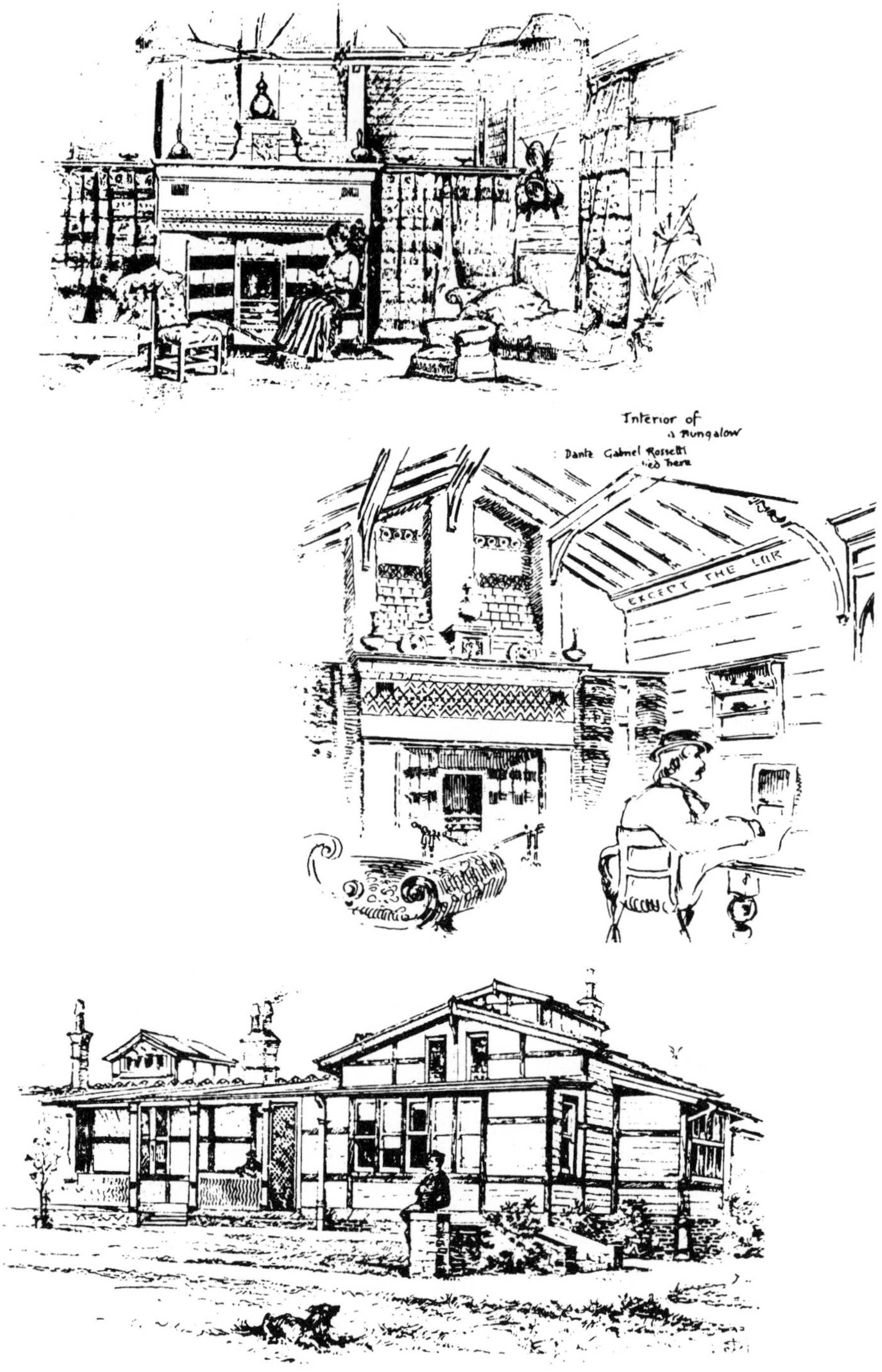

Figure 2.6   The artistic simple life: inside the 'Rossetti Bungalow', 1880s. (*British Architect*, 12 May, 1882; *Art Journal*, 1886) (*Michael Darby*)

might have come across the 1868 catalogue of Derbyshire ironmonger, James Handyside, where, apparently for the first time, a design appeared of a huge cast-iron bungalow for export to Bombay. Either of these – or some other source – might have sparked off the idea. Yet the date and conditions of its production were circumstances which had deeper roots in history. It is only of incidental interest to note that the first of these earliest bungalows in England was to house an eminent physician and the last, the deathbed of a Bohemian painter and poet.

Any of these – or some other source – might have sparked off the idea in Taylor's head. Yet it was symbolic of the meaning and purpose of these earliest bungalows in England that the first was to house an eminent physician and the last, the deathbed of a Bohemian painter and poet.

Conclusion

The 'invention' of the seaside bungalow provides a good example of the way in which the forces behind industrial capitalism, always on the look-out for investment and profit, generate new environments and building types. 'Needs' are constantly invented, especially in the spheres of recreation and leisure. What began in the 'Age of Capital' with the invention or proliferation of the winter garden, pier, and bungalow, or the glittering theatres and restaurants of the metropolis (King, 1980a:24) continues today in the casinos, leisure parks and time-share holiday apartments of the leisure industry. The drive is towards consumption, and specialisation, as well as exploitation of class differences, helps to achieve this end. Contemporary with the bungalows were new modes of fashion: clothes for the country and others for the seaside. The money invested in the spacious bungalows at Birchington also helps to explain other contemporary housing in London, the Peabody Buildings or the condition of the homeless described in Mearns' *Bitter Cry of Outcast London* published just as the third phase of bungalows was completed (1884).

The artistic associations and patronage of Birchington were equally a product of the times. The era of the railway and foreign investment also provided the economic base for the flourishing of Victorian art (Hobsbawm, 1975). It was a time when painters made fortunes selling to a growing bourgeois clientele. In the 'great Victorian boom', the number of architects more than doubled, from less than 3,000 to almost 7,000 in the thirty years after 1851 (Kaye, 1960:173). When the bungalow where he died was being built, Rossetti, having started as a critic of bourgeois society, was happily living off its profits (Nicoll, 1975:144).

Seddon's activities as developer apparently faded in the mid 1880s, possibly because the Birchington Bay Freehold Land and Estate Company had entered the field in 1882. With a capital of £150,000 in 30,000 £5 shares, the three directors (an ex-Indian army colonel from London, a city solicitor and an ex-mayor of Cambridge) had by then begun developing the resort. Everywhere, according to their prospectus (in Cambridge University Library), the development of freehold land offered the best investment, the Liverpool Land Company's 20 per cent being a case in point. At Westgate, land was selling between £2,500 and £4,500 an acre and at Birchington, the bungalow settlement had no doubt helped to 'greatly increase the value of land in recent years'. But no more were built and the developments were of a more traditional kind. After Birchington, little is heard of the seaside bungalow until the end of the decade when investment in building, slack during the 1880s, again started to rise. By then, however, the bungalow had also moved inland.

Architecturally, the bungalows were to be of no little importance. Within a decade, the idea had been taken up on opposite sides of the globe, in Australia and on the North American east coast; it also went to South Africa. Though they received limited professional attention when they were built, thirty years later, when the bungalow came into its own, the designs for these early developments were published in full in the *Building News* (1905-6).

Today, so accustomed are people to the plain, horizontal forms of modern outer suburban or country building that the significance of these early examples – economic, social and architectural – has been overlooked (cf. Figures 8.1 (p. 250), 2.2 (p. 79) and plate 104). As a specialised form of leisure building, their spacious, land- and time-consuming single-storey form was the outcome of a new political economy of design made possible by the economic and transport developments of a market economy: their 'simplicity' was a social product of the material excesses of the time. In the early decades of the next century, the bungalow, with its origins in colonialism, was to contribute to a new, outer suburban phase of capitalist urbanisation.

Chapter 3

Britain 1890-1914

A cottage is a little house in the country but a Bungalow is a little
country house

R.A. Briggs, *Bungalows and Country Residences*, London 1891:vii

In these days of commercial enterprise, with our enormously
increased facilities for transport, both over sea and land . . . the
entire world has become the market for the architect and builder

P.T. Harrison, *Bungalow Residences*, London, 1909:41-2

Introduction

In the thirty years before 1914, the seaside resorts rapidly grew in size, becoming the principal places of leisure for the growing middle class in the towns. With some exceptions, however, the bungalow was relatively slow to 'take off', making its impact at the seaside mainly from the later 1890s.

More important as a pointer to future change was the appearance of the bungalow in the country. It heralded a major, if not radical, shift in the use of rural land. As the urban proportion of the population grew from about a half to almost four-fifths in the sixty years after 1851, the countryside was to gradually assume a new role. It was one only slowly adopted in the years before the First World War and then, only by an urban middle and upper middle class. But from the 1920s, and especially after the Second World War, this new function came to equal, if not surpass, the traditional agricultural use of rural land. As an increasing global division of labour took agricultural workers away from the land, the country became a place for mass leisure, a resource consumed by people living in towns.

This provides the first theme: the changing use of land as it became subject to the emerging world economy. Tracing the introduction of the country and suburban bungalow provides some insights into these developments.

The second theme concerns the symbolic meaning of architecture. Between 1880 and 1914, the bungalow came to be invested with symbolic meanings: as it was, by definition, physically separate and away from the town, it symbolised not just the 'flight from the city' but also, at a time when many social conventions were in flux, an ideal of Bohemianism and the 'simplification of life'. Its unassuming, single-storey form also had political overtones, although not till the bungalow arrived in North America were all these ideological meanings fully explored.

Two other themes are touched on: the development of prefabrication in housing and its results, and the beginning of the mass market second home.

The changing use of rural land

Until the second half of the nineteenth century, agriculture had been the predominant, if not the sole, economic activity of rural England. The great estates were the basis of rural society, with the landed aristocracy living in country mansions yet with extensive interests, and property, located in the towns. When – as in the eighteenth century – fortunes were made by city merchants, economic and social substance was often given to the fact by the purchase of a country house and estate. Landed interests dominated British political and social life. In the early and mid Victorian age, as Mark Girouard has shown, industrial profits were converted into rural property: some 500 country houses built or re-modelled between 1835 and 1890 were financed from industry or commerce (1971b).

In the country, the main business was agriculture. Outside the market towns and villages which linked agriculture to the nation's economy at large, the variety of buildings expressed this function: farms, rented from the larger estates, housed the families working on the land, their various outbuildings containing livestock, implements, machinery and the produce from the land. In the village or on the estate, cottages housed workers who lived mainly by selling their labour, and a small proportion of freeholders had buildings of their own. For the mass of the rural population, the villages and fields provided space for recreation, for country games, fairs, festivals and clandestine poaching, in an annual calendar where spare time was governed by the demands of work, the weather, 'Nature's day' and the rhythm of the seasons. The village green and inn were the primary, in many cases the only, specialised places for leisure. For the landed gentry, the land itself provided opportunity for traditional field sports and in the larger country houses, ample recreational space existed in the gardens, conservatories, billiard room, libraries or study.

By the 1880s, however, fundamental economic and social changes were beginning to affect the countryside, preparing the way for the function of 'urban playground' which it fulfils for many today. A hint of this had already occurred in the early nineteenth century with the fashion, among city merchants and others, for the 'rural retreat'. Yet many of the 'ornamental cottages' designed between 1790 and 1840 as part of the cult of the picturesque were as much to look at as to live in. They were relatively few in number and even where used as 'a retreat from the hurry of town life', the restrictions of horse-drawn transport limited them to being 'a few miles out of town' (Bartell, 1804:4; Elsam, 1803). Many, in fact, were outer suburban villas (Slater, 1978; King, 1980b).

In the second half of the nineteenth century, 'changes in the countryside were certainly the most widespread of all changes in the geography of England' (Coppock, 1973:602). They were a result of the economic and technological and consequent demographic factors referred to earlier. With a huge expansion of railways around the world, steamships, telegraphic communication and such innovations as refrigeration in ships, agriculture everywhere gradually became subject to the emerging industrial world economy.

Certain areas such as the North American prairies became massive exporters of grain. The demands of the industrial economy multiplied the market for agricultural products, both domestically, through the growth of cities, and internationally. And as more and more land was brought into cultivation and agriculture fully commercialised, peasant economies began to disappear and everywhere there was a major 'flight from the land' (Hobsbawm, 1975).

This process became especially pronounced in the third quarter of the nineteenth century as railways opened up hitherto inaccessible regions to export production. This period also saw the beginning of attempts to develop certain overseas areas, either formal colonies such as

Australia and Bengal or informal ones like Brazil, as specialist producers of exports for the 'developed' world – wool, indigo, jute, coffee and tea. It saw the expansion of plantations and, as we shall see below, the bungalow was also important here.

The international trade in agricultural produce was now in being, generally leading to extreme specialisation or even monoculture in the exporting regions as well as having drastic effects on farming in Britain. It was the real beginning of an international division of labour which, with technological changes in farming, over the coming decades was greatly to reduce the numbers working in agriculture and simultaneously increase the numbers living and working in towns (Roberts, 1978; Barratt Brown, 1978).

In the fifty years after 1860, agricultural workers in Britain were to fall from some 19 to 9 per cent of the workforce (Coppock, 1973:596). The specialisation which had begun in the society and city was now extended to a global scale: some countries became producers of agricultural and primary products, remaining largely rural, while others became industrial and urban. Britain was historically the first example of the latter and, as part of the development, much of what was once rural, agricultural land was turned over to urban, residential use, from production to consumption.

Between the 1870s and 1900, the newcomers to the country were a wealthy and largely metropolitan bourgeoisie, whose ranks had been swelled by the growth of industry and commerce, the department stores and the beginnings of the mass market (Fraser, 1981). Expanding railways and, after 1900, the motor car, brought country areas increasingly within reach of the towns. In the third quarter of the nineteenth century, route mileage for railways in England increased by 130 per cent (from just over 5,000 to almost 12,000 miles). Helped by improved horse carriages and hard-surfaced roads, this meant deeper and more frequent penetration into rural areas. By 1912, over 16,000 miles of rail was in place (Coppock, 1973:646). The motor car, introduced effectively in England after 1895, grew rapidly in popularity – for those able to afford it – and between 1900 and 1912, the numbers on British roads increased from some 800 to 80,000 (Robertson, 1978).

For centuries, the countryside had been the preserve of the aristocracy, for income, residence and mainly for recreation. As the scale of urban leisure had grown, however, the developing seaside resorts had, for the upper and middle class, provided a variety of places to stay, each with its own social image and prestige. In 1881, according to *The Architect* (17 September:185) it was still apparently true that 'the typical aristocrat is apt to despise seaside delights. He prefers to spend the autumn either at his own 'place in the country', or at the place of some friend, or somewhere abroad. The growing seaside resorts, on the other hand, had to be designed for 'the middle classes and though inferior people have also to be considered in these places, it is not to any appreciable extent'.

This situation was to change markedly in the next thirty years. Taking the aristocracy as their model, the urban upper and middle class were to start searching for a 'country pad'. With the example, money and transport to do it, and an expanding architectural profession to produce the designs, they were persuaded by an increasingly fashionable ideology. This was not simply a complaint about 'bad air' and the physical conditions of towns; it was a protest about the 'strains and stresses' of industrial life and the constraints of a formalised social routine. 'To have a country cottage, or better still, a bungalow', was to permit temporary escape from the city. For the growing middle class, it was the beginning of an idea now better known as a 'second home'. It catered for temporary use, initially, for some weeks in the summer but, from the later 1880s, for the emerging temporal unit of the 'week-end' (King, 1980b). Situated in Berkshire, Surrey, Sussex or Kent, the houses were within 30 or 40 commuting miles of London. Sited in bucolic surroundings, the countryside was an aesthetic rather than economic resource. Designed to accommodate not just a family but also servants and guests, they were purpose-built environments for the passing of leisure time. It was in this role that the bungalow was introduced into the country and it is in the interdependent relationship of the bungalow to its surroundings that the function of country as recreational resource is most clearly understood and seen.

The bungalow in the country

An early (though not the first) example was the estate of bungalows constructed in the depths of the Surrey countryside, near East Grinstead, in 1887. Some 30 miles from London, the estate (its name, 'Bellagio', conjuring up romantic associations of the lake-side haven on Italy's Lake Como), was reached – not without significance – either from London or Brighton by the railway which ran between them. The nearest station was Dormans, opened in 1884, and the estate was reached via a 10-minute carriage ride through the thickly wooded area of what today is Dormans Park. By 1891, there were some forty 'bungalow residences', large and small, 'dotted about the copse-clad slopes'.

> The surrounding country shows fertile meadows on every side . . . belted here and there with dark patches of woodland. If you want peace and quiet, Bellagio is decidedly the place to get it, for here in your bungalow, hidden away amongst wooded slopes, you can be lost to the outer world as completely as you wish.

When completed, there would, according to the *British Architect* (1888:74), be 'no more delightful rural retreat for tired Londoners than Bellagio'.

Figure 3.1   Country pad: the bungalow as 'little country house'. Surrey, 1887-91.
'a cottage is a little house in the country but a Bungalow is a little country house' (R.A.Briggs, 1891)

Figure 3.2 and Figure 3.3 As an increasing international division of labour took agricultural production from the land, 'rural areas' were re-defined as 'country-side' (sic) and consumed for recreation by the urban middle class. The five editions of R.A. Briggs' *Bungalows and Country Residences*, 1891-1901 catered for these new requirements, having considerable influence in spreading the bungalow ideology on both sides of the Atlantic. Some of Briggs's more substantial bungalows were built at 'Bellagio', now Dormans Park, in the emerging 'stockbrokers belt' of Surrey. Briggs calls Figure 3.2 a 'Bungalow House' (see p. 96)

The bungalows had been designed and built by architect R.A. Briggs. In *Bungalows and Country Residences*, the first book of architectural designs on the bungalow to be published in England, and an important landmark for the ideology which developed around it, Briggs spelt out the contrasting images of town and country, demonstrating in the process the needs which his bungalows were designed to fulfil. The bungalow appealed

> to people of moderate means in a City like ours where grime and smoke, bustle and hurry make us long for the country and its freshness, where at a small expense we may pass a quiet week-end 'far from the madding crowd' to strengthen us for the next week's toil. A House in the country with its attendant expense would be beyond our means but a Bungalow can be built and maintained at a comparatively trifling cost.

Briggs distinguished between a bungalow, generally of one storey though sometimes with bedrooms in the roof, and a bungalow-house. This had verandahs and balconies, a second 'storey' accommodated in the roof space and a more informal architectural style. As with the Birchington developments of two decades before, Indian images had been the source of his inspiration, though with increasing consciousness of empire at the end of the 1880s, other colonial ideas had also played a part.

> What is a bungalow? . . . our imagination transports us to India . . . to low, squat, rambling one-storied houses with wide verandahs, latticed windows, flat roofs and with every conceivable arrangement to keep out the scorching rays of the sun. . . . Or else we think of some rude settlement in our colonies, where the houses or huts built of logs of wood, hewn from the tree and with shingle roofs gives us an impression, as it were, of 'roughing it'.

This was not the kind of bungalow suitable for England, nor what Briggs meant when he used the term which, for him, also had social connotations.

> A Cottage is a little house in the country but a Bungalow is a little country house, a homely little place, with verandahs and balconies, and the plan so arranged as to ensure complete comfort with a feeling of rusticity and ease.

Cheapness and economy were also important, and a compromise could be made with the accepted notion of the bungalow as a house on one floor by having solid walls for one storey but then making some bedrooms in the roof. Built in this way, bungalows were 'very cheap in comparison to houses as the great aim in the design [is] simplicity'. The leisure function was embodied in both the building and the estate. The houses, with billiard rooms, lounge, six to eight bedrooms and spacious gardens, made ample provision for guests. Despite the search for seclusion, there was 'no reason to be dull, for fishing was to be had (in two trout lakes), tennis, cricket and football at the recreation ground and social intercourse at the clubhouse'. *The Caterer and Hotel Proprietor's Gazette* (15 August, 1888) reported that this had 'a capital kitchen, from which the steward provides breakfast, lunches, dinners according to order by telephone from the respective bungalows'. At the entrance to the estate, where later bungalows and houses were built by other London architects, C.F.A. Voysey and Wimperis and Arber, was a lodge where 'custodians' kept out intruders.

In the ten years following the establishment of Bellagio (1887-97) the *Building News* ran competitions for the design of a 'seaside', 'countryside' and 'hillside bungalow' and later, for a 'bungalow club'. For the 'country-side bungalow', the function was made explicit.

Bungalows, or free and easy dwellings in the country, erected on sites out of the way of the ordinary run of holiday-seekers, or on some river-bank or unfrequented shore, are nowadays becoming more the fashion with people whose business compels them to spend the greater part of their time in London or our larger towns. To have a country cottage, or better still, a bungalow, with space and surroundings within doors somewhat in character with the comforts of home, and none of the horrors peculiar to lodgings, affords an attraction which warrants the necessarily frequent railway journeys to and from the shop or office during the summer months, while the family are enjoying the freedom of a country-side stay in some rural retreat (1893:6).

The idea of the bungalow as 'a little country house' was particularly associated with 'Bungalow Briggs' as he became known to architectural friends. His book had 'remarkable success', being printed in five editions between 1891-1901 and, as will be seen below, helping to transport the bungalow from a country to a suburban setting. 'These little dwellings have become very popular in England as they appeal not only to the economical side of our nature but also to our artistic feelings', wrote Briggs in 1894. 'What we mean by a bungalow is an artistic little dwelling, cheaply but soundly built . . . popped down in some pretty little spot with just sufficient accommodation for our particular needs.' It should be 'a homely, cosy little place, with verandahs, oriels and bay windows'. Where local authorities allowed, walls would be of wood, covered with tiles, weatherboard or roughcast. Inside features were to be 'of the

The Garden Front

Bungalow at Belladio

Figure 3.4   Imperial image transferred, 1891.
'What is a bungalow? . . . our imagination transports us to India . . . to low, squat, rambling one-storied houses with wide verandahs, latticed windows . . . or else we think of some rude settlement in the colonies where the houses . . . give us an impression . . . of roughing it' (R.A.Briggs, 1891)

Figure 3.5   Space and gender: the bungalow as 'bachelor's summer residence'.
As in the later American 'Craftsman' bungalows, appropriate symbols, in this case, the
crossed swords and visor, add a suitably masculine flavour. In a bachelor's summer residence,
women apparently visit in pairs (R.A.Briggs, 1891)

simplest description' with white painted woodwork throughout. Functionally, the bungalow
was a 'second home': it enabled 'paterfamilias to enjoy his brief holiday in comfort and at a
moderate expense, the year's interest on the capital cost being less than a month's house hire
at a seaside resort' (1894:21). According to the *Builders Journal* (1895:342), Briggs had
erected 'a vast number' of these 'delightful little dwellings' in all parts of the country.

The exploitation of the countryside for leisure is well demonstrated in Briggs's designs as
well as numerous competitions in *Building News*. The raison d'être of the bungalow was in
those aspects of its location, siting and design which allowed the fullest use of the senses –
visual, aural, olfactory. They also provided for the particular social functions which the
bungalow was designed to fulfil. In 'the bachelor's summer residence,' a surrounding
verandah provided 'magnificent views'. Cut and clipped yews 'with a rustic summer house
under a spreading tree for a book' framed the bungalow in a 'quaint and picturesque setting'.
For the *Building News* 'countryside bungalow', the viewing facilities on the verandah,
extending round three sides, were supplemented by a belvedere tower. Inside, maximum time-
passing activities were accommodated. Family members and guests (in six bedrooms) might
relax, 'for shrimps and tea', in the large (20 by 18) hall/sitting room. A writing room and
library could be used for quiet rest. The smoking room should not be too isolated 'for comfort
of the kind so needful in a bungalow after a pull on the water or a game of tennis' (1893:6).
The 'hillside bungalow' intended 'for a gentleman' was to be on a site 'a few miles from
London' and was to act as 'a summer residence' (1898:700). There were to be two best
bedrooms and two extra ones for female servants, generous living and drawing rooms, a large
billiard room and provision in the basement for golf irons and bicycles. In the riverside

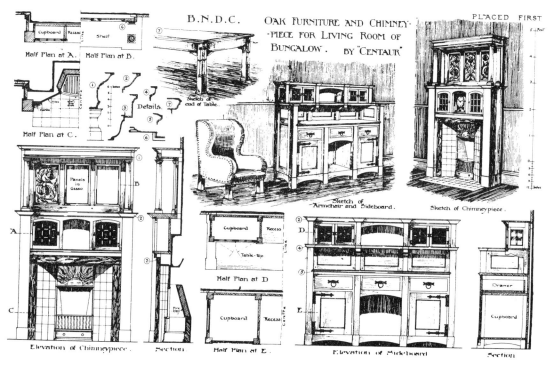

Figure 3.6 Bungalow furniture:
'plain and simple,' for the gentleman who has everything (*Building News*, 10 June, 1898)

bungalow of 1898, with seven bedrooms, a boathouse was incorporated under the billiard room. As 'the rough and ready freedom of Bungalow life' suggested 'an avoidance of delicate detail', special furniture was required, 'distinctly plain and simple, straightforward in construction and more like joiner's work than cabinet-makers's' (1898:810). In the 'week-end bungalow' the 'countryside character externally ought to prevail, as being out of accord with all fuss and vulgar self-assertion' (1906:428).

Even in these early days, 'getting away from it all' could also mean taking it all with you. A few years later, the 'bungalow by the sea' was aimed more at the motor user who 'in the rush of modern fashion, seeks a haven for a few hours at least, from the turmoils of town life.' Though the bungalow suggested an experience of 'roughing it',

> we all know that such a client expects to be surrounded with the amenities of home and . . . the common items of luxury, even down to the minute details to which the well-to-do are accustomed. . . . The client himself may pose as a Spartan and his women-folk may talk exquisite nonsense about roughing it but experience proves how ephemeral all this 'poca a poca' really becomes.

None the less, what was wanted in a bungalow design was 'the gaiety of a sort of Bohemian freedom, away from the over-bearing etiquette of town residence'. And though privacy was generally desirable 'during tub-time in the house', mixed bathing 'may not be *de trop* out of doors' (1910:67).

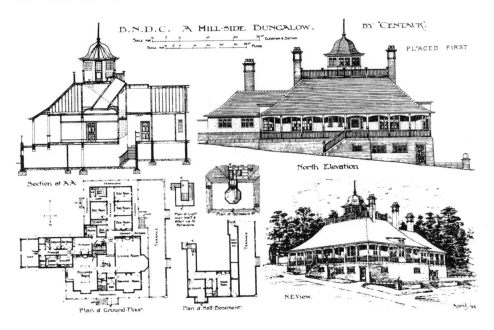

Figure 3.7   Capital bungalow, 1898.

As an imperial capital and centre for investment on a world scale, London was unrivalled at the end of the century. Some of the surplus capital flowed into leisure building, as in this proposal for a 'hill-side bungalow, a few miles from London, for a gentleman' who apparently also had a surplus of time.

Outside, the site, terrace, encircling verandah and belvedere tower encourage time spent consuming, as 'views', the countryside around; inside, the generous dimensions, billiard room and basement with storage space for golf irons and bicycles indicate the leisure function. As a 'horizontal container for the consumption of surplus free time', the economic and social significance of the bungalow can also be appreciated in comparison to the multi-storey, multi-unit 'philanthropic dwellings' for the poor being built in London about the same time (*Building News*, 20 May, 1898)

The bungalow and the Bohemian

Whatever its form, the significant characteristic of the bungalow was its 'apartness' and consequent social isolation. In what a later generation was to label 'the Naughty Nineties', the bungalow's 'free and easy', Bohemian image is easy enough to grasp. In *Gal's Gossip* (1899), Arthur Binstead, 'the most authoritative guide to the Bohemia of the 1880s and 90s' produced 'the truest tidings of London's demi-monde ever written' (Booth, 1927, viii). The heroine (a chorus girl or actress from a West End theatre), recounts her exploits, month by month, each from a different address: The Flat, St John's Wood; Hotel Metropole, Brighton; The Gables, Bottomparley; The Lady Author's Club; Off Cowes, Isle of Wight; the Grand Hotel, Paris. In May, she meets a friend, Mabel Morrison, who 'couldn't really stand Westgate . . . too many invalids there and . . . everyone keeps asking you what *you* are "down here for" '; in July, our heroine moves from the flat in St John's Wood to 'The Sprouts, Bellagio' and 'up to the present, I have not found country life nearly so dull as I thought it would be.'

I must tell you that Charlie* and I have taken the delightful semi-detached bungalow between Horley and Crawley that I told you about in my last; indeed, we have been living in it for the past fortnight. I think it exquisitely rural. We are over a mile from a house of any sort, and nearly two from a tavern. Charlie has hit upon such a pretty name for it, 'Dryazell'. Is it not charmingly sylvan? As far as I can judge, our next door neighbours are particularly quiet people, but it may be that they are only keeping so (as the walls are very, very thin) in order to overhear what we say.

* Not, of course, her husband. Charlie had an eyeglass and was a friend of 'Jocelyn-Johnson who parted his hair and name in the middle'.

The events of *Gal's Gossip*, with its references to Gaiety chorus girls, ornate garters, bedroom windows with no blinds, girls in the nude and the Gatwick steeplechases, might not all have occurred at Bellagio but a distinct reputation was established which lingers on to the present. The 'Bungalow Utopia' quickly acquired a Bohemian reputation'. A subsequent inhabitant recalled the 'gay skating parties on the lake with fairy lights hanging in the trees'. In the mid 1970s, there were still 'persistent local traditions about the goings on at Bellagio, from the [former] Prince of Wales downwards'; 'the place acquired a very "fast" reputation and local residents shunned it'.[1]

This meaning which the bungalow acquires as arty, Bohemian, a symbol of the unconventional, is seen at its best in George Gissing's novel, *The Whirlpool* (1897). Gissing had a keen sense for what was going on around him and the novel, a brilliant commentary on the social world of the 1890s, with its references to amateur photography, cycling and 'the simple life', captures many of the overtones surrounding the bungalow at this time.

The 'whirlpool' is London, with its stifling social life of gossip, keeping up appearances, problems with houses and servants, and entertaining. Much of the story revolves round a series of tensions: the dissatisfactions of a small-scale rentier class of owning property, with its attendant responsibilities, and yet a wanting 'to be free'; between the social climbing of London and an idealised 'simple life' in 'the country' or leaving it all for a 'rugged' one in the colonies; between the wishes of a woman drawn at one time to the life of the Bohemian artist and at another, to that of a lady with social conventions to respect.

The villain of the story, Cyrus Redgrave, is a mysterious, somewhat shady bachelor, a 'man of the world' and, a 'polished capitalist'. He has 'a little place' at Riva, on Lake Garda in Italy (an interesting parallel with Briggs's 'Bellagio'), another in the Pyrenees and a taste for other men's wives. In London he is conventionally dressed, but abroad in Bregenz he wears 'flannels, a white necktie loosely knotted and a straw hat'. At forty, 'the passions were sportive, half fantastical as though . . . they had grown to ripe worldliness.' He was, in his own words, 'a natural Bohemian, liking nothing so well as to disregard ceremony'.

When not abroad, Redgrave lived at his sister's house at Wimbledon. The large garden was in fact 'a sort of little park' and here, among the trees, he had 'built himself what he calls a bungalow' carefully hidden by shrubbery. 'One is free there', Redgrave says, 'a member of the family whenever one likes; domesticated; all that's respectable; and only a few steps away, the bachelor snuggery, with all that's. . . .' As his housekeeper noted, 'the rooms had French windows – a convenient arrangement. The front door may be locked and bolted but people come and go for all that.'

The central incident of the story takes place in the bungalow. One evening, the young wife, nervous at the thought of compromising her social position, visits. 'The thought of stealing into his bachelor house . . . startled and offended her self-respect.' Stepping from her carriage, she finds 'a house of unusual construction, with pillars and a verandah'. Her senses are dazzled and confused. She enters, crosses a floor of smooth tiles, under electric light 'ruby-coloured by glass shades' and enters a room illumined, 'until the servant turned on a soft radiance like that in the hall', only by a fire. 'She sensed the atmosphere of luxurious refinement, its colour, perfume and warmth at once allured and alarmed her. . . . She wished to indulge her senses . . . but she also wished to turn and escape.'

Redgrave is away, but the visit and what the woman's husband later believes to have taken place, cause him to race over to the Wimbledon bungalow, with dire consequences for both Redgrave and himself.

The moral symbolism with which Gissing invests the bungalow, using it as part of a larger moral topography of metropolitan districts and dwellings (Alma wanted 'an interesting house to live in. Nobody's ancestors ever lived in a semi-detached villa. What I should like is one of those picturesque places in Surrey, quite in the country yet within easy reach of the town') – was to be echoed some years later by Gissing's friend and mentor, H.G. Wells. Like Briggs's designs for a bachelor's bungalow, Gissing also provides insights into a society dominated by masculinity as well as by wealth.

The bungalow in the suburbs

As an artistic, small country house for summer or temporary use, or even for permanent occupation, the bungalow became steadily more popular for a wealthy upper middle class from the early 1890s. At a time when average incomes were less than £80 a year, there were perhaps 2 or 3 per cent of the population for whom a country house or second home at £1000 or £2000 was within reach (Thompson, 1975:12). Briggs's houses were in this bracket although he also included designs at £250 and £550 (Figures 3.3, 3.1).

That some of these bungalows were of two storeys rather than one confirms the notion that, for this class, the bungalow was defined as much in terms of its use and image as any more prosaic criteria. There was, however, increasing professional opinion that the term should keep its traditional meaning. According to *The Builder* (1891:33):

> No doubt any one is free to call his house a bungalow if it pleases him but the
> word . . . was, we believe, originally applied by Europeans living in India to the typical
> wide-spaced, and low-verandahed house all on one floor . . . and we think it might as
> well be kept to its original meaning. A house may, however, conform to the bungalow
> type architecturally without being literally of one storey.

Indeed, even in 1878, the *Building News* had felt it necessary to inform its less cosmopolitan readers that the term was used in India 'for a country house of one floor only'. Yet some were obviously being built in England:

> In this country, the term is similarly applied to single dwellings on one floor. (And then
> apparently drawing on the Indian prototype with its distinctive type of roof), the general
> characteristics of them being a square plan with the entrance at the side or in the centre, a
> high-pitched pyramidal roof, with sometimes the chimney made the central feature
> (1878:685).

Ten years later, this 'structural meaning' had obviously been fully accepted among the English public at large. According to Murray's *New English Dictionary* (1888), it was 'a one-storied house (or temporary building, e.g. a summer house) lightly built, and usually with a thatched roof'.

Among architects, the notion was more flexible. According to one of the more eminent, Professor Robert Kerr, the bungalow's single storey should be 'of especial spaciousness and simplicity' and have a verandah. The plan should be 'very liberally treated, with superabundance of light and air and the rules of aspect fully observed'. Though these requirements largely confined the bungalow to 'the open country and sea' (Sutcliffe, 1898:52), it was already moving into, or extending the suburbs. In provincial cities, the wealth generated by the growth of the mass market enabled increasing numbers of people in commerce or the professions to move to more spacious surroundings, a move made possible by tramways, now reaching out of built-up areas and for some, the ownership of a car. However, developments were already taking place in the prefabricated bungalow which foreshadowed the disrepute which was to overtake it some thirty years on. In the most extensive discussion of the English bungalow printed in the nineteenth century, the *Building News* attempted to clarify just what the concept meant.

> Some people have the idea that the bungalow is of necessity a very temporary kind of structure – something like a dismantled railway carriage deprived of its wheels and fitted up as a residence . . . such an idea is at variance with the fact for all the bungalows herein described are extensive permanent houses built with bricks and mortar, covered with slate and tiles, except in a few cases where they are built specially with wood-framed walls, match boarded and roof-felted, to permit of rapid removal and re-erection elsewhere at a minimum cost. An extensive verandah is associated with a bungalow in the popular acceptance of that term, but this is not a special feature of the bungalow as naturalised in the British Isles (1895:399-400).

As the house-type was clearly gaining in popularity, the *Building News* pointed out its advantages. With domestic service becoming scarcer and more expensive, it saved the labour of servants and occupants, particularly in climbing stairs; invalids in wheelchairs had access to all the rooms; neither children nor adults could fall on stairs; removal of furniture up and down stairs was avoided; loss of life by fire was lessened as occupants could climb out of the windows; there was security from the spread of fire as the walls of the rooms were carried up to the roof; gas, water and bell wires could be laid and removed more easily; soil and water pipes could not leak and damage ceilings and walls. Another contemporary (no doubt anticipating the 'old people's bungalow' of the future) drew attention to the problem in two-storey houses of carrying coffins downstairs.

There were no disadvantages for the occupier, though costs were higher and the plot larger than for a house of similar accommodation. For three living rooms, six bedrooms and the usual offices, a roof of 2,300 superficial feet was needed in comparison to one of 900 feet for a three-storey house of similar accommodation. Plot sizes would be 1,600 feet compared with 560 superficial feet. Moreover, the bungalow, owing to its limited height, required more room all round than a higher house as no two rooms could overlook the same frontage and there were no upstairs rooms on a high level to command hedges, boundary walls or shrubberies that might, if too close to the house, 'completely block the view'.

Evidently, the bungalow was already being used as a 'retirement dwelling'.

The neighbourhood should be good, that is, the surrounding property should be of good class and likely to be maintained. If the locality is retired, it will always be well to be within reach of pleasant company. People who have spent their lives in a busy, noisy city naturally seek at first the quiet of the country or the seaside.

For such a purpose, clear air and pleasant surroundings were essential. The air near large towns was 'vitiated by respiration, combustion, sewage effluvia and deleterious gases from chemical works and gasworks'. The plans which accompanied this extended discussion all included accommodation for servants.

In the decade spanning the nineteenth and twentieth centuries, the bungalow, sometimes large, rambling and spacious, began to appear in the equally spacious suburbs. In retrospect, its development is easily understood. The great railway cities of the Victorian era were, by today's standards, dense and closely packed, the characteristic forms of housing often in terraces, rows, or perhaps working class tenements and 'buildings'. Houses of three or more storeys were not uncommon. In the United States, skyscrapers had been introduced. The middle and upper class suburbs of the nineteenth century were generally of two, three or four storey villas, many semi-detached, for large Victorian families with cellars and attics for the

'[This] design for a bungalow . . . in its own grounds – that is to say, with a garden of at least 20 feet on each side – will be a useful example for those who intend building in the country or suburbs.'

work and rest of servants. Suburban extensions in the late nineteenth and early twentieth centuries resulting from increased capital investment and transport developments, whether in railways, the electric tramway, and later, the motor car and bus, reached out into cheaper land. And with British agriculture increasingly depressed by competition from the world market, outer suburban land also became cheaper, especially after the First World War. The idea of a dwelling appropriate to these new, more spacious country or outer suburban plots, with accommodation principally on one floor, was, in retrospect, a revolutionary development. There had, of course, always been single-storey cottages, but these were essentially artisan or proletarian dwellings. The Edwardian middle class had to rediscover the convenience of single-storey living on a larger scale.

The first identified reference to the bungalow as suitable not just for the seaside and country but also for suburban locations is in 1891 and it occurs in that year not only in Briggs' up-market book of designs, *Bungalows and Country Residences* but at a much more modest level, in the *Illustrated Carpenter and Builder*. For Briggs, the bungalow was not only suitable for second homes in the country but also, for the country-like setting of the outer suburb. In his Preface he refers to 'the desire . . . for artistic and appropriate dwellings . . . among the large number of persons of moderate income . . . hitherto content to reside in the ordinary suburban villa of a stereotype pattern.' And as with many other aspects of nineteenth century urban life, there was also a 'sanitary' motivation for the suburban bungalow. According to hygienist Dr G.W. Poore (*The Dwelling House*, 1898), the standard Victorian four or five storey middle class house in the city had added immensely to over-crowding. Lacking sunlight and ample circulating air all round, it had an additional hazard in the inadequate ventilation of the staircase. In his view, detached houses in the suburbs were in every case more healthy and, as in the plan of the south-facing bungalow which he included, the 'sanitary advantages' of a large single floor area were 'very great'.

Figure 3.8   Hints of a suburban revolution, 1890 (see also Plate 48)

Whilst the effect of capitalist industrialisation was to concentrate people in cities and towns, the same market forces combined with transport developments to expand the suburbs around them.

Yet in these areas, growing rapidly from the mid nineteenth century, traditional two-, three- or four-storey houses continued to be built, whether terraced, detached or, increasingly, the semi-detached villa. Even in 1912, an observer visiting the USA from England, could write:

To the dwellers in city streets, or in suburban districts around our large towns, in which dwellings of three or more stories, closely huddled together, seem to be the order of the day, the delights of the Bungalow, as it exists in the United States, are absolutely undreamt of . . .

In California, the shift towards the single-storey separate dwelling, characteristic of the later consumer-orientated 'sprawling suburb' was already taking place in Los Angeles with the introduction of the California Bungalow from 1905. In Britain, it was to begin, though on a much more modest scale, with 'bungaloid growth' in the 1920s.

This illustration is the first identified reference in Britain to the bungalow as recommended for suburban as well as country locations. That the design was sent to the journal from an English reader in Santiago, Chile, suggests that the bungalow was already in the early stages of becoming part of an international free market culture. (*Illustrated Carpenter and Builder*, 13 February, 1891)

The recommendations of Briggs, the *Illustrated Carpenter* and Dr Poore seem to have been adopted relatively slowly for the same point about the suitability of the bungalow for the new suburbs was being made again two decades later, though this time inspired by examples from Pasadena, California (see page 145). However, given the conditions for its development, some appear to have been built. In a newer suburb of Leeds, The Bungalow with billiard room and six bedrooms, and inspired by Briggs's book and other 'Arts and Crafts' ideas, was constructed in 1900, its early occupants being the owners of a new department store selling consumer goods in the city (plate 50). In commercial and industrial cities such as these, the political economy of empire which helped provide the economic base for suburban expansion was fully appreciated at the time. A year or two after The Bungalow was built, a statue of the late head of this empire was erected in a park closer into town; Queen Victoria sits on top, the plinth supported by two figures representing Industry and Peace; round the foot of this large plinth, supporting the whole, are inscribed the names of the four continents on which the imperial economy rested – India, Africa, Australia and Canada. The 'Arts and Crafts' sculptor was the same George Frampton whose early career had started with the bungalows at Birchington, and whose later work included the statue of Queen Victoria in Calcutta.

In these years then, the bungalow idea was 'in the air', the term itself being much in vogue with a 'Bungalow Dog Kennel' (no doubt for a dachshund) exhibited at the Royal Agricultural Society meeting at Leicester (1895) and a Royal Bungalow Restaurant at the 1901 International Exhibition in Glasgow.

Bungalow prefabs on the beach, 1880-1914

In the late 1880s, the permanent seaside bungalow was still very much a middle- or even upper-class phenomenon, located at the 'better resorts'. When E.C. Brewer compiled the second edition of his *Dictionary of Phrase and Fable* in 1895, he noted the 'English bungalows at Birchington and on the Norfolk coast at Cromer'. Like Westgate, Cromer was much favoured by the wealthy, the literary and the artistic; its visitors included the Empress Elizabeth of Austria, Oscar Wilde, J.M. Barrie, Ellen Terry and Lords Tennyson and Curzon (Girouard, 1971). Personified by the writer Clement Scott (1897) as 'the art-loving, red-haired intense descendant of Pre-Raffaelitism', it hosted 'Girton and Newnham girls' and 'learned gentlemen and professors writing poetry for high class magazines'. Here, two somewhat unorthodox bungalows with a hint of the fashionable Japanese taste had been built in the 1890s. It was thought that Cromer 'would never be vulgarised'; the new houses would grow old and 'the bungalows will be toned down to the landscape'.

Before the early 1880s, the seaside bungalow seemed slow to catch on. From then, however, advances in transport and growing sophistication in the construction of portable buildings were to bring rapid changes. The thirty years before the First World War saw a boom in the major resorts. Places like Southend, close to centres of population, doubled in size.

Between 1901 and the First World War, Blackpool's population grew from 47,000 to 61,000; Bournemouth's, from a similar figure to almost 80,000 (Walvin, 1977:91). The drift to the south-east (including its resorts) had already begun. In the two decades before the war, south-east England registered the highest proportional gain in urbanisation in the whole country (Friedlander, 1966), and much of this gain was in the seaside resorts, like Bournemouth, Brighton and Hove, where permanent residence was becoming increasingly common. And in 1903-4, there was a housing boom, especially at the seaside (Saul, 1962).

Yet in these growing resorts, accommodation for summer holidays was still, with exceptions such as Blackpool, Skegness or Cleethorpes, primarily for a middle class clientele. In the 1850s, people visiting Brighton had usually rented houses or, for the less well off,

---

10   HARRISON SMITH BUILDINGS LIMITED, BIRMINGHAM.

ORNAMENTAL BUNGALOW.

Design No. **29**

A picturesque Bungalow, designed for those who rather favour the half circular bay window or oriel.

A substantial-looking Bungalow, and artistic in every detail. The octagon-shaped roof over oriel and the gables give it a unique appearance, the dark overlays and white background also add to its charm, and it will always prove an attraction to your friends.

GROUND FLOOR PLAN

HARRISON SMITH BUILDINGS LIMITED, BIRMINGHAM.   13

SIX-ROOM BUNGALOW.   Design No. **37**

Plan **A**

Plan **B**

We will survey the site for proposed Residence, and make all the necessary plans, and give you first-class information as to construction, style, and most advantageous position for your future home.

Figure 3.9   Shift to the suburbs: twentieth-century home. About 1905-10.
Described as 'composite buildings' in the catalogue of Harrison Smith Buildings, Birmingham these bungalows made use of prefabricated methods (*Alan Crawford*)

lodgings. 'To live in public in a hotel' was considered 'disgraceful' (*World's Work and Leisure*, 1903:18).

From the 1880s, however, as the resorts attracted increasing capital investment – in housing, municipal works and entertainment facilities – the large holiday hotel was introduced. And though a block of flats had been constructed at Bexhill early in the century, 'flats architect' S. Perks (1905) believed that 'flats at the seaside are not a success [and] are not wanted.'

The opportunity of having one's own bungalow, or at least, renting someone else's, came about from two kinds of change: a minor revolution in the manufacture of portable buildings and subtle changes in recreational behaviour on the beach.

The use of cast iron in building, begun in the 1780s, developed especially in the first half of the nineteenth century. As Gilbert Herbert has shown, these were the pioneering years for prefabrication. With the invention of corrugated iron in the late 1820s, a new material was found which was to revolutionise building techniques. From the 1830s, corrugated iron and timber buildings were being shipped all over the globe, stimulated by emigration and the gold rushes to California and Australia. By the last third of the century, the prefabricated corrugated iron building – for temporary houses, sheds, barns and factories – had become 'commonplace and unspectacular' (1978:65, 115). By then, the industry was producing some 200,000 tons a year, some three-quarters of which were exported. The domestic market, however, was now about to increase, stimulated by export production.

The portable cottages and gamekeepers' lodges manufactured during these years were primarily for the aristocratic estate. From the later 1880s, however, many factors had combined to create a wider demand for leisure buildings (Meller, 1976), and it was to meet this market that firms like Boulton and Paul (Norwich) and Coopers (London) began producing iron buildings for country and seaside use.

The advent of the prefabricated, 'temporary' bungalow from the later 1880s was to bring a major change in the morphology of the seaside, and one associated with changes in public behaviour on the beach. In the space of a hundred years, building was gradually creeping closer to the water's edge, colonising the shore. As we have seen, the earliest seaside visitors had been lodged in existing cottages. The next stage was marked by purpose-built accommodation; typically, this was the substantial terrace, located at a distance from the shore, with an intervening thoroughfare separating buildings from the beach. The 'marine residences' of this time, even the bungalows at Westgate, were similarly on firm ground, with access roads often separating them from the shore.

The small, prefabricated and lightweight bungalow, however, placed as close as possible to the high-water mark on the beach, marked a third stage in the colonisation of the coast. From then on, further advances could only be made by the erection of pile dwellings in the sea or, in the later twentieth century, by the appropriation of shallow waters with flotillas of small boats.

An early, and possibly the first, example of this process was on the Sussex coast, west of Brighton, between the ancient ports of Shoreham and of Lancing, some one and a half hours' train journey from London. The site was a strip of beach sandwiched between the sea and the backwater of the Adur estuary. In the late 1880s, this had been occupied only by a coastguard station, a cholera hospital and recently erected chemical plant. Between 1890 and 1896, however, some dozen bungalows were built. By 1902, there was a continuous line of over two hundred, each occupying adjoining square plots, with 66-foot frontages and all within 20 yards of the high-water mark. Within another ten years, the line extended for a mile and a half

ROSE LANE WORKS, NORWICH. 177

No. 411. Portable Iron Bungalows for Leasehold Property.

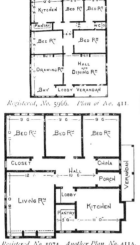

Registered, No. 5966. Plan of No. 411.

REGISTERED DESIGN, No. 5966.

This Bungalow is constructed of strong deal framing, covered on the outside with galvanized corrugated iron, sheet felted between the iron and the wood framing, and is lined inside with matchboarding. Strong floors. Eaves-gutters, down-pipes, locks, and window fasteners included. Erected by our men on purchaser's light brickwork foundation, he providing assistant labour. Outside woodwork painted three coats. Windows glazed with 21-oz. sheet glass.

Cash Price, about £240 0 0

Exclusive of Stoves, Chimneys, and all inside Fittings.

For Stoves, see page 202.

Registered, No. 5974. Another Plan, No. 411A.
Erected by our men on purchaser's brickwork foundation, he providing assistant labour.
Cash Price £220 0 0
Exclusive of Stoves, Chimneys, and all inside Fittings.

No. 310. BUNGALOW, SHOOTING LODGE, &c.

Cool in Summer. Warm in Winter. No possibility of Damp.

Can be inhabited the moment they are finished.

REGISTERED COPYRIGHT.

This Bungalow or Shooting Lodge is constructed of strong deal framing, covered on the outside with galvanized corrugated iron, lined inside with matchboarding, sheet felted between the iron and wood framing. Strong floors. Eaves-gutters, down-pipes, locks, and window fasteners included. Outside woodwork painted three coats. Windows glazed with 21-oz. sheet glass. Erected by our men on purchaser's light brickwork foundation, he providing assistant labour.

Cash Price, about £360 0 0

Exclusive of Stoves, Chimneys, and all inside fittings. For Stoves, see page 202.

From JOSEPH COLLIER, Esq., Queenstown.
We like the Iron Cottage very well, and think it ought to make both a comfortable and durable house.

From Messrs. D. & P. T. MACDONALD, Athole Arms Hotel, N.B.
The Iron Building is now erected, and is much admired by every one, and has turned out perfectly to our wants.

REGISTERED COPYRIGHT.
Plan for another Bungalow. No. 310A.

Figure 3.10 Prefabrication: corrugated iron and timber bungalows, (Boulton and Paul catalogue, 1889).

down the coast. Bungalow Town, with its own railway station marked on cyclists' maps, had been established (O.S. maps; *Building World*, 1902:1).

The settlement had apparently begun when a local resident noticed three or four old railway carriages towed to the beach and used as net stores by local fishermen. From then on, his role had been that of entrepreneur. Plots were marked out and let, the tenant paying a ground rent to the lord of the manor in whose control lay the beach. Rent and taxes for the plots, at 25 shillings per year, were collected by the manager who also arranged the purchase and removal of railway carriages from the Brighton Railway. Costing £10 each without wheels, these were taken on horse-drawn trolleys to the beach for a further £2 or £3 and erected on a foundation of sleepers. The inside was stripped, though the doors and windows remained intact (plates 51 and 52).

Other Shoreham bungalows were more conventional, many designed and built in the first years of the century by Dorchester's Borough Engineer, P.T. Harrison. In 1909 he published *Bungalow Residences*, bringing the bungalow idea to a broader, more popular public than that addressed by Briggs. For Harrison, the word bungalow could refer, on the one hand, 'to a commodious and well-appointed residence in the tropics' or, on the other (no doubt with Shoreham in mind), to 'a superannuated railway carriage adjoining a plot of beach or waste ground'. Though Harrison's designs were small, simple and, at about £300 to build, available to a more modest middle class clientele, the idea was very similar to Briggs's more up-market plans. The bungalows were 'intended for residence in this country either for summer months only or as a permanent residence'. The aim was:

> to convey a sense of unrestraint and easy comfort . . . some bungalow dwellers situate
> their bungalows so as to afford as much change as possible from the conditions of living
> in towns by seeking the simple life . . . situation and environment are, of course,
> instrumental in making bungalow homes so attractive. They usually possess a liberal

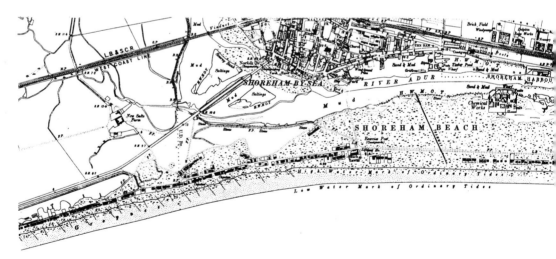

Figure 3.11   The shape of things to come: the colonisation of the shore, c.1900.
Beginning in the early 1890s, by 1902 more than two hundred bungalows had been established on the beach between Lancing and Shoreham, Sussex, within easy reach of London by rail (Ordnance Survey map, Sussex, West, 1912; Survey, 1909)

amount of garden or ground around them, being built in districts where land is comparatively cheap.

The isolation and privacy which Briggs had provided for was equally important to Harrison's less affluent clientele. Turning his back on Shoreham, he now described the idea: 'No one would entertain for a moment the idea of erecting rows or even pairs of bungalows because by so doing their principal charm as well as their distinctive character would be destroyed.' Rather, they were to be erected,

> for the most part at the seaside or in the country in positions chosen for the quality of the air, or for recreative facilities or other attractions . . . (it was) an added pleasure if the site commands views of white cliffs and restless sea, of verdure-clad hills or winding river.

Harrison's bungalows contained a central room, a living room, four small bedrooms (including one for a servant) and, significantly, a bicycle store. Set on sleepers, they, like most of the others by now, were timber-framed, with external weatherboard walls and inside surfaces in matchboard. The roof was of corrugated iron. Painted white, and with details picked out in green, with names like 'The Nugget' or 'Mon Repos', they were bought by local landladies who hired them out at 2 guineas a week.

The explanation of the creation of this and other 'bungalow towns' in the next decades was due not just to prefabrication, developments in transport and a general rise in living standards. There had also been changes in attitudes surrounding the practice of bathing on the beach. In the mid Victorian period, the moral climate of many seaside resorts had become increasingly strict, formalising behaviour and introducing new social codes. Bathing suits, for example, had become compulsory and the segregation of sexes before bathing had been generally enforced. By the turn of the century, however, more liberal views prevailed. Influenced perhaps by French practice, mixed bathing began to be allowed (apparently, first at Bexhill in 1901) (Howell, 1974:121). Men if not yet women, appeared in shorter, more 'rational' swimming garb, including bathing trunks; the old, 150-year-old habit of changing in bathing machines and being hauled, in total privacy, across beach to water, was being abandoned in favour of using static bathing tents providing privacy only when actually undressing. It was now acceptable not only to be seen in bathing dress on the beach but even, among certain classes and in particular resorts, to change there.

Moreover, the emphasis on health at the seaside was already shifting from the quality of the air to the quantity of sun. Where earlier, nut-brown skin or reddened neck were marks of ill-bred country labour, now, the sun-tanned cheek was becoming a sign of health and leisure. These changes, slight and not everywhere applicable, helped to permit the idea of the beach bungalow at the turn of the century. It was part of a growing belief in the merits of the outdoor life – an 'open air craze that had brought outdoor sleeping sheds', camping and the development of the caravan, purpose-built for holiday touring (plates 53-61).

Contemporary postcards of Shoreham suggest that visitors were of relatively modest social origins, coming generally from London and, as many doubtless could not swim, only paddling and relaxing on the sand. It was a later writer who spoke of 'one of the most attractive features of life is the delightful "dip" in the morning. You rise betimes, and walk straight from the bungalow and woo the waters.' Bathing was a pastime which could be indulged in 'virtually free of the tiresome restrictions prevailing in the orthodox seaside resorts'.

It was obviously the more liberated, then, or those with no social reputation to lose, who patronised these early bungalows at Shoreham, Herne Bay or Clacton-on-Sea where, in the first years of the century, a manufacturer of portable buildings had set up some of his own. Here, 'every convenience' was provided in furnished and unfurnished bungalows, containing from two to ten bedrooms, and reception rooms, for between 1 and 10 guineas a week. They were also available for sale (Cooper, c. 1900). Other bungalow settlements were established at Heacham (Norfolk), Selsea (Sussex), at Moretown in the Wirral (Cheshire) where simple bungalows could be bought for as little as £20. Even before the First World War, both these places were to run into trouble for allegedly contravening public health bye-laws, passed under the Public Health Act of 1907. Some places, like the Hightown Bungalows on the dunes north of Liverpool, were little more than modest outdoor sleeping huts: the important fact was that the land was more or less free (plate 67).

What the invention of the prefabricated bungalow had done was to bring a type of land into use which had not been used for building before. Before planning laws brought controls, the beach below high-water mark, and even sand dunes above, were often treated as common land or were available for temporary use (personal communication, John Walton, 1982) with only a token rent to the lord of the manor. At Shoreham, trouble occurred when he sold the beach (by then full of bungalows) for £30,000 and the new owner demanded £250 from each of the owners to stay there. By the end of the nineteenth century the 'local bourgeoisie' were steadily to gain the upper hand in the control of beaches (*Westminster Gazette*, 8 April, 1903).

Despite these problems, the bungalow habit had obviously caught on. With the erection of the Royal Bungalow on Snettisham Shore, near Sandringham in 1908, it received a seal of approval. Built in a self-conscious 'hand-crafted' style of yellow stone, with white woodwork and a green slate roof, the inside walls were decorated with shells and varied-hued pebbles from the beach. Inside, the queen had a small room for herself (with a low hearth fire of rough bricks surmounted by a beam of rough oak) and another for the servants. Across the ridge a carved board proclaimed 'NISI DOMINUS – MCMVIII' (*Building News*, 1908:485) (plate 46).

The seaside towns had always offered the occasion for abandoning social constraints; they were 'peculiar cities where tens of thousands rushed into a social vacuum'. The bungalow town was an extension of the development. It contained the socially adventurous, the avant-garde, the more liberated members of the community. And as Bellagio was immortalised in fiction, so also was Bungalow Town.

H.G. Wells's *In the Days of the Comet*, a fascinating blend of socialism, science fiction and romance, was published in 1906. The hero, a young clerk of modest background, is in love with Nettie, the daughter of the head gardener on a large Midlands estate. Having walked all one hot afternoon to see his beloved, he is dismayed to discover that she has been taken out (and off) by the university-educated son of a wealthy industrialist. Taking his revolver, the hero follows the couple to 'Shaphambury' on 'the coast of Essex' where he asks an old inhabitant about the Bungalow Village. 'Ah, Artists and such. Nice goings on! Mixed Bathing. Something scandalous'; the village was situated 'six lonely miles from the town'.

> Two people were bathing in the sea. . . . They waded breast-deep in the water . . . a woman, with her hair coiled about her head, and in pursuit of her, a man, graceful figures of black and silver. . . . Each wore a tightly fitting bathing dress that hid nothing of the shining, dripping beauty of their youthful forms.
>
>   I came over the little ridge and discovered the bungalow village . . . nestling in a crescent lap of dunes. . . .

This place . . . was a fruit of the reaction of artistic-minded and carelessly living people against the costly and uncomfortable social stiffness of the more formal seaside resorts of that time. It was . . . the custom of the steam-railway companies to sell their carriages after they had become obsolete . . . and some genius had hit upon the feasibility of turning these into habitable little cabins for the summer holiday. The thing had become a fashion with a certain Bohemian-spirited class; they added cabin to cabin, and these little improvised homes, gaily painted and with broad verandahs and supplementary lean-to's added to their accommodation, made the brightest contrast conceivable to the dull ridigities of the decorous resorts. Of course, there were many such discomforts in such camping that had to be faced cheerfully and so this broad sandy beach was sacred to high spirits and the young. Art muslin and banjos, Chinese lanterns and frying, are leading 'notes'. . . . But . . . to the poor man, to the grimy workers, beauty and cleanliness were absolutely denied; out of a life of greasy dirt, of muddied desires, they watched their happier fellows with a bitter envy and foul, tormenting suspicions.

The bungalow as symbol for the simplification of life

This image of the bungalow town as, in Wells's phrase, 'a queer village of careless sensuality' and of the bungalow as a symbol of the artistic, Bohemian and, in other contexts, with vaguely political overtones, was at its height at the turn of the century. For two brief years between 1899 and 1901 a slim magazine made a fleeting appearance on the fringes of the London scene. Edited by Max Judge, *The Bungalow* was devoted neither to building nor architecture but to things 'artistic, literary, topographical and Bohemian' (1899:1).

Bohemianism was a constant theme. Many people, it seemed, were true Bohemians at heart, having 'a sneaking fondness for an easy, natural mode of living'. Driving was a pastime 'always associated with Gay Bohemianism' as railway travelling was not only commonplace but there 'one has to become a passenger in such or such a class, to be a Smoker or non-Smoker, ticketed and numbered in good English fashion'. How glorious it was 'to drive away from the haunts of Industrialism into the sweet fresh air of the country where nature reigns supreme'. The essence of Bohemianism was 'the spirit which prompts one to throw overboard all the formalities of the world and to shock Mrs Grundy'. On holiday, the true Bohemian would not pack half a dozen shirts, two or three suits and shaving paraphernalia but would dress in his oldest clothes, take no luggage and rest in a barn or shed rather than a hotel. His greatest delight was 'to get away from the city to some distant place, there to live a more natural life, to mix with country folk and do as they do; or by the sea, to become a temporary fisherman.' In short, a Bohemian was 'one who lives a simple life, where he can be in close communion with Nature'; one 'bent on living his own life, unfettered by the tyranny of convention . . . the true Individualist.' (plates 59, 60, 61).

The rejection of the city was central to this philosophy. The 'simple life' was essentially life in 'the country'.

When you have lived in London for many years and have become hardened by the daily crush and turmoil of the city; when you have grown weary of the ceaseless new attractions week by week and when you feel that you are gradually being developed into a machine, you begin to long for 'long calm days and long calm evenings' . . . at your desk in the office it is always the same, week after week, the days to be got through as soon as possible . . . think for a minute of the delight of rising in the country, think of the charms of the meadow in the early hours and then betake yourself with your work, from London, and settle down seriously to country life.

However, as another contributor pointed out, 'living in the country on the whole is not productive of idealism unless you can afford it.'

These ideas, about art, the pressure of social conventions, anti-industrialism, were all symbolised in the magazine's title. In 'A Word about Bungalows', the symbolism was made explicit. It had been said that 'building vertically or horizontally is influenced by social questions'. In the skyscraper, one saw the vertical idea; in the bungalow, the horizontal. There were, however, social factors which influenced these two broadest divisions of building. Nobody, according to the editor, has his liberty, but perhaps

> the man in the bungalow has most. There is no limit to his building. Room after room can be added, as he wants and according to the position of the sun, so he can select *his* position in the shade of the never-ending verandah. . . . In the cities of Northern Europe, where men from all parts find themselves thrown together, a limit is at once placed on everything. The houses have to arrange themselves in order and instead of spreading themselves out they must mount higher up, and then comes the fight for the best position! The wealthy first, then the poor – nearer heaven! Everyone is on a level in the Bungalow – you are either *above or below* in the towering city dwelling.

Yet Judge was also prepared to recognise the 'realities of life', the industrial base on which modern civilisation was built. The bungalow, after all, had originally been erected in India 'as a help to work rather than an encouragement to idleness'.

> We cannot all live in Bungalows and it is as well. If we had done so, the European race would not have developed itself as it has developed, neither would the arts and crafts have flourished if it had not been for that struggle for existence in a thickly populated city. Get away from India and you get away from Bungalows, but we can use the word as typical of a comfortable existence and a free unrestrained life.

These sentiments, if not yet explicit Socialism, had drawn heavily on the teachings of Morris and Ruskin whose names figure frequently in *The Bungalow*'s pages. When Ruskin died, a long editorial praised the changes that his writings had brought in questioning established conventions that 'everything is to be sacrificed to "respectability" and worldly success'. The race for wealth had too often meant the crushing of the nobler instincts. Ruskin had taught the artist to despise convention and to follow nature; he had proclaimed to rich and poor their common brotherhood and the social responsibility of all members of the community (1900:1).

Some years earlier, in *The Simplification of Life* (1884), Morris's friend, Edward Carpenter, had expressed similar misgivings about the complexity of modern life, its materialism and overbearing social conventions. The tendency in the past had been to accumulate. Yet 'every additional object in the house requires dusting, cleaning, repairing, storing – anti macassars require wool, wool requires knitting needles, needles require a box, the box requires a side table, etc. etc.,'. It was obvious that 'immense simplifications of our life are possible.' The fact that there were so many religious enthusiasts in Arabia was due to the great simplicity of their life and landscape (1905:34-5). 'Simplicity of life, even the barest, is not misery but the very foundation of refinement,' Morris had written three years before (Davey, 1980:23).

The same ideas had been behind the foundation of 'alternative' communities. In an age of religious doubt, the void was filled by utopian socialism, devotion to good works, vegetarianism, the reverence for manual labour and, as a substitute for formal faiths, nature mysticism and the implicit religion of 'country life'. Whatever their other beliefs, the devotees of these ideas were firmly convinced that 'the city must go'. Richard Jefferies' own brand of nature mysticism was centred around contact with the earth and solitary communion with nature, to be away from 'the pettiness of house-life – chairs and tables'. A new interest in 'primitive peoples' led to the foundations of anthropology and in the world of letters, R.L Stevenson went off to seek solitude in a bungalow in the Pacific (Marsh, 1978:30-5).

As Sheila Rowbotham has shown, such ideas were characteristic of a time when the division between ideas on art, politics, religion, nature, cosmic consciousness and living was far less clear than it became in the 1920s (1977). Just what the readers and contributors of *The Bungalow* were looking for was not immediately apparent; it was a new kind of life which they were not quite able to express: 'an indefinable, inscrutable, perplexing something which many of us are groping after in a misty haze' (1899:11).

Yet apart from the discussions on Bohemianism, there were also essays on travel, on 'ocean solitude', picnicking, art exhibitions, poetry, architecture and book reviews. In 1900, a Bungalow Club was proposed for 'individuals who are inclined to a literary or artistic life'. It was to be 'a Bohemian institution where the objects are carried out with as little formality and stereotyped method of procedure as possible'. There were to be meetings in London where papers were read, visits to museums and art galleries, exhibitions by members in their own rooms, summer meetings in districts of historic and architectural interest and excursions into Kent, Surrey and Berkshire. During the year, the club members gathered in West Hampstead to hear Mr H.O. Newland speak (once again) on 'Bohemianism'; a paper was read on 'Architecture and History' in St John's Wood and at the studio of one of the members there was an exhibition of Japanese prints, posters and enamels, some drawings of D.G. Rossetti, lent by his brother William and watercolours by Ruskin. Those present included leading figures in London's literary and art world – Christine and W.M. Rossetti, J.L. Paton and others. 'With tea, art and agreeable company, the atmosphere was passed in true Bohemian fashion'. As it was intended that 'formal and official documents of proceedings should be a negative feature of the Club', little more is known of the club's activities. Like the fugitive journal itself, it disappeared into the past.

The bungalow re-exported

In the later nineteenth century, as industrial production grew, the empire – both formal and informal – expanded. Larger markets were necessary and raw materials required for the increasingly sophisticated industries which developed from the 1880s.

Yet to expand overseas markets a basic infrastructure of railways and public utilities were needed. In the later decades of the century, vast amounts of capital were exported to set up this infrastructure, particularly railways, much of it transferred from the depressed market in agricultural land (Cottrell, 1975; Roberts, 1978). And with the capital to build railways, in South America and the Far East, or open mines, went British engineers to supervise and maintain them.

Here, and elsewhere, plantations were being set up, in Assam, Ceylon or Brazil, to develop specialised crops for production and export, again to be managed by British staff. The raw materials of the second, electrical phase of industrialisation – rubber, copper, zinc or asbestos – were needed from Malaya, South Africa and Latin America. With other factors, these developments led to imperial expansion, not least on the African continent.

The managers of these tasks, however, and the officials who, in many cases, were to transform self-sufficient peasants into wage-earning labour, had to be housed. By the later 1880s, the exportable bungalow, specially designed for conditions in the tropics, had been developed. As discussed in Chapter 6, although prefabricated iron and timber houses had been exported for almost a century, only in the later nineteenth century did an appropriate, mass-produced, tropical design emerge. By the turn of the century, firms in London, Glasgow, Liverpool and Norwich were sending bungalows abroad.

Typical of these were Boulton and Paul of Norwich, previously involved with the manufacture of conservatories and horticultural equipment. In the overseas investment boom of the early years of this century, they supplied bungalows to the managers of rubber plantations in Malaya, to the resident railway engineer in Lobito, West Africa, and to others in East and South Africa, Chile, Argentina, Egypt, the Sudan, as well as despatching bungalows to Messina, South Italy, following the disastrous earthquake in 1906.

By the First World War, the export of capital had reached enormous proportions, with some £4,500 million invested overseas; people too had emigrated in large numbers, some

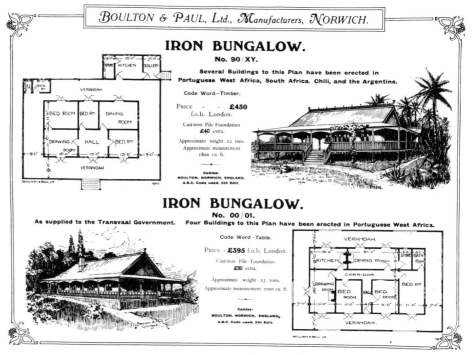

Figure 3.12   The bungalow in the international division of labour.
Exported from industrial Britain, the machine-made, prefabricated bungalows were for the use of planters, engineers and other colonial officials exploiting agricultural products and raw materials from what later became known as the 'third World' (Boulton and Paul Catalogue, 1907) (Drawings, 1903) (*J.D. Paul*)

three million leaving Britain in the first decade of the century (Barratt Brown, 1978:137). Many of them took their particular views of privacy and housing with them. It was for these that G.S. Samson produced two editions (1910, 1920) of his *Houses, Villas, Cottages and Bungalows for Britishers and Americans abroad*, coming out strongly in favour of traditional British ideas in contrast to those of other Europeans also living in the colonies:

> The Continental, and especially French system, that obtains in even quite small towns abroad, of living in large, barrack-like buildings, divided into little *appartements* or flats, the lower floors occupied by the rich and the upper ones by those of lighter purses (with) . . . the garrets . . . (for) the poor, – this system does not recommend itself to the British mind. There is little privacy, there are no gardens, and there is a mixture of classes and people which does not appeal to our tastes.

Included were plans for a specifically 'colonial bungalow' and, as 'each year more foreigners take to our plan of living in villas – even be they quite small – in the suburbs rather than living in the towns themselves in these barrack-like flats' (1910:18-19), he no doubt hoped that the practice would spread.

Just how far the early-twentieth-century growth of bungalow settlements in England was stimulated by their production for export to the colonies is an open question.

Figure 3.13 Back to the land: the effects of a global economy.
Competition from world markets was to lead to agricultural depression in Britain. The small holding movement in the early years of the twentieth century was one attempt to counter the trend (Boulton and Paul catalogue, 1907)

Back to the land

From the early 1870s, overseas competition was to bring about a collapse in the agricultural land market, and the migration of workers from the land. Concern at these developments was to result, in 1906, in a *Parliamentary Report on the Decline in the Agricultural Population of Great Britain, 1881-1906*, where housing for agricultural labour was seen as a central problem. After the 1880s, few houses had been built for farm labourers, either speculatively or by landlords and many cottages were falling into decay (Burnett, 1978:132).

In middle class circles, concern for agriculture and the condition of its workers was frequently linked with overcrowding in the cities. It gave rise to books such as Ebenezer Howard's *Garden Cities of Tomorrow* (1903), where each cottage was to have its own cultivable plot. The promotion of urban allotments and smallholdings was seen as a possible solution both to reduce urban overcrowding as well as regenerate agricultural land. The pressures of the international market economy were steadily making themselves felt, with 150,000 people leaving rural areas every year as dairy produce came increasingly from abroad. The Small Holdings and Allotments Act of 1907 was offered as an answer, encouraging the establishment of smallholdings up to 50 acres and smaller allotments of less than 5. For these, Boulton and Paul produced a series of functional, and hence 'modern'

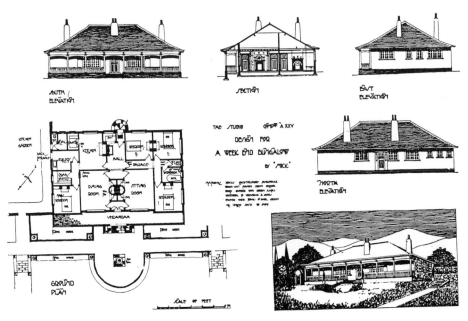

FIG. 3. DESIGN FOR A WEEK-END BUNGALOW. BY "MICK"

Figure 3.14 Changes in the social organisation of time: the 'week-end bungalow', 1906.
Over the space of a century, industrial capitalism was to restructure both time and space. As a unit of non-working free time, the middle-class 'week-end' emerged between 1880 and 1900, helped by having specialised buildings and places in which to spend it (*The Studio*, 1906)

Figure 3.15 Second home: design for a week-end bungalow near Glos'ter for a London bachelor, £350, 1909
The deck chair and sun-dial symbolise some of the supporting motives behind the bungalow ideology (*Building News*, 21 May 1909)

bungalow designs in timber, at prices from £83 for a bunglow (22' by 12') with living room, bedroom, food store and verandah to £216 for a larger (50' by 15') three-bedroom version.

Yet combined with this concern for the agricultural worker was a parallel interest in getting 'back to the land'. It was all part of the move towards 'the simplification of life', manifesting itself in the establishment of agrarian communities, garden cities, the New School movement stressing the value of life in the country, light and air, manual work and, like the hero in Virginia Woolf's first novel, *Night and Day* (1911), 'the idea of a cottage where one grew one's own vegetables and lived on fifteen shillings a week'. Needless to say, the simple life, back-to-the-landers were a small, middle class minority in a society marked by vast conspicuous consumption of the upper class on one hand and immense poverty on the other (Marsh, 1978:35-6; 'Home Counties', 1905). For some, it was a desire for a small-scale farm; for others, simply to live in the country. The motives were similar to those of Briggs's clients, though without the sexual overtones. In the country 'for a time at least, the rattle of the motorbus may be forgotten with the many other obtrusive indications of the triumph of machinery, indispensible as such may be in these days of rush and luxury.' (Harrison, 1909)

The idea of the bungalow as a 'small country house' which Briggs's patrons had adopted from the aristocracy in the 1880s had now, twenty years later, filtered to a lesser bourgeoisie. It resulted from depressed land prices, rising living standards, transport innovations, further developments in prefabrication and, with reduced working hours, changes in the social organisation of time with – in the decades spanning the turn of the century – the emergence of the 'weekend' (King, 1980b).

Figure 3.16   Country bungalow: builder's version, 1902.
'This type of house is prevalent in India and in most of our colonies, and is being increasingly adopted in the United Kingdom as a convenient and comfortable form of summer residence' (*Building World*, January 25, 1902:319)

Combined with an extensive railway network, the bicycle, or after 1900, the motor bike, car and bus, released thousands of people from the city at the weekends. The logic of these developments was to have not only a particular place to go to (the seaside or the country) but a particular dwelling there when one arrived. For the wealthy middle or upper class who could afford an architect-designed bungalow at £500 or more, or increasingly, a renovated labourer's cottage, this was the 'weekend cottage', the earliest reference to which seems to be in 1904. Yet a cheaper market was now developing.

There had, according to the author of a sixpenny handbook on *The Home Beautiful* (1908), 'during the past few years, been a very large increase in the number of small cottages intended principally for occupation at week-ends, when the tired business man can get away for a few hours to recuperate in the pure air of the country after the toil and worries of city life.' Formerly, 'expense had stood in the way of those of comparatively little income from indulging in such luxuries, but modern ingenuity had shown that the outlay need not be large.' For example, Oetzmann, Hampstead Road, London had produced a bungalow cottage, with three bedrooms, hall, kitchen and living room, which could be built for between £200 and £230. For another £45, it could be furnished complete. The brick-built bungalow, roughcast in white with red-tile roof, the latticed porch fashionably decorated with the Arts and Crafts heart motif, was exhibited at the Anglo-French and Coronation Exhibitions of 1907 and 1910. Reproduced in books and on hundreds of postcards it was to make a large impression.

For others, however, there was the prefabricated wood or wood and corrugated iron bungalow.

Thus, Cooper's of the Old Kent Road, employing over 300 men on their 6-acre premises and selling almost 10,000 greenhouses a year, were making and selling small bungalows at £140 each. In Birmingham, Harrison Smith (telegraphic address in 1904, 'Bungalows, Birmingham') had a three-bedroom 'week-end holiday bungalow', 22 by 17, in deal at £103, carriage paid. For £30, one could buy three railway carriages, plus £10 each for delivery and, including modifications, construct a bungalow for £100.

Bungalow · Hawkchurch · Devon
Arthur W. Yeomans f.r.i.b.a. Architect Chard

Ground Plan

Figure 3.17 Country bungalow: architect's version, 1904.
Both this and Figures 2.2 and 8.1 indicate some of the underlying forces behind the
development of 'modern' architecture (*Building News*, 22 April, 1904) (See also plates 21,
88)

By this time, many new materials were being introduced. In the two decades before the First
World War, cast iron and steel were to be supplemented, if not displaced, by a variety of new
materials which, combined with timber, were to revolutionise building methods. Though their
widespread adoption was not to be felt till after 1918, they were already making an impact.
And as the bungalow had come from and then gone out again to the empire, so some of its
raw materials were also derived from there: rubber for 'ruberoid' roofs, asbestos, zinc for
corrugated iron, tropical hardwoods as well as the sisal carpets, rattan stools, bamboo screens
and furniture and Indian mats, which furnished the 'simple life' inside.

Asbestos cement, invented in 1889 and used for making sheets and tiles, was introduced
into Britain from Austria from about 1904. In 1910, Turner Brothers, the British Uralite
Company and Bell's United Asbestos Company started production in Britain (Bowley,
1960:118-20). A year or two later, Bell's were advertising an all-asbestos bungalow. Pre-cast
reinforced concrete blocks had been invented in 1875 (Morris, 1978; Shaw, 1878).

Concrete tiles were introduced from 1893 and the Belgian firm of S.A. Eternit was also to
sell large quantities of his patent tiles in Britain from about the same time. In 1898, the Patent
Millboard Company, founded at Sunbury on Thames, began making a material ideally
suitable for lining bungalow walls. Plasterboard, a North American invention of 1904, was
introduced into Britain but made little impact before the First World War (Bowley, 1960). The
Ruberoid Roof Company, with their patented rubberised finish, had been founded in 1891.
About the same time, the Wire-Wove Company of London developed panels of expanded
steel lathing, covered with plaster, to replace wooden lathes. In 1906, they offered a one-

Bungalow : Sea side · Cottage · Residence · ✱ view of Sea front ·

Concern for the problems of damp and 'rising emanations from the ground' were behind Dr W.H. Brock's patent for 'improvements in the construction of sanitary houses and bungalows', 1884 (*Patent Office Library*).

Figure 3.18   *Inventions: the bungalow as agent of change, 1878-1884*
Prefabrication was gradually to revolutionise construction, making a big impact on housing and leading to a de-skilling of building labour. Before its suppression from the later 1930s, the self-built bungalow was to embody many of the new developments.
   An early exponent, W.H. Lascelles, inventor of a patent cement slab system, **commissioned designs from architect R. Norman Shaw to help sell his idea** (*Designs for Cottages*, 1878). The term was probably picked up from contemporary developments on the north Kent coast.

bedroom, weekend bungalow for £100. Compared to £200 for a conventional brick bungalow at Herne Bay, Boulton and Paul, using ferro-concrete panels and brick, were offering weekend cottages, at between £134 and £345 ('Home Counties', 1905; Country Gentleman, 1905).

As many of these materials presupposed a frame construction rather than load-bearing walls, a single-storey design was inherent in their use. This was seen at the Cheap Cottages Exhibition at Letchworth in 1905, held to encourage the design of £150 cottages for rural labourers and the use of prefabrication. Bungalows were built using 'Uralite Kent Board' panels and tiles, 'Mack' partition slabs, machine-made roof tiles and internal walls of expanded metal covered with plaster (*Architectural Review*, 18, 1905:155-7).

These, and similar opportunities had been aired by 'Home Counties' in *Country Cottages. How to Build Them and Fit Them Up* published (and reprinted three times) in 1905. The book had come out of a series of articles in *The World's Work and Leisure* between 1903 and 1904, and had been addressed to a range of weekenders including 'a London clerk, with bicycle, on thirty shillings a week' as well as retired service officers, returned colonial civil servants, 'professional men and merchants', journalists and barristers.

Sites were within 30 miles of London. Essex and Suffolk provided the cheapest; Hertfordshire, Buckinghamshire and Berkshire were more expensive. Sussex, Kent and Surrey, for long the favoured areas for the wealthiest class from the metropolis, were dear. Here, the motor-owning class reigned supreme.

The main obstacle to such back-to-the-landers came from district councils. Here, local bye-laws were used by some to prevent the building 'of any dwelling the external walls of which were not constructed of good bricks, stone or other hard and incombustible materials properly bonded and solidly put together'. The origin of the controversy lay initially in the Public Health Act of 1875 which had introduced regulations governing building structure and materials and was aimed at preventing unstable, insanitary and inflammable buildings. This had been followed by a set of model bye-laws issued by the Local Government Board in 1877 and available for adoption by local authorities (Harper, 1977).

In 1890, however, rural authorities were granted legislative powers previously only available to urban councils. Thus, bye-laws originally designed to govern building methods and materials in towns could, if the district council so chose, be adopted in the very different circumstances of rural areas. The effect was to prevent the use of many of the new materials and construction methods developed during the course of the century.

The attack on the outmoded bye-laws came from a combination of interests: people campaigning for cheaper housing for rural labourers; architects objecting to restrictions on innovation in design for middle class clients, middle class 'back-to-the-landers' anxious to build a bungalow in the bush. In many areas, the regulations were apparently used to preserve vested interests. According to 'Home Counties', builders saw prefabricated dwellings as a threat to their livelihood; for tradesmen, the settlers' search for 'the simple life' was bad for trade (as also was their practice of having groceries delivered from London stores); parsons were shocked by their views and 'irregular church attendance'; landowners' aesthetic sensibilities were offended by 'rambling huts sprawled all over the district'. All interests might therefore combine against these 'wild folk from the towns with no visible means of support' ('Home Counties', 1905:4).

How such bye-laws were adopted and enforced, however, clearly depended on the social composition of councils. In large parts of Essex, Cambridge and Hampshire there were few bye-laws restricting bungalow development; yet Surrey, Sussex, Kent and Berkshire, the preferred areas of the metropolitan elite, were 'comparatively bye-law ridden'.

The anti-bungalow lobby, however, was already on the alert, especially among architects, whose professional role as arbiters of taste was threatened. Reviewing engineer Harrison's book on *Bungalow Residences*, the *Architectural Review* thought it 'a doubtful policy to issue books of this kind . . . they give to the layman that amount of knowledge which is a dangerous thing. The thoughtless individual is likely to go to the builder, book in hand, and say "Build me one like that" ' (1909, 26:310).

The controversy over the bye-laws eventually resulted in their revision. And in the event, they not only permitted the bungalow to flourish but, in a strange legislative irony, confirmed its distinctive size, location and form. Where wooden houses were built, for reasons of stability, they were only to be of one storey and to ensure stability, they were not to exceed 600 square feet in area nor 6,000 cubic feet in volume. To eliminate risk of fire, each had to be at least 200 feet distant from any other building not in the same curtilage. These were regulations which had clear implications for the future form and pattern of bungalow settlements (*Building News*, 1899:250).

Conclusion

When viewed in a long-term perspective, the introduction of the country and suburban bungalow in this period could be seen as part – indeed, a symbol – of the beginning of a process of 'counter-urbanisation' (Berry, 1976b), though itself part of an emergent structure of world urbanisation in which economies were inextricably linked. Though introduced as a 'country' house, the bungalow was essentially an urban dwelling. It was *in* the country but not *of* it. It was a product of the despoliation of the city which industrial capitalism had brought about – environmental pollution, overcrowding and the 'stresses and strains' of urban life.

Though relatively few were built in suburbs and country before the First World War, the idea of the bungalow and the philosophy from which it sprang were firmly established. After 1918, the idea gained immensely in popularity.

Over this period, from about 1880 to the 1930s, the perception of rural land, of agriculture and of something which became known as the 'countryside', underwent a change. With almost 80 per cent of the English population urban in 1911, the countryside began to be invested with an aesthetic and ideological identity of its own. For the largely middle class population who assumed this view, it was a perception which was far more widespread, and also different, from the earlier view of the Romantic poets. The journal *Country Life* had been established for an urban bourgeoisie in 1896. In 1903, *The Country-side*, 'a journal of the country, garden, nature and wildlife', was begun and later, *The Countryman* established, each devoted to a townsman's concept of country-lore. Like the term 'week-end', 'country-side' in the early twentieth century was hyphenated. The hyphen gradually disappeared as both institutions became rooted into social and cultural life. With the growth of the media and car ownership, the idea of the countryside as a recreational resource, as assumed by the *Countryside Commission* or discussed in Marion Shoard's *Theft of the Countryside* (1980), became accepted. In the last thirty years, to spend 'a weekend in a country cottage', even if not one's own, has become, for many of the middle class population, a form of leisure which rests on the institutions of 'weekend' and 'countryside' established half a century before.

Already in 1902, in a perceptive article on 'The Coming of the Motor', Henry Norman, MP, had foreseen the impact of the car. Arguing that everyone who kept a horse could keep a car for less money, he demonstrated how its vastly increased travelling radius would lead to 'a revival of country districts'. 'Thousands of the town-dwellers of today will be the country-

No. 662.

BUNGALOW   Maison Coloniale   Casa de Campo

As supplied to the Transvaal Government.

Constructed to Specification "A, " D," and " E." See opening pages of catalogue.

Specification " A."
Code—TABLE.

Specification " D."
Code—TABLEZICIB.

Specification " E."
Code—TABLEZICOC.

Modèle livré au Gouvernement du Transvaal.

Construite selon spécification "A," " D," et " E." Voir les pages au commencement du catalogue.

Mot du Code—TABLE.

Mot du Code—TABLEZICIB.

Mot du Code—TABLEZICOC.

Como la suminstrada al Gobierno del Transvaal.

Edificada según especificación "A," " D," y " E." Véanse las páginas al principio del catálogo.

Clave—TABLE.

Clave—TABLEZICIB.

Clave—TABLEZICOC.

Figure 3.19   *A bungalow, by any other name . . . 1903*
The Hindi/English/French/Spanish terminology here is not only evidence of the bungalow's ubiquitous function; it also represents (where bungalow = colonial house = country house) the projection of a basic division of labour between town and country, through colonialism, onto a world-wide scale (see Williams, 1973).

dwellers of tomorrow . . . to the car-owner, it is virtually the same thing whether his home is one or a dozen miles from the railway station.' The car would 'bring into the market at good prices a great number of country places unlettable and unsaleable today.' In ten years, horses would not be seen on the streets of London. (*World's Work and Leisure*, 1902-3:362)

In these ten years, many country areas were to be turned into commuter suburbs. Hindhead, in Surrey, was typical. A valley close by was 'discovered' as a residential centre and a building boom followed, speculative architects and builders buying up plots of land so that, between 1890 and about 1910, the population of 500 increased to 2,000. A once-quiet high road was 'noisy with the motor cars of the richer residents', the country 'invaded by the leisured class'. Where donkeys had grazed in 1900, ten years later, 'the well-to-do have their tennis or afternoon tea' (Bourne, 1912:6, 16, 129).

On the nearer suburban areas where the smaller bungalows were coming up, Masterman was equally perceptive. 'The Suburbans' were the creation not of industrial, but of commercial and business activities of London. The middle classes had reconciled the pressure between the standard of comfort and limitation of income by reducing family size. This had led to a 'headlong collapse of the birthrate' in the last twenty years (c. 1890-1910) in all save the poorest class (1918:59, 69, 161). These were to be the new patrons of the spreading suburban bungalow, both then and in the years to come.

The beginnings of the mass market, purpose-built second home (both in North America and Britain) which the turn-of-the-century bungalow and country cottage represent, is also of major importance. It gives a longer history to an institution previously only located in the 1960s. The ideology behind it is not dissimilar to that of the 'Bohemian' and simple life of the turn of the century. It was the product of a bourgeois society, an urban equivalent, as Hobsbawm points out (1975:297), of the eighteenth-century *fête champêtre*: playing at not belonging to it. The 'simple life' has meaning only for those with surplus wealth to attain it.

The period which witnessed the introduction of the bungalow also saw the beginnings of attempts to control the development of cities and towns. The Town Planning legislation of 1909 and the creation of the Institute of Town Planners four years later was the formal and public response by the state and professional groups to the problems of urbanism in Britain. Yet no attempt was made to change the basis of the market economy or to bring land, urban or rural, into national ownership. Instead, for those who could afford it, the real response to urbanism was both informal and private, and used the institutions of the market to escape to far-flung suburbs, country bungalows and second homes (King, 1980d). In the decades to come, the urbanisation of the countryside was to lead to constant conflict and reinforce social divisions between country and the town.

Chapter 4

North America 1880-1980

Bungalow of Dreams

Our little love nest
Beside a stream
Where red, red roses grow
Our bungalow
Of dreams

Far from the city
Somehow it seems
We're sitting pretty in
Our bungalow
Of dreams

Just like two love birds
We'll bill and coo
I'll whisper love words
For only you

A bit of heaven
Beside a stream
I know you'll love it so
Our bungalow
Of dreams

Bix Beiderbecke, RKO Recording, c. 1928

Introduction

If the development of the modern bungalow had taken place in Britain, then it certainly matured in the USA. Here, in a way that is only now being realised, its significance was immense. As in England, it was not only a precursor of the contemporary purpose-built vacation home; of more economic and social importance, it was instrumental in the development of the modern mass suburb. The prototype for this, the 'fragmented metropolis' with its tens of thousands of low-density, single-family dwellings, was Los Angeles: it is therefore no coincidence that something called the 'California Bungalow' developed in the early years of this century as a new and distinctively modern form of home. In this guise, it was – in the words of a recent authority – 'to exert the greatest influence upon the domestic architecture of the country' (Current, 1974:10), to be a harbinger of modern house design. The bungalow's later popularity in Britain was not unconnected with these developments.

In recent years, considerable interest has been shown in the three main topics with which this chapter is concerned. In architecture, the American bungalow has become the subject of increasing attention; in geography and leisure studies, vacation homes are an important field of research, and thirdly, in the political economy of urbanisation, a renewed interest has arisen in understanding the relation of suburbanisation to the functioning of the market economy (Walker, 1978, 1981:Gottdiener, 1977).

This chapter aims to throw light on all these themes and, if only in an implicit and indirect way, to show the inter-relations between them. Previously, architectural studies have, with some exceptions, primarily considered the bungalow from a somewhat narrow viewpoint of 'style'; its economic and social importance have been largely overlooked. Where earlier writers have classified the phenomenon according to region, designer or style, this chapter suggests that its significance can be more clearly understood by using the simple functional distinction suggested above, namely, the bungalow as summer residence and its use as permanent suburban home – even though the distinction was not always so clear-cut. It was, for example, the image of the bungalow as a 'simple yet artistic' summer dwelling that was at least partly responsible for its adoption as a suburban home.

A study of this second role provides some interesting insights into the large-scale suburbanisation which took place in North America in the early years of this century. What recent studies have brought out is the function of suburban development in attracting investment capital and generating market demand. Yet whilst capital is obviously essential for their development, the actual shape which suburbs take depends on many influences, social, cultural, technological, political and, not least, ideological. It is this last factor, ideology, understood simply as the prevailing ideas and beliefs of dominant interests in society, with which much of this chapter is concerned. Other research will be needed on the economic basis of suburban expansion and the development of the mass vacation house in the early years of the twentieth century. What this chapter explores is the role of the 'bungalow ideology' in promoting both and, in the process, bringing about architectural change.

The first theme of this chapter then, is the relation of ideology to architecture: how do social and intellectual beliefs mould the dwellings and landscapes in which people live? The second theme concerns the relationship of a dwelling to its setting: in the massive growth of early-twentieth-century suburbs which technology, cheap energy and the free play of market forces brought about, the bungalow was developed as an ideal suburban home. Finally, the chapter considers the role of the American bungalow in the emergence of modern architectural design.

Summer cottage

The bungalow as summer cottage
In the opinion of Glaab and Brown (1976:99), the modern American city emerged between 1860-1910. In these years, the percentage of city-dwellers increased from less than 20 to over 45 per cent, the rapid growth of the 1880s partly resulting from the building up of a national system of transport. In the same decade, as the forces of capitalist industrialisation increasingly concentrated production in cities, railroad mileage doubled and the migration of rural people moved citywards rather than to the West. Not only were Americans increasingly urban, but the size of the largest cities grew. In the second half of the century, the number of

100,000 plus cities rose from two to seventeen (Walker, 1978:185). This was especially so in the north-east where America's oldest, largest and wealthiest metropolises – New York, Boston, Baltimore and Philadelphia – were located.

It was near these cities – and Chicago – that the summer resorts of America had developed, mainly since the Civil War. The expression of conspicuous consumption and surplus capital, they lay along the north-east seaboard, or, for Chicago, on the larger lakes. Of them all, Newport, Rhode Island, was probably the most well known and here, from the 1840s, visitors began building their villas and 'cottages', the small houses placed round hotels to accommodate the overflow of guests. Later, the term came to be applied to the huge mansions and palaces serving as 'summer cottages' for New York and other elites (Amory, 1952; Downing and Scully, 1952).

The 1880s brought a big increase in these developments. 'The eastern coast', wrote Charles D. Warner in 1885, 'with its ragged outline of bays, headlands, indentations . . . from Watch Hill . . . to Mount Desert, presents an almost continual chain of hotels and summer cottages. In fact, the same may be said of the whole Atlantic coast from Mount Desert to Cape May' (i.e. from Maine to New Jersey) (Wolfe, 1956:504). As in Britain, the growth of industrialised production had swelled the ranks of the commercial, professional and rentier class, providing architects and builders with a growing clientele. But, too, the increase in building activity at this time seems also to have been linked with the international movement of capital and its investment in the built environment. As Brinley Thomas has shown, in the 'Atlantic economy' of the nineteenth century, the long waves of investment in the built environment moved

Figure 4.1   American connections: bungalow as 'summer cottage' 1, 1880
Similar economic, political and cultural conditions in the USA and Britain ensured that the bungalow idea could take hold. This is the earliest identified evidence of a 'named bungalow' in North America, in this case, at Monument Beach, Cape Cod, one of the many 'second home' areas for the increasingly wealthy urban population further inland (*American Architect and Building News*, 27 March, 1880. *Clay Lancaster*)

inversely to each other in Britain and the United States. In England, the bungalow had been introduced as part of larger urban developments in the early 1870s when investment in building was on the increase. As this declined in Britain during the 1880s, it rose rapidly in the United States. The two movements were not independent of each other but tied via the migrations of capital within the framework of the international economy of the time (Harvey, 1977:118). Though further studies are needed on the financing of summer homes and resorts, it seems more than a coincidence that the bungalow was to arrive in America at this time.

The earliest known American bungalow to be named as such was part of these developments. Built in 1880 at Monument Beach, Cape Cod, by a Boston architect and probably for a Boston client, its simple structure, broad verandah and location on the shore suggest that, for both, 'bungalow' meant a simple seaside vacation house, irrespective of its two-and-a-half storey form. That the term is apparently first used in North America in this way suggests not only that the idea had come from England but, with neither explanation of the word nor description of the house in the *American Architect and Building News* where it was illustrated, readers were expected to be familiar with its use (Lancaster, 1958).

Yet in the middle 1880s, the idea of the bungalow as a simple summer cottage, a purpose-built 'vacation home', was still comparatively new. When the second known example appeared, in a book of cottage designs by New York architect, Arnold Brunner, in 1884, it figured as the frontispiece and received a definition. ' "Bungalows" as the one storey houses used in India are called, seem adapted to some parts of America particularly as summer cottages.' For New Yorkers interested in up-state country relaxation, it was seen as 'attractive to those disliking going up and down stairs', the verandah 'a particular American feature'.

Noting that the cottage habit had diffused to the less affluent bourgeoisie, Brunner had produced designs for 'medium and low cost houses' (the latter between 500 and 1,000 dollars) by various architects and directed to a growing New York middle class. 'In view of the rapid growth of "Art Ideas" and the general improvement in taste in the last years', he believed there was 'a demand for dwellings reasonable in cost yet artistic and homelike.' If these remarks anticipate the social and aesthetic ideas of the 'Arts and Crafts' ideology, other comments seem to confirm them: 'during the last few years . . . our conception of what a country house should be has entirely changed. Simplicity, elegance and refinement of design are demanded and outward display, overloading with cheap ornamentation, is no longer in favour.' Though at about 3,500 to 4,000 dollars, his bungalow was hardly for the mass.

This concern with simplicity and artistry, echoing back to the early 1870s in Kent and, as we shall see, forward to California and the new-style American home of the 1900s, forms a key to later developments. And whilst Brunner reaffirmed the single-storey definition, his own bungalow had one and a half storeys with bedrooms in the loft – a feature to become characteristic of the American type. Of less than a dozen bungalows known to have been designed in North America in the nineteenth century, and mainly in the last decade, all apparently functioned as 'summer cottages', in the mountains, the country or by the sea, and practically all in the North Atlantic states (Lancaster, 1984).

At one level, the actual idea of the bungalow seems to have arrived in North America by way of an increasing professional network, an interchange of books and journals, including the English *Building News* and *The Studio*, with Briggs's article of 1894; Brunner, for example, seems likely to have picked up the term from Shaw's *Sketches for Cottages* (1878), and by 1901, Briggs's *Bungalows and Country Residences* had gone into five editions since it first appeared in 1891. Yet the 'need' for something called a bungalow, or at least the perception of that need, and the preconditions for it, had had to be created as well. 'Everyone

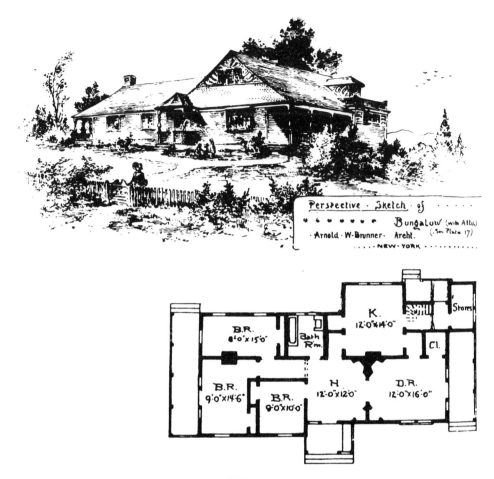

Figure 4.2   Bungalow as 'summer cottage' 2, 1884.
Improved communications and the increased spread of professional literature were two of the factors responsible for the transfer of the bungalow idea round the Anglo-Saxon world.

New York architect Arnold Brunner used this design as the frontispiece for his *Cottages or Hints on Economical Building*, 1884. As it was meant as a second home for people with plenty of material goods, 'simplicity, elegance and refinement' were demanded rather than 'outward display'. The cost was some 3,500-4,000 dollars

wants some little place, some little corner in this big world which can be called his own,' wrote Frank Lent, in *Summer Homes and Camps* at the end of century.

The idea of home is each year entering more and more into arrangements for the summer. It is often the case that the members of the family see more of each other during the leisure of the summer than during all the rest of the year. Many families make it a point to gather under one roof at least every summer, and there are many cases where the summer residence is the only home, the family living there six or eight months continuously and spending the remainder of the year in travelling or living in hotels.

BUNGALOW, PHILADELPHIA.

Figure 4.3   Country bungalow, USA, 1900.
As in Britain, the definition of a bungalow related as much to function as to form (*Building News*, 7 September, 1900)

Such, according to one of their architects, was the plight of wealthy bourgeois families fleeing from the city.

In 1890, New York, with well over $2\frac{1}{2}$ million inhabitants was, next to London, the largest city in the world. Of an increasingly urban population, half were concentrated in the North Atlantic states where Massachusetts, with two-thirds of its inhabitants in towns and Boston a growing city of half a million, was the most urbanised state of all. Other states where summer cottaging developed – Rhode Island, New York and New Jersey – contained the largest number, and wealthiest section, of the country's city population. On the west coast too, 'getting back to Nature' was equally in vogue.

About a hundred years later, a study of the second-home phenomenon in the USA concluded that 'sufficient income and sufficient leisure time' provided the opportunity for vacation house ownership in the later twentieth century. Other factors, including 'capital accumulation, status attainment and the desire to engage in outdoor recreation' provided the motive, while improvements in transport, and the availability of vacation house types and sites offered the opportunity (Ragatz, 1970). Yet with the architect-designed bungalow at Monument Beach providing the chance to fish, gaze at scenery, boat or chat idly in the verandah, most of these opportunities and motives seem to have been present, for some at least, in the 1880s if not before (Figure 4.1).

Back to Nature – the bungalow and the Arcadian myth
These few examples, however, only hint of things to come. Apart from Brunner's scanty reference, there seems to have been no discussion let alone theorising about the bungalow in America until the early twentieth century. From then on, between about 1905 and 1915, bungalow books and articles – as well as the phenomenon itself – proliferated on all sides.

The full impact of urbanisation seems to have struck America's intellectuals and writers at the close of the nineteenth century. In his study of American reactions to urbanism, Peter Schmitt describes how the modern metropolis not only refashioned the physical environment of townspeople but also profoundly altered the way in which they perceived the natural world outside the city. For its inhabitants, there developed an 'Arcadian myth', a 'back-to-Nature' movement which attracted wide support amongst the urban middle and upper middle class, creating institutions and attitudes which remain firmly entrenched today. It was similar, yet also different, from what was taking place in Britain at the same time.

The urge for the out-of-doors, the rugged life and the rustic was not a rejection of city life. In Schmitt's words, the middle class city-dwellers who looked 'back to Nature' at the turn of the century did so to escape the minor irritants not 'the problems' of urban life (1969).

> Poverty, crime and disease disturbed them less than did the press of crowds along antiquated sidewalks, the rattle of wheels on cobblestone streets or soft coal smog. Such folk heartily approved the opportunities for social and economic success, the education and . . . cultural advantages that accompanied urban life. They simply realised, as every suburban mother knew, that the city is no place to raise a family (ibid.:3).

The attraction of 'Nature' was, of course, not new; it had flourished in the eighteenth century and in the Romantic thought of the nineteenth. But as the twentieth century drew close, the back-to-Nature movement shifted from being a luxury of the rich to a preoccupation of the urban middle class. Nature and the country were redefined to suit urban tastes; 'nature study' was introduced into city classrooms, 'country clubs' established on the edge of towns, bird lore encouraged for city ornithologists and the 'wilderness novel' developed to give city men 'the breath of real life but without its inconveniences' (ibid.:125). And for city gents who could afford it, it encouraged a temporary return to the wild, a search for solitude in the bush.

It was these ideas which led, from the turn of the century, to the flood of nature and 'wilderness writing'; if W.H.H. Murray's *Adventures in the Wilderness: or Camping Life in the Adirondacks* (1869) was an early manifestation, the build-up occurred in the first decades of the century with titles like *In the Open* (1908), *Outdoor Philosophy: The Meditations of a Naturalist* (1912) and *Tenting Tonight: a Chronicle of Sport and Adventure* (1918). The most well-known, Jack London's *Call of the Wild* (1901) was one of the six best selling novels between 1900 and 1930. Newly founded family and home-maker magazines such as *House Beautiful* (1896), *House and Garden* (1901) and *American Homes and Gardens* (1905) regularly contained articles on nature lore and the 'simple life'. It was these which helped to promote home ownership, encouraged the pursuit of nature in the suburbs and, when it arrived, sang the praises of the bungalow.

The 'back-to-Nature' movement was related to another ideology affecting intellectual circles at this time, the social and aesthetic movement of the 'Arts and Crafts' which had developed in England from the 1880s. In rejecting the consumer society, it was a moral and humanist attack on bourgeois civilisation and materialism, its belief in 'unity with nature', the pursuit of simplicity and the handmade being the source for changes which later took place in the arts. By the early 1890s, the ideas behind the 'spiritual crusade' of the Arts and Crafts were being taken up in the USA (Kaufmann, 1975; Naylor, 1972; Winter, 1975).

It was from these two ideological strains that, after the hesitant start outlined above, the bungalow as 'summer cottage' was really to blossom out. The second more or less simultaneous development – the bungalow as suburban dwelling – was not unconnected with the first.

Arts and Crafts and The Craftsman *bungalow*

Of all the house and architectural journals founded at this time, one of the most important for the bungalow's development was *The Craftsman*, edited by Gustav Stickley from New York.

Just what connection there was between the ideas behind *The Bungalow* published in London between 1899 and 1900 and those of the English artists and writers associated with the 'Arts and Crafts' only more detailed research might disclose. Further digging might uncover the links between these names and their aesthetic and social ideas as they crossed the Atlantic (with Gustav Stickley, for example, who visited England in 1898) to emerge in North America and especially in the pages of *The Craftsman*. For where *The Bungalow* was an ephemeral literary gazette having no connections with building or design, *The Craftsman*, fusing architecture with social reform, was devoted to the development, both in theory and practice, of the three main principles of the Arts and Crafts philosophy – simplicity, harmony with nature, and the promotion of craftsmanship. The bungalow was to become the incarnation of all three.

'Published in the interests of art and labour', *The Craftsman* ran from 1901 to 1916. Stickley, the founder of the United Artists and Craftsmen, aimed 'to promote and extend the principles established by Morris in both the artistic and socialistic sense' (*The Craftsman* 1901:1).

From the start, *The Craftsman*'s pages were sprinkled with quotations from Kropotkin, Walt Whitman, Ruskin, Edward Carpenter and Arts and Crafts enthusiasts such as C.R. Ashbee; in 1905 it added the sub-title, 'an illustrated monthly magazine for the Simplification of Life'. From 1903 on, regularly included in its issues were designs, plans and discussions of the bungalow.

'Of late years it has become more and more the approved thing to own the country home or camp and to go there year after year,' reported the journal in 1906; and 'for any place, whether in mountain or valley that is really "in the country" the best form of summer house is the bungalow.' Here was a dwelling which embodied the essence of the Arts and Crafts philosophy. It was 'a house reduced to its simplest form where life can be carried on with the greatest amount of freedom; it never fails to harmonise with its surroundings . . . it was never expensive because it was built of local material and labour; and it was beautiful as it was planned to meet the simplest needs in the simplest way.' Three years earlier (1903) Stickley had made the point even more explicitly: the American bungalow was 'nothing more or less than a summer residence of extreme simplicity, economic construction and intended for more or less primitive living'. With its low-pitched, sweeping roof, the single-storey dwelling was literally *closest* to Nature both in form and in site. The stress on low-lying horizontality was 'a subject of congratulation that the countryside is no longer *affronted* with lean, narrow, two-storey houses'. Similarly, the simple wood construction, cedar and redwood shingles (which in time 'came to look like autumn leaves') combined with 'the rough stone of the large chimney to tie the building to its surroundings and give it the seeming of a growth rather than a creation.'

This close identification also influenced the interior: walls might be in dull olive yellow burlap, the exposed ceiling in wet mossy green, woodwork should be of hemlock or cypress, the exposed stonework fireplace of weathered limestone.

The design for '*The Craftsman* Bungalow' used field stone set at random, rough hewn timber walls, a stone fireplace with an elk's head over it. Stencilled on the one-and-a-half foot frieze were 'conventional objects relating to primitive life'. . . . 'Great care should be taken . . . to omit every article that is not absolutely essential to the comfort or convenience of the occupants, it not being intended to make the building . . . a cheap museum . . . as frequently happens in the summer cottage to the great disturbance of the simple life.'

Between 1905 and 1907, designs for 'Forest', 'Craftsman', 'Hillside' and other bungalows appeared among Stickley's 'Craftsmen Homes'. Though the prices ranged from 300 dollars upwards, Stickley's sympathies were for the simplest which he saw as appealing to the rising number of middle class professionals like the young lawyer building a bungalow a thousand feet up from the shore of Lake Michigan. There was a growing concern to develop the bungalow as a natural, essentially American product, appropriate to 'the new wilderness areas being used by vacationers'.

Going back to Nature was 'part nostalgia and part therapy'; the country was a place where wealthy city-dwellers could live for a time the uncomfortable life which none of them would ever dream of making permanent. As early as 1878, C.D. Warner's *In the Wilderness* had described 'the instinct of barbarism that leads people periodically to throw away the habits of civilisation and seek the freedom and discomfort of the woods. It was not so easy to understand, however, why such passion should be strongest in those who are most refined and trained in intellectual and social fastidiousness' (Schmitt, 1969:8). Yet it was just this group, secure in health, wealth and social position, for whom 'the primitive' had an appeal:

> To those of us who live and work amid the artificiality of city life there is something irresistably attractive in the idea of being close to the heart of nature, wearing old clothes and living for a time the free and easy life which we like to imagine was lived before the call of the city became insistent.

Robert Court wrote thus in an early reference to 'Vacation Homes in the Woods'.

Similar sentiments were expressed by Bliss Carman writing on 'The Use of the Out of Doors' in *The Craftsman* in 1907:

> we are crowded and hustled and irritated to the point of physical desperation in our thoroughfares and markets, our tenements and tiny apartments, our shops and street cars. . . . Give us more air and sun and ground under foot and we will give you fewer instances of unfortunate morality, knavery, greed and despair.

This concept of 'the primitive' and 'the rugged life' is best illustrated by William Comstock's *Bungalows, Camps and Mountain Homes* (1908, 1915) or Henry Saylor's *Bungalows. Their Design, Construction and Furnishing (with suggestions also for camps, summer homes and cottages)* (1911). Bungalows, according to Saylor, had become 'a fad for many wealthy city men who want some sort of retreat in the woods where they can entertain as freely as in the city'. Here, irrespective of cost, they constructed their own idea of 'the simple life' which, as some cynic observed a few years earlier, was 'a final evolution reached by a system of unlimited complication' (Schmitt, 1969:17). It was in this spirit that someone else had defined a bungalow as 'a house that looks as if it had been built for less money than it actually cost' (Saylor, 1912:1).

What such simplicity and ruggedness meant was a low rambling mass, wide verandahs and over-hanging eaves; a building of a picturesque and informal type buried deep in the wood or by a lake or the seashore. Wherever it was, the natural environment should be undisturbed, trees left standing and materials chosen to secure 'the intimate relationship between home and surroundings that conveys an impression of peace and stability rather than strife and unfitness' (plate 68).

Living simply required complex thought. Time was worth spending on planning as, while avoiding the formality of the city household, the bungalow had still to be as comfortable, and with all its convenience and privacy. It was an important point, best expressed perhaps by Elon Jessup's book, *Roughing it Smoothly* (1923) or an article in the *Woman's Home Companion* in 1916, 'The old-fashioned log cabin is the new-fashioned summer camp, with all the comforts of modern life and all the picturesqueness of pioneer days.'

Sleeping out of doors was the touchstone of the outdoor philosophy. 'To sleep outdoors for a month' was 'better than a trip to Europe', a comment presumably meant for those who could afford to do both. To fulfil this need, the sleeping porch became an essential feature of the bungalow, whether as summer cottage or suburban home.

Whatever the outside – hewn logs, brick, stone or shingles, provided it 'harmonised with nature' – the interior should reflect 'the simple life'. At all costs, plastered walls had to be avoided in favour of raw brickwork, 'natural' timber or boulder finish. The fireplace – meriting a whole chapter in Saylor's account – was the symbolic centre: 'a bungalow without a fireplace' was like 'a garden without flowers'. The ideal was a large, ceiling-high mass of plain bricks, stones or rough boulders, finished with a suitable mantel, 'an old railroad tie' for example, 'supported on five or six wrought iron spikes' (plate 69). Sturdy 'craftsman furniture' of brown oak was best for the living rooms, as also were other 'natural materials' such as willow, wicker or woven grass. 'If there was one place more than another where white and gold vases or gilt clocks or other symbols of city wealth were unfitting', wrote Stickley, 'it was in the bungalow living room.' Except for a few handmade oriental rugs, floors were bare. On the porch, carefully contrived informality prevailed: potted plants, a coarse woven grass mat. One table might have 'a few good books and the current magazines'.

Such basic requirements were supplemented by the owner's props, well illustrated in the interiors of Comstock's mountain bungalows. Here, for the urbane, educated city-dweller, were the – essentially male – symbols with which he transformed himself into 'primitive man', a Daniel Boone or a Davy Crockett. Fishing nets hang from the ceiling, snow shoes and frying pans on the walls, hardwood chairs, guns, fishing rods, shooting hats – symbols of what the Great Outdoors man, President Theodore Roosevelt, called 'the strenuous life'. Here too are the clues to the intellectual origins of it all, the college pennants bearing 'Swarthmore' or 'Yale', the beermugs, the shelves of books on built-in cupboards (plate 70). Small wonder then that the greatest 'wilderness writer' of them all, Jack London, 'the ideal of strenuous Americanism, apostle of scientific socialism, spirit of world-wandering', ex-coal heaver, worker on the Yukon goldfields and best-selling author of *Call of the Wild* decided in 1906 to come to Sonoma County in California where 'out of his own rock and sand he purposes to erect a spacious bungalow'; here to find 'the wild joy of living' (*The Craftsman*, 1904:614-19).

For those unable to afford such architect-designed bungalows, Saylor's book included more modest versions, the portable bungalow, the camp shack or tent-house. For city folk, more used to working at a desk than a bench, manual toil took on its own romantic appeal. Building-it-yourself became a popular middle class urban philosophy, typically expressed by the wilderness writer S.E. White in his trilogy *The Forest*, *The Mountain* and *The Cabin* completed in 1911. There was 'a real joy in the smell of the newly cut wood and its gradual transformation under the tools that never palls' (Schmitt, 1969:169).

In 1907, with 'the bungalow fever still upon us', *Indoors and Out* devoted almost its entire issue to the phenomenon. 'We have contracted [the fever] in daily intercourse with our friends; the germ continues to reach us through our evening mail. We want every one of our readers to own a bungalow . . . and we shall continue to publish bungalows so long as our readers impart to us the bungalow bacillus.' It was time for 'our savage selves to go outdoors and whoop. City life and indoor conventionalities should be forgotten.' Using a haphazard collection of bungalow pictures and drawing freely on Briggs's book, the editor discussed:

the word, bungalow . . . one that was in everyone's mouth who talks of rusticity and ease in the country . . . conveying a sense of roughing it a bit, living more or less in the open air for pleasure, a hint at extemporised conveniences with a suspicion of Bohemianism and a laxity of conventional conduct.

Masculine territory: the bungalow as domain of the male

> Among the shrubbery and shade trees
>   The brisk little bungalow stands,
> Its swinging white gate speaking welcome
>   While its dignified doorhook commands.
>
> Its windows so clear and so gleaming
>   Look out with suggestions of pride,
> The walls neatly shingled and beaming
>   Speak well for the cosy inside.
>
> Here neighborly spirits shine clearly
>   And family life is implied
> From the smoke of the brick-built dutch chimney
>   To the billowy curtains inside.
>
> Here the home of American manhood
>   Independent and true in his life
> With a welcome for friends and for neighbors
>   To share with his children and wife.

> 'The Bungalow', *Keith's Magazine on Home Building*, 33, April 1915:246
> (from R. Winter, *The California Bungalow*, 1980:18)

Bungal-Ode
By Burgess Johnson

> There's a jingle in the jungle,
>   'Neath the juniper and pine,
> They are mangling the tangle
>   Of the underbrush and vine,
> And my blood is all a-tingle
>   At the sound of blow on blow.

As I count each single shingle
  On my bosky bungalow.

There's a jingle in the jungle,
  I am counting every nail,
And my mind is bungaloaded,
  Bungaloping down a trail;
And I dream of every ingle
  Where I angle at my ease,
Nought to set my nerves a-jingle,
  I may bungle all I please.

For I oft get bungalonely
  In the mingled human drove,
And I long for bungaloafing
  In some bungalotus grove,
In a cooling bung'location
  Where no troubling trails intrude,
'Neath some bungalowly rooftree
  In east bungalongitude.

Oh, I think with bungaloathing
  Of the strangling social swim,
Where they wrangle after bangles
  Or for some new-fangled whim;
And I know by bungalogic
  That is all my bungalown
That a little bungalotion
  Mendeth every mortal moan!

Oh, a man that's bungalonging
  For the dingle and the loam
Is a very bungalobster
  If he dangles on at home.
Catch the bungalomotive;
  If you cannot face the fee,
Why, a bungaloan'll do it –
  You can borrow it of me!

from H.H. Saylor, *Bungalows, Their Design, Construction & Furnishing etc.*
New York, 1911, pp. 2-3.

Suburban home

Suburbanisation: the Los Angeles experience

> I just got off the sunset train
> I'm from the Angel Town
> The Golden West Los Angeles
> Where the sun shines all year round
> I left a girlie back there
> She's the sweetest girl I know
> She said 'Goodbye'
> I'll wait for you
> In the Land of the Bungalow
>
> Chorus
> In the Land of the Bungalow
> Away from the ice and snow
> Away from the cold
> To the Land of Gold
> Away where the poppies grow
>
> I just can't keep my tho'ts away
> From California's shore
> The Land of Flow'rs & Winter Show'rs
> How I miss you more and more
> As soon as I can get away
> I know that I will go
> Back to the girl
> I love the best
> In the Land of the Bungalow
>
> Away to the setting sun
> To the home of the orange blossom
> To the land of fruit & honey
> Where it does not take much money
> To own a little bungalow

In the Land of the Bungalow (1929) George F. Devereux (lyrics)
(from R. Winter, *The California Bungalow*, Los Angeles, 1980)

It was a somewhat different version, however, which became the typical suburban home for millions of Americans in the two or three decades after 1905. If universal car ownership combined with federal support for private developers to bring widespread suburbanisation after the Second World War (Checkoway, 1980) the origin of the phenomenon – tracts of small, single-family, privately owned dwellings, each on its own plot – was in the age of the electric streetcar of half a century before (Singleton, 1973; Walker, 1978).

In the early nineteenth century, American cities had been fairly compact. From the 1830s, economic, social and technological developments had led to gradual suburbanisation. Suburbs had not developed simply from improvements in transport: investment was also required and the economic and social motivations of people moving to them also need considering. The steady change to industrial and capitalist forms of production encouraged a growing division of labour and, as the surplus wealth which industrialisation created combined with the steam train, horse railway and cable car to produce the suburbs, the emerging social hierarchy of the workplace was increasingly reflected in the different residential areas round the town. The growing social differentiation which suburbanisation brought about, to become the typical pattern for free-market societies in the twentieth century, was to be exploited for profit by all those with interests in property and land – developers, builders, estate agents, architects and, not least, by the house-owners themselves. All benefited from the growing market in suburban land and the higher values which social segregation introduced.

Hence, though transport developments were not the sole reason for the expanding suburbs, the introduction of the electric streetcar in the late 1880s and early 1890s was none the less a major impetus to their growth (Glaab and Brown, 1976:145). Suburban living, previously limited to a wealthy few, became available to the many. By the end of the century the 'middle class suburb' had become established; the large-scale production of the automobile was to follow, not create, the emergence of the modern mass suburbs in the early years of the twentieth century (Tobin, 1976). Though suburbs had grown immensely in eastern and mid-western cities, the classical case of suburban explosion was California: Los Angeles became the prototype, and archetype, of the fragmented suburban metropolis now typical of the USA (Fogelson, 1967, from which is drawn much of the following).

Until the 1850s, California had been a barren land, the territory of neighbouring Mexico. The Gold Rush brought the first real influx of population and, in 1850, the incorporation of the state into the American Union. In the following thirty years, growth was relatively small, but, with the transcontinental railway linking California to the east in 1885, the great migration began.

The reasons why people came, who they were and where they were from, all, in their own way, contributed to the kind of residential environment which later emerged – not least to the development of the California Bungalow. At the turn of the century, newcomers to Los Angeles were mainly middle class, rural mid-western or at least native white Americans. 'Unlike the typical American metropolis, Los Angeles did not have at any time in its modern history a vast group of European immigrants' (ibid:33). Mexicans, Japanese and blacks also migrated to the city but they were a minority confined, in the early years, to downtown areas.

For the majority of newcomers, the motivation to migrate was not just economic; some came to retire – wealthy people from the mid-west or east, attracted by the warm, dry California climate and the attractive suburbs of Los Angeles or the more upmarket Pasadena, a fashionable resort in the 1890s and soon to provide the setting for the exotic California bungalows of the architects Greene and Greene. Others came for a holiday, spurred by the health-giving properties of southern California. Between 1890 and 1910, the proportion of over-55s in the 'city of the angels' doubled from 8 to 17 per cent and by 1920, at 21 per cent, it was larger than in most other eastern or western American cities. From the start, California seemed to attract a self-selected population – the innovative, creative, entrepreneurial and democratic. More easy-going than their countrymen in the east, the new Californians were less formal and perhaps more idealistic.

Late-nineteenth-century San Francisco had a reputation of being free and open, artistic and, according to Kevin Starr, its own 'Bohemian Club'. At the turn of the century, discarded tram-cars set on floating rafts made pleasant houseboats for the arty: 'there are', reported *World's Work* in an article on the 'Open Air Life' in 1903, 'worse things than a railway car as the foundation for a bungalow.' A few years before and contemporary with Shoreham's Bungalow Town, an entrepreneur had set up a 'streetcar village' in the shadow of San Francisco variously called Ocean Side, Ozona or Carville. Other 'carvilles' had mushroomed on the Atlantic sea-board, as well as America's rivers and lakes (Lancaster, 1960:215). Robert Fogelson describes how, at the turn of the century, there seems to have been a profound change in American values: people were less willing to devote their lives simply to improving their material condition of life. Though not renouncing wealth, there was none the less a shift in favour of self-realisation, a move to a life that could be enjoyed. California, with its benign climate, open society, exotic landscape and a familiar developing suburban environment offered 'an easier, more varied, less complicated and well-rounded life'.

After the collapse of an initial land boom in the 1880s, the real development of Los Angeles got under way. In the first three decades of this century, the city population soared from just over 100,000 to well over a million; the largest increase, of over 200 per cent, occurring between 1900 and 1910, with a massive surge between 1904 and 1906. Overall in the USA, there was a spurt of investment in building (Harvey, 1977). It was precisely in these years that the suburban bungalow boom seems to have begun.

Gary Tobin (1976:95) suggests that suburbanisation is best explained by reference to four related factors: the availability of resources; prevailing values – both individual and social; particular institutions and the availability of technologies, especially transportation. In terms of all four, early-twentieth-century California provided an ideal setting. Its resources included almost endless supplies of relatively cheap land made available by the electric railway, a bouyant economy and a fairly wealthy population; for its inhabitants, the 'Arcadian dream' of life in a rural setting and of owning a single-family home, were the supporting values; of the institutions, the free operation of developers, sub-dividers and railway companies – provided the plots and sometimes houses; and technology was there in the form of the new modes of transport.

In California, electric railway interests combined with real-estate development led to rapid and extensive suburban development round Los Angeles. Men such as Henry Huntington, with his Pacific Electric Railway and Huntington Land and Improvement Company, and others provided the tens of thousands of plots on which people could build their homes. Elsewhere, other developers put up bungalows and houses which newcomers later bought. Though the car was to supersede the railway, it was the private sub-division of land, and the shared assumptions of railway companies, city authorities, highway builders and, not least, the million inhabitants, which were to create the most widely scattered metropolitan suburbs up to that time. In the words of Robert Fogelson,

> the unique dispersal of Los Angeles reflected not so much its chronology, geography or technology as the exceptional character of its population – relatively affluent and secure, the native Americans had a much wider choice than European immigrants of housing and communities, to both of which . . . they gave a conception of the good community which was embodied in the single-family houses located on large lots, surrounded by landscaped lawns and isolated from business activities.

Though many Californians had come from single family homes in the mid-West, for others, it was a reaction against the city they knew.

> Not for them, the multi-family dwellings, confined to narrow plots, separated by cluttered streets and interspersed with commerce and industry. Their vision was . . . the residential suburb, spacious, affluent, clean, decent, permanent and homogeneous – not the congested, impoverished, filthy and immoral great city (1967:144-5).

California's vast countryside was transformed into Los Angeles's sprawling suburbs; the purchaser bought his lot and on it he, or someone else, built his home (plates 72 and 73). By 1930, Los Angeles had more single-family, and fewer multi-family, dwellings than any comparable metropolis; of its more than a third of a million families, a staggering 94 per cent were living in single-family homes (ibid.:146). Instrumental to the emergence of this new suburban ecology was an innovative, small, single-family, 'simple but artistic' dwelling – inexpensive, easily built, yet at the same time attractive to the incoming middle and aspiring middle class population: the California Bungalow – a term in use by 1905 if not before (*AR*:1905)* It was these developments which explain the thousands of 5 to 25 dollar bungalow drawings and plans which appear in increasing profusion from about this time (plates 73, 74, 75).

The California Bungalow

The metamorphosis of the bungalow from vacation home to permanent house was helped by transferring the ideology which had brought the first about – the idea that one could live 'close to nature' in a 'simple but artistic home'. It was the 'back-to-Nature' syndrome applied to the commuter's house. The idea was best expressed in *Radford's Artistic Bungalows*, one of many similar books published in 1908.

> The bungalow is the renewal in artistic form of the primitive 'love in a cottage' sentiment that lives in some degree in every human heart. Architecturally, it is the result of the effort to bring about harmony between the house and its surroundings, to get as close as possible to nature.

It was 'a tangible protest of modern life against the limitations and severities of humdrum existence'. And 'though primarily intended for the wilds, this style of home has been seized on eagerly by home builders in every hamlet of the land, in every town and city'. It was 'a radical departure from the older style of cottage, not only in outward appearance but in inside arrangement' (Wilson, 1910:2).

Until the early twentieth century, in the east and mid-west of the USA, 'bungalow' had simply meant a summer house, 'a temporary country house of ample dimensions . . . perhaps of somewhat unfinished or inferior construction', a low building with an air of informal charm (*AR*, 1905:217). The 'comfortable bungalows in California', the best at between 3,000 and 5,000 dollars, though with cheaper versions at 300–2,200 in the influential *Ladies Home Journal* of January 1904 – an early reference to the phenomenon – were apparently for summer homes. Yet it also seems to have been taken up as a permanent residence about this time. 'Instead of being perched on a hill top and surrounded by rocks and grass, it was situated on a street and surrounded by suburban villas.' Low and spacious, simply built, inexpensive and 'trying to be "artistic" ', the one or one-and-a-half-storey suburban bungalow was set snug to the ground, with overhanging eaves, shaded porches and rough stones for chimneys and foundations. The essential feature was that 'there should be as little

---

* *AR Architectural Record.*

70 Ideology and environment: 'roughing it' – the all-male interior.
Curtis ranch house, Altadena, California (*Robert Winter*)

71 Ideology and architecture: the rugged California bungalow, 1923.
Uplifters Club Grounds, Rustic Canyon, Pacific Palisades. The figure on the left is reputedly Frank Baum,
creator of 'The Wizard of Oz' (*G. and O. Rice Robert Winter*)

72 The fragmented metropolis: suburban Los Angeles, 1920s (*Robert Winter*)

"REPRESENTATIVE CALIFORNIA HOMES"

(1912 Edition)

Price 50 Cents, Postpaid to Any Address

A Typical Street View Showing a Row of Pasadena Bungalows

E. W. STILLWELL & CO.
217 Henne Building, 122 West Third Street, Los Angeles, California

73 The suburban vision: California bungalows as the ideal.
Los Angeles was to become the prototype of the sprawling city. The foundations were laid by the speculations of combined transport and realty developers. The California bungalow was part of the package (*Deryck Holdsworth*)

FLOOR PLAN
No. 418

418—This bungalow is a perfect example of bungalow architecture, and has proved to be one of the most popular styles ever designed. The unique feature of the exterior is the introduction of cobblestones for the massive porch columns. The well-proportioned roof and wide overhanging eaves lend an individuality to this design that has met with favor in every part of the United States. The shingles are laid in alternate courses and stained a golden brown to complete the scheme. The principal rooms of this house are models of convenience and comfort. The dining room has beam ceiling and panel walls, with a large built-in buffet. The bed room arrangement is good and affords ample closet space.

Estimated cost $4600.00
Price of plans as shown or reversed   15.00

This is a style of bungalow which has been popular throughout California and the West Coast for years. The lines of the house are very graceful and the whole effect is remarkably attractive. The porch cornice is supported by brackets and the gable is the familiar half-timber construction. Cobblestones set into the brick of the chimneys is unusual and relieves the otherwise straight, hard lines. The rafter ends are exposed with curved fancy ends.

The plan of the house offers every convenience usually found in the California bungalow. The living room has two low bookcases under the high windows at the sides of the fireplace. A wide open arch with columns supporting it divides the front of the house into the dining room and living room. The kitchen has a fine cabinet and in addition a large ventilated cooler. Where a cellar is not necessary, the stair space can be used for closet and enlarged porch room. This house has a more graceful finished appearance than many of the extremely rustic bungalows.

Estimated Cost $1950.00
Plans $10.00

74, 75 All-American style: bungalow pattern books, USA.

According to a number of American scholars, bungalows represent one of the first common house-types to break regional boundaries and become a national phenomenon in the first decades of this century. As plate 80 suggests, it also went further afield (Jud Yoho, *The Craftsman Bungalow Book*, 1913; E. W. Stillwell, *Representative California Homes*, 1912 *Deryck Holdsworth*)

A Row of Cozy Bungalows in California.

76 Close to nature: the ever-clinging vine, c.1912.
According to the ideology, the vines ensured that the bungalow 'clung closely to the ground'; they also helped secure privacy when the bungalow was near the sidewalk. Note the caption (*Robert Winter*)

77 Close to nature: stranded in the suburbs.
A contemporary wrote, 'the suburban husband and father is almost entirely a Sunday institution'; during the week, the men left on trains to work among their colleagues in the city but for the wife 'left standing behind the struggling vine of her brand new piazza' the day 'was often dreary' (H. H. Saylor, *Bungalows*, 1911)

78 The American bungalow matures: Tampa, Florida, 1920s.
Tampa grew rapidly at the turn of the century, though the majority of its 26,000 population still lived at
the urban core. In the 1920s, the bungalow, with improved mass transport and the automobile, began to
open up the more elite suburbs to middle-income families. By then, bungalows on Grand Central Avenue
had developed double storeys at the rear.

79 American bungalow, Japanese style: Delaware Avenue, Tampa, Florida, 1920s.
The developers of Tampa's suburbs capitalised on the nationwide popularity of the bungalow style to help
them sell their lots. Between 1910 and 1930, some four thousand bungalows were built (Ricci, 1979)
some adopting the fashionable Japanese style introduced in earlier decades (Lancaster, 1963) (*both
plates, Tampa-Hillsborough Public Library System and James M. Ricci*)

80 Australia (*Book of Australian Bungalows*, 1923. *D. L. Johnson*)

Capitalism and culture: the suburban bungalow round the Anglo-Saxon world, 1920s.

Historic cultural links between different market countries across the world were to transplant the same prefabricated bungalow styles to the new tram and automobile suburbs of the 1920s. Mail order catalogues were one of the mechanisms.

81 United States: South Florida Fair, 1920 (*Tampa-Hillsborough County Library System and James M. Ricci*)

"ROSEDENE."

the artistic bunga-
low-home built
by Mr. T. W.
Marshall in Firle
Road, Peacehaven.

82 England: Peacehaven, Sussex, 1926 (*Peacehaven Estates*, c.1926)

83 Canada: Artistic Bungalow Company, Vancouver. 1921 (*Deryck Holdsworth*)

84 United States: Rhode Island, Sea View, Riverside. 1920s (*Robert Thorne, 1980*)

With bolts left sticking up around the edge of this floor, the framework of the building can be bolted down and you have a garage standing on a cement platform, which is very convenient construction.

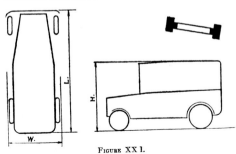

FIGURE XX 1.

TABLE OF AUTOMOBILE SIZES.

Kind	Length (L)	Width (W)	Height (H)
Small Electric	10′ 7″	5′ 6 ″	7′ 2 ″
Large Electric	13′ 0″	5′ 8 ″	7′ 2 ″
Small Four Cylinder	12′ 5″	5′ 6 ″	6′ 8 ″
Large Four Cylinder	14′ 10″	5′ 8 ″	7′ 0 ″
Small Six Cylinder	14′ 1″	5′ 8½″	6′ 9 ″
Large Six Cylinder	15′ 10″	5′ 8 ″	6′ 10½″
Ordinary Eight Cylinder	15′ 5″	5′ 8 ″	6′ 10½″
Twin Six	16′ 5″	5′ 8⅛″	7′ 0 ″

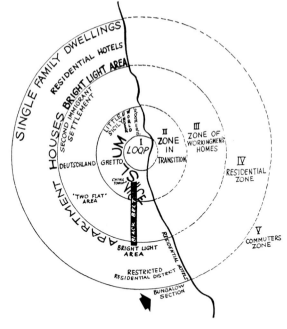

85, 86, 87 Urban theory and the bungalow

Though some early bungalowners had cars, they rarely had garages. In 1923, C. E. White (*The Bungalow Book*) gave some thought to accommodating the automobile which, as Chicago sociologist, E. W. Burgess, had discovered when constructing his famous 'concentric zone' theory of the city in 1925, was making a big impact on the urban fringe. That his 'commuters' zone' was also the 'bungalow section' is sufficient comment on the influence of private property and personalised transport on the production of bourgeois theories of the city (H. Saylor, *Bungalows*, 1911; C. E. White, *The Bungalow Book*, 1923; E. W. Burgess, 'The growth of the city' in R. E. Park, *et al. The City*, 1925)

88 The bungalow, the 'Chicago School' and the architecture of Frank Lloyd Wright (original caption). Much discussion has been generated in the United States about 'the invention of the bungalow' and its association with architects Greene and Greene, or influence on F. L. Wright and others in the 'Chicago School'. As discussed in the text, the same factors which gave rise to the bungalow were also influential in producing the architecture of these well-known names (H. H. Saylor, *Bungalows*, 1911)

89 'Bungalow on the Point', Wood's Hole, Cape Cod, Massachusetts, 1912 - 14. Aeroplane influence has been attributed to this example, designed by 'Chicago School' architects, Purcell, Feick and Elmslie, with second storey overhanging, at right angles, the long ground floor. Drawing by Clay Lancaster.

A RANCH BUNGALOW EMBODYING MANY MODERN IDEAS:

90 Ranch bungalow. Burbank, California, 1912. American authorities see the present day ranch house – the characteristic consumerist suburban dwelling – as developing from the earlier bungalow (*The Craftsman*, May, 1912, p.209, *Clay Lancaster*)

91 Suburban revolution, USA: 1890s – 1920s.
In the USA more so than in Britain, the bungalow was to effect the transition from the vertical inner, to the horizontal outer suburb.

92, 93 Steps towards metropolitan sprawl, 1920s – 1980s.
In 1925 – about the date of the middle example – the residents in Burgess's bungalow section (see 88) commuted by electric trolley or car, the latter stored in a garage at the rear. The shift from public to privatised transport took place after the Second World War: the expansion of suburbs and the auto industry went hand in hand with the emergence of the two car, double garage ranch house – one car for work, the other for shopping and driving the children to school.

In the words of Harvey (1973:270-1), the effective demand for automobiles, 'the linch pin of the contemporary capitalist economy . . . has been created and expanded through the total reorganisation of the metropolitan built form so that it is all but impossible to live a "normal" social life without a car . . . A need has been created out of a luxury' (*Author*, Lexington, Kentucky, 1983)

94, 95, 96 The California bungalow conserved: Los Angeles, 1980 (*Robert Winter*)

97 Sawmill suburbs: San Antonio, Texas 1920s. Photograph, 1980 (*Deryck Holdsworth*)

98 Vancouver, British Columbia, Canada, 1921. Photograph, 1980 (*Deryck Holdsworth*)

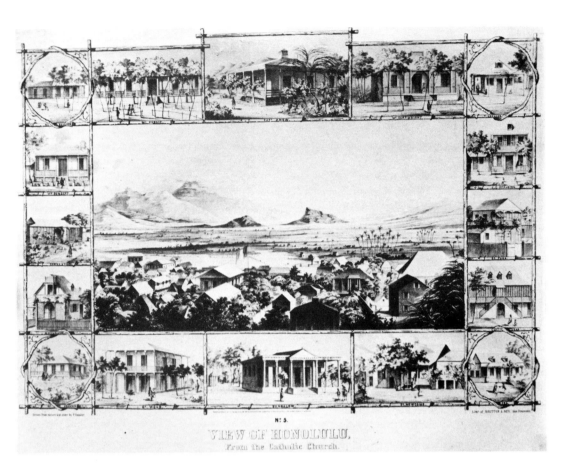

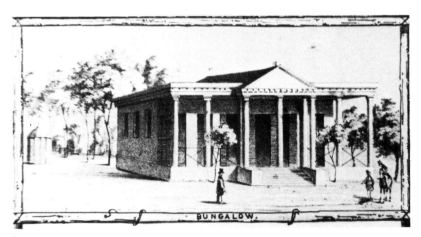

99, 100 World economy and cultural sphere: the bungalow in the Pacific. Honolulu, 1854.
The first European to make contact with the Hawaian Islands was Captain James Cook in 1778. From 1820, the Hawaiians were increasingly influenced by New England missionaries and by mid century, there were frame houses, schools, churches and merchant settlements. The British occupied Honolulu in 1843, apparently bringing the bungalow idea from India (Lithograph published in San Francisco, 1854. *Clay Lancaster*)

101, 102 Builders' vernacular: the mass transport bungalow in Britain, 1930s (cf plates 12–15)

103 Prefabricated bungalow, Sheldon Road, Cambridge, 1920s. (*Author*, 1977)

104 Architect's bungalow, 1926 (R. Phillips, *The Book of Bungalows*, 1926)

105 May Figgis writes on the back of
the postcard, 'This is a photo of
my little place,' Xmas, 1926.
Brighton, Sussex.

106 An anonymous owner writes 'Ours is the 6th bungalow from the front of the picture. I can see the name
"Clarendon" under the magnifying glass and I have counted them up from there'. Postcard,
Kingsdown Park (?), about 1930.

107 Hillingdon, outer London.
Photograph, 1979 (*Author*)

108, 109, 110 The bungalow in the age of the car: riverside, seaside and suburb. Shepperton, Middlesex; Lancing Park, Sussex; Hillingdon, outer London, 1920s – 30s.

distinction between indoors and out', an effect achieved not only by the design, location and materials, but by covering it all over with vines (David, 1906) (plates 76, 77). Describing 'the bungalow at its best', one architect had planned his dining room so that

> the occupant will feel as much as possible that he is out of doors. The walls are converted into large windows, quite unbroken by sashes and designed so to frame the views of grass, trees and foliage. . . . In this instance, the wooden enclosure of the room is so far as possible broken down so that its inhabitants may live, at least with their eyes, out of doors (*AR*, 1906:305).

In May, 1906 *The Craftsman* published an article on 'The Bungalow. Its possibilities as a permanent home'.

The bungalow as suburban mass house

> There's a little side street at the edge of the town
>   That sloped from the brow of the hill
> Where the shadows lie deep from the sun going down
>   And the harsh city noises are still
> The white wings of peace seem to brood in the air
>   Of this little side street that I know
> And Phyllis so fair is awaiting me there
>   In our own little Bungalow.
>
> The stern wheel of toil – let it drive as it may
>   At even its driving is done
> And my cares fall away at the close of the day
>   As the morning mist melts in the sun
> In the quaint inglenook, with my pipe and my book
>   I sit by the firelight's glow
> With Phyllis so fair, with the light on her hair
>   In our own little Bungalow.

> *Representative California Homes*, Stillwell & Co, Los Angeles, 1912, p. 3.

This ideology, to become increasingly adopted in domestic design of the twentieth century, was not only behind the architect-designed bungalows of California; it was also in the popular culture of the suburban house. The bungalow, in some American cities at least, was to be the ultimate development of social and architectural trends already in motion. In the words of Gwen Wright, between 1873 and 1913, the form of the American middle class house underwent a major transformation

> from an exuberant, highly personalised display of irregular shapes, picturesque contrasts and varieties of ornament, supposedly symbolising the uniqueness of the family, to a restrained and simple dwelling, with interest focussed on its scientifically-arranged kitchen. The twentieth century model house was more visibly like others in a planned, homogeneous community (1980:3).

The bungalow, after all, was not just simple and artistic; it was also cheap. The ideology behind it combined with, even if it was not just produced by, the economic interests of both owners and developers. For the crowds flocking to California, it offered the opportunity of a detached, single-family dwelling which they had never experienced before. The 'simple life', 'back-to-Nature' ideology legitimised an economic choice. Advances in prefabricated building meant that self-built bungalows could now be constructed from as little as 400 dollars. In *Practical Bungalows for Town and Country* (1906, and reprinted three times in the next ten years), the first of literally dozens of American bungalow books published before the end of the 1920s, Frederick T. Hodgson described the Californian bungalow as 'the best type of cheap frame house which had been erected in this country since the old New England farmhouse went out of fashion'. Coming from one of the foremost building-journalists in the country, such a statement must have carried some weight.

Though only about thirty out of Hodgson's three hundred designs were actually for bungalows, these could be constructed for between 700 and 1,100 dollars compared to over double the price for two-storey houses. Plan prices were a mere five dollars. In the mild dry climate of California, where much of life was lived outdoors, the construction could be relatively flimsy and substantial foundations and cellars ignored. Moreover, the new, informal lifestyle of California meant that 'much of the interior finish . . . considered necessary to the adornment of the house, even of a mechanic' in other parts of the country could be dispensed with, and redwood sheathing, for example, substituted for plaster work.

In the ten years after 1906, bungalow books and articles (many originating in California) flooded on to the market, helping to disseminate the idea throughout the States. *Radford's Artistic Bungalows*, 1908, contained over 200 designs; H.L. Wilson's *Bungalow Book*, 1910, included 'a short sketch of the evolution of the bungalow from its primitive crudeness to its present state of artistic beauty and cosy convenience'. Bungalow books were issued by the Standard Building Investment Company, the Building Brick Association of America, the Architectural Construction Company, Bungalowcraft, California Ready-Cut Bungalows, amongst others. Bungalow articles proliferated, not only in the building and architectural journals but in the new home-making magazines, *House and Garden*, *House Beautiful*, *Ladies Home Journal* or *Keith's Beautiful Homes Magazine*, stimulated by massive suburban development.

In April 1907, *Indoors and Out* devoted their entire issue to the bungalow with pieces on 'The evolution of the bungalow in California', 'the word bungalow – whence it came and what it has come to mean', a bungalow 'in Gothic style', 'Bungalow entertaining' and 'How to furnish a bungalow'.

Worried about what was happening to the image, journalist Felix Koch went off to make a survey, 'In search of bungalows. What we found' (*House and Garden*, 1908). His results were none too reassuring; the name was being adopted for any small house, simply as a fashionable cachet. So widespread had both the term and the phenomenon become that many must have asked with the readers of *Arts and Decoration* in October 1911, 'What is a bungalow?' Everyone had his own garbled version of its origin – whether in India or in the indigenous Californian barn – though few seem to have been conscious of its diffusion via England: the only authentic account resulted from the chance visit of Rudyard Kipling's father to his son in the United States in 1911. In 'The Origin of the Bungalow' written for *Country Life in America* just before he died, John Lockwood Kipling, Curator of the Bombay Museum, brought the only informed account to a country with little direct acquaintance with the genuine Anglo-Indian dwelling.

Not that such academic discussions troubled the rapidly growing suburbanites for whom the bungalow had become the ideal home. According to *Country Life in America* (July 1912) there was 'a rampant craze for the Bungle-oh' and when Mary Austin visited and then wrote about *California. The Land of the Sun* (1914), it was the results of this craze which left one of the strongest impressions:

> In this group of low hills and shallow valleys between the Sierra Madre and the sea, the most conspicuous human achievement has been a new form of domestic architecture.
>
> This is the thing that strikes the attention of the traveller; not the orchards and the gardens which are not appreciably different in kind from those of the Riviera and some favoured parts of Italy, but the homes, the number of them, their extraordinary adaptability to the purposes of gracious living. The Angelenos call them bungalows, in respect to the type from which the latter form developed but they deserve a name as distinctive as they have in character become. These little, thin-walled dwellings, all of desert-tinted native woods and stones, are as indigenous to the soil as if they had grown up out of it, as charming in line and the perfection of utility as some of those wild growths which show a delicate airy fluorescence above ground, but under it have deep, man-shaped resistant roots. With their low and flat-pitched roofs, they present a certain likeness to the aboriginal dwellings which the Franciscans found scattered like wasps nests among the chapparal along the river – which is only another way of saying that the spirit of the land shapes the art that is produced there.

The Californian image in Britain

As a popular dwelling specially created for the suburbs, the bungalow became established in America a generation before it fully took root in Britain. In the process of diffusion, the *Building News* again seems to have played a role. In May, 1912 a glowing account of 'The American Bungalow' appeared suggesting the reasons for its success:

> To the dwellers in city streets, or in suburban districts around our large towns, in which dwellings of three or more stories, closely huddled together, seems to be the order of the day, the delights of the Bungalow, as it exists in the favoured spots in the United States, and notably in such a paradise as Pasadena, are absolutely undreamt of. To those who love a simple life, in which comfort obtains without the chains of ceremony and in which empty pretensions find nothing to feed upon, there is no dwelling so absolutely congenial and restful as a well-planned, one-storey, and roomy bungalow.

Here, for British readers, was summoned up the Californian ideal:

> Picture such a dwelling, in a garden of flowers, growing in all the freedom of uncultivated Nature; surrounded with peach and orange trees laden with golden fruit; and with its pergola almost bending under its load of luscious grapes – picture all this under an azure sky, and fanned with a perfume-charged breeze – and compare it with the best our speculative builders are offering today in the so-called 'garden suburbs'.

Although the English climate could not be transformed into that of southern California, 'we can', suggested the author, 'easily learn a lesson from what architects of that country are accomplishing in the direction of domestic accommodation and home comforts, at very moderate expenditure. We can surely accomplish something of a kindred nature, especially in districts where land is plentiful.' The editor of *The Builder*, H.H. Statham, was equally impressed by the California bungalow when writing his *Short Critical History of Architecture* (1912) about the same time.

The plans accompanying the account showed what might be done. The smallest American bungalow usually comprised a single living room, opening directly from a verandah, a kitchen, two bedrooms, one of which could be very small, a bathroom, and two or more closets. For all-the-year-round bungalows, a small cellar could house the central hot-air apparatus. The most important feature was the general living room which occupied a similar position to the old English 'house-place' still seen in some dwellings on the dairy farms of Cheshire and elsewhere. The living room was entered directly from the verandah and two windows looked out on to it. In addition, there was a large projecting window at the west end (the verandah always faced south) fitted with box seats, and two windows in the 'inglenook' adjoining the fireplace at the east end. The dining room was usually entered from the living room through a wide opening, framed by book cases and often hung with portieres and the large window in this room was also fitted with a box seat. The kitchen communicated directly with the dining room by a swing door, and was fitted up with cupboard, drawers, a sink and two washing tubs, in addition to the stove and hot-water cylinder. The two bedrooms were provided with the usual wardrobe closets.

The living room had a large fireplace; on each side of the chimney breast were low cupboards and drawers surmounted by glazed bookcases. The roof of the verandah was supported on square posts of wood, resting on stone piers. These, as well as the foundations, were commonly built of rough rubble or cobble-stones laid in cement and producing 'a good rustic effect'. Chimneys were often similar.

Many bungalows were of one-and-half storeys with two additional bedrooms in the roof. The type was sufficiently widespread to be illustrated for many years in Funk and Wagnall's famous dictionary, along with different bungalow forms from Africa (Belgian Congo) and the East Indies. Typically, the average Californian and suburban variety was of timber, stained green or grey, or earthy brown with asphalt dissolved in turpentine. In 1907, a four-roomed bungalow with electric light and gas heating could be built for about 800 dollars; a ten-roomed one for about twice that sum (Lazear, 1907).

Compared to the older town houses from which many of their purchasers had come, the main difference in the bungalow was the open plan which increasingly characterised American houses in the twentieth century. Victorian hall and parlour had disappeared. Instead, the often centrally placed living room, linked by open arch to dining room, took on a new symbolic function as the family room. Many features were 'built in' – sideboard, bookcases, folding wash-stands, disappearing beds and a kitchen full of labour-saving gadgets. The kitchen cabinet, by Hoosier, McDougall and others, to make such a major impact in England in the 1920s, was already being advertised in the *Ladies Home Journal* in America in 1903. The more expensive bungalows boasted a sleeping porch, a major concession to the philosophy of 'out of doors'.

The greatest rationalisation of space took place in the bungalow kitchen – a good decade before it was to follow in Britain. Servants had disappeared, not just because of labour shortages but, to a lesser extent, from the 'progressive' rejection of the master–servant relationship in the home. And as most of the household tasks had to be performed in the kitchen, 'every step saved there saves untold energy through a lifetime of occupation in domestic duties'. Where possible, everything should fold away: the ironing board was hinged and folded into a wall closet; a linen dryer slides into a ventilated drying closet; a folding table was fixed against the wall. The kitchen cabinet took the place of a pantry or others might prefer a 'pantryette'. With only two or three people in the house, a 'breakfast nook' could be squeezed into the kitchen plan. Fittings for the bungalow kitchen should be 'as condensed as the equipment of a yacht' (Comstock, 1908).

Later, as the technology of electricity developed, it had an increasing effect on kitchen design. The telephone, giving immediate communication to shops, made storage space less necessary: stocks stayed on grocery shelves rather than those of suburban homes. In a dozen areas electricity was applied, including the kitchen cabinet, range, oven, percolator, sewing machine, fridge, heating system, washing machines, cleaners, to create the modern functional bungalow of the early 1920s (White, 1923). At the front, especially in California, a pergola disguised the transition between 'in' and 'out' of doors, integrating the bungalow carefully into the suburban bush. Other bungalows were built round a patio or in the form of a bungalow court, two of a variety of new types of lay-out which architects and others thought would lead to new democratic and progressive communities at this time (Winter, 1980; Wright, 1980).

If the accommodation was fairly uniform, the styles were certainly not. Individuality in façade, form, or colour and style was the attribute which gave it an appeal. Though beginning as 'a simple home', over the years the styles developed – Swiss chalet, Old English, Spanish, Japanese-Swiss, Mission style, Tudor and Colonial (plate 79). What most recommended it was the scope for individual expression: 'each individual can construct himself a shell that fits his personality in a way that no conventional architecture will admit of, at a price within the limits of the smallest purse . . . the individual who can express himself in his environment is greatly developed by the process – happier in himself and more interesting to his neighbour' (Lazear, 1907:73).

The compact bungalow: California, 1914

> This is the song of the bungalow,
> With a buffet built in the wall
> And a disappearing bed beneath
> That won't disappear at all;
> A song of the folding Morris chair
> That never will fold until
> You plant your weary carcass there
> And sprawl in a sudden spill;
> The song of the dinky writing desk
> That hangs from a sliding door
> Which sends you kiting galley west
> Until you write no more;
> The song of the pretty porcelain tub,
> With a flour bin below,
> And a leak that springs on the bread-to-be
> While on the floor runs liquid dough;
> A song of the handy kitchenette
> That is almost two feet square
> And all undefiled by the sordid job
> Of cooking dinner there;
> A song of the lidded window seat,
> Where no one could ever sit,

And of plate racks that come crashing down,
And of shelves no book would fit;
A song of pantry and bureau drawers
That will never go in or out –
Oh, a song for all 'built-in features'
That we read so much about.

Kind friend, if you capture a bungalow,
Keep it, and your soul, unmarred,
By taking a kit and a sleeping bag
And living right out in the yard.

'Ballad of the Bungalow', *Architect and Engineer*, 36, 1914:111 (from Robert
Winter, *The California Bungalow*, 1980:54).

The bungalow in decline

The 1920s were to see the biggest bungalow boom as well as its decline. When, as Robert
Winter reports, in the early part of that decade Woodrow Wilson described American
President Warren Harding as 'bungalow-minded' (a comment on his limited capacity to
think), the term had obviously fallen from grace. Yet in the United States as a whole, this was
the most rapid period of suburbanisation to date, stimulated by the enormous growth in
automobile ownership and the consumer boom which went with it. In seven years from 1922,
car production in America doubled to reach over 4½ million, a level not attained again until
the middle of the twentieth century. Though central cities grew by under 19 per cent, areas
outside them expanded at double that rate. In Los Angeles in the 1920s, many suburbs grew
by a staggering 300 or 400 per cent (Tobin, 1976:104; Fogelson, 1967:151).

In Los Angeles, the sixth – and last – edition of the Bungalowcraft Company's *New Spanish
Bungalows* appeared in 1930. By then, an unprecedented decentralisation had set in. Industry,
department stores, and hotels, keen to cut down costs and simultaneously increase profits,
were pursuing both labour and consumers out to their far-flung suburbs. In response to the
influx of single people, entrepreneurs began to maximise their investment in land by building
apartment houses. From the early, and especially mid 1920s, single-family houses as a
proportion of all dwelling units decreased as the proportion of multiple-family dwellings rose.
Early bungalow developments, like the areas north and south of Wilshire Boulevard, were
already being 'apartmentised' in the early 1920s (Fogelson, 1967:151; Winter, 1980).

According to Clay Lancaster, probably more bungalows had been built in the quarter
century after 1905 than cottages in the 125 years before. And in addition to California, it also
took a strong hold in Florida where, in places like Tampa, in its developed and distinctive
style, it became the characteristic type of suburban dwelling (Ricci, 1979). Since its
introduction, however, the range and meaning of the American bungalow had matured, an
impression confirmed by the last significant monograph, C.E. White's *The Bungalow Book*,
published in New York in 1923. After some twenty years of development, here were some
perceptive reflections. 'All that bungles is not bungalow,' wrote White with some feeling. The
word had become 'hard-worked, vacillating, meaningless but it had become so firmly rooted
in American minds that it is now practically sanctioned by good usage.'

Hence, when the hero of Scott Fitzgerald's *The Great Gatsby* (1926) went with 'an old

Dodge' to a 'commuting town' in the east and took 'a weather-beaten cardboard bungalow at 80 dollars a month', the image was immediately recognisable. According to White, the bungalow was accepted in America as an ideal. Beginning in a small way it had swept the country. For several years it had held high place in the esteem of the public.

these little dwellings have come to stay and one may safely say that the bungalow of the early days has developed into a really sensible type of domestic architecture, suitable to American living conditions . . . founded not on cost merely but on convenience, appearance and comfort.

Apart from having all the room efficiently planned on one floor (a development increasingly perceived by apartment dwellers) it had other benefits: adaptability to any site, with 'the low horizontal, simple roof line partaking of the spirit of the prairie'; less expensive materials could be used without offending aesthetics, and a free and less laborious manner of design could be employed.

So widespread had the bungalow idea become in California that it was applied elsewhere: a bungalow church, and a bungalow school. The bungalow court – a series of bungalows grouped round a central place – had, in 1909, pioneered what might today be seen as 'sheltered housing'. And, as Robert Winter suggests, it was from this idea that the motel (the term was first coined in 1925) was to develop.

By the 1930s, all this was past, the term out of fashion, replaced by 'cottage' or house. The introduction of the bungalow duplex, or semi-detached bungalow in England, was seen to bring degeneration. With the depression, suburban development dramatically declined. Following the Second World War, and especially from the 1960s, bungalows began to be swept away; rising land prices brought in apartment houses and after the Second World War, the condominium. The shopping centres, freeways, and wholesale redevelopment were all to take their toll (see frontispiece).

The basic bungalow: North America 1920

> The first untaught need of the savage
> 　The first unskilled work of his hand,
> Was a shelter from storm and from ravage –
> 　The first step by reason o'er-spanned.
>
> And down through the ages uncounted
> 　Since the first dim striving began
> To the marvelous labor surmounted
> 　That mark the far progress of man.
>
> Though toiling with ploughshare or sabre –
> 　Wherever his lot has been cast –
> a home at the end of his labor,
> 　Has been his first need and his last.
>
> And ever to mark his advancement,
> 　To match his refinement of mind,

The home has its added enhancement
    Has been bettered and brightened and fined.

He has learned that in worth, not in seeming,
    The fullness of life must be sought,
And into the home of his dreaming
    This essence of truth has been wrought.

He has found that in fineness and fitness
    Lie beauty and charm, not in show.
As his latest achievement bears witness,
    The beautiful Bungalow.

> Stillwell & Co., *Little Bungalows*, 1920 (from Robert Winter, *The California Bungalow*, 1980:26).

Appraisal

The American bungalow in social perspective

American experts, Lancaster and Winter both agree that it was from the bungalow that the later 'ranch house' was to develop after the Second World War. Though far more spacious, and consuming an infinitely larger site, the fundamental characteristics of the latter were the same: a single-family, predominantly single-storey dwelling, located in its own grounds, and evolved specifically for the modern suburb (plate 90).

Recent studies of post-war suburbanisation in America, and to a lesser extent that of earlier decades, have brought out the connection between the suburban process and the dynamics of the market economy (Checkoway, 1980; Gottdiener, 1977; Walker, 1978, 1981). The automobile and truck industries, tyre companies, oil interests, highway engineering and construction firms, mortgage finance companies as well as a host of interested professionals – lawyers, estate agents, surveyors, architects – all depend on continuing suburban sprawl. Once constructed, the tracts of suburban housing provide a captive mass market for everything from a motor mower to a barbecue set, and other consumer goods essential to the suburban way of life.

In the emergence of the bungalow, as also other middle class housing of the time, changes resulted from the developing market economy. In the later nineteenth century, various activities were gradually moving out of the house. The commercialisation of bread-making, and of some food preparation (with the introduction of tinned foods), combined with the availability of department and grocery stores to reduce duties in the house. Ready-made clothes and commercial laundries dispensed with other tasks. As more women were drawn into the labour market, servants became less common. Children's education was increasingly subsumed by nurseries and kindergartens, and the state made high school education compulsory. These and other factors brought a gradual shift to smaller dwellings, with fewer and smaller rooms. Feminists and other housing reformers endorsed the idea of simple, more efficient houses and apartments. Simplicity and rational design were also a product of the 'germ culture'; progressive social and political ideas suggested that ostentatious houses were disapproved. These and other factors were to result in the notion of the 'minimal house' in the first decade of this century (Wright, 1980).

Yet, as this chapter has suggested, other ideological factors were important as well. Not the least of these were enduring American values in the separate single-family home. At a time when apartments were regarded as 'communistic', the vast majority of Americans endorsed the single-family, separate house as their ideal.

'A single house region', quoted one commentator, 'once infected (sic) with an apartment house tends to accumulate other apartments, and the neighbourhood tends to change from a stable, home-owning population to a shifting, renting class, a class lacking in neighbourliness and civic pride and leading an impoverished family life' (quoted in Schwartz, 1976:26). The development of the small, cheap, yet none the less attractive and individual bungalow was to extend the rustic suburban ideal to millions. It embodied a form of modern popular architecture, conferring the respectability, privacy and sense of territorial possession sought by an aspiring middle class. For an increasing number of people it became their main symbol of home, the psychic fulfilment of the American dream. And California was attractive because it provided the ideal conditions for the fulfilment of that dream (Winter, 1980). In this sense, it became a suburb for the rest of the country, even indeed for migrants from the crowded cities of Europe.

Simply stated, suburb is just a geographical expression; suburbia, on the other hand, connotes a combination of suburbs and inhabitants in a distinctive way of life. It is a style of life often depicted as middle class, family-centred, conformist, alive with humdrum social activity, the acquisition of status symbols and a drive to 'keep-up-with-the-Joneses.' Whether this image is true or merely a myth has exercised scholars for three decades (Schwartz, 1976). In the 1950s it was thought that middle class suburbia would become the dominant life style of the consumption-orientated, post-industrial society of America, a lifestyle represented by 'the ranch house, lawn, barbecue and two-car garage' and the 'functionally designed churches, schools and shopping centres'. With such symbols would be a set of activities: long-distance commuting, transience of residence, an obsession with the repair and appearance of the home, 'not to mention lack of privacy and an intolerance of the offbeat '. The bureaucratisation of work was paralleled in the suburbanisation of residence: both attracted society's least venturesome souls, moving to further standardisation and the suppression of individualism (ibid.).

This classic theory of suburbia was later rejected as a myth: living in a particular place can hardly, in itself, induce a particular style of life. More recently, however, this 'suburban myth' has again received support as a viable representation of suburban life (ibid.). Yet missing in this discussion is a consideration of the actual dwelling forms in which suburbanites live. The suburbs in these discussions are of a particular kind: a land of privately owned, not rented, property; though in theory multi-family apartments could cover the suburbs, in practice it is the single-family, detached ranch house, with its own lawn and surrounding plot which permits the barbecue, the 'obsession with repair and appearance of the home'. The question, therefore, is not whether a particular kind of 'residential area' encourages a certain lifestyle but whether this middle class, 'suburban' lifestyle is associated with a particular type of tenure and dwelling. Without an understanding of the ideology behind the development of the bungalow (and implicitly, the contemporary ranch house), the emergence of the suburb both as a social as well as physical and spatial phenomenon cannot fully be understood. The 1920s bungalow can be seen as symbolic of the beginnings of the contemporary, consumer-oriented American home, with its associated problems of residential segregation (O'Donnell, 1978).

The Currents call the bungalow California's 'first truly suburban vernacular' (1974:10). Yet it was also a nationwide type. Much more than the earlier American cottage, it was devoid of regional variation; the pattern books, the bungalow firms, the magazine articles and advertisements, the growing mobility of the population ensured that, after the First World War, the bungalow – and later, the ranch house – became familiar all over the USA. Whilst Chicago's centre might be different from that of Philadelphia, the suburban bungalows of each were increasingly the same. People moving from one suburb to the next were assured of the same type of dwelling and culture.

The bungalow became in fact, a distinctively *national* type, a fact recognised by Stickley and fostered by others like Matlack Price: 'If architects would take the bungalow more seriously . . . there may be evolved a highly desirable and essentially American type of dwelling, bearing no similarity whatever to the tropical affair from which its name has come' (1916:202). All over North America, the bungalow replaced distinctive regional types. Entrepreneurs like Jud Yoho, 'The Bungalow Craftsman' or 'The Bungalow Man' from Seattle, spread the idea. Radford's 'artistic bungalows' were built 'as far north as Hudson Bay and south as the Gulf of Mexico', as well as the Pacific and Atlantic coast and in Australia and South Africa.

By 1912, the bungalow had taken root in Canada, the *Vancouver Sun* popularising Jud Yoho's *Craftsman Bungalow* designs. Real estate companies such as the newly established Bungalow Finance and Construction Company of Vancouver not only adopted the housing model from California but also the Los Angeles Investment Company's system of sub-division. Between 1895 and 1915, such companies had paid out over 600 per cent cash dividends on suburban developments and with the new garden suburb idea imported from England, the Californian bungalow proved the ideal house. The Prudential Investment Company established a million-dollar syndicate to deal in land and homes in Western Canada and used modern, prefabricated factory produced bungalows in its various suburban schemes. 'To all intents and purposes, the suburban landscapes of Vancouver and Victoria were California North' and by the late 1930s, a perceptive observer was commenting on 'English-style hedges surrounding California-style bungalows' (Holdsworth, 1981, 1982).

Contemporary studies of the bungalow's popularity have seen in it an expression of 'individualist democracy', a form of populism in housing and symbol of the Progressive era in politics. Clay Lancaster, too, suggests that its emergence 'was inevitable following the establishment of democracy on this continent.' (1984).

If these assumptions are generally true, they also require a footnote. A dwelling can be understood only in relation to the settlement of which it is a part, a settlement which is both a physical and social entity. In the classic early-twentieth-century suburbs of Los Angeles, developers saw that a homogeneous population and use of land were no less essential to the suburban vision than a proper lay-out. Hence, restrictions were devised prohibiting blacks and orientals and fixing minimum costs for houses in order 'to group the people of more or less like income together'. They also forbade commercial and industrial activities and, in many suburbs, outlawed all but single-family homes, the foundation, according to most Los Angeles residents 'of this country's security'. Hence, for the thousands of Mexicans, Japanese and blacks who lived amidst commerce and industry in the ghettos of central Los Angeles 'there were a million white Americans who resided in the suburbs sprawling north to Hollywood, east to Pasadena, south to Long Beach and west to Santa Monica' (Fogelson, 1967:145-7).

The suburb, and the bungalows of which many were created, seems also likely to have provided the means by which the most effective form of social segregation could be achieved (see also O'Donnell, 1978). Early-twentieth-century bungalows in Los Angeles were almost certainly built for middle class whites (Fogelson, personal communication 1980); as restrictive covenants and deeds excluded blacks and other racial minorities, a question which needs examining is whether the social contribution of the cheaper bungalow extended the 'privilege' of segregation to a much larger proportion of the white, Anglo-Saxon population of California.

Moreover, in the male-dominated world of the time, few men reflected on the likely consequences of distant suburbs for the female members of their family. The image of the bungalow as a cosy, family-centred haven of rest – sometimes with a specifically-provided 'sewing room' in the half storey upstairs (Lancaster, 1984) – was one which emerged from the masculine province of the city. Moving to their rustic bungalow bliss in the early decades of this century, women especially soon found that there were two sides to the coin: being far from the madding crowd could also mean isolation and loneliness. 'The suburban husband and father is almost entirely a Sunday institution,' complained a writer in *Harper's Bazaar* in 1900; life in the suburbs could discourage 'the young wife in lonelyville', wrote a contributor to *Good Housekeeping* some years later. The men left on trains to work among their associates in the city but for the wife 'left standing behind the struggling vine of her brand new piazza' the day was often dreary (Schmitt, 1969:20-1). It was not just that the cosy houses and bungalows encouraged this 'family-centredness' but the covenants restricting industry and commerce deliberately excluded the possibility of local employment for wives. On the other hand, the ample provision of schools and churches were to be instrumental in fostering the type of female community activity associated with middle class suburban lifestyles prior, and even subsequent to, the feminist revolution of the 1970s.

As with suburbs, there had been an equally long tradition of 'summer cottaging' in North America well before the bungalow arrived, and many of such cottages had been purpose-built. Yet the significance of the bungalow as vacation house is that the ideology that both created it and determined its form has persisted right up to today. Earlier cottage designs had drawn their inspiration from historical sources such as the 'Gothic'. Though such styles also had their ideological underpinnings, the shape, site and materials of the bungalow drew far more on the modern understanding of 'function' and the ideology of the arcadian dream. The idea of 'living with Nature', with 'natural materials blending with the environment', still pervades some of the basic architectural canons of today. The ideology of the vacation bungalow in the woods of 1910 persists in the American Forest Code of the present: vacation cabins, it states, should

> harmonise as much as possible with the natural environment . . . [they] fit the ground more readily when horizontal lines predominate and building outlines are low and sprawling . . . rough wood and stones are considered the best materials . . . smooth materials lack the rugged appearance necessary in most mountain sites.

Architectural significance

It is not the aim of this book to examine what, in a somewhat restricted sense, might be called the architectural significance of the bungalow or its relation to questions of style. Yet equally, it would be perverse not to make some comment.

More perhaps than in any other field of historical writing, explanations for changes in architecture, even in the social sciences (Lloyd, 1981:192) frequently rely on the 'Great Man Theory'. Charles and Henry Greene are occasionally credited with the invention of the

California bungalow, and Frank Lloyd Wright with the 'prairie house' which, in Lancaster's view, is virtually a bungalow.

Since 1970, however, various writers have seen the California bungalow as one of the mainsprings of modern domestic architecture in the USA. Its development was to exert 'the greatest influence on the domestic architecture of this country', and the vogue for bungalows in general has been seen as one of three key factors in the development of the 'Prairie School' of Frank Lloyd Wright and his contemporaries (Brooks, 1972; Current; 1974; see also Lancaster, 1984).

What should be apparent from this chapter is that the idea and form of the bungalow resulted not from a single person or source but from a wide range of inter-related economic, cultural, ideological, social and technical factors which only become apparent when the architecture and urban design of early-twentieth-century America is compared with other historical and cultural situations discussed elsewhere in this book, for example, the present-day socialist experience of the Soviet Union, the 'restrictive planning' context of Britain or even, the contemporary experience of the so-called 'third world'.

The question is not so much whether Frank Lloyd Wright was 'influenced by' the bungalow (as was already implied by Matlack Price in 1916) but rather that the same forces producing the early-twentieth-century bungalow were also significant in producing the domestic architecture of Frank Lloyd Wright: a free market in land; a huge capital surplus created by industrialisation and its selective appropriation by a wealthy bourgeoisie; suburban expansion made possible by investment, railways, the trolley bus and the automobile (though Wright's early single-storey 'spreading' designs were in fact 'pre-automobile'). As more land and money became available, large houses were increasingly built on one storey and the natural, even more economic, form of roof was either flat or one of a very low pitch. It is more than a coincidence that Wright was born about the same year as the bungalow arrived in the west (plates 88 and 89). As Amos Rapoport once said, many of the most important decisions about design are taken long before the designer is ever called in. What is needed to understand these phenomena is a political economy of design.

As for the bungalow book designs, many were anonymous, or the product of little-known draughtsmen or architects. Given the basic economic, social and cultural conditions, the actual shape of the bungalow drew on many sources: in its more sophisticated 'high-style' form, Japanese influences were important (Lancaster, 1963). It was also, as was the case in Britain (and Anglo-India too), a continuation of an older cottage form, the product of a long-established cultural tradition. Frederick Hodgson suggested something of this as early as 1906:

> The little bungalows of which we are speaking are rarely designed by architects at all . . . they are . . . the sort of thing that the ordinary California country carpenter knows how to build . . . the result of a popular tradition . . . a genuine expression of popular and wholesome habits of country life and habits of country building.

The name, however, was important. It came, via England, from India and it carried a positive image. It was exotic, new and had 'the same sort of charm as the word "Mesopotamia" to a lady in Maine' (*AR*: 1905:222). Though there were many bungalow styles, it remained a unity, in Lancaster's words, 'a modern, informal, individual and artistic house, suggesting simplicity and style'. Whatever the various influences, there can be no doubt that the American bungalow marks a clear watershed in the domestic architecture of the nineteenth and twentieth centuries. On one hand, the vertical, formal, cluttered and historically derived styles of the Victorians; on the other, the low, horizontal, informal, 'open plan' and functional design which has come to characterise 'modern' architecture of today; the first, in the inner railway suburbs of the city, the second, in the far-flung auto suburbs of the metropolis, or the more distant setting of the 'second home'.

For those further interested in pursuing these themes, including the transplantation of the bungalow ideology both to and through the USA, a closer examination of the ideas and people associated with the 'Arts and Crafts' might yield something new. Wright's first single-storey designs date from the early 1890s; the Greene brothers began building their earliest bungalows about 1902-4 following a visit to England by one of them in 1901 (Makinson, 1977). Whatever their individual contribution, these architects all seem to have shared the same economic, social and cultural assumptions, the arcadian dream, a commitment to the expansion of suburbs and a deep-seated belief in the institutions of both the family and of private property which, as part of a long-established American cultural tradition, have been historically expressed in the detached, single-family house. The expanding capitalist industrial economy of late-nineteenth-century America encouraged both the widespread adoption of these aspirations as well as the socialistic revolt against the bourgeois, industrial urban system itself.

It is, indeed, only in this context that the original bungalow idea can be understood. It was produced by what might be called an industrial or urban 'dialectic'; 'nature' had meaning only for city folk living apart from it; 'living simply' made sense only to those with a surfeit of material goods; having a 'simple' informal second home was attractive only to those with a complex, formal city house; raw wood, grass matting and coarse fabrics derived their meaning only in contrast to the elaborate decor, finished materials and consumer luxuries of the urbane city; the 'Great Outdoors' appealed only to those with warmth and comfort within. How could people be 'different' if they had nothing to be 'different' from? Yet too, the bungalow was also a genuine protest by an artist-intellectual class, with no great means or second home, against capitalistic materialism. Their goal, in Robert Winter's words, was 'ostentatious simplicity'.

When suburbanisation surged again after the Second World War, it was a more affluent society in which it took place. For this, the small bungalow was far too modest and the split-level executive ranch house took over from earlier forms. Though enclaves of bungalows were left, many disappeared through fire, road-widening and freeways. With ever-increasing land-values, bungalows were razed to the ground and the market pressures replaced them with apartments, condominium flats and, further out, by split-level ranch houses.

Current interest in the bungalow comes from a second phase of just those social forces which originally brought it about: a revolt against what are seen as 'urban excesses': 'high rise apartments . . . restless travel, incessant amusement, pointless accumulation of gadgets' (Lancaster, 1984). In the United States of today, old bungalows – ideally situated between inner city and outer suburb – take on a new lease of life. For the author of 'Lyric encore for a dated house' (*House Beautiful*, May, 1973) 'Millions of bungalows stand in our cities waiting for imaginative eyes to recognise their potential for contemporary living'. In California, amenity societies arrange walks to admire their charms: others are designated historic monuments (Winter, 1980). For conservationists, knowledge is created: in July, 1983, the *Bungalow Magazine* was re-started by the grandson of its 1917 editor and Vance Bibliographies produced a bibliographic guide to *The Bungalow Style*. The re-cycling movement has obviously begun.

Chapter 5

Britain 1918-1980 – Bungaloid growth

'the bungalow now stands for all that is vile and contemptible'

Thomas Sharp, *Town and Countryside. Some Aspects of Urban and Rural Development*, London, 1932:32.

Introduction

In the first half of the twentieth century, the bungalow was the most revolutionary new dwelling type to become established in Britain.* During this time, and especially between the wars, it took its place in the vernacular building tradition. Its widespread adoption was due to economic, social and other changes and, not least, its suitability for the areas of residential development which expanded during these years: the outer suburbs, along main roads, the coast and previously undeveloped countryside.

Yet the bungalow was more than an innovatory dwelling form. It became, for an influential social elite, the focus of ridicule and wrath, a symbol of environmental change which they altogether deplored. With other new features in the landscape, the proliferation of the bungalow and especially its siting, materials and form gave rise to major changes in the law: control of the appearance of buildings and the extension of statutory planning from 'town' to 'country' environments. In helping to bring about the most important planning legislation up to that date (the Town and Country Planning Act of 1932), the bungalow had a significant part to play.

This chapter continues the themes pursued earlier, namely, the effect of economic and social change on the built environment, though it takes up demographic and political change as well; conversely, it also shows how changes in that environment give rise to new institutions and ideas. It explores the question of control over the aesthetic quality of that environment, highlighting the inherent conflict of interest beween people with different ideas and the power to carry them out. Finally, it pursues the theme of 'dual residence', developed in Chapter 3.

The first part of the chapter examines the reasons for the phenomenal growth in numbers and popularity of the bungalow between the wars; the second demonstrates how this expansion raised more fundamental questions relating to control over building development. In the conclusion the larger social issues reflected by these developments are explored.

---

* The other obvious innovation, the multi-storey block of flats, did not make its main impact till the 1960s and, by the 1970s, its impetus was fading (see A. Sutcliffe, ed. *Multi-Storey Living. The British Working-Class Experience*, 1974).

Bungaloid growth

The setting: the inter-war building boom

The environmental changes which took place between the wars were arguably more substantial and far-reaching than any occurring in a similar period before. True, the growth of industrial towns in the previous century had had immense social and physical effects and throughout that century, industry and railways had, by 1891, made England by far the most urbanised country in the world (Weber, 1899). The proportion of almost 80 per cent of the population living in towns which the 1901 census recorded did not change significantly in the following fifty years.

Yet it was precisely this distinction between town and country, the 'built-up areas' and 'rolling countryside' which, for certain people living at the time, became so obviously blurred in the decade after 1918. With electrification of railways and the huge extension in motorised traffic, unprecedented building began. The most rapid and noticeable increase in this traffic happened between 1919 and 1929 when the largest rise so far registered in the number of motor vehicles (120,000 to over 2 million) had taken place. Before 1914, motoring had been a luxury enjoyed by a few: there had been no cheap car for mass transport in Britain. Yet by 1926, a small Ford cost less than £130 and by the end of the 1920s, the Austin Seven and Morris Minor were selling at about the same price; 1930 saw the largest number of public service vehicles on the road up to that time.

The break-up of landed estates, a process begun with the agricultural depression of the 1870s, continued unabated. Rising taxes and death duties were only some of the reasons why the landed aristocracy rationalised their finances, selling off huge tracts of land to invest the money more profitably both at home and overseas. In 1914, only some 10 per cent of agricultural land in England and Wales had been occupied by its owners. By 1927, this proportion had risen to 37 per cent; one quarter of England and Wales had passed from being tenanted land into the possession of its farmers in a hectic flurry of selling in the years after the war. A transfer on this scale, and so rapidly, had probably not occurred since the Norman Conquest (Massey and Catalano, 1978:69; Pollard, 1979:144; Thompson, 1963:332).

These changes, brought about by international market forces, resulted especially from the imperial connection and it was not just regional economies which were affected (Massey, 1979:236) but the degree, and nature of urban and suburban development. The global division of labour, referred to earlier, with the development of urban industrial countries on the one hand and rural agricultural ones on the other was fully appreciated at the time. As Prime Minister Baldwin stated in 1936, 'the United Kingdom is today predominantly an industrial and commercial country . . . our overseas trade consists in the main of the exchange of industrial goods for food and raw material from Empire and foreign sources' (Sheail, 1981:29). The cutting off, during the war, of Russian and Danubian supplies of grain, had encouraged an expansion of overseas producers to meet British and other European markets. Canadian, Australian and Argentine producers enormously expanded their markets, flooding the world with cheap grain. With agricultural prices in Britain falling, despite protection, 70 per cent of the value of British food was imported. The arable area fell by a third between the wars and as the flight from the land continued, the number of agricultural workers was reduced by a quarter (Sheail, 1981:24; Pollard, 1979:138).

With these developments, low-density suburbs expanded into previously rural land and new by-pass and arterial roads provided cheap roadside sites. Remote stretches of coastline came within reach of mobile city populations. Subsequent studies were to show that between

1920 and 1939, the total acreage of built-up, urban land in Britain increased by 50 per cent, from 2.2 to 3.2 million acres, or from 5.9 per cent to 8.6 per cent of the total area of land, a far greater increase than that of subsequent years (Hall, 1973, 1:69). And whilst these changes continued through both decades, it was in the middle 1920s that their effects, at least for some, first became apparent. It was no coincidence that 'ribbon development' and 'bungaloid growth' were both terms coined between 1925 and 1927.

The housing boom was central to these developments. In 1918, there had been some 8 million houses in Britain. In the twenty years that followed, half as many again were to be built, three-quarters by private enterprise, the rest by local government. The rate of building was unprecedented. In the half-century before 1914, the stock of housing had increased by 10 to 15 per cent each decade. In the 1920s, this rose to 18 per cent and in the 1930s to 25 per cent. In 1927, the 258,000 houses constructed exceeded all previous annual records – until 1933 (304,000). Between 1936 and 1938 over 360,000 houses were being planted annually on the ground (Hole and Pountney, 1971; Richardson and Aldcroft, 1968). There were many reasons for this boom. The housing shortage of 1914 had been exacerbated during the war and by 1919, there was an estimated shortage of over three-quarters of a million homes. The coalition government's response was the (Addison) Housing Act of 1919 giving generous subsidies to local authorities to build publicly owned 'council' houses. Later Housing Acts (1919, 1923, 1924) subsidised both public and private development.

Whilst an overall population growth took place in Britain between the wars, it was the increase of $3^1\!/_2$ million separate families which, with generally rising real incomes, falling building costs and the expanding building societies, helped to fuel housing demand. Both the number and size of building societies increased tremendously, with shares and deposits growing ninefold in the years between the wars. Throughout the period, there was a general, though uneven, tendency for interest rates to fall, with 6 to 7 per cent prevailing in the 1920s and 5, even 4, per cent in the early 1930s. As others have shown, houses could be purchased for a deposit of less than 5 per cent (£20 on a £400 house) and in some cases, with hardly any downpayment at all (Boddy, 1980; Burnett, 1978; Jackson, 1973).

Economic change, the result of national and international developments, brought related social and geographical change. Whilst the north-east, north-west and Wales with their heavy industries were in decline, the new, electricity-based industries and service sector of the economy was growing rapidly in the south. Other developments enlarged the size of the middle and lower middle class, the main beneficiaries of the housing boom. The realm of government was being extended, multiplying the number of ministries and the civil servants which they employed. As commerce and trade expanded, the number of white-collar jobs increased. The growing building societies, insurance firms and banks all enlarged the salary-earning class. Teaching, scientific work and public services added further to middle class ranks.

The widespread adoption of bus services and, in London, the extension of the electric train, meant that the effective area of building was greatly increased, the bus encouraging circular rather than tentacular development round towns (Hall, 1973, 1:81). Here, land previously of little use for building was cheaply bought for speculative development; in the years between the wars, over 800,000 houses were built in rural districts, seven-eighths of them by private developers (Sheail, 1981:24).

If these were some of the main factors behind the general expansion of housing – not least, the universal 'semi' – there were others which particularly favoured the bungalow.

The California connection

How far was the adoption of the bungalow as a permanent suburban dwelling influenced by the earlier example of the United States?

As we have seen, the suburban bungalow phenomenon occurred a generation earlier in the United States than in Britain. There, the huge output of bungalow books and plans took place long before 1920 when the first British book to treat the bungalow as a serious suburban proposition was produced. Only in a later one of these, published in 1924, did W.I. Chambers suggest that, contrary to prevalent belief, 'bungalows originated in California and not in India'.

There are other odd clues: the promotion of the California bungalow in the *Building News* in 1912 (p. 145 above); pictures of the American bungalow in later editions of Phillips' *Book of Bungalows* (1926), copies of Fred T. Hodgson's *Practical Bungalows and Cottages* (1916) and Charles E. White's *The Bungalow Book* (1923) in the British Museum. More curious, a 1920 edition of H.H. Saylor's influential *Bungalows*, published in New York, was discovered in 1980 in a second-hand bookshop near a centre of 1930s bungalow development at Uxbridge. The most substantial evidence is from Peacehaven, begun in 1915 by a Canadian developer. This will be examined below. More important perhaps than the proven connections is the fact that, in both these technologically developed, free-market societies, one perhaps a decade or so ahead of the other, similar influences were at work. It was part of what later was increasingly referred to as 'the Americanisation' of English life (Hebdige, 1981).

Bungalow types

The bungalow boom began straight after the war and continued throughout the 1920s and 1930s. Essentially a private enterprise phenomenon, it apparently peaked towards the end of the 1920s. On both sides of the Atlantic, bungalow consciousness was at its height, figuring in popular fiction with Carolyn Keene's, *The Bungalow Mystery*, C.F. Oursler's *The Bungalow on the Roof* and Taffrail's *The Lonely Bungalow*, all appearing in 1930-1.

In Britain, the bungalow was basically a non-urban, suburban or country dwelling ideal for permanent housing and for temporary weekend or holiday use. Three common categories might be identified, distinguished roughly according to size, location, materials and form.

Most prevalent was the small, often square, brick or brick and concrete rendered 'builder's vernacular', with slate, clay or asbestos tiled roof. If slate, the lines of the hipped roof were typically marked by ridge tiles in contrasting red or cream. This might be found in outer suburbs, singly or in groups, along arterial or country roads, on isolated country sites or flanking early-twentieth-century suburbs of popular seaside towns. Low, often with round-headed porch and garden to front, back and sides, this often filled up the roadside plot which developers had left behind. A sprinkling, or maybe just one, announced the entrance, and exit, to country villages and towns (plates 101, 102).

Less common was the more lavish 'architect's bungalow' (plate 104). Larger, 'individually designed', more expensive to build, this was noticeable because of its site: in the country, on rising ground, with more extensive, often landscaped garden. Alternatively, it was in the 'better' suburb or wealthier seaside resort where the lack of height was compensated by a larger, more privatised plot.

For use, though less frequently, as a permanent home was the semi- or fully prefabricated form. This might be brick-based and make greater or lesser use of timber cladding, concrete panels or asbestos sheets. Roofs were of asbestos tiles (in green, red or grey), diagonally laid, or sheeting of 'ruberoid' finish, felting or corrugated iron. In this class, a wide variety

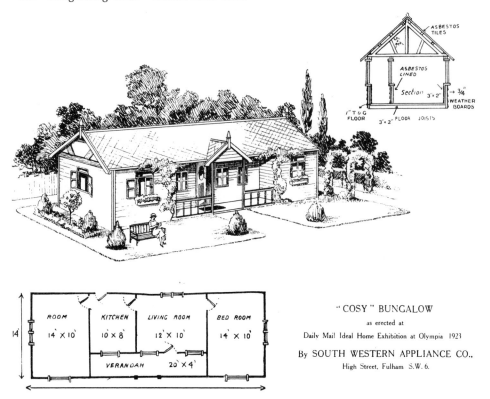

Figure 5.1 Bungalow prefabrication, 1923 (*Daily Mail Bungalow Book*, 1923)

appeared depending on the economic status of the owner, availability of materials and degree of local authority control. Found on the edge of seaside or rural towns, on semi-marginal land or isolated country tracks, this class included the converted railway carriage, country bus and self-built weekend hut (plate 103).

Throughout the period, myriad reasons favoured the proliferation of all three types: social and economic change, prevailing beliefs and ideas, the structure of the building industry, developments in materials, new modes of transport and the availability of sites. It was these and other factors which, in rapidly encouraging its growth, forced the image of the bungalow to the forefront of a hostile, upper middle class mind.

Ideological appeal

In a society committed to a belief in private property, the bungalow, irrespective of size, had an obvious threefold appeal. Possession of even the smallest often provided the cheapest entry into the property-owning class. Moreover, as a symbol of private property, the detached and territorially separate bungalow – the irreducible minimum of a house within its own grounds – was patently second to none. And for the middle class who could afford it, the 'bungalow in the country' provided the perfect opportunity to emulate the style of a country-house-owning elite.

At a time of unprecedented increase in home-ownership, this appeal was never very far away. Thus, the author of *An Ideal Bungalow* (1927) wrote, 'it is good to feel the land is your own and that you can hand it down to your descendants with all that has been built on it'. Keeley's *Bungalows and Modern Homes* (1928) begins with a quotation from Cowley: 'I never had any other desire so strong, and so like covetousness . . . that I might be master at least of a small house.' The shift to private ownership was a major trend of the time. Before the war, some 80 per cent of all households had lived in rented housing: owner-occupiers, at only 10 per cent of the whole, were few and far between. Local authority tenants, perhaps 1 per cent of all, were concentrated in large cities, London, Liverpool and the north. The years during and after the First World War saw the rapid demise of privately rented housing with rent control, high building costs, alternative forms of investment and the rapid growth of building societies deterring the private landlord. With the provision of council housing on a large scale from 1919 the tenure situation changed drastically: twenty years later, over 30 per cent of all households were owner-occupiers and 14 per cent were council tenants. The polarisation between forms of tenure had begun (Burnett, 1978; Glynn and Oxborrow, 1976).

The bungalow extended the pride of ownership to thousands who had not had it before. At Christmas 1926, for example, May Figgis of Brighton sent her greetings to Mrs Maslem of 'Chalfont', Frand Avenue, Bournemouth, with a photograph postcard of her pebble-dashed asbestos-tiled bungalow, 'Killiney' in Chatsworth Road, writing on the back, 'This is a photo of my little place – to bring you all good wishes of the season.' (plate 105). Another proud new owner in the crescent of Kingsdown Park (which could be anywhere) marked the picture postcard with a cross and wrote: 'ours is the sixth bungalow from the front of the picture. I can see the name 'Clarendon' under the magnifying glass and I have counted them up from there.' (plate 106).

The belief in private property was backed by another ideological appeal, an almost universal commitment, among governments, the public, developers and the majority of architects and planners, to the ideas of the 'garden city': low-density, open development with twelve or fewer houses to the acre, each surrounded by garden, trees and grass. The garden-city movement, a cause as much for social as environmental reform, had emerged at the turn of the century. Bourgeois in composition, it combined an upper class preference for country living with prevailing social concern about the depopulation of agricultural land. Expectations of increasing land-values in garden cities were combined with social assumptions about the community benefits supposedly gained by detached, cottage-type houses arranged in the semi-rural, village type of setting.

Expounded by contemporary architects and the newly founded town planning profession, the Garden City idea provided a model for emulation. 'You have often cherished the desire to live in the open unspoiled country rather than amid the dull monotony of London's suburban streets' advertised one builder on the cover of R. Rawling's *Houses and How to Buy One* (1925, price sixpence). Essentially an ideology, garden-city ideas were promoted as a science of town planning, their basic assumptions adopted in official housing and planning legislation (Cherry, 1974).

When town extension schemes were adopted under planning laws, the continuous street or terrace, characteristic of eighteen- and nineteenth-century urban development, was outlawed: 'not more than four dwellings shall in any place be built under one continuous roof' (Sharp, 1932:144). With little dissent, the combined, 'town-country' idea, characteristically expressed in the reproduction, en masse, of the detached house or 'semi-' situated within its own grounds, was to become an experience shared by representatives of all social groups:

demonstrated by the aristocracy at the top; aspired to, and often achieved, by the middle class in between; and imposed, in the new council estates, on the working class at the bottom (Swenarton, 1981). The bungalow was very much part of the trend.

Economic factors: state subsidies[1]

The large-scale provision of council housing began effectively in 1919. The Housing Act of that year offered substantial subsidies to local authorities, requiring them to provide housing for working people at rents which they could afford. Yet with labour scarce and building costs high, private-enterprise housing was slow to get under way. As a stimulus, the Housing (Additional Powers) Act was passed later that year. At a time when houses were being built in Essex and Cambridgeshire for £500-£600, if somewhat more expensive elsewhere, this provided a lump sum subsidy of between £130 and £160 to 'anybody who builds a house in a satisfactory manner', according to a specified size, before the end of 1920. Within a year, this had been raised to £230-260, the dwelling to be finished by the end of 1921.

By July of that year, between 25,000 and 30,000 private subsidy houses had gone up. To the annoyance of some MPs, however, many of these hardly conformed to Parliament's intentions. 'Weekend bungalows, chauffeur's cottages and gamekeepers' houses were surely not meant to be paid for by subsidies from the taxpayer,' complained a leading member of the Commons. Only about one-third of the subsidy houses had been occupied by what he called the working class. 'Many were really houses of the middle class type built by people themselves.' Many, indeed, were probably middle class bungalows, both large and small.

'The extraordinary interest which is being taken in bungalows', began R.R. Phillips's *Book of Bungalows* (1920), 'gives the occasion for this book.' Addressed to 'the needs of one class – that middle class upon whose shoulders every new burden is thrust', it ran into two further editions (1922, 1926) whilst other government subsidies were in force. 'In the matter of housing', said Phillips, 'the middle class have to shift for themselves and many are turning to the bungalow as a solution to their difficulties', a statement somewhat belied by giving the conditions of the government grant. 'With the aid of a government subsidy . . . many people contemplate building a bungalow for themselves.'

The grants were generous, with between £230 and £260 available for bungalows and houses of not less than 700 or (for £260) 920 superficial feet, depending on the number of rooms. The largest bungalow qualifying for a grant might have a floor area of 1,400 feet overall, and have four bedrooms, one of which Phillips thought would do for a maid. Reduced by one-third, the subsidy was also available for timber bungalows and converted ex-army huts. For this, both Phillips and Gordon Allen (*The Cheap Cottage and Small House*, 1919) provided plans showing how the standard hut (60 by 15) could be 'economically converted into a comfortable bungalow'. Boulton and Paul were typical of a number of firms commissioned by the Ministry of Health to erect prefabricated housing in timber, concrete and asbestos sheeting to meet the shortage. Their standard wooden bungalow (46 by 19) contained four bedrooms, living room, bathroom, kitchen and other offices, with asbestos slate roof and asbestos cement interior lining. Without the cost of land it could be erected by the owner for about £460 or by the firm for another £115.

Whilst the subsidy no doubt stimulated bungalow growth, the government's main policy was to provide local authority estates. With the Conservative government and Housing Act of 1923, this was completely reversed. Less generous than the Act of 1919, the new measure provided a subsidy to private builders and local authorities of £6 per house for twenty years; alternatively, on completion, the cash would be paid as a grant of £70-£100 to the builder.

But local authorities might build only if they convinced the Minister that they could make better provision than private enterprise (Burnett, 1978:277-9).

Conservative aims were to stimulate the private sector until it could eventually provide housing unaided by the state. It is clear from the Parliamentary records that, by reducing the size of houses qualifying for the grant (now lowered to a superficial area of 620 square feet) and by specifically referring to one-storey dwellings in the Act, the aim was to house the maximum number of families in small, separate dwellings. Larger houses took more labour and capital to build. And though single-storey dwellings had to be between 550 and 880 superficial feet, in certain circumstances the minimum area could be reduced to 500. The stage was set for a further small-bungalow boom. Despite warnings that, as before, loopholes would be found to subsidise 'seaside cottages' and 'country bungalows' for use as 'a secondary house', the Act went on to the books.

The first Labour government came to power the following year. Housing policy was again turned on its head. The Act of 1924 restored to local authorities their earlier working class housing role, yet the government continued to give private grants. As the third (1926) edition of Phillips's *Book of Bungalows* pointed out, 'assistance is given also in respect of private ownership and bungalows come within the scope of the grant.' In order to qualify, the applicant had to satisfy the local authority that it was needed, yet, as there was no set method by which this was done, 'it is primarily a matter for the applicant's conscience . . . and the local authority's consideration'.

Seizing the opportunity, the Concrete Association republished (1924) six thousand copies of their earlier (1918) *Concrete Cottages and Bungalows*. For the more popular market, however, there were other manuals such as *The Builder*'s book of *Bungalow Designs* (1923), W.I. Chambers, *Bungalows* (1924), or 'Economist's' one shilling special, *An Ideal Bungalow. How to Build it well and at lowest cost and pay for it in a few years as rent (Eligible for the Government Subsidy)* of 1927.

Combined with reduced building costs, the subsidies were to have telling effect. Between 1920 and 1922, some 80,000 houses a year had been built, the majority by local authorities. Between 1924 and 1927, the number rose from 146,000 to an unprecedented 258,000, most of them privately built. And when the private subsidy was stopped in 1929, some 90 per cent of all houses finished in the previous five years had been subsidised by government (Richardson and Aldcroft, 1968:56).

Just how many of these, whether subsidised or not, were bungalows seems impossible to say. Yet the grant was obviously worth proportionately more for a cheaper than a more expensive house. It might be noted in passing that of some thirty books (including new editions) on bungalows ever published in Britain before 1939, at least twenty appeared between 1918 and 1932. The evidence lies elsewhere: the elitist attack on the bungalow began in 1926, the term 'bungaloid' coined the following year. The real proof, however, is on the ground; to misquote the memorial to Sir Christopher Wren, 'Si bungalum requiris, circumspice'.

Economic factors: land, materials and labour
Apart from subsidies, there were other economic factors favouring bungalow growth. With the effective area for development opened up by bus, train and car, outer suburbs provided cheaper land. In London, the better sites, closer to transport terminals, commanded a higher price, and merited larger detached houses or at least a 'semi-'. Yet further out, on cheaper, less desirable land, the bungalow provided semi-rural advantages at considerably lower cost. In

the far-flung suburbs of London, served by electric train (Upminster, Hornchurch, Rainham, Uxbridge or Hayes), bungalows were thick on the ground. Given the annual cost of a season ticket 'the further out one lives, the cheaper should be the house' (plate 110).

Another opportunity presented itself with the extensive programmes of road-building. In London, the Ministry of Transport plans for 1920-4 involved an outlay of over £4 million on a network of some 200 miles. By 1926, many arterial roads and by-passes were completed or under way (Jackson, 1973: 112-14). Here, following commercial logic, builders bought land fronting the road, building bungalows and houses and saving considerable costs on service roads, sewers, electricity or water pipes. Other cheap sites became available because of developments in the bungalow itself. Light, prefabricated materials were readily carried to marginal land. Wooded hills were especially attractive and hillsides, as a leading town planner pointed out in 1926, previously too steep for horse and cart to labour up, were now within reach of a truck carrying prefabricated materials (Abercrombie, 1926:11). Elsewhere, as by the upper reaches of the Thames, land too unstable for permanent building was just right for the weekend bungalow.

Freed by motor bike or car from the major transport routes, the bungalow, unlike more substantial housing estates, was not confined to areas with services already installed. New technologies now made these dispensable. 'There is no need to hesitate about buying or building your ideal bungalow "far from the madding crowd" on the score of "no lights" or having electricity expensively laid from the town', announced the promoters of Carbic gas. Gas could be generated in a lean-to shed and light produced by acetylene lamp. Alternatively, mini generating sets 'suitable for the smallest bungalow or the largest country house' were on sale in 1922. Water could be piped from the nearest farm or well and the Elsan Closet and cesspool coped with sanitary needs (*Daily Mail Bungalow Book*, 1922).

The prefabricated bungalow was part of a quiet revolution in materials and construction which had started before the First World War. Post-war shortages of skilled labour and its continuing high price were important factors encouraging the use of substitutes for traditional materials and methods. Now, with improvements in road transport, prefabricated materials became much easier to move. The *Daily Mail Bungalow Book* of 1922 included a host of advertisements for new materials which cut down on labour-intensive skills, especially brick-laying, roofing, plastering and joinery.

Asbestos cement tiles, available from about 1910, were a popular innovation. Reducing roofing costs by 40 per cent, they were light (one-sixth the weight of ordinary slates, one-third of roofing tiles) and relatively large. They thus reduced the costs of labour to lay them as well as the roofing structure below. Asbestos sheeting, wood and fibreboard, jointless flooring, 'machine-reduced standard stone' (for facing walls), cavity bricks, were all available to simplify, cheapen and above all, release the bungalow from dependence on skilled labour, specialised plant and access to major transport routes. They also gave scope for personal taste. 'A dining room, furnished in Jacobean style receives the completing touch when panelled in "Sundeala" wallboard with oak-stained wooden strips covering the joints.'

Bungalow construction was also appropriate to the talents of the typical small firm. In the inter-war years, this was short on skills and had little or no heavy plant. In 1930 over 80 per cent of all building firms employed less than ten men and half of all building labour was unskilled (Richardson and Aldcroft, 1968:335). For the small-time firm, the bungalow had a triple attraction. It was subsidised: it cost little to build and whilst a pair of 'semis' required two buyers for the builder to recoup the costs, the bungalow needed only one. Simple to construct, it required little more than a barrow and ladder, in terms of specialised plant. At a

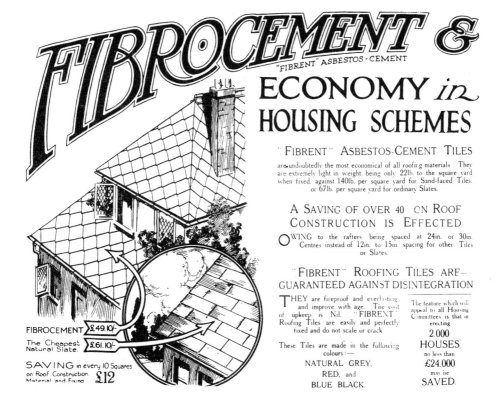

Figure 5.2 Innovatory materials: asbestos cement.
Introduced in the early years of the century, the impact of new materials occurred mainly with the development of motor transport in the 1920's (*Daily Mail Bungalow Book*, 1923)

push, they could be tackled by a handyman and his family, as contemporary records suggest.

It was this small size, enabling the owner to exercise total control over his property which helped to give the bungalow such an appeal. In this respect, it had considerable advantages over the ubiquitous semi-detached. The bungalow owner controlled the site, the full height of *all* four walls and even, the whole of the roof. All were literally within reach. The marks of ownership, the identity of possession, could thus be made complete.

Social factors
A variety of demographic and other social developments were also promoting the growing popularity of the bungalow. In the fifty years after 1871, average family size had been falling steadily; the birthrate, 35.5 per thousand in 1871 and 25.4 in 1911, had fallen to reduce the average number of children per family from 3.5 to 2.2. Yet if class differences are taken into

account, it was in the non-manual, middle and lower middle families where the pattern of one or two children increasingly became the norm (Halsey, 1972). For whatever social or psychological reasons, birthrates plunged in the years after the war, from about 23 per thousand in 1921 to an all-time low of 14.4 in 1933. The greatest percentage fall (from 17.89 to 16.7) occurred between 1926-7 when the bungalow boom seems to have been at its height. There seems good reason, therefore, for the Dean of St Paul's to link the increasing lack of babies to a preference for bungalows and cars (see below). Yet marriage was more popular than ever. In 1901, only about 35 per cent of the population had been married. By 1931, this had risen to some 43 per cent and in the next twenty years, the proportion was to exceed 50 per cent (Burnett, 1978:257). As Henry Hall and the BBC Dance Orchestra recorded in 1933 (with a marginally ambiguous symbolism), the bungalow was the ideal for many about to get wed:

> Underneath your window
> Every night I stand
> Pleading for your wonderful caress
> Listen at your window
> And you'll understand
> What it takes to bring me happiness
>
> Three little things are all I desire, dear
> A bungalow, a piccolo and you
> Three little things set my heart on fire, dear
> A bungalow, a piccolo and you

The numbers of elderly were also increasing with the population of over-60s growing from about $1\frac{3}{4}$ million to $3\frac{1}{4}$ million between 1901 and 1921. All over the country, but especially in the seaside towns of north Wales, the east coast and especially in the south, for those who could afford it, the bungalow became the place to spin out the last years.

In terms of housing aspirations, it was a dwelling with a broad-based social appeal. It allowed the working class to 'move up' and the middle, to 'move down', both social strata combining as patrons of the new form. For the better off middle class, hit by increased taxes and poorer since the end of the war, the bungalow's advantages were regularly spelled out. It was not 'over-costly to build . . . was less expensive to furnish' and, with all rooms just on one floor, it was 'the easiest house to run'. In the over-worked phrase of the time, it was a 'labour-saving' home.

According to *The Ideal Bungalow* (1927), many people had learnt to appreciate this aspect by living in war-time army huts, a viewpoint confirmed by correspondents to the *Daily Mail*. Moreover, as suggested above, many such huts had filled the housing gap in the years just after the war. Yet by 1922, a volume of correspondence to the *Daily Mail* was suggesting that the army hut and corrugated iron and wood building had had their day. 'A big public demand was growing for the bungalow of the better type' and there was a need for designs to meet it.

For the impoverished post-war middle class, domestic service had become increasingly dear and difficult to find. The growth of shop, light factory and clerical work had provided alternative jobs for younger women. And in a more democratic atmosphere after the war, they were not only more expensive, but were less willing to be exploited. Not without cause did the

THE BUNGALOW KITCHENETTE

The bungalow bedroom

COMPACT ARRANGEMENT OF THE LIMITED
SPACE IN A BUNGALOW DINING-ROOM

The extending bungalow for week-end parties

Figure 5.3   Reduced circumstances: the compact bungalow, 1936.
(W.Heath Robinson, 'Bungaloid' in *How to Live in a Flat*, 1936, Gerald Duckworth & Co
Ltd 1936, 1976 Estate of W.Heath Robinson)

author of the popular *Book of Bungalows* (1920) also produce three editions of *The Servantless House*.

Social attitudes were modified to accommodate these changes. 'One does not lose caste these days by moving into a smaller house,' wrote Gordon Allen in *The Small House and Cottage* (1919). Old urban and suburban houses had become obsolete: they were too large, lacked newly available technology, were costly to maintain and often in the wrong place. Now, with the help of bus, train or car, dwellings could be twenty miles away from one's work (Allen, 1919:12). By contrast, the bungalow was small, compact and had no stairs. Not only did it reduce areas to be cleaned; without the presence of servants, the need for social space separating employer from employed also disappeared.

Figure 5.4   The political economy of the bungalow kitchen, 1924.
The industrialisation and commercialisation of food production drained many functions from the kitchen, considerably reducing its size. In the same year as the bungalow appeared in the West (1869), H.J.Heinz and the Campbell Soup Company started their industrialised food operations, and household manuals in the USA noticed the increasing number of factory bakeries. In the early decades of this century, the larder was to be gradually replaced by the kitchen cabinet, the 'Hoosier' having appeared in 1903 in the USA.

Also in 1869, a speaker at the annual meeting of the British Medical Association had referred to 'beastly contrivances' for limiting births, contrivances increasingly adopted by 1924, the date of this illustration, when Mummy (not, of course, Gladys) is preparing the sixth birthday of what is probably her only child. As the Dean of St Paul's hinted about the same time, the bungalow was to be a house type increasingly associated with consumption. (see page 179) (Trager, 1980; W.I. Chambers, *Bungalows*, 1924)

As Americans had discovered twenty years earlier, the major labour-saving area was the kitchen. Here, a range of new equipment was introduced, much of it via the USA. High, cavernous wall-cupboards of old were replaced by the 'Easiwork' or 'Hoosier' kitchen cabinet. The latter, obtainable from the Bungalow Department, Ideal Furniture Stores, Liverpool, with its 'forty work-reducing features . . . saved miles of steps . . . providing places for 400 articles within arms length, saving the journey from larder to cupboard, or cupboard to the sink'. The 'Bungalow Stove' boasted over-hanging plate racks where just-washed dishes dried and warmed for later use. Dirt-producing coal ranges were replaced by gas or electric stove. Electricity 'gave an absence of dirt' and was 'immensely labour-saving both in cleaning time and the laying of fires'. Serving hatches and the 'service trolley' dispensed with the need for servants to carry things about and vacuum cleaners were easily pushed around one floor. Where a maid was kept, in a dwelling now with far fewer rooms than before, each room had to perform multiple functions. Here, new technology helped out. The 'Servall' grate 'cooks, roasts, boils and heats 30 gallons of water' then, after various folding operations, 'as an open fire, transforms your kitchen into a cosy sitting room' (Chambers, 1924).

'Simplicity' was the recurrent theme. 'Let it be remembered that if the bungalow stands for anything, it stands for an unaffected sort of life.' Pretentious furniture should be avoided, as should 'essays in a Jacobean or Georgian manner' appropriate to a country house. Walls should be of plain paper or coloured distemper and stains for floorboards were 'simple, hygienic and artistic and also economical'.

Nothing more clearly conveys the continued validity of Briggs's maxim that 'a cottage is a little house in the country' but 'a bungalow is a little country house' than the illustrations in the middle class bungalow books of the time. Each stands complete, a miniaturised version of the country seat, with no other buildings in sight. In plan descriptions, the key words are simple, neat, convenient and compact; yet also roomy, ample, quiet, dignified, old-world and picturesque.

Private ownership and simplicity were important attractions of the bungalow style of life. A third was explained by prevailing ideas of health: a belief in sunshine, fresh air and the merits of open-air life. This meant not only a country or a seaside setting but a site, if possible, on gently rising ground. Activities previously pursued indoors were now, weather permitting, taking place outside: eating, sleeping and everyday social life. The changes, with their implications for design, were similar to what had earlier occurred in the USA.

For eating and relaxation, the verandah was important. If this was well-sheltered, meals might be taken out of doors in all kinds of weather. Verandahs were usually at the semi-private area at the front; for outdoor sleeping, a more private 'Sleep out' was provided round the back (Keeley, 1927). A 'Sun parlour' was attractive and as the bungalow 'leads one to live an outdoor life' chairs should serve equally well in and out of doors. Casement windows were preferable to sashes as, being thrown open, they gave an 'abundance of air'. With no servants available, breakfast might have to be in the kitchen, in which case 'a large east window should admit the morning sun'. The horizontal, wide window allowing more sunshine than the narrow vertical sash was gradually introduced. The obsession with sunshine was no doubt also responsible, if subconsciously, for the symbolic rising sun which decorated the gates, gable ends and garage tympani of thousands of bungalows in the 1930s.

Such bungalows were for the better-off middle class, the managers and senior executives earning £500 to £600 a year. Though the cheaper of Phillips's examples cost £550 to build, the majority of these architects' designs were in the £1000-£1500 range, with more over the higher than the lower end of the limits (Jackson, 1973; Keeley, 1928).

For the larger market, a more modest version was around. This was the 'spec-built' builder's vernacular which expanded on all available sites. Untroubled by architect's worries, this was often the cheapest form of house. For £25 down and between nine and twelve shillings per week, the bungalow appealed to a previously property-less class: senior clerks, supervisors, lower grade civil servants, young teachers and skilled workers if they were earning more than £3 10s a week. In distant London suburbs (Hillingdon, Greenford or Uxbridge), in the middle 1920s bungalows were selling for £450 to £475, compared to £685 to over £1000 for a detached or semi-detached house. In the early 1930s, entire bungalow estates went up at Upminster, Hornchurch and Hayes. Better class two- and three-bedroomed bungalows were on sale at £550 in the far commuter zones of Watford, Harrow or Orpington in 1938. In 1930, the *Evening News* was offering five hundred 'Bungo-palaces' at Sidcup, in Kent. Outside London, especially for bungalow 'semis', prices were much cheaper. For £395, one could have a bungalow in 'sunny Worthing' or elsewhere on the south coast, and in some Midland towns the price was as low as £250.

For those willing to build themselves, there were plans and instructions around, such as 'Economist's' *An Ideal Bungalow*. In these, the same criteria applied by the rural aristocracy were, if possible, to determine the choice of the site. This should have 'open country', be 'well wooded and have pleasant scenery around'. If, in the suburbs, this was somewhat unrealistic, 'have a site with an open space or at least a gap in the houses on the opposite side of the road'. To establish territorial rights, 'do what is necessary to enclose your property – a low fence in front of neat paling or feather-edged boards'.

The sense of ownership was enhanced by visibility, from within and without. For health, aesthetic and social reasons, the site should be 'a little higher than the surrounding country and one that rises slightly from front to back'. External appearance was governed by both tradition and economy. Granite chippings or pebbles could be thrown on the cement rendering and the whole painted cream, the spaces between 'black and white work' finished in white cement paint. With a government subsidy, 'the capital cost was almost none'. Building societies would advance 75 to 80 per cent of the total cost of £500; alternatively, money could be borrowed from a life assurance company or the district council.

With motor traffic now flooding the countryside, new entrepreneurial opportunities opened up. Set back from the road, the bungalow, fronted by different distributors' pumps, was ideally suited for a service station or for the ambitious couple supplying thirsty travellers with teas. For motorists, wheeling along at a slightly greater height than today, the triangular expanse of grey or blue-slated roof was exactly right to notify, in large white letters, the presence of PETROL, TEAS or CAFE. For the smallholder, encouraged back to the land with promises made in the war, and given even more generous subsidies in the Housing Act of 1924, the slightly set-back bungalow gave room to advertise eggs, tomatoes or bags of fresh manure. Behind, the poultry sheds, greenhouses or garage could expand almost infinitely.

Encouraged by rapid improvements in transport, many firms were producing fully prefabricated bungalows for more rural areas, whether for permanent or weekend use. In the late 1920s, the South West Appliance Co and Hurlingham Bungalow Company, both of Fulham, advertised in the popular press, weatherboarded, asbestos-tiled models, 33 by 22, with five rooms at between £110 and £155. Where the purchaser built it himself, the cost of foundations, carriage and construction hardly exceeded £250.

Bungalows by the sea

The most prolific area for expansion was the seaside, both hinterland and coast. By the mid

1930s, there were four main areas for permanent and vacation bungalows, each within 50 to 70 miles of major centres of population: the Sussex and Hampshire coast, North Wales (between Llandudno and Prestatyn) and the coastal strips of Lancashire and Yorkshire. Shorter working hours, the growth of holidays with pay, better rail and road provision and, in 1931-35, an almost 40 per cent increase in motor vehicles, were seen as some of the principal reasons.

Between the wars, a double migration was taking place. On the one hand, industrial restructuring moved people from the declining north and Wales to London and the home counties; the latter gained some 1^34 million people overall (Richardson and Aldcroft, 1968:87). Yet at the same time there was a shift within the south-east region itself, with a drift towards the coast. With immense transport improvements to the south-coast resorts, functions only nascent before the war now rapidly grew in size: to their role of pleasure ground, they added that of retirement resort, suburb for London commuters, and destination for thousands of day excursionists. All favoured building development, not least, of bungalow estates.

A major factor in this development resulted from the growing numbers of the old. In the forty years before 1901, the proportion of over-60s in England and Wales had remained steady at just over 6 per cent. With falling birthrates, improved medicine and higher standards of living, this had doubled by the later 1930s to reach almost 14 per cent in 1951. In the early twentieth century the average expectation of life had been about 55 years; by 1951 it was rising to 70 (Halsey, 1972). Where, for those rich enough to choose, could they spend the final fifteen years of their lives?

In the later nineteenth century, the wealthy had retired to inland spas like Bath, Cheltenham and Tunbridge Wells, though by the early 1900s they were increasingly moving to the coast. In 1921, the population of Worthing, Hove and Hastings contained twice as many over-60s (over 14 per cent) as the population of England and Wales as a whole (7.8 per cent). In the following ten years, these and other towns on the Sussex coast (Bexhill, Eastbourne and Bognor) took over the role of 'retirement resort' from the older inland spas.

The people who retired to the drier, sunnier climate of the coast were both healthier and wealthier than those they left behind in the towns. Compulsory retirement at 65 became common from the 1920s and occupational pensions were increasingly introduced to supplement those that had been started by the state. The seaside bungalow was to meet a ready market and a growing specialised want. Sampling a proportion of retired people by the sea in the early 1970s, one researcher found over 40 per cent at Bexhill and even 70 per cent of those at Clacton were living in bungalows built since the 1920s (Karn, 1977). The ageing and commuters helped to swell the growth of Sussex resorts during these years.

Of these cases of 'bungaloid growth', none was more famous than Peacehaven. The site of Peacehaven, lying at the foot of the Downs between Newhaven and Rottingdean, had been bought by a Canadian developer, Charles Neville, in 1915. The development provides most evidence for the influence of North American real-estate practices – and the role of the bungalow in them – on inter-war British urban development. The atmosphere of 'a mid-Western prairie town', conveyed by the sprawling rectangular layout and haphazardous development, which one observer detected in 1975 was more than a coincidence (Dickens, 1975). Like other Australian and Californian developments, there were common elements.

Neville was a Canadian, with land interests in Saskatchewan where, in 1913, with the North American bungalow boom getting under way, he had developed estates known as Belgravia, Coronation and the Garden Suburb of Mayfair. One of a number of entrepreneurs

THIS SEA-SIDE BUNGALOW, VALUE £300, TO BE GIVEN AWAY.

ALSO 20 PLOTS OF FREEHOLD LAND GIVEN AWAY.

PARTICULARS WRITE Minster Development Corpn., 68, Cheapside, E.C.

No. 9147   KEEP THIS CARD AND TAKE IT TO MINST
IT MAY BRING YOU A VALUABLE PRIZE.

ONE PLOT GIVEN AWAY BY BALLOT. ON EACH OCCASION.

THE NEAREST OCEAN FRONTAGE.

The most picturesque part of the Isle of Sheppey, Kent. A locality with a very promising future. Abounding with interesting historical associations. Near Sheerness, the base of the Home Fleet.

Magnificent views, extending over North Sea, the Thames, Medway and Swale Rivers and thirty miles of Kentish Hills. Particularly bracing air. Cliffs 200 feet high. Good beach and stretches of sand.

Its many charms and its geographical position ensure its success.

That's why Freehold Land there must prove a good investment, and is well worth the consideration of all investors—especially as plots in really fine positions near the sea can be secured now at most moderate prices and on easy terms if desired.

SPECIAL EXCURSIONS FOR PROSPECTIVE PURCHASERS—LIMITED NUMBER ONLY.
EVERY MONDAY   2/6   EVERY THURSDAY
BY STEAMBOAT.   BY EXPRESS TRAIN.
RETURN FARE.

For Sea Sun Sand and Scenery see Kinmel Bay

The Sunniest Site in Great Britain

Free Gift of a £1000 Seaside Home

AT KINMEL BAY
A RISING SEASIDE RESORT ON THE WELSH RIVIERA

Kinmel Bay a Project of Immense Size and Possibilities

How to Make Money from the Land, the Safest of all Investments

Figure 5.5   Capital investment: 'how to make money from land, the safest of all investments', 1910-20s. The most well-known use of the give-away bungalow as a device to sell land was at Peacehaven, Sussex; other postcards suggest that the seeds of an 'informal economy' were present in the plotlands settlements of Shell Beach, Canvey Island and the Isle of Sheppey, Kent, well before 1914.

operating along the south coast at this time, he bought 415 acres of Sussex coastline in 1915 at £15 an acre. The following year, he held a national competition for the name of the resort which he was proposing to develop, with £20,000 as the first prize and fifty freehold building plots for other prizes. Instead of fifty, some two and a half thousand 'prize' plots were given away, with each of their recipients required to pay three guineas for the conveyance entitling them to the site. As a result of these and other dubious practices, Neville made profits of £30 an acre, £12,000 overall (ibid.).

Despite Establishment protests, an area of 3,000 acres was laid out, in the words of Peacehaven Estates Limited, as 'a Garden City'. In 1921, the first bungalow was built, according to Neville, the first anywhere in England after the war – a doubtful claim, though one perhaps suggesting that Neville believed he was introducing the bungalow from America. Indeed, a few of his designs, with pylon pillars and pergola, were evidently inspired by California, even though the majority were in the emerging British vernacular tradition (plate 82). The dwellings were in fact 'mostly of the bungalow type, neat, pretty and clean', a type equally suitable for the bank, butcher's, golf house and shops. According to Neville's own newspaper, *The Peacehaven Gazette*, the incentive to purchase was 'to own a little bit of England'. The newly established cement works, converted from an aerodrome hangar, provided ready-made building blocks which went well with the asbestos-tiled roofs.

Amongst the 'rush of settlers' were those who had 'retired from business and wanted a healthy home by the seashore', Londoners, 'professional men wanting a place where their families can stay in the bad months and whom they can join at the weekend'. Other 'shrewd friends' had purchased plots to sell at a profit within a few months. Plots were priced according to location: 'all the cheaper class of bungalows were congregated together, superior structures are on the better class land.' A speciality was the two-bedroomed bungalow with verandah and cellar, complete on a 25 by 100 plot for £500, though others could be had for £350. Between 1922 and 1929, the population grew from 25 to over 4,000. By then, Peacehaven was appealing not only to the retired and weekender but to commuters, contrasting the clean, quiet and relaxed life of the town with the strain, stress and noise of London streets. For amusement, there was the Lureland Dance Hall, the hotel ('a Mecca for Motorists'), golf course, three churches and a cinema. The major attraction, however, was domestic:

> When the golden sun sinks in the West
> In its glow I can see from afar
> My bungalow sweet
> In its rural retreat
> Like a bright and insidious star
>
> As the shadows of eve gently fall
> And the toilers turn homeward to rest
> Sure the thoughts of my heart
> Take the flight of a dart
> To that gay little Peacehaven Nest
>
> Its the place for a kind loving wife
> And for children a haven of bliss

> And the rich fertile ground
> Makes all products abound
> Never Eden of Dreams was like this

After 1925, a 'gift house' worth £1,200 was offered each year in a national lottery to boost sales. The lucky winners in the first two draws were a south London music teacher and a South African businessman (Peacehaven Estates, c. 1927).

Neville had an obvious gift for publicity, with his promotional concert parties – with Flora Robson – and booklets and postcards which circulated throughout the country. In 1936, he unveiled a clifftop memorial to King George V which lies on the Greenwich meridian: one side of this records the event; on the other are listed the distances to various parts of the empire, a fitting and prescient acknowledgment of the emerging significance of the bungalow which he did so much to promote.

Bungalow development was also related to the introduction of the inner-city, multi-storey flat. Among business people, 'The evolution of the town flat is a real indication of the coming demand for bungalows' for the weekends. L.H. James wrote in the preface to *The Modern Bungalow* (1935). For those wealthy enough to own both, each type of residence had, for W. Heath Robinson, its distinctive social function: the flat, 'for entertaining people through whom they hope to obtain introductions to members of the Peerage' and the bungalow, 'for weekend relaxation' (*How to Live in a Flat*, 1936). Others explained the growing phenomenon of dual residence by reference to social and economic changes. The small service flat had been made possible 'by the dissolution of the old, binding family loyalty which kept the middle class in acrimonious association until marriage or death parted its members'. The growth in women's employment meant that 'the business girl prefers to share a flat with some other girl' rather than face a boarding house or 'the horrors of a hostel'. Increasing affluence and the pressures of industrial capitalism were seen as encouraging young married couples to live in a service flat, run a car, patronise the cinema and 'streak along the great traffic roads, down to the sea and back, in a haze of fuel fumes' to visit 'their week-end bungalow by the sea or country cottage'. For the 'active children of the Commercial Machine Age', 'movement occupies their leisure' (Gloag, 1938:196).

Weekend retreat

In the more relaxed years after the war, the open-air life became increasingly popular, with the cult of hiking, camping and youth hostels (founded in 1930), partly influenced by the *wanderbewegung* from Germany. Habits established at the turn of the century now had a wider social appeal. According to S.D. Adshead, Professor of Planning at London University,

> Young married people of the middle class flock to bungalow towns. There they can live a sort of aboriginal existence for a time. There is always a great attraction in a primitive existence, and it is here that the bungalow craze comes in. The demand is increasing very rapidly. The whole of the hill-side behind Douglas, in the Isle of Man, is now utilised as a summer encampment, where thousands of tents are erected, and fortunes have been made in running this primitive town. In other places there are very large developments in bungalow buildings – for instance, at Shoreham. The enormous demand for tents and bungalows is far ahead of the supply, and a bungalow city, where a sort of 'Swiss Family Robinson' existence can be lived for a few weeks in the year, is a demand . . . which town planners must direct their attention to very seriously (1923).

In the course of some forty years, the notion of 'countryside' as a 'vast park or pleasure ground' had moved down the whole social scale. Briggs's 'country bungalows' of the 1880s were bourgeois versions of the elite's country seat; Phillips's 'weekend country bungalows' of 1920 were geared to middle class needs; by the later 1920s, there were plenty of proletarian bungalows around. Though many firms supplied portable versions, for the more enterprising weekender it was possible to make one's own. A 'simple, weekend bungalow', with a living room, two 12 by 12 bedrooms and kitchen could, exclusive of site, water and sanitation, be built by one man, unaided, for less than £90 in 1929. All that was needed was a sympathetic farmer and a truck to take one to the site (Vant, 1929).

Near large cities, informal settlements of self-built housing providing pleasure and recreation for the mass grew up. For Liverpool, there was a bungalow town at Moreton, in the Wirral. At Whitesand Bay in Cornwall, working families from Devonport and Plymouth built a holiday village of asbestos chalets and bungalows. Similar settlements developed in Sussex at Rye, Winchelsea, Sheppey, Tatsfield, Biggin Hill and Fairlight, and a cluster of railway bungalows at Pagham Beach. All round the coast, within reach of major towns, a proletarian colonisation of seaside land was taking place. Other chalet towns developed at Withernsea near Hull, and along the upper reaches of the Thames, though here, the 'bungalow towns' were of a better class and, according to Professor Adshead, were places where actors and actresses went for the weekend.

One of the largest of the villages was that at Pitsea and Laindon, at the eastern end of Essex. Here, in the late 1920s, came people from London's East End, buying land for as little as £5 per plot and, after establishing possession with a tent, built their weekend bungalow for a cost of less than £50. By 1945, inflated by war-time migration, some 25,000 people were living in 8,500 houses, a settlement which became the nucleus of Basildon New Town. Equally organised was Jaywick Sands, south of Clacton-on-Sea. Here, in 1930, a farmer bought 24 acres of tidal land and, after advertising in the East London papers, sold it off in 30 by 15 plots, at £30 each. The place of the motor car was commemorated in its narrow avenues, each named after leading makes of cars, Austin, Hillman, Vauxhall, Bentley or Daimler. Without drainage and water supplies, the bungalows at Jaywick, at first only for holidays, were gradually improved and used for permanent occupation (Ward, 1976, 1977, 1980).

As time went by, the owners, making use of waste or re-cycled materials, as well as their craftsmen's skills, turned what were initially weekend chalets into bungalows for permanent use, homes to which they later retired. Not having the money to buy more conventionally built dwellings, or the requisite economic and social status to qualify for a mortgage, the house-builder (and often his family) substituted their labour for capital. In years to come, as the houses were improved, they came to match, and even surpass, the 'professionally' built dwellings of the speculative developer.

Comparable, in many ways, to the self-built settlements of so-called 'third world' cities today, the history of these inter-war bungalow settlements has, with rare exceptions, been largely overlooked (Noble, 1973; Ward, 1976, 1977, 1980). A combination of cheap land and transport, prefabricated materials, and the owner's labour and skills had given back to the ordinary people of the land the opportunity denied to them for over two hundred years, an opportunity which, at that time, was still available to almost half of the world's non-industrialised populations: the freedom to build one's own house. It was a freedom that was to be very short-lived (plate 113).*

---

* Since this chapter was written, Dennis Hardy and Colin Ward have researched and published extensively on the 'plotlands issue'. See their *Arcadia for All: The Legacy of a Makeshift Landscape*, Mansell, 1984 (in press).

A RAILWAY CARRIAGE BUNGALOW

SUGGESTING HOW A DISUSED CORRIDOR COACH MAY BE ADAPTED

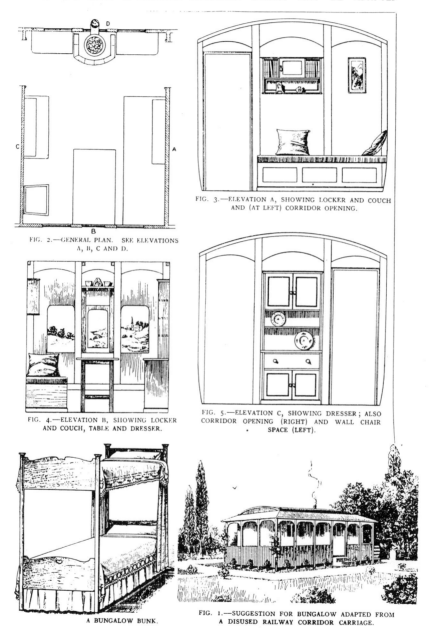

FIG. 2.—GENERAL PLAN. SEE ELEVATIONS A, B, C AND D.

FIG. 3.—ELEVATION A, SHOWING LOCKER AND COUCH AND (AT LEFT) CORRIDOR OPENING.

FIG. 4.—ELEVATION B, SHOWING LOCKER AND COUCH, TABLE AND DRESSER.

FIG. 5.—ELEVATION C, SHOWING DRESSER; ALSO CORRIDOR OPENING (RIGHT) AND WALL CHAIR SPACE (LEFT).

A BUNGALOW BUNK.

FIG. 1.—SUGGESTION FOR BUNGALOW ADAPTED FROM A DISUSED RAILWAY CORRIDOR CARRIAGE.

Figure 5.6 Proletarian weekend retreat: the railway carriage bungalow, 1925.
What the bourgeoisie had in the nineteenth century was gradually achieved by the mass in the twentieth – until it was later suppressed (*The Woodworker*, vol. 29, 1925)

Environmental control

The bungalow under attack 1925-47

Mushrooming bungalows were only part of the widespread landscape change taking place during these years. Advertisers had seen the potential of prominent roadside sites; garages, petrol pumps and restaurants blossomed along country lanes. New roads were built, existing ones widened out, trees chopped down to hasten traffic flow. Poultry farms, rural industries and smallholdings were established, hillsides enriched with extensive plantations of pines and electric pylons carried power across the landscape. 'Historic houses' were sold and transported, stone by stone, to the United States. In country towns and villages, council estates grew up, housing rural workers; in city suburbs, private and council developments expanded in all directions.

From the mid 1920s, these changes became the object of a small but increasingly powerful campaign. Mediated through the Establishment and professional press – *The Times, Observer, Spectator, Country Life, Architectural Review, Architects' Journal, Garden Cities and Town Planning* – the attack came from the architectural and planning professions, landed interests, 'country' activists and an intellectual and literary elite.

The focus was on what was generally described as 'the spoliation of the countryside', a protest, on aesthetic grounds, about the environmental changes taking place. Of these, the widespread proliferation of the bungalow seemed somehow to epitomise the developments which the campaigners deplored.

> 'Every road is becoming a nightmare of ugly hoardings or still more ugly individual designs', protested a spokesman of the campaign, 'another factor . . . is the extraordinary ugliness in many villages of garages and petrol pumps . . . of peculiarly conspicuous colouring. . . . The distressing sacrifice of rural beauty involved in the uncontrollable erection of bungalows and unsightly buildings in conspicuous positions should be dealt with by a joint body representing the whole of the artistic, learned and other societies interested in the protection of rural England' (*Observer*, 30 May 1926).

A frequent topic for criticism was 'ribbon development', a term apparently coined about this time by Patrick Abercrombie, Professor of Town Planning at Liverpool, to describe continuous roadside building. 'Soon this green and pleasant land will only be glimpsed from our country roads through an almost continuous hedge of bungalows and houses,' he wrote to *The Times* (6 April 1925).

Architects were at the forefront of the attack. In pre-war days, the 'chief lament of the housing enthusiast' had been the operation of bye-laws which had controlled the sizes of rooms and forbidden the use of cheap materials. With the post-war need for housing, this control had largely disappeared. Yet 'everyone who loves the English countryside must be appalled by the rash of squalid little bungalows which disfigures even remote beauty spots,' wrote an influential member of the profession (Weaver, 1926:2). Whilst the large, architect-designed bungalow costing £800 to £2000 was perfectly permissible, the self-built or folk vernacular of the builder ought not to be allowed. The great majority were 'banal with embellishments of the most monstrous kind . . . worried with "features" and dotted with bits of carving, coloured glass and flower baskets. . . . One begins to deplore the whole genus to which it belongs.' There were 'whole collections of them, by the seaside especially, which stand as evidence of what a bungalow ought not to be' (Phillips, 1920:2). Colonies of weekend and summer chalets were, according to Professor Abercrombie, springing up all over the

THE TIMES SATURDAY AUGUST 29 1981

Man in tussle over bungalow demolition has fine cut

From Our Correspondent, Luton

A £1,760 fine imposed by magistrates on a man who refused to demolish his bungalow was cut to £176 by a judge at St Albans Crown Court yesterday.

John Andrews had been fined £10 a day for not obeying an order to demolish the building because it was erected without planning permission.

But Judge Stockdale told him on appeal: "This is a larger fine than those imposed on many serious criminals." He reduced it to £1 a day, or £176.

Earlier, Mr Stephen Aitchison, for Dacorum District Council, Hertfordshire, said that Mr Andrews should have demolished the bungalow. Twice he had been refused planning permission to replace an existing wooden bungalow on the site in Potten End, near Hemel Hempstead.

The judge said: "It is not appropriate for this court to go into great detail about such breaches of the law. We are concerned with litigations, and whether there has been a deliberate flouting of the law, and there has certainly been nothing of that kind. He has been in breach, but that is only of a technical nature.

After the hearing Mr Andrews, car delivery agent of Water End Road, Potten End, said the hearing was his first victory in a three-year battle with planners.

He bought the site in 1977 with a dilapidated wooden bungalow on it. There was also a council notice ordering work to be done before the bungalow was occupied.

Mr Andrews applied for permission to knock it down and rebuild it in brick, but he was twice refused because of the council's green belt policy.

In 1979 his proposals were approved under the Building Regulations and work began.

Mr Lawrence Marshall, for Mr Andrews, said: "Professional advisers thought that was sufficient. But in September that year, like a bolt out of the blue, came a notice from the council saying planning permission was required."

Work stopped immediately, although £10,000 had been spent. An enforcement order followed, saying that the building should be pulled down.

In January Mr Andrews was fined £100 for failing to comply with the order. In July the fine of £1,760 was imposed.

Mr Marshall maintained that Mr Andrews was told at one stage that if he had rebuilt the original bungalow piece-meal, "one wall at a time", he would have been all right.

Mr Andrews, who has complained to the Ombudsman, said outside the court: "I am hoping that common sense will prevail. I live in a caravan on the site and obviously it would be better for that to go, rather than the bungalow, and that is what the local people want.

"I am sure there is a compromise solution."

Figure 5.7   The bungalow persecuted (*The Times*)

country, representing a natural desire of town folk for country life. Though this trend was 'better sociologically' it was 'artistically deplorable'. The preserver of rural amenities could not allow 'any sort of old junk cabin to deform his choicest beauty spots'.

A *cause célèbre* at this time was the proposal to develop some 470 acres of land on the south coast, fronting the Seven Sisters, east of Beachy Head, as a bungalow town. 'The Sussex Coast has enough of these experiments', protested *Garden Cities and Town Planning* in 1926. Rural areas should be 'sterilised to prevent them turning into ugly bungalow towns,' wrote the Librarian of the Garden City Association to the *Observer* (7 September 1926), an opinion apparently shared by the paper's middle class readers. Holiday-makers, returning home from the seaside resorts in September 1926, had come back, according to the editor, 'surprised and indignant at the blindness of local authorities . . . many of the beauty spots in the south coast,

Cornwall, Devon, Wales were being disfigured by badly designed bungalows erected by speculative builders with or without the state subsidy.'

Taking up the theme, the 'Weekend' page ran a readers' competition. According to the *Oxford Dictionary*, the bungalow was a lightly built, one-storeyed or temporary house. However, 'in the light of later knowledge of its nature and habits on the south coast and elsewhere', the *Observer* offered a prize for a new definition. The entries were 'rich in the critical and uncomplimentary': 'the superlative of hut, i.e. positive, hut; comparative, railway carriage; superlative, bungalow'; 'a cross between a small country house and a marquee; has inherited the vices of both'; 'a slight parasitical execrescence on the fair face of Nature; sometimes infectious'; 'a small collection of rooms sprawling over the garden, a little higher than the hollyhocks'; 'a domestic building on which the builders bung a low roof and a high price'; 'a one storied house built to admit light, air and rainwater'. Most perceptive, though understandably not winning the two guinea prize, was 'the poor man's home; the middle man's pleasaunce; the rich man's abomination' (26 September 1926).

For the preservationists, the problem was as much to do with the decline of agriculture as the growth of holiday-making. In promoting a policy of zoning areas for development and 'sterilising' others against it, the critics had found in the bungalow a rallying symbol for all they deplored, 'ribbon development', a lack of architectural control, infiltration of 'country' areas and urbanisation of the coast.

Whilst these criticisms were based on the shared aesthetic values of middle and upper middle class groups, a prominent member of the Establishment saw the bungalow as a symbol of social and moral decay. It represented an upheaval in the social order manifest in landscape terms. For William Inge, Dean of St Paul's, writing in the *Evening Standard* on 'social life in the next hundred years' the middle nineteenth century had been 'the golden age of the middle class' but now,

> under universal suffrage, the helplessness of the middle class is painfully apparent. . . .
> Before the end of the century we may see such a state of things as exists in America.
> Increasingly high death duties made it impossible to found a family which 'has always
> been the main object of an Englishman's ambition'. . . . Now that the possession of
> wealth is treated as some sort of crime, the old ostentation is rapidly disappearing . . . in
> the next twenty years, there will be very few country houses left. They are among the few
> beautiful things that we have to show our visitors but they are doomed. The whole face of
> the country will be spotted with bungaloid growths within which childless couples will
> sleep after racing about the country in little motor cars (7 September 1927).

The Dean's mellifluous-sounding phrase was quickly absorbed into the language of environmental pathology. The medical analogy was expanded; the bungalow was 'infectious'; areas 'broke out into a rash of red-roofed bungalows'; there was a 'fever of bungalow-building'; places were hit by 'an outbreak' or 'plague' of bungalows. Bungalows and 'other fungoid growths erupted all over the landscape'. According to the *Evening Standard*, in the spring of the following year,

> Motorists . . . lured by the fine weekend into making their first country excursions of the
> year have returned to London with almost blood-curdling stories of what they saw
> revealed by the clear February sunshine along the great arterial roads. They report the
> existence there, in distressing numbers, of what Dean Inge has so admirably called
> 'bungaloid growths' and . . . wonder how these are permitted to come into being.

Country Homes

CUBICAL CONTENTS (approx.), 26,000 cubic feet.

Description.

An imposing elevation, in which the Garden suggestion shows great possibilities of a simple yet pleasing treatment.

This Bungalow contains a large Entrance or Sitting-out Porch. Living Room. Dining Room. Kitchen and convenient Offices. Four Bed Rooms and Dressing Room. Bath. Lavatory, &c.

A corner or end-on Site could be used as well as a wide frontage for the erection of this type.

DESIGN No. B.14.
(COPYRIGHT.)

WIDTH OVER ALL   ..   ..   .. 30 ft. 0 in.
DEPTH ..   .. 65 ft. 0 in.

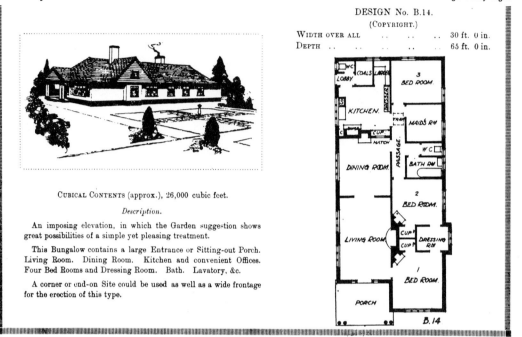

CUBICAL CONTENTS (approx.), 36,600 cubic feet.

Description.

An excellent example of a Bungalow Residence, with ample accommodation for average family.

A gabled Porch suitable for sitting out under, leads to large Living Room, which gives access to Dining Room at one end and large Verandah at the other. The Dining Room enjoys a similar but smaller feature.

Three Bed Rooms and Maid's Room. Kitchen. Offices. Bath Room and w.c. are all contained in this rectangular plan, being economical in cost of erection and maintenance.

DESIGN No. B.3.
(COPYRIGHT.)

WIDTH OVER ALL   ..   .. 63 ft. 0 in.
DEPTH ..   .. 42 ft. 0 in.

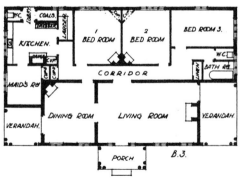

Figure 5.8   Room for the maid: middle class bungalows, early 1920s (*Country Homes*, n.d. c.1920)

Something had gone awry with the scheme of arterial roads where there was arising 'a ragged fringe of paltry and shabby buildings'. The low rateable value this created had the effect of depressing the area; in addition, a magnificent opportunity, civic and aesthetic, to create different development was being thrown away (20 February 1928). The passion for arterial roads was being indulged in 'without sufficient safeguarding against the reflex consequences' reported *Garden Cities and Town Planning* (February 1927). The Ministry of Transport and county councils were cutting these through more or less virgin land at vast public expense without providing proper use of the frontages, upon which, 'there settle down, like bees, swarms of bungalows, built by speculative housing companies, without serious control of lay-out or external design' (ibid., February 1927). Other protestors broke into verse.

The jerrybuilder lay dreaming in
His golden fourpost bed;
He dreamt of an endless ribbon
Of bungalows pink and red,
With fancy work on the gables
To every purchaser's choice:
And he dreamt in the back of his conscience
he heard old England's voice –

'Don't build on the By-Pass, Brother:
Give ear to our last appeal
Don't advertise where it tries the eyes
And distracts the man at the wheel.
You've peppered the landscape, Brother,
And blotted out half the sky:
Get further back with your loathsome shack,
Let the By-Pass pass you by!'

The jerrybuilder made answer:
'I'm English, I wants me rights.
Wot are the by-pass fields to me
But Desirable Building Sites?
I've peppered the landscape proper,
But me pocket 'as to be filled.
If I wants to build on the By-Pass,
I'm bloody well going to build!'

'Don't build on the By-Pass Brother:
It won't suit anyone's book;
An endless street is nobody's treat,
With roofs wherever you look.
Before you smother the country
We only hope you'll die:
You ought to be hung with the ribbons you've strung . . .
Let the By-Pass pass you by!'

They swung out a big new By-Pass
When the first was a choke-full street:
The glorious day isn't far away
When London and Liverpool meet,
And nothing remains of England
Where the country used to be
But the roads run straight through a housing estate
And a single specimen Tree.

'Don't build on the By-Pass, Brother;
Allow us a breath of air:
We like to see an occasional tree,
More so as they're getting rare;
You're poisoning all the country
Like a dirty bluebottle-fly:
Don't clutter the tracks with your loathsome shacks:
Let the By-Pass pass you by!'[2]

For the self-appointed guardians of architectural taste, the bungalow had become the symbol of all that was bad. In the most widely read of their manifestos (*England and the Octopus*, 1928:140-2) by architect Clough Williams-Ellis, bungalows were said to constitute

> England's most disfiguring disease, having, from sporadic beginnings, now become our premier epidemic. So few areas are still immune that it is unnecessary to give instances, though Peacehaven . . . (is) the classic example of this distressing and almost universal complaint. [Having begun as] a perfectly reasonable type of building [it had been] meanly exploited to its own degradation and the disfigurement of the country at large. For besides being the cheapest sort of human habitation . . . the reach-me-down, 'carriage-paid-to-any station' bungalow is also extremely adventurous . . . in fact, the intrusive impertinence of the bungalow knows no bounds (plates 114, 115).

Before the war, rows of villas had sprung up

> along the line of the public services . . . as do weeds along an open drain; but the bungalows are not thus regimented – they penetrate into the wildest country as lone adventurers or in guerilla bands.

Though the demand for bungalows was 'very reasonable' whether for a weekend or holiday camping place or regular home,

> it is only with the anti-social placing of these little buildings and their gratuitously flashy or exotic appearance that fault is found. Laid out with sense and designed with sensibility, a seaside 'Bungalow Town' might be charming.

Increasingly influential, the lobby recruited the Prime Minister, Stanley Baldwin, whose speech on 'the destruction of the English countryside' was reported in *Garden Cities and Town Planning* under the heading, 'Bungaloid Growth'. At Brighton, according to the Town Planning Advisory Committee, there had been, since the war 'an appalling change for the worse in the appearance of the coast line, from the Solent to the South Foreland:

What Dean Inge calls 'bungaloid growths' – the phrase seems likely to be called a technical term – have sprung up to such an extent and with such rapidity that . . . it will not be long before the entire coast is one long line of ferro-concrete and Ruberoid roofing.

By 1929, the opprobrium attached to the term by this influential Establishment had become so strong as to induce self-defensive stances by authors catering for a larger, if less-influential public. 'On every hand there are complaints of bungaloid growth,' apologised S. Vant, in *Bungalows and How to Build Them* (price 6d); 'it is to be regretted that the word "bungalow" seems, in many areas, to have been confounded with the shorter and aptly descriptive word, shed.'

The campaign gained increasing momentum. Aired regularly in the establishment press, it was taken up by the intellectual and literary elite

'This sceptered isle, this earth of majesty . . . this blessed plot, this earth, this realm, this England. . .'
Nina looked down and saw inclined at an odd angle an horizon of straggling red suburb, arterial roads dotted with little cars, factories, some of them working, others empty and decaying, a disused canal, some distant hills sown with bungalows, wireless masts and overhead power cables.
'I think I am going to be sick', said Nina
(Evelyn Waugh, *Vile Bodies*, 1930; quoted in Cherry, 1972:151).

In *The Horrors of the Countryside* (1931) philosopher C.E.M. Joad described how, after passing through twenty miles of 'continuous London' on a journey to the coast, at Haywards Heath,

the red rash breaks out again in a scurf of villas and bungalows, and from there to Brighton, the bungalows are with us more or less all the way, increasing in numbers and virulence as one approaches the coast.
The South Coast has now become one more or less continuous town. Brighton stretches out to meet Shoreham, Shoreham to Worthing, Worthing to Littlehampton. . . . Large towns are girt by rows and rows of small houses, stretched out interminably into the countryside, fringed with allotments and threaded by motor roads. . . . At Camber Beach, near Rye . . . before and behind the dunes, a bungaloid growth has sprung up of quite unspeakable ugliness and vulgarity. Shacks and old tramcars have appeared on the beach. A dozen shabby stalls, built apparently from sugar boxes or petrol tins, press tea, sweets and aerated waters on your unwilling attention. . . . All around the coast the same destruction of . . . privacy and beauty is going on. Consider Shoreham, for instance, or Peacehaven.

For an intellectual minority, this democratisation of the environment had become a burning issue, presenting the guardians of culture with the crisis of their lives. At one of the major centres of high culture, two passionate crusaders, increasingly influential in future years, produced *Culture and Environment* (1933), a primer in 'the training of critical awareness' for use in schools and adult education. Drawing on George Sturt's *Change in the Village* (1911), they offered a catechetical approach for examining cultural change.

Do you know of any ugly building, furniture, tools etc. before 1820? Account as far as you can for your findings.

Compare the bungalow quarter in 'Star Dust in Hollywood' with Sturt's village before it changed. Which would you rather live in?

A lengthy biography recommended *England and the Octopus* and the publications of the Council for the Preservation of Rural England (Leavis and Thompson, 1933:136-8).

The Council for the Preservation of Rural England

'She was more than ever proud of the position of the bungalow, so almost in the country'.
(Angus Wilson, *A Bit off the Map*, 1952)

The driving force behind the campaign was the Council for the Preservation of Rural England (CPRE). The initiative in starting it had been taken, in 1925, by leading architects, Guy Dawber, the President of the Royal Institute of British Architects, and Patrick Abercrombie. The Council was an umbrella organisation for some two dozen groups representing the principal 'country' interest: professional, social, political and economic (RIBA Journal, 18 December 1926: 138-276). Whatever else might be said about its motives, and a membership which cut across normal political and ideological positions, the Council represented the middle and upper class viewpoint of an established and propertied class with vested interests in the land. Its regional committees were headed by the aristocracy; the membership was composed of senior serving or retired officers, Justices of the Peace, prominent landowners, writers and university scholars (RIBA Journal, 18 December 1926; Alison, 1975).

The late 1920s saw an increasingly vigorous campaign. Grouped housing, planned according to architectural rules, should replace 'ribbon development'; some areas should be zoned for housing, others for agricultural and recreational use; advertising should be further restricted and 'architectural control' exercised over building development. In short, the powers of local government to plan urban development introduced on a limited scale in the Housing and Town Planning Act of 1909, extended (and in the case of larger towns, made compulsory) in legislation of 1919 and 1925, should be broadened to encompass not just towns but the whole of 'country' areas.

As part of its campaign the Council published a series of regional reports. Well, even lavishly, produced, with expenses privately guaranteed, introduced by a socially prominent literary figure (John Buchan, G.M. Trevelyan, Sir A. Quiller Couch) and advised by the architectural profession, they illustrate the preservationists' concern. Unlike the great reports on mid-nineteenth-century towns highlighting poverty and problems of poor public health, these reports were not concerned with social issues, with the pressures of capitalism or even with agricultural decline. Their focus was essentially aesthetic. The criticisms expressed were with the quality of contemporary building and above all, with the 'invasion' of the whole countryside.[3]

Such issues were not regarded as problematic. It was, for example, sufficient for the report on *The Thames Valley from Cricklade to Staines* (1929) to state, 'some are of simple and charming design, the others are notorious for their architectural vulgarity. . . . The riverside inn close by is expressive of an age when architectural manners were better understood.' (1929:50). According to their rules of taste, new developments were 'hideous', 'outrageous', 'offensive' or 'incongruous'. Suburbs were 'desecrated by a mass of uncontrolled vulgarity'. It was assumed that 'there are some fundamentals of good taste which should be obvious to the common man', yet 'the vague inclination for meaningless ornament is a depressing attribute of the age'. Though these reports covered rural advertising, garages, bridges, roads, industry, landscape and all new building, the bungalow, as usual, came in for special attention.

At Coln Brook, a 'colony of bungalows' had been erected which 'are probably the worst disfigurement to the riverside in the Region surveyed'. Near Appleton 'two bungalows of incongruous materials' had been built in a country lane. Elsewhere, 'blue slate roofs with red hip and ridge tiles is a combination which should never be permitted.' Between Staines and Pangbourne, low-lying land, previously thought unfit for building, had been 'covered for long distances with riverside bungalows'. These 'ought not to be allowed on floodland and their architecture should be controlled.'

Economic and social changes were altering the riverside scene.

> From the Stuart period and through the Georgian, great houses were built along the banks (of the Thames) and at the end of the Georgian period, interest was divided between park-like scenery, wide stretches of low-lying land and intermittent villages and towns. The Victorian period had seen its banks dotted with villas of the wealthy, reposing amidst a richly wooded country, with cedars, acacias and weeping willows, spreading their branches over the smooth lawns. The twentieth century has seen a great incursion of small houses; long stretches of meadowland and much of the flood-land are now dotted with bungalows. Many of these are by no means unattractive, with their landing stages and little gardens brilliant with geraniums, lobelia and rose-embowered pergolas. . . .
> While there are still miles and miles of pleasant park-like scenery . . . and many eighteenth and nineteenth century villas . . . the bungalow with its sham half-timber, its tinsel and more ephemeral trimmings is rapidly creeping up the banks . . . the fashion for building big villas has practically ceased.

Instead, there was an 'ever present menace of smaller houses down to bungalows and shacks'.

For the compilers of the report, the Earl of Mayo, and architect-planners, Professors Abercrombie and Adshead, what was necessary was 'Architectural Control, covering siting, design and materials of new building' and 'the elimination of meretricious ornament'. The opportunity to exert this had, in fact, been suggested in the planning act of 1909 and in 1927, by a 'model clause' of the Ministry which could be adopted by local authorities. This allowed the setting up of an advisory committee consisting of a local Justice of the Peace, and an architect and surveyor recommended by their respective professional organisations. However, the best safeguard against 'disfigurement' was 'possession of the land by the owners who would not allow it' (ibid.:64-5).

Similar views prevailed elsewhere. If Cornwall was to preserve its 'subtle beauty' 'the flimsy type of ill-designed bungalow and suburban villa that disfigures the Sussex coast should never be allowed to violate the headlands of Cornwall.' A 'debasement of taste throughout England' had taken place from the late Victorian period and 'incongruous' and 'garish' new materials had been introduced. According to the Cornwall report (Thompson, 1930):

> One material produced in this country on a large scale since the war, namely, asbestos, had done more than any other to encourage 'jerry-building' and the disfigurement of rural England . . . for reasons unknown, the manufacturers have assumed the English purchaser wants a temporary roof of salmon pink colour and the speculative builder has apparently concurred with the decision . . . asbestos is infinitely cheaper than green slate and if of a conspicuous pink colour is more likely to catch the eye of the prospective and indiscriminating purchaser.

In an appendix to the Report on Derbyshire a lengthy list of materials was included which were 'specifically unsuitable to the Peak District'. These included red, orange and pink bricks; red, reddish, pink and purple machine-made tiles; vividly coloured concrete tiles; coloured glass, as used in ornamental windows; red, reddish brown and purpley red paint; crude harsh colours of every kind; pink and red asbestos slates, and diamond-shaped slates of any colour; half timber, either constructional or imitation; rocky faced pre-cast concrete blocks or imitation stone; in brief, most of the materials which had been marketed in the previous decade. In the Report on Ryedale, the Committee suggested that even if grey asbestos tiles were used, they should not be laid diagonally.

In these reports incontrovertible rules of colour were assumed.

> Hundreds of vulgar villas complete with fussy facades, creep up out of Sheffield . . . and shatter the harmony of remote villages. Pink bungalows suddenly appear in the heart of a wooded dale or austere moor, ruining areas of noble scenery.

In the Cordwell Valley, in Derbyshire, a handful of bungalows had 'pink asbestos roofs which shatter the peaceful loveliness of the surroundings'.

The bungalow was singled out as having 'special problems': the square plan was generally used, giving rise to an 'ugly roof' and 'badly shaped chimneys'. The walls, being one-storey high, 'are quite devoid of dignity' as they were 'overpowered' by the roof. The effect of bungalows and houses built in close proximity or placed alternatively, was 'always unfortunate', the 'broken roof line is most unpleasant'. Bungalows and houses should be kept in separate groups. It was scarcely possible, even for the skilled architect, 'to give a dignified appearance to the ordinary bungalow or block of two villas owing to their lack of size.' Instead, they should be grouped into blocks of four or six (plates 116 and 117).

Discussing 'Disorder and vulgarity', these arbiters of taste deplored the fact that 'each house strives to be different from its neighbours'. Bungalows were a 'doll's house type of building' which was sadly out of place on the edge of a moor. The smaller a country building, the plainer it should be. A new bungalow should have 'the elementary decency and good manners to cover the nakedness of its red-brick walls with plaster and whitewash' (Williams-Ellis, 1928:162).

The Town and Country Planning Act, 1932[4]

The campaign succeeded. In 1928, the CPRE had drafted a Bill in which the name 'town planning' would be altered to cover 'rural planning', to simplify rural planning procedures and to give county councils town and rural planning powers. The aim of the new Act of Parliament, passed in 1932, was to simplify existing legislation, widen the application of planning power from town to country, and 'prevent the desecration of the countryside'. The preamble referred to 'the protection of rural amenities' and 'the preservation of buildings and other objects of interest and beauty'. Local authorities were given the right to regulate not only the size and height but also the 'design and external appearance of buildings'. 'Thus, architectural beauty is at last officially admitted to have an existence as much as the foundations and the drains,' announced *Garden City and Town Planning* with satisfaction, in August, 1930. The 'aesthetic lobby', it seemed, had won the day.

In the debate on the bill, the contribution of the CPRE and RIBA in forming public opinion and 'promoting interest in the subject' was fully acknowledged. As might be expected, the 'bungaloid' image was to come in useful. With historic castles increasingly being exported to California, Sir Stafford Cripps was worried about the unequal exchange. He had had the sad experience, 'living in one of the most beautiful parts of England' (the Cotswolds), of seeing people coming in 'to put up small buildings of the bungaloid type' while others 'were removing buildings entirely to be erected in other parts of the world'.

In the event, the Act was to have limited effect. For various reasons, 'ribbon development' went on. In 1935, the Restriction of Ribbon Development Bill was introduced. Though Abercrombie's original objection to the phenomenon had been social, economic and aesthetic, creating what he assumed would be socially incohesive settlements, expensive to service (with roads, sewers and power), the burden of the criticism was on aesthetic grounds. During the debate on 25 June 1936, the issue was not seen as 'a transport problem at all. It is a sociological and aesthetic problem.'

> We are against ribbon development because we are against uglification – we are against bungaloid and other fungoid growths which are now stretching out from every big town into the countryside . . . we often find on a road, a hundred small bungalows, all of one elevation and size, which are neither useful nor beautiful.

Yet the long discussion of the bill, on a phenomenon in progress for over ten years, merely encouraged developers to take advantage of the delay. The Act made it illegal, without the consent of the highway authority, to build within 220 feet of the centre of main roads and therefore pushed building lines further back. Yet agricultural buildings (including, it must be assumed, the occasional smallholder's bungalow) were to be exempt. In the debate, only the lone figure of Sir Francis Freemantle spoke up on behalf of people who liked to live by the side of the road, people who enjoyed watching traffic as others enjoyed watching railways, a feeling 'not confined to the working class'.

The 1932 Act was permissive rather than compulsory. It followed that only relatively wealthy authorities, whose elected representatives shared the same assumptions and values as the people responsible for bringing the Act onto the book, could take advantage of its new powers. This was particularly so as the Act had immense implications involving compensation for land prevented from being developed.

Thus Surrey County Council, with the highest rateable income *per capita* in England, had been the first county to get a private Bill through Parliament restricting building development in the country in 1931, prior to the passage of the general planning act a year later. Similarly, Middlesex and Essex, with their wealthy and interested middle class constituents, had promoted legislation to preserve the by-passes according to the image of their choice.

'Architectural control' was exercised in a similar way. In the debate, the Minister (Hilton Young) had seen difficulties in legislating on matters of taste. In his view, such questions were best left to local magistrates, 'with an intimate knowledge of the district in question' or 'a committee of specialists, of architects and people of that sort with special knowledge of the subject'. In effect, this meant that those with social and political power exercised the aesthetic criteria of the class to which they belonged.

Where members of the CPRE or its constituent bodies were powerful, there was now quite extensive legislation by which building development could be controlled. And it is clear from CPRE publications that where their members found self-built bungalow settlements visually or socially offensive, public health legislation was invoked to restrict or prohibit them.

The mid 1930s saw greater expansion than ever. Each year, over 360,000 houses were built, a greater number than either before or since at a time when the population was only four-fifths that of the 1970s. The impact of these developments was immense. In 1938, a government report recognised that one-third of all dwellings in the country had been built in the previous twenty years, almost three-quarters of them by private enterprise. By the mid 1930s, the market for middle class dwellings was well-nigh saturated. Builders were having to reach to lower markets, with smaller dwellings; hence, the bungalow persisted, continuing to figure in the environmental protests of the pre-war years and symbolising, for leading architect-planners, the nadir of environmental control.

In *Britain and the Beast*, a collection of essays by prominent political, literary and other figures, edited by Clough Williams-Ellis (1938), the bungalow took a further rap. For H.J. Massingham, the English village was being 'swallowed up by the bungalow plantations – the newest form of enclosure'; for Sheila Kaye-Smith, the complaint was of the disappearance of 'old world charm': the thatched roofs coloured like dead bracken, the walls of ruddy golden brick of Kent and Sussex, which suggested a 'natural growth', were being replaced by 'the bungalow coloured pink that can be seen nowhere else save in boiled crustaceons'. Yet there was sympathy for the bungalow-dweller. Even 'a hideous bungalow set down in the midst of the loveliest of rural landscape' was the sign of a desire for 'something better than a house in a town street' according to a 'professional countryman', A.G. Street.

Everywhere, rapid suburbanisation had taken place. Near Oxford, 'lorry-drivers and bus-travellers are pitchforked into the road near . . . a stucco bungalow with a raised tower that fulfils no other function beyond giving the cafe its name.' In the Lake District was 'Bill Brown's bungalow; the poor chap had saved for years to build the little shack for himself.' He couldn't afford an architect and 'the best we can do is to see he uses grey asbestos instead of pink for the roof and trust the thing won't look too bad . . . from a distance.' In 1928, Patrick Abercrombie had referred to 'blasphemous bungalows'; ten years later, according to another architect, 'the mere mention of the word "bungalow" makes excitable people nearly as furious as a whisper of the shameful word "drawing room" does among the Chelsea highbrows' (Briggs, 1937:68). As the 1930s drew to a close, planning ideas were increasingly turning to issues other than the purely physical and visual, to questions of unemployment, social amenities, defensive strategy in face of possible air raids and notions of regionalism. Yet as the 1932 Act was not compulsory, people still maintained a relative freedom to build. It was a freedom drastically removed in the new planning legislation of 1947.

Conclusion

Since enclosures and the rise of the industrial state, a ruling class had owned and controlled the rural and urban environment, and had shaped it according to taste. In the country the form of building, as well as landscape, was governed by a powerful land-owning class; in the new industrial towns, building developments were in the hands of equally powerful groups. In many conventional urban histories, it is often stated that such cities 'grew in totally unplanned ways'. This is a misreading of the situation in that they grew according to the 'natural', albeit unstated, plan or logic resulting from the structure of economic and political power, expressed in local cultural traditions.

When explicit 'town planning' was instituted in the form of building, health and housing legislation, the resulting environments ('bye-law housing' and 'garden city' design) similarly expressed the values, social, moral and aesthetic, of a newly powerful middle and upper and upper middle class (Swenarton, 1981). As others have pointed out (Ashworth, 1972), the history of town planning in Britain was the history of a middle class social and architectural movement whose ideology was accepted as a norm and institutionalised through legislation.

Throughout this time, the majority of the population – the folk, the common people, the proletariat – whichever term is appropriate, were a dependent class, not least regarding housing, let alone any question of 'taste'. They owned neither property nor land. Owner-occupiers, with dwellings and territory over which they had total control, represented less than 10 per cent at most of all households in the early twentieth century. In the countryside, the mass of the population were dependent tenants; in the towns, housing was owned by greater or lesser landlords. Everywhere there were explicit or implicit restrictive covenants. Taking building materials as 'given', the appearance of housing was determined according to culturally derived and socially enforced values (as regionally varied as these were), of landlords operating with the informal mechanisms of economic and political power. The mass of people expressed no personal 'taste' in housing because they owned neither land nor property to display it. As Alf Doolittle – of Shaw's *Pygmalion* – said of morals, the poor 'can't afford them'.

What happened after 1918 was that the ruling class lost this architectural and environmental control. Changes happened which they could not contain. They therefore organised themselves to gain access to formal means of control, to legislation and the manipulation of public opinion, to ensure that the environment should as far as possible be preserved in the image of their choice. What this class was trying to achieve was the aesthetic control of what, in the forty years before 1914, had become a recreational preserve of the traditional aristocracy as well as the urban, upper middle class, as discussed in Chapter 3. It was a combination of interests which had given rise, for example, to the Country Gentleman's Association (1900), the 'weekend cottage' and the discovery by middle class architects of the 'vernacular tradition'. The countryside was still the private territory of an educated elite. The view of the 1920s and 1930s that the 'country is intrinsically a better place to live in' was a relatively new view, dating from the late nineteenth century. Prior to that time, and before industrialisation, the town had been the preferred environment, the symbol of progress, security and culture; the country was for production. Only for the minority did it have any attraction; for the majority it represented the outposts of wilderness of nature (Boumphrey, 1938:109). In an earlier age, the Game Laws had been passed in the interests of a landowning class, defining those who contravened them as 'poachers' (Williams, 1973). In a more subtle way, the new planning legislation, in theory in the interests of all, was an attempt to preserve landed interests, and by defining self-built housing as 'unsightly' or 'non-conforming', effectively kept it off the land.

The initiative in setting up the preservationist lobby came from the professional environmentalists, the architects and planners. Of the latter, the larger proportion were architects, from middle and upper class origins (Cherry, 1974:43; Kaye, 1960:45-7, 51-2), sharing the values of others grouped in the CPRE. Before 1932, and to a somewhat lesser extent through the 1930s, the theory and ideas of planning were strongly influenced by architectural ideas, which, at this time, were largely dominated by visual and aesthetic concerns (cf. Sharp, 1932). It was significant, therefore, that in the all-important Act of 1932 the title was to reflect not a concern with economic activities such as 'industry and agriculture' or, as later, the spatial distribution of populations and a concern, in 'urban and regional planning', with economic development and growth. Instead, it expressed the traditional social and visual categories of environment of the middle and upper class lobby who had promoted it, the 'town' and 'country' planning act of 1932. At a time when urban and rural areas were becoming increasingly interdependent, legislation was introduced which aimed to keep them apart.

Protests against change in the environment were, of course, hardly new. What was different in the inter-war period was not only the size and rate of change, and the perception of it, but the organisation of the lobby against it. Here, the major difference resulted from the rise of the professions and their increasing influence, particularly architects, surveyors and, after 1913, town planners. With their annual conferences and statements reported in the press, their specialised journals and, consulted by the government, growing status, they became increasingly influential in forming public opinion. The revolution in communications was also important. Apart from causing much of 'the problem', the motor car gave members of this lobby the opportunity to see the changes which they deplored. The things of which they complained were mainly 'views from the road' (it is incidentally remarkable how few bungalows can be seen from the train). Cars enabled people to move and organise. The press also expanded during these years and establishment views were promulgated by the increasingly influential monopoly of the BBC whose weekly paper, *The Listener* was also important in promoting these views.

Why was the bungalow so deplored, the symbol of all that was bad? The reasons offered by the preservationists' lobby have been sufficiently stated above. There were, however, much more fundamental explanations.

In a word, the popular bungalow, in its design, materials and location, undermined all the basic principles on which the professional architect based his career: that there were inherently absolute rules which governed questions of design: colours or materials which 'harmonised' with the landscape, rules about 'proportion' and beliefs about 'communities' which resulted from grouped dwellings. Where the planner wanted to cluster buildings together, and keep them all in one style, the bungalow-owner insisted on staying apart. Where they insisted on creating a 'community', the bungalow-owner preferred to be on his own. The vast majority of bungalows presented the professional environmentalist with a blatant contradiction of every belief on which he based his professional role. They soiled a cherished cultural ideal, the image of the bucolic, romantic landscape decorated with simple cottages and cows. By pre-empting, even usurping, the architect's role as 'designer', it challenged his very existence.

It is a commonplace of sociology to suggest that the established or ruling values of a society may be studied in their purest form by looking at its upper class (Dahrendorf, 1970:39). Yet it was precisely in the values governing their residential preferences that the idea of the 'bungalow in the country' had its origin. When middle class critics complained that 'it is a rare experience to come upon a landscape in southern England that is not flawed by at least one modern bungalow, planted, as bungalows almost invariably are, so as to command, and in commanding, to ruin the maximum possible area' (Joad, 1931:124), they had only the aristocracy to blame.

In the years between the wars, the preservationist lobby won the right of 'architectural control'. For some, the argument was simply elitist and paternalist. 'There never was a time when public opinion was so vulgar, or so ill-trained, or so powerful.' Whilst the people's claim to the countryside was paramount, they were, as with nineteenth-century arguments against extending the franchise, 'not yet ready to take it up'; hence, the countryside should be 'kept in trust' until such time as education made them fit for the responsibility. For those with such views, the only solution was to give back the countryside to the large landowners. For others, 'in these democratic days' (of 1938) it was impossible to impose the cultural views of a minority on the mass of the population. Yet with the disappearance of the controlling landowners, such a minority had to take responsibility (cf. Williams-Ellis, 1938). What was clearly at issue were two sets of cultural rules: those of an elite, both professional and social, and those of the mass, or folk, both builders and owners, and the latter were rapidly gaining in ascendancy. For the elite, the rules were based on principles they called 'order and simplicity'. These principles they had been able to enforce when backed by the power of the state. For them, the ideal model was the post office in 'neo-Georgian style' and especially, the new local authority estate. Such 'corporation estates' had 'the merit of plainness and a certain unity of style'. 'Had there been no new housing but Council housing since the war, we had been in far happier case today so far as the look of England is concerned,' wrote a major pillar of the CPRE. On such estates, accommodating ever-growing numbers of the more affluent working class, bourgeois architects, with public money behind them, had been able to impose their ideas of taste, a taste whose origins lay in their reconstructed version of rural village life. The design of the houses reflected these ideals. The lay-out of the estates exhibited a calculated 'order' which only a local authority could impose. The location of the estate, again decided 'from above', was often in the poorer part of the town. Above all, in being denied the opportunity to modify the house façade, the tenants demonstrated their subjection to local authority rules. In short, architectural control was achieved by, as well as expressed, social control.

Making pseudo-sociological assumptions, the architect-planner believed that housing, especially in country village or town, should be in physically 'close knit groups'. Such groups symbolised 'the socially cooperative basis of the group of people it houses'.

The 'new romantic villas and bungalows', however, 'with their pebble dash, their half-timbered gables, the picturesque leaded lighted windows' in the 'new squandering suburbs' displayed not only 'unsightliness, a disorder and vagueness' but apparently the greatest sin of all, 'a violent individualism' (Sharp, 1932).

Yet it was precisely these rules, about lay-out, location and appearance of façades, drawn up by architects and imposed with local authority power, which expressed the tenant's dependent status. The fact was not unappreciated at the time. According to the Conservative Attorney General, Counsel to the CPRE, 'it might have been expected that the high standard of design imparted by architects since 1919 to the best types of Council houses would have helped to educate public taste.' Yet this was not so. On the contrary, there had been 'a psychological reaction against the Council house . . . a revolt against (its) artistically good simplicity and excellent design'. The reaction had manifested itself in a demand for the kind of house which was 'an abomination'; a house bought because its 'exterior is so different from the decent exterior of the Council house that the casual observer must see at a glance that its owner is *not* living in a Council house – it may even have been chosen in the belief that people will think it has cost more' (Scott, 1936:32-3). No better examples exist than the illustrations in the 'Ideal Home' books of the mid 1930s. Here, all key words of the description, each invested with deep social and cultural meaning, and describing the most important symbolic elements of the facade, are capitalised. 'House in TRADITIONAL style'; 'This design FEATURES the PORCH'; 'The BEAUTY of HALF-TIMBERED work'; 'with a ROOF of THATCH'; 'in TUDOR style for the ENGLISH countryside'.

Yet whilst architects were imposing their aesthetic views on a captive working class, first in the 'villagey' estates and subsequently, in mammoth 'Modernist' flats in larger cities families slightly higher up the social scale were planning with their feet. Leaving the 'old communities' supposedly expressed by urban streets, they were moving to 'better areas' and a territorially expressive, private personalised house, or a bungalow out in the bush.

If the 1932 Act had been relatively ineffective in establishing their objectives, the post-war legislation of 1947 saw the architect-planners firmly in control. The principles won in 1932, if not always enforced, were now strongly reaffirmed. Since that date, the 'distinctive philosophical strain of planning', according to Professor Hall, has been the notion that 'the planner has the right and responsibility to try and shape the life of the community through physical arrangements.' It is a right which included the two principles established in 1932: to determine the location of houses and decide on their 'aesthetic appearance' from outside. The three freedoms retained by the poor in the poor countries of the world were lost by the poor in the richer ones, the freedom 'of community self-selection, the freedom to budget one's own resources and the freedom to shape one's own environment' (Turner, 1976).

The bungalows of the inter-war years are now of little interest to anyone but their owners. What Joad wrote in 1931 has, in the event, proved correct: 'our children growing up in a world of garages and bungaloids . . . not knowing what they have lost, will not miss what they have never known.' And ironically, as botanical investigation has shown, asbestos-tiled roofs have proved to be particularly attractive to a certain species of green-gold algae, especially in smoke infected regions. After fifty years, the red-roofed bungalows have faded imperceptibly into the landscape.

The issues they raised, however, have remained very much to the fore. In 1940, it was foreshadowed that 'the great danger is that the preservation of beauty may come to be regarded as a class issue' (Boumphrey, 1940:30). This is how it was to frequently turn out. For the rich, there was an 'architecturally-approved' house in a National Park. For the poor, the self-built bungalow, whether for permanent or holiday use, was ruled out of court. The caravan that took over its role was to be mainly confined to a compound that, for planners, was preferably kept out of sight.

Chapter 6

Africa 1880-1980

'The Indian bungalow is the one perfect house for all tropical countries.'

Dr J. Murray, *How to Live in Tropical Africa*, London, 1895:314.

Introduction

According to a leading authority on urbanisation and development, one of the most pressing problems of African countries in the second half of this century is the provision of shelter for the rapidly growing urban and rural population. In the urban areas of most of these countries, this problem has been compounded,

> by the imposition of official housing standards, usually of colonial origin and often not wholly appropriate . . . by the adoption of foreign housing designs, and by the dependence on imported construction technologies that place the costs of house building well beyond the means of a vast majority of the population of the country' (Mabogunje, 1979:291).

This comment states succinctly what part at least of this chapter is about. Yet as Professor Mabogunje has discussed elsewhere (et al., 1978), these problems are only part of a much larger issue. The design of dwellings, the materials and manner of their construction, their size and contents, and their arrangement in settlements are perhaps the most visible signs of any civilisation and culture. In discussing housing standards we are talking about forms of civilisation, about the extent of economic development, ways of life, social priorities and the distribution of wealth between rich and poor. And in mentioning colonial origins, foreign design and imported technology, Mabogunje recognises that these matters depend not simply on a local but a global or international situation. What, in fact, we are considering is a topic far larger than 'housing': it is the impact of colonialism and Westernisation on the life and material culture of Africa.

For the present, however, the discussion can be limited to the question of standards. In many developing countries, whether Asian, African or Latin American, official standards exist which regulate housing and urban development. Even though they cannot always be enforced, norms are set down controlling everything from the size of rooms to the width of roads. According to experts from these countries, most of these standards are still based on both Western technology and social philosophy and can be criticised on a number of grounds (Mabogunje et al., 1978).

For example, they are said to take little note of local experience, resources or culture; construction practices are insensitive to local resources and in most countries, 'traditional' forms of shelter built in local materials rather than concrete are often considered 'sub-standard': 'modern' is taken to mean 'Western', and modern housing means Western housing. In most tropical African and Asian countries, living and sleeping, perhaps with some overhead shelter, often takes place outdoors for most of the year; in the traditional houses of the ordinary people rooms serving specialised and exclusive uses are rarely found. Yet in 'modern' housing, this is what is usually supplied. As most of the standards were either inherited from the colonial past, or subsequently imported from developed countries, the technology used is invariably Western: mass production and prefabrication are often advocated to achieve housing targets. Human resources, the major asset of developing countries, are often overlooked.

These reports also stress the disjunction between 'official' housing and the local economy. The result is that huge differences arise between the economic rent for government-built housing and the rent-paying capacity of the people. The Western orientation of standards, in size, design or facilities, increases disparities between different groups of people. Dwellings become associated with social and economic status. The old colonial pattern is replaced by a new, indigenously evolved yet equally alien housing style and lay-out. In Nigeria, for example, though Europeans have left the 'European Reservations', new 'Government Residential Areas' are developed, still using similar designs and building technology.

Two sets of standards exist, the 'official' and the 'cultural'. When rural people move into urban areas, they bring their cultural standards with them. Yet once settled, they are either obliged to comply with the 'official' or else they tend simply to aspire towards and copy them. 'For the huge majority of people who have migrated to cities, the set of standards operated by local authorities constitutes the single most important obstacle to their settled existence in the urban areas to which they have migrated' (ibid.,:10-15).

How did this situation come about? How, in less than a hundred years (and half that time for most), did vast numbers of Africans, previously living as members of extended families, farming on family-held rural land, and living in grass or mud-built dwellings in compounds, come to move into towns and cities, living in nuclear families, working for wages, and inhabiting concrete houses and bungalows, situated in residential suburbs? One aim of this chapter is to throw some light on these questions; they are ones which form part of a much larger and complex theme. In a brief chapter such as this, only a few impressionistic ideas can be explored and these relate mainly, though not entirely, to West Africa even though some of the generalisations apply more specifically elsewhere. The investigation of the development of the bungalow provides a useful place to begin.

The significance of the bungalow in Africa

Though single-storey 'house and verandah' dwellings were known in South Africa at least in the early years of the nineteenth century (Lewcock, 1963), the bungalow designed and named as such reached Africa in that century's last few years. Why it arrived at this time, how it was introduced, and the role it played in incorporating sub-Saharan Africa into a global economy, are the other themes of this chapter. As elsewhere, its importance was considerable.

It was, in the first place, a technological device – a form of shelter for British colonial officials providing protection against malaria and reducing the effects of tropical heat. In its construction and design, it drew on over two-and-a-half centuries of tropical experience from India, South-East Asia and the Caribbean, incorporating ideas from other Europeans and the people over whom they ruled. And at the turn of the century, it used the new materials, science and technology developed in industrialised Britain. Like quinine, the railway or Enfield rifle, it was what Donald Headrick has called a 'Tool of Empire' (1981), which helped a handful of colonial officials exercise control over an expanding territorial domain.

Secondly, as a distinctive form of housing, the bungalow was an important element in the vast process of urbanisation which, during the course of the twentieth century, was instrumental in transforming the economic, social, cultural and political life of Africa. To oversimplify the complex issues discussed below, it was part of a change which, in many parts of Africa, transformed a peasant economy to a capitalist one, a society based on lineage and kinship to one increasingly structured by class, a rural family system based on the extended kin or descent group to an urban one where nuclear forms became increasingly common. In short, the bungalow was part of a physical and spatial process of urbanisation which incorporated modern Africa into a capitalist world economy.

Finally, as part of this same process, the bungalow was also a model, a European form of housing designed for one person or a nuclear family which, in its form, materials and construction, was to play a significant role in the social and cultural transformation of West Africa's urban elite.

If these seem ambitious, even outlandish, claims, it might be as well to clarify just what is meant, in this context, by the term 'bungalow': for this, no better authority exists than the Governor of Lagos, W. Egerton, writing to the Secretary of State for the Colonies, Lord Elgin, in 1906: 'the term "bungalow" . . . is strictly only applicable to a house with no floor above the ground floor but I gather it is used in your Lordship's despatch to include *any house built for European occupation*' (Colonial Office, 1909). Although they might have two storeys rather than one, they invariably had other common features: they were 'detached', contained a number of specialised rooms, and were built according to European (English) standards and technology. Most importantly, they provided for one person or for a nuclear family where the children were generally living elsewhere.

European interest in Africa

Though trading links between Europe and Africa go back to the fifteenth century, for much of the first half of the nineteenth, sub-Saharan Africa remained largely unknown and of little interest to Europe, including Britain. The formal ending of the slave trade had suppressed much of the economic activity in West Africa, and European, African and other merchants were gradually developing more legitimate commerce. A few intrepid explorers had penetrated the interior, and Sierra Leone was established as a Crown Colony for freed slaves in the early years of the nineteenth century. For the most part, however, European contact, in the form of merchants, and from the 1840s, missionaries, was strictly confined to the coast.

Increasing British interest in West Africa from mid century, and somewhat later, direct involvement in the form of colonial rule, was the outcome of economic and political developments both in Britain and Europe. From the late eighteenth to the mid nineteenth century, Britain, as the 'first industrial nation' had been practically unchallenged in producing and selling goods both to her own domestic as well as overseas markets. From then, however, and especially after the 1870s, as Germany, France, Belgium, the Netherlands and the United States industrialised, British exports increasingly felt the winds of competition. The growing interest in finding markets in the 'undeveloped' parts of the world, whether the formal empire of India and white colonies of Australasia, or the informal empire of South America and Africa, was less an attempt to conquer new markets than an easy way out of her failure to dominate her competitors (Porter, 1975; Cain and Hopkins, 1980).

The cotton trade provides a good example. As Porter writes, African peasants were needed as customers for Lancashire textiles just as African groundnuts and palm oil were needed to make lubricants for the machines, and soap to wash the hands of the machinists. By the mid 1880s, the importance of colonies was recognised by the major industrial powers of Europe, as markets, as suppliers of raw materials, as well as sources on the spot for cheap labour. Whilst these developments were to take the British, and the bungalow, into Sudan, Egypt, further into Malaya and elsewhere, the process and its urban consequences are best examined in West Africa.

The Act of Emancipation freeing slaves on British soil had been passed in 1807. Its logical extension was the attempt to stop the slave trade as a whole. Lagos, one of the most important slaving ports, was bombarded and occupied as a British colony in 1851. Five European merchants set up business in 1852, soon to be joined by others. Exploration up the Niger established trading relations and missionaries extended their influence to the east and west. With the discovery of quinine as an antidote to malaria, factories and trading posts were gradually established up the river.

Yet trade required political stability. On the one hand, inter-tribal warfare threatened British traders; on the other, increasing competition came from French merchants. The Niger region, along with the rest of Africa, became the area for the rivalry of European powers. At the Treaty of Berlin in 1884 the Lagos region and Niger delta were conceded to the British, the other powers accepting the extent of her sphere of influence to an indeterminate distance inland. In January 1900, the British government took control of the whole of Nigeria from the Royal Niger Company, previously in charge of its administration and commerce.

Early urban enclaves

This rapid expansion posed the colonisers with a new set of problems. In the earlier years, British consuls, officials, merchants and missionaries had, by and large, lived in the relatively small urban enclaves on the coast except, of course, when travelling inland. Yet these places were the traditional 'white man's grave', with malaria as the ever-present danger. As the settlements grew, and as Europeans stayed longer, they became increasingly critical of their conditions. Though senior officials seem to have been fairly well provided for, many Europeans lived in what, for them, were congested and unhealthy surroundings. At Accra in the Gold Coast Protectorate (established 1868), there were, according to the explorer Henry Stanley writing in 1873,

> many pretentious houses, whitewashed, attracting attention from their prominence above the clay-brown huts among them. Almost to the extreme left was the Commandant's house, aloof and exclusive, its wide veranda denoted luxurious coolness, its wide space around it informed you that at one time or another some occupant had been assiduous to procure unpolluted air . . . to the extreme right was another large house with wide verandas and abundant grounds around it . . . [this was the Basel Missionary House] . . . between these houses, the body of the town of native and European buildings jammed itself . . . the huts of the natives have been established everywhere, without regard

to order . . . the streets are uniformly narrow, crooked and oppressive from the filthy habits of the natives . . . a hundred thatched roofs in all stages of decay and native improvidence.

Some ten years later, conditions were even worse:

Gutters were uncut and drainage non-existent, so that the anopheles and other deadly insects swarmed in the pools lying under the windows and at the doors of the houses and proceeded to infect their victims (Acquah, 1958:23, 27).

Equally unhealthy conditions were seen to exist at Freetown, Sierra Leone though Lagos seems to have been somewhat better.

In the last decades of the nineteenth century, conditions in the port cities seem to have combined with the massive extension of British rule to focus attention on accommodation and health. To ensure that economic activities flourished, orderly government and peaceful conditions were essential. Though colonial officials were few – three or four officers might be in charge of a division of nearly a million people, assisted by a handful of Nigerian clerks, and police – they needed adequate shelter. Though some of the early officials in rural areas seem to have lived in temporary shacks and African huts, administrators such as Lugard realised that to operate effectively, adequate shelter was essential to give protection from malaria, heat, humidity, tropical rainstorms, insects and animals, as well as provide for a minimum of social activities (Lugard, 1965:143; Gann and Duignan, 1978:229).

The bungalow as tropical house type

The history of tropical building – or more accurately, building and architecture for Europeans in the tropics – is, despite its importance, a much under-researched topic. Since the fifteenth century, Portugese, Spanish, Dutch, British, French, Danes, and later, Belgians, Germans and Americans have moved from temperate areas of the world to colonise and settle in the tropics. In the process they have made, though often slowly and with reluctance, adaptations in dress, diet, behaviour, dwelling and settlement forms, though rarely have the newcomers adopted the dwellings of the indigenous peoples, even if they have used their materials and techniques. Even from much earlier times, different colonising powers have borrowed from each other: the Romans from the Greeks, the Turks from the Arabs.

Yet apart from some studies of individual cases, little has been written in a systematic sense on the amalgam of economic, cultural, political, social, technological and material factors which explain why particular forms of shelter and settlement took on the forms they did.

Whatever the forms of shelter developed since the sixteenth century by British colonists in the West Indies, North America, India, Australia and South Africa, by the second half of the nineteenth, if not before, knowledge was being systematically assembled both in Britain and overseas concerning the most appropriate forms of housing for Europeans in the tropics. The particular problems of health and 'tropical medicine' had been discussed since the seventeenth century (Renbourn, 1963), and interest in the design of housing was to gradually increase among medical and military officials, engineers and travellers; later, manufacturers of 'portable buildings' exported to the colonies were also to take an interest (Herbert, 1978).

Apart from the odd exception, the design of portable houses sent to Africa, Australia or California in the early nineteenth century seems to have made little concession to the different

EAST INDIA VILLA.

Figure 6.1   Exploring culture: portable dwellings, 1836, 1854.
With some exceptions, early portable houses sent to tropical colonies were not particularly
adapted either to the climate or life-style of their future occupants. Increasingly knowledge
and experience from mid century gradually brought changes in the design (J.L.Loudon, *An
Encyclopaedia of . . . Cottage Architecture*, etc. 1836): S. Hemming, *Hemmings Patent
Improved Portable Houses*, etc. 1854)

climate, let alone lifestyle, or social conditions of their inhabitants. After the 1850s, however,
they became increasingly adapted to tropical requirements, incorporating a verandah, roof
ventilation, raised plinth, piers, and eventually quick assembly methods. Specialised
knowledge developed by military engineers in India became available in Britain; by the end of
the 1860s there was sufficient interest for the problem of providing domestic accommodation
for Europeans overseas to be discussed at the Royal Institute of British Architects. With

DRAWING 155.
ILLUSTRATION OF PLANTER'S OR OVERSEER'S IRON HOUSE, AS DESIGNED BY FRANCIS MORTON AND CO. (LIMITED) FOR HOT CLIMATES
CONSTRUCTED ON FRANCIS MORTON AND CO.'S (LIMITED) IMPROVED PLAN TO SECURE THE NECESSARY COOLNESS, AND COMFORT OF THE OCCUPIERS.

Prices on Application.   Please state accommodation required, number of Rooms, sizes of Rooms, &c

OUR ONLY CORRECT ADDRESS IS—

FRANCIS MORTON & COMPANY, LIMITED, NAYLOR ST., LIVERPOOL.

London Branch—36, Parliament Street, Westminster.
Glasgow Branch—Bank of Scotland Buildings, George Square.

ESTABLISHED OVER QUARTER OF A CENTURY.

Figure 6.2   The developing tropical house, 1873
Expansion of the capitalist world economy in the later nineteenth century took an increasing
number of Europeans overseas, many as planters and 'overseers' to manage the production
and export of raw materials to the countries at the core. Improvements were gradually
introduced into dwellings exported overseas; in this case, a single verandah, ridge ventilation,
a double roof and ventilated plinth aimed 'to secure the necessary coolness and comfort of the
occupiers' (Francis Morton, *Catalogue of Portable Buildings*, 1873. Liverpool Public
Library)

growing numbers of merchants, missionaries, doctors, engineers and government officials
and, at the end of the century, settlers in West and East Africa, it was perhaps logical that in
the late 1880s or early 1890s, both the generic form of dwelling used by Europeans in India,
as well as the term used to describe it, were seen as appropriate for Africa. Typical was Dr
John Murray's manual on *How to Live in Tropical Africa*, published in 1895.

After considering a number of alternatives, the author described the Indian bungalow as:

built on a masonry platform $2\frac{1}{2}$ feet above the ground. The platform is beautifully level
and smooth on top, where it forms the floor of rooms, passages and verandah, being
covered here and there with native mats. . . . The verandah is 9 or 10 feet wide, and has a
tiled roof, which is supported on pillars; it extends almost or quite round the house. The
doors and windows open directly on the verandah, which is shaded in parts by shrubs,
and generally bamboo sun-screens or 'chics'. The windows seen above the verandah are
for ventilation merely, as there is no upper storey in bungalows. The house is thatched
with reeds and grass, the roof being about $2\frac{1}{2}$ feet thick, and rising to a ridge 15 feet
above top of the walls, which it overhangs some $3\frac{1}{2}$ feet at eaves. For Africa, the

The Indian Bungalow.

Figure 6.3 The Indian bungalow: 'the one perfect house for all tropical countries'
By the 1890s, the bungalow, already used in the tropical world in form if not always in name, was being developed as a 'tool of Empire' for exporting to colonies abroad. (J. Murray, *How to Live in Tropical Africa*, 1895)

platform should be raised, say 15 feet above the ground in malarial districts; and a space of 3 or more yards wide outside of this should be cemented. Then would come flower pots and a low hedge, on outside of which should be a snake fence, made of broken stones and glass in infested districts.

The final sentence of the book reads 'the best form of tropical housing is the Indian bungalow'. By then, the term 'bungalow' had become synonymous with tropical housing for Europeans; this, by definition, was in the colonies. Hence, before the French adopted the term 'bungalow' some decades later for a rather different use in their own country (see below, p. 252), 'bungalow' meant 'maison coloniale'. For the eminent German Professor of Hygiene at Heidelberg, Dr Ernst Rodenwaldt, whose *Tropenhygiene* of 1938 reached two later editions 'these bungalow houses are still seen as the most ideal form of tropical house'. For the first decades of German colonial experience before the First World War, the Germans adopted the bungalow from the British.

The idea of the bungalow, then, seems to have reached West Africa about the early 1890s, whether prefabricated and exported from Liverpool, or through being used as a model for new residential developments.

Urban improvements began in the 1880s. In Lagos, for example, some of the huge surpluses being generated by the export of palm products, rubber, timber, cotton and other crops were invested in urban development and expansion of the European residential area of Ikoye

(Baker, 1974:29-30). From 1885, a vigorous sanitation policy was set on foot to clean up Accra. A public reservoir was constructed, large areas of the bush cleared, roads were widened and drains built. Between then and 1900, the government erected secretariat buildings in the vicinity of Victoriaborg, a new spacious development on the outskirts of the town. Here, bungalows were erected for European officials, changing the previous practice whereby they had lived in hired houses or rooms in James Town. A few wives had joined their husbands in these houses and had found them uncongenial; the authorities too had found such accommodation unhealthy and voted money for the new developments.

> The bungalows were wooden structures, erected on concrete pillars; they had much window and floor space and proved a great improvement on town dwellings. A place of recreation for Europeans was also erected. From then on, Europeans in Government service worked in offices mainly situated away from the town centre and for the most part, spent their leisure in the residential area. Later, European firms provided similar accommodation for some of their European staff and hence, increasing residential segregation of Europeans and Africans resulted (Acquah, 1958).

These changes in the location and housing of Europeans in West Africa in the late nineteenth century were largely the outcome of the medical research (and what turned out to

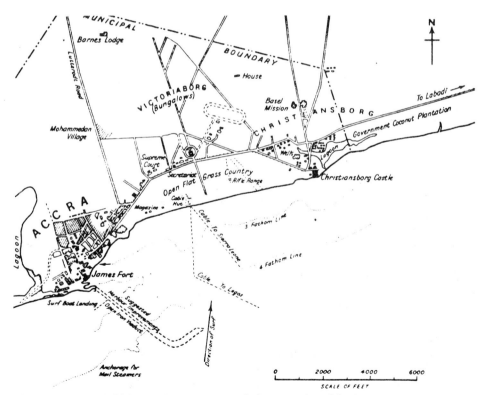

Figure 6.4 Accra, Gold Coast, 1903: moves towards the segregation of the city
In the early years of this century, the European population moved from the old indigenous city to the bungalow suburb of Victoriaborg (I. Acquah, *Accra Survey*, 1958)

be erroneous assumptions) of Dr Ronald Ross. In 1897, Ross had established that malaria was caused, not by infected 'emanations from the ground' but from the bite of the anopheles mosquito. Two years later, Ross, previously with the British army in India, with other colleagues from the Liverpool School of Medicine, went out to Freetown, Sierra Leone, in order to test his theory (Spitzer, 1968, on which the following account draws). Two solutions were possible: the first, based on the discovery that the anopheles bred in small pools, aimed to eliminate the disease by killing the larvae in such pools before they hatched. This method, however, would require sanitation operations after every rainy season. A more permanent method which fitted better with the growing late nineteenth century prejudices about the association of British with indigenous peoples, was the principle of 'health segregation'.

Ross has been shocked to find Europeans in Sierra Leone not only not using the punkah and mosquito nets common in India, but also living in houses which were small, crowded together and also not segregated from those of Africans. As Africans were seen to be carriers of the disease parasite in their blood, any anopheles mosquito that bit them became a source of infection to another person subsequently attacked. However, as mosquitos attacked their victims only at night, segregation was only necessary during night time. The solution proposed and adopted was a European enclave in the hills surrounding Freetown.

Workmen began clearing the bush in 1902 and, using pre-fabricated kits sent out from England, 24 bungalows and a governor's residence were completed by 1904. An expensively constructed railway was finished in the same year. Like its Indian counterpart, the segregated settlement, 800 feet above the Atlantic and five miles out of town, was known simply as 'Hill Station' (plates 118, 119).

According to a contemporary visitor, the government was to be congratulated 'for having provided so great a boon as these (twenty four) bungalows where comfort, rest, change and sea breezes' were to be enjoyed, 'an incalculable improvement upon the unhealthy town quarters of former times'.

The 'very spacious bungalows' were so conveniently arranged and healthy that several of the officials had their wives with them. Each stood in its own grounds, 'a liberal space being allotted for the garden'. In addition, there were 'an excellent tennis ground, croquet lawn and golf course . . . wherever there were more than one or two British officials, there was always a tennis court'. In another suburb (Cline Town), more bungalows were provided for the European heads of the railway workshop, maintenance engineers, traffic managers and others. That of the locomotive superintendent was stone built and marked 'a new departure on the construction of bungalows out here'; each of the three main rooms were 20 by 20 and 11 high. From the 'very spacious verandah' one could 'inhale fresh air and breathe freely and you look with calm pleasure on to a quite English landscape with herds of cattle grazing lazily on the grass fields.' With 'an absence of tom toms and unsavoury odours, it was a place in which a European and his wife should be perfectly happy, and enjoy good health for . . . their twelve month tour' (Alldridge, 1910:104-36).

By the early years of the century, the rapid introduction of the railway had opened up the rural area for exploitation of agricultural products. Almost 140 miles inland was Bo where the railway station had recently been completed. Behind it was a large compound, 'though more like a park, carefully laid out with trees, through which run well-kept private roads'. Here were nine bungalows 'several being of spacious dimensions, forming three sides of a large quadrangle'. Originally built for the railway construction staff, they had been taken over by the colonial government for official residences with tanks for storing water gathered from corrugated iron roofs. 'Though the mention of such roofs is shocking to English taste,' few people in England appreciated their value as waterproof coverings.

The bungalows were occupied by the district commissioner, medical officer, school principal, and the largest by the circuit judge and his wife. At the time of the visit, the judge's wife was the only European woman living in the bungalows and, 'though feeling the want of female society' there were advantages: if anything was wanted 'you only had to wire for it and it arrived by the next train.' As Bo was one of the healthiest locations in the colony, the government had chosen it for the site of a school for the sons and nominees of native chiefs (ibid.). In future years, the lifestyles of the local European community were not to go unnoticed. As for the establishment of 'Hill Station', its 'health' premises were to prove mistaken: it simply served to segregate Europeans from Freetown Creoles and lead to a deterioration in relations between races (Spitzer, 1968).

African dwelling and settlement forms

These developing European settlement and housing forms were typical of other colonial enclaves at this time. Their significance is best understood in comparison with African forms and their relation to the pre-colonial economy and society. And despite an immense variety of peoples and forms of economic and social organisation in Africa, certain generalisations can be made (Amin, 1977:140; Mabogunje, 1980).

Though there is a long urban tradition in Western Africa, predominant forms of settlement in pre-colonial Africa were rural, with an economy of peasant agriculture (Hull, 1976; Mabogunje, 1968). The basic functional unit of society was the extended family. Fundamental to an understanding of the economy is its relationship to land: the extended family is the unit that generally owns land and whose members relate to this land on the basis of values and rules sanctioned by the society. In West Africa, much land is also controlled communally with effective control vested in local chiefs. Land belonged not only to its present cultivators but to their ancestors and their descendants. As an African chief is reputed to have said, 'land belongs to a vast family of which many are dead, few are living and countless members are still unborn' (Coulson, 1971:203). Traditionally, no African society recognised the sale of land though with the introduction of cash crops, this gradually changed.

The kinship relation also determined the organisation of labour and residence. Usually, this was based on the allocation of tasks to different age grades who worked on family land, or on other community tasks. Crops and animals were raised with the aid of a variety of tools. Surplus crops were stored in containers which ranged in size from simple pots to large granaries or barns. In many rural communities, according to Mabogunje (1980), land is divided into two categories, one near the homestead, intensely and permanently cultivated, the other further away which is allowed to lie fallow in alternative seasons.

The residential forms to which this system of economy, technology and social organisation give rise take the form of a compound comprising a number of individual huts or a continuous building of many rooms. Such compounds may be isolated or grouped into hamlets or villages. The different types of dwelling, construction materials and techniques, and the spatial organisation of the compound, have been discussed and illustrated at length. Among different peoples and regions, an immense variety of dwelling-forms and lay-outs exist (plate 117): yet what they have in common is that they are all related to the form of economic activity and its associated social organisation (Denyer, 1978; Hull, 1976; Oliver, 1970, 1975).

Amongst only a few people was a single building the norm, and this was found mostly

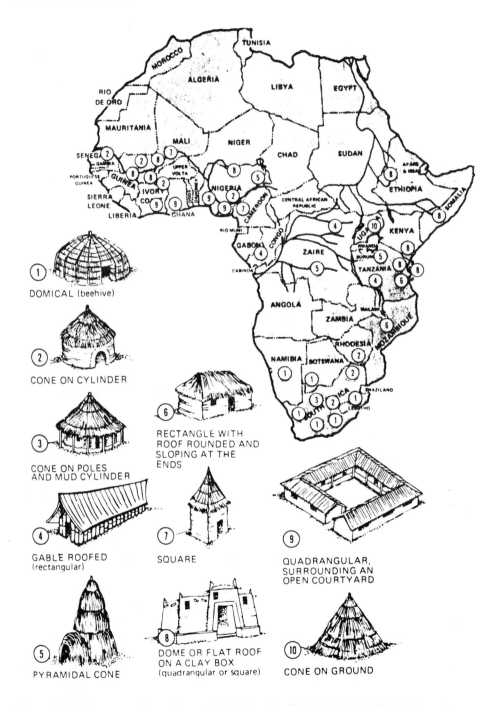

Figure 6.5   Major structural forms of precolonial African dwellings (R.W.Hull, *African Cities and Towns before the European Conquest*, 1976, W.W.Norton, New York)

where buildings were square or rectangular rather than circular. The more usual arrangement is for compounds to have many separate buildings, each one, in effect, a 'room' of the homestead, with one special purpose – a kitchen, man's bedroom, wife's bedroom, grain store (Denyer, 1978:21).

In the pre-colonial towns and cities, the design of buildings was likewise the product of family and tribal structures as well as religious, political and economic institutions. In such towns and cities, compounds usually looked inward on an open courtyard. This inner space provided a communal area for washing, cooking, craft work, relaxation and perhaps prayer. At the centre of the Hausa compound were the dwellings of the compound head, his wives, children and immediate relatives, and separate units for storage and cooking: each wife had her own hut for herself and her young children. The most common organisation of a compound was that each wife had a cluster of units reserved for her own use (Hull, 1976).

The Yoruba compound, unlike that of the Hausa or Nupe, was an enclosed space, generally a square, bounded by a mud wall about 7 feet high. Inside, the compound was divided into numerous rooms housing a number of related families. Until the early twentieth century, most of the houses of the compounds were roofed with thatch; the smallest walled area might cover half an acre, those of the chiefs, several acres. A compound housed an extended family

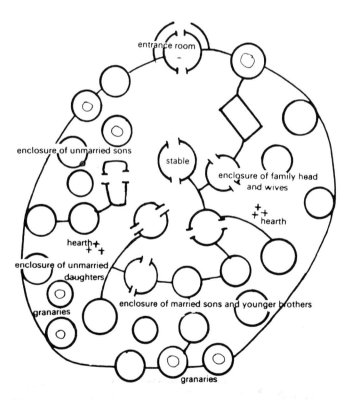

Figure 6.6 Social and spatial organisation in a peasant economy: plan of a Nupe chief's house, central Nigeria, about 1940 (S.Denyer, *African Traditional Architecture*, 1978, Heinemann Educational)

comprising a man's immediate, though polygamous, family, the families of his grown male children and sometimes the families of his brothers as well as slaves belonging to each family.

The basic unit of residential organisation in Nigerian towns, however, was the 'quarter' or 'ward', consisting of groups of compounds. Depending on the city or state, ward identity might be based on one or more considerations: ethnic, military, occupational, social or religious. Wards were further combined into political quarters in the larger African communities. Pre-colonial Kano (plate 121), in northern Nigeria, had 127 such wards, each associated with particular ethnic or religious groups; Benin city, on the other hand, was largely of one ethnic group, though the city was divided according to craft organisation and ritual priesthoods connected to ancestor worship. Long before Europeans arrived, there was in many cities segregation based on race, ethnicity and culture, probably a device for maintaining control over strangers.

Differences in social and political status were often reflected in house style, building materials and the proximity of the dwelling to the royal compound, as in Benin city. In Kumasi, Benin and Abomey, two-storey houses were the exclusive right of the monarchs. The *afins* or palace compounds of the Obas of Yoruba towns had a distinctive *kobi*, resembling a porch; these were architectural marks of rank and only houses of the Obas and a few other high-ranking officials could possess them.

In many African communities, dwellings were arranged according to the occupants' social or political status. In Yoruba towns, the Oba's afin was situated in the centre of the town, next to the marketplace. In Southern Africa, Zulu *kraals* were organised in such a way as to demonstrate which parts were occupied by the major, and which the lesser, wives.

'The layout articulated a design intended to minimise social friction and to assign every family member his or her rightful place . . . the kraal layout was a physical expression of the institution of polygamy' (Hull, 1976:90) (plate 120).

The impact of colonialism

The impact of colonialism on house and settlement forms was part of its overall drastic impact on the economy. Traditional structures were undermined and gradually destroyed by the penetration of the capitalist mode of production. Specifically, this meant the further monetisation of the economy (which had begun before the colonial impact) with the basic factors of production, land and labour, turned into commodities to be bought and sold. This is the starting point for understanding the development of a market in land, the construction of property as well as the ability to buy and rent it from the profits of wage labour (Mabogunje, 1980:80 et seq.).

The ownership of land began to be individualised, in the process eliminating all claims on it originating in kinship or neighbourhood organisations, though family land did persist. Peasants moved into cities, even though, in West Africa, many retained rights over land which could be exercised if they returned home. In addition, land was subordinated to the needs of the rapidly expanding urban population, created by the market economy. The agricultural surplus, previously supplying the neighbourhood and local town, was now shipped abroad to feed the inhabitants of the expanding metropole of Britain. In the words of Mabogunje, 'Farmers in the tropical and sub-tropical zones were drawn into the vortex of an industrialising, urbanising Europe, based on capitalist production.' Land was taken over for cash crops – groundnuts, palm oil, or newly introduced coffee, cocoa or tea for export.

Lancashire textile interests promoted cotton plantations (Porter, 1975:192). Yet in this process, as Europeans 'pushed', Africans also 'joined'.

The replacement of the peasant economy by the capitalist mode of production, even though it was not always total, required, to use Mabogunje's phrase, 'a more appropriate spatial order'. Fundamental to this was the establishment of law and order to ensure the conditions for colonial economic production. The two main elements in re-structuring the peasant economy and re-orienting it to the metropole was a new transport network based on the railway, and a new system of towns. These concentrated the rural surplus and organised the available labour force.

To ease the transition of land from collective to individual and commercial ownership, legal, administrative and commercial rules developed in European countries came increasingly to be applied to land in African countries. In East Africa especially, where there were large settler populations, extensive tracts of land were set aside for European occupation. And for land under indigenous proprietorship, individual holdings were introduced. As the land tenure system became more complex, farmers, driven off the land, became labourers in the towns, contributing to a new class structure.

Colonial settlement: the dwelling

The new colonial settlements were part of this 'more appropriate' spatial and administrative order: on these, the basic dwelling unit was the colonial bungalow. An insight into the nature of this is provided by a unique report (Colonial Office, 1909).

As indicated above, Ross's discoveries had important implications both for the siting and design of European living accommodation in Africa. Moreover, the rapid penetration of the Nigerian interior, over two hundred miles from the coast, meant that at least some minimum, even temporary, accommodation was now an urgent necessity for both military and civilian personnel. Previously, some housing had been provided for government officials in the coastal area in the form of timber and iron bungalows sent out from England by the Crown Agents. Yet there were many complaints about these. It was to gather their collective experience that the Colonial Secretary, Lord Elgin, wrote to the Governors of Sierra Leone, Gambia, the Gold Coast, Lagos, and the High Commissioner of Northern Nigeria in 1906. Their replies, together with other appendices, drawings and photographs were published in 1909.

Perhaps the first point to notice is the extent of Indian influence, either implicit or explicit. Elgin himself had spent five years as viceroy of India in the 1890s; F.D. Lugard, High Commissioner for Northern Nigeria and subsequently largely responsible for developing the administrative and urban structure of Nigeria, had been born of missionary parents in Madras and had served in the Indian army. Lugard's Director of Public Works was also an old 'India hand'. W. Egerton, the governor at Lagos, had, in his own words,

> the advantage of 23 years service in one of His Majesty's tropical possessions [Malaya] and one in which the designers of houses enjoy the experience of generations of Indian officials and of the native races in designing houses most suitable for occupation in countries adjacent to the Equator.

The correspondence was summed up on behalf of the Crown Agents by a Royal Engineers colonel, R.D. Lloyd, with over twenty-nine years of service there who believed that:

we cannot do better than follow the experience of India. . . . It is well known that West Africans [i.e. European colonial officials in W. Africa], until military and civil officers of Indian experience began to arrive, knew or cared little of the usual precautions required to make life in the tropics bearable.

The correspondence represented the collective experience of British officials as it had evolved over two-and-a-half centuries, specifically mentioning the West Indies, India, Ceylon, Malaya, Burma and West Africa, as well as recent American experience in the construction of the Panama Canal.

The criticism concerned both the materials and the design; rooms were too small and too low-pitched to hang a punkah (another import from India); windows were too small for ventilation and the anti-mosquito wire gauze covering led to 'impossible heat and stuffiness'. Yet, whilst most writers expressed dissatisfaction with the portable bungalows, their merits were also appreciated. With the rapid territorial expansion, buildings were needed which were light, transportable and quickly erected with unskilled labour. For Lugard, opening up some 300,000 square miles of 'unexplored' territory in Northern Nigeria, prefabricated housing had been essential. In cantonments (another concept from India), necessarily on a river or railway, he had adopted wooden bungalows as the cheapest and best form of shelter, despite the fire hazard. Yet at outstations such as Sokoto, Kano and Kuka, over 250 miles from a river or railway, the cost of transport had made them impracticable; bungalows were therefore built of local stone or brick with perhaps doors, window frames, rafters and light iron roofing sent up from the coast.

Portable bungalows also provided flexibility in location; the first site selected was often not the best. Moreover, the advantages of the light, portable bungalow were also seen in the swampy, unstable ground of the Niger delta where a more substantial stone or brick house would have required the expensive sinking of piers.

While this historical evidence sheds light on some of the explicit assumptions behind the introduction of the bungalow, it says little or nothing about the implicit ones.

A better understanding is gained by referring to the two societies with which it was associated, the 'pre-industrial' African and the metropolitan British, with its capitalist industrial economy.

Most obviously, the reason for its existence in Africa was political: it housed the representative of the colonial power in the same sense as, in the indigenous African village, the most prominent dwelling housed the tribal chief. Yet from an economic and technological viewpoint, the imported bungalow had no or little connection to the indigenous economy. Its materials and manufacture were undertaken in Britain, the product of power-driven machinery using inanimate sources of energy – steam or electricity. Few, if any, local materials were used. However, local labour, under colonial supervision, seems likely to have been used for putting it up, and if paid for, came from the surplus appropriated from the local African economy. If built of local materials, the overall design meant that construction techniques were imported.

From a social and cultural viewpoint, the bungalow was a form of shelter designed for a single person, or nuclear family, often with servants, but socially (though not administratively) unconnected with the surrounding population. By the nature of this task, the official was on his own, or resided with a handful of colleagues, in an alien environment. Unlike the local population who built their dwellings collectively, as members of a kin or community group, the official was isolated; the community to which he belonged was thousands of miles away.

Thus, where the Yoruba chief lived collectively in a compound, and the compound was part of a quarter, the resultant dwelling was part of a collective unit. And while this had an economic, social, cultural or religious rationale, it also made sense in climatic terms. The thick-walled mud housing, each house unit fused to the next, allowed little heat to penetrate.

In comparison, the colonial official was a social isolate. This fact, together with a commitment to long-established cultural preferences and the nature of his political office, meant that the colonial dwelling was equally isolated and 'detached'. As such, it presented its inhabitants with problems of coping with an unaccustomed 'tropical' climate which the occupants of indigenous dwellings did not face. The most obvious of these was that of keeping the sun off the external walls; hence, the development of and concern with the verandah.

Such a 'social' explanation for the form of the bungalow, however, is clearly only partial. There were also historical, economic and cultural reasons why colonial officials lived in single, 'detached' dwellings, the same reasons which had led British emigrants to build detached, single-storey cottages in other parts of the tropical world where they were not in a comparable colonial situation, i.e. the southern states of North America, the West Indies or Australia.

In the late nineteenth century, the colonial administrator came from a society where, among the bourgeois class to which he belonged, one separate dwelling increasingly housed, and was the property of, one (nuclear) family; where, after almost two centuries of capitalist industrial development, house space had, for this class, been constantly enlarged and divided into separate and distinct specialised rooms to accommodate both different domestic activities and functions (cooking, eating, sleeping, bathing, relaxation), differences of social rank, age and gender (with spaces for servants, children and different sexes), but more especially to accommodate the accumulation of consumer goods made available through the mass market which industrial capitalism had created: soft furnishing, specialised equipment, a variety of clothes, cooking utensils and the general accoutrements of living.

These material developments had led, as we shall see below, to the development of certain attitudes and expectations about standards: social expectations of comfort, of states of health, of privacy, of aesthetic satisfaction in terms of internal and external appearances of dwellings, of 'outlooks', and 'views', and of houses as symbols of social position and status. Culturally, they also had particular expectations about the use of space, about explanations of disease and especially, about the tolerance of temperatures and climatic extremes. In comparison, Africans had quite different attitudes, expectations and explanations. A further social assumption, partly resulting from the perception of climatic differences though more from social ideas about privacy – and one that contrasted especially with African practice – was that all domestic activities, eating, sleeping, bathing, should, in general, be undertaken inside the house, out of sight of the indigenous inhabitants.

These considerations, however, were all implicit; the two most explicit requirements were, according to the report, the need to preserve the health and the comfort of the inhabitants.

A major fault of existing bungalows was the problem of over-heating caused by corrugated iron roofs. The complaints of the eminent traveller, Mary Kingsley, in *Travels in West Africa* (1895), were typical:

> corrugated iron is my abomination. I quite understand it has its points and I do not attack it from an aesthetic viewpoint. . . . There is, close to Christianborg Castle at Accra, Gold Coast, a patch of bungalows and offices for officialdom and wife that . . . in the hard bright sunshine look like an encampment of snow white tents among the cocoa palms, and pretty enough withal. . . . But the heat inside these iron houses is far greater than

inside mud-walled, brick or wooden ones, and the alterations of temperature more sudden; mornings and evenings they were cold and clammy; and draughty they are always, thereby giving you chill, which means fever, and fever in West Africa means more than it does in most places.

The main remedy was to provide space or insulation between the metal roof and the ceiling below. In Australia, double corrugated steel, with an air space between, was used. Other methods included fixing a layer of felt on the lower side of the rafters to give a 6-inch gap to the roof, though this required leaving the gutterboarding open and the space was then invaded by bats, birds and lizards. Another method, brought from India, was a 3-inch layer of charcoal placed over the ceiling, the effect of which was to lower thermal temperatures on average by some 2 degrees Fahrenheit. Roof ventilators, enthusiastically developed by engineers in England, proved disastrous in the Nigerian climate. During tornadoes, high winds swept rain into the ventilators and thence, through the ceiling. In one case, a director of public works had found the occupants of a bungalow sitting round the dining table wearing their solar topis to keep the rain from dripping on their dinner.

Many of the new roofing materials developed in Britain at the end of the nineteenth century had been imported and tried out by Lugard. For the rest-house at Burutu, Southern Nigeria, glazed tiles had been shipped in, only to be found broken on arrival; the felt sent out for house roofs in Wushishi had perished before it was used. The earlier houses built at Lokoja had been roofed with Willesden canvas; yet this had first rotted and then been torn to shreds by the tornadoes. 'Asbestile' had proved 'little better than cardboard' and 'Uralite' had too high a degree of conductivity. 'Eternit' slates had also been imported. The patented wire-wove bungalows (concrete slabs reinforced with wire mesh netting) had cracked and let in the rain. In the end, Lugard, like the others, had reverted to corrugated iron.

The problem of housing colonial officials in West Africa was very different from India: there, labour was cheap and skilful, materials plentiful and inexpensive, and much more money, as we shall see below, was spent on housing by the government, private concerns and Indian owners. Tiles were burnt on the spot, or flat-terraced roofs used. These had not yet developed for colonial use in Africa.

What all correspondents agreed was that the bungalow, whether wood, brick or stone, should be raised on wood or concrete piers off the ground. For some, these should be 4, for others, 8 feet. The rationale for this had changed over the years. 'It dated back to the time, comparative recent, when the cause of malarial fever was generally attributed to exhalations from the ground.' Yet despite later discoveries about the real causes of malaria, earlier practices were not abandoned. Raising the bungalow off the ground ensured greater dryness, ventilation, freedom from dust 'in all countries a potent carrier of disease', and invasion from insects. 'Undoubtedly, mosquitos will be fewer in a high than a low bungalow'; the greater the superficial area covered, the higher the bungalow. Moreover, the added height of the white man's house no doubt gave psychological, even moral, advantages. Whatever the origins of the bungalow on piers, the British were credited with having adopted the principle from indigenous tropical peoples in contrast to the practice of Dutch, Spanish and Portuguese colonisers whose more solid, stone or brick-built houses had been placed firmly on the ground. Unlike the lightly constructed bungalow, these were also much more susceptible to earthquake damage (Rodenweldt, 1938).

The alternative to bungalows on piers was one of two storeys with living accommodation upstairs and the ground floor, to a greater or lesser extent, built as an 'arcade', kept for

EUROPEAN BUNGALOWS.
SAPELE.

SCALE 40 FT TO 1 INCH.

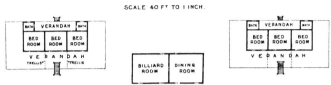

(C.3) EUROPEAN BUNGALOW, SAPELE.

ABOUT THREE YEARS OLD, ONE OF THE FIRST TYPE OF PERMANENT BRICK HOUSES.
THE SIDE VERANDAHS HAVE BEEN ADDED LATER - THE ENDS OF THE HOUSE BEING
WITHOUT PROTECTION RENDERED SOME ROOMS ALMOST UNINHABITABLE AT CERTAIN
HOURS OF THE DAY. THE VERANDAHS ARE OF THE CORRECT OPEN TYPE BUT THE
ROOMS ARE TOO SMALL; IT WOULD HAVE BEEN BETTER TO HAVE HAD LARGER
ROOMS AND TO HAVE REDUCED THE SIZE OF THE VERANDAHS PROPORTIONATELY.
HAD THE BASEMENT BEEN RAISED 3FT MORE THE ACCOMMODATION WOULD
HAVE BEEN DOUBLED FOR ALMOST THE SAME SUM OF MONEY. THE BASEMENT
SHOULD HAVE BEEN EITHER LOWER OR HIGHER TO GIVE MORE SPACE;
EVEN AS IT IS BASEMENT PROVIDES FOR BOX AND STORE ROOMS.

HEIGHT OF EAVES 7 FT

SCALE 20 FT TO 1 INCH.

EUROPEAN BUNGALOWS.
WARRI, 1906.

C.4.

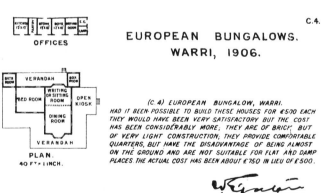

(C.4) EUROPEAN BUNGALOW, WARRI.

HAD IT BEEN POSSIBLE TO BUILD THESE HOUSES FOR £500 EACH
THEY WOULD HAVE BEEN VERY SATISFACTORY BUT THE COST
HAS BEEN CONSIDERABLY MORE; THEY ARE OF BRICK BUT
OF VERY LIGHT CONSTRUCTION; THEY PROVIDE COMFORTABLE
QUARTERS, BUT HAVE THE DISADVANTAGE OF BEING ALMOST
ON THE GROUND AND ARE NOT SUITABLE FOR FLAT AND DAMP
PLACES. THE ACTUAL COST HAS BEEN ABOUT £750 IN LIEU OF £500.

PLAN.
40 FT = 1 INCH.

SCALE 20FT = 1 IN.

ESTIMATED COST £500.

HEIGHT TO EAVES 7 FT

Figure 6.7 The bungalow transferred: official colonial housing in West Africa, 1906 (Colonial Office, West Africa, *The Design of Bungalows for Government Officials in West Africa*, 1909)

storage or office space. This had occasionally been the pattern in the Gambia but, according to the governor, it was not to be encouraged. 'With the office so near, one is always liable to calls, and this becomes very trying in a climate that has such an effect on the nerves as does that of the West Coast of Africa.'

Unaccustomed to what was perceived as 'the hot, steamy and oppressive climate of West Africa,' the paramount need was to keep cool. For this, generous dimensions and the 'perflation of breezes' were seen as pre-requisites. 'The ideal bungalow should be spacious and lofty,' wrote the governor of Sierra Leone. Verandahs should go all round the house and be 'as wide as money will allow' – one 12 feet wide was 'a great additional comfort in a house'.

Colonial settlement: social space

The scale of accommodation varied according to social rank and region. Fairly typical were the four types of two-storey bungalows provided in the Gold Coast for senior officers (married or single), junior officers (married), junior bachelors, and those for up-country quarters. For the higher ranks, the ground floor contained dining room, store room, pantry and box room; the first floor, a sitting room, 2 bedrooms, 2 mosquito rooms, 2 bathrooms, 1 or 2 earth closets, 1 kiosk (or porch) and an 8' verandah; outbuildings included a kitchen, lamp room, boys' room, forage room, stables for two or three horses and a drying closet. Bungalows for junior bachelors were smaller, with only one bed and bathroom and without store rooms, mosquito rooms (protected by mesh), kiosk and lamp room, and with stabling for only one horse. In the following, all figures refer to feet (30 cm).

Room sizes were determined both by cultural and psychological factors: 'larger rooms are, of course, more comfortable, as the feeling of roominess in a tropical house produces a feeling of coolness'. On these grounds, the typical bedroom size for a junior officer was about 16 by 16, 20 or 24 by 16 for a dining room, and 8 by 8 for a bath or store room. For senior officials, the dining room might be increased to 38 by 16, and other rooms, to 10 by 8. Room heights were to be a minimum of 11, giving ample room for a punkah.

The Indian experience of the Crown Agent's representative, Colonel Lloyd, led him to conclude that these dimensions were too small. There was, after all, the question of proportion to consider: for large rooms, 'double cubes, such as 40 by 20, are handsome and useful'. A 'nice size' for a bedroom was 14 by 18; a drawing room of 17 by 24 would accommodate eight people and a dining room of that size, twelve guests.

The rationale for the large size and also number of rooms was the concern for coolness: 'for the sake of airiness, the sleeping room should contain little furniture but the bed and wardrobe; this necessitates a dressing and bathroom and also a store room to keep his belongings.' These included a wardrobe, chest of drawers, washstand, bootrack, writing table and 'articles of a private nature'. The bed, according to the West African pocket book, should be kept away from the wall on both sides, incurring a loss of 24 square feet from the room area. Moreover, 'every young officer should have a second room for the sake of health so that in the event of his not being well enough to go out he might not have to spend the whole of the day in one room.'

Other social considerations governed the number of bungalows on a station. Even where a number of officers were stationed together, it was thought that each should have his own bungalow. Lugard's view, that officers should dine and relax in a central 'mess house', using their bungalows primarily for sleeping was generally not shared by others. More typical was the Gold Coast practice: 'In order to ensure comfort and privacy, each bungalow should stand in its own compound and be allotted to one officer only, and in no cases should offices be contained in, or form part of the bungalow.' In the view of the medical officer, it was often the case that a three-roomed bungalow was shared by two officers 'who cannot hit it off'; one wanted his lunch at 11.30 and the other, at 12.00 and there was only one kitchen. The other officer's 'boys' were always about the place and if anything was missing 'it was only natural to the native to accuse the other servants'. Moreover, the choice of a young officer's companions was not always discreet: 'there is a tendency to keep late hours, to introduce third parties, and for contentions to arise among the servants. . . . Losses of property are frequent when servants of two masters are in one bungalow.' The objection to incorporating offices likewise stemmed from a distrust of the native Africans. Even if the office was only used by the bungalow's occupant, there was still 'the traffic of natives to and from the bungalow and through the compound'.

The size of the bungalow was an important indicator of status. In Ceylon, for example, quarters were provided not exceeding twice the annual salary of the occupant: the maintenance of these differentials was crucial; 'any officer compelled to live in quarters that did not come up to the standard of accommodation due to his provision and salary should receive compensation in lieu'.

The most essential part of the bungalow was the verandah, an element which – though significantly absent from the large majority of traditional African and Asian dwellings – had long been a feature of European colonial houses in the tropics. Ostensibly, its function was to keep the sun's heat off the walls; but the verandah had for long been one of the main eating, living and sleeping areas of the colonial bungalow (King, 1976:148-52). The verandah, a minimum of 8' wide, or 10 and 12 feet for more expensive houses, and preferably all round the house, combined with the need for all rooms to go through from front to back, to ensure the 'perflation of the breezes', to result in large, and hence, expensive houses, to say nothing of the effects on land use. As the Governor of Lagos pointed out, with front and back verandahs 12' wide, and a room of 15', it meant a roof span of 39' for the sake of one room. Yet verandahs were deemed essential and 'those less than 6 feet pertain to stinginess and badly-proportioned design'.

Increased awareness of the danger of mosquitos favoured the enclosed verandah, which might then be used, according to some, as an office, sitting or dining room; an enclosed verandah also reduced the extent to which roof eaves needed to be brought down. Most agreed that bungalows were best only one room deep; to fill verandahs with bathrooms and store rooms defeated their purpose. This was where one-and-a-half centuries of Indian experience was put to good use: bathrooms in the corners of verandahs did not interfere with through air circulation for the rooms. Alternatively, bathrooms could be located in the rear annex, connected to the bungalow by a mosquito-proof bridge.

With the discovery of the mosquito origins of malaria, attention moved from raising the bungalow off the ground to keeping mosquitos out of the house. Apart from changes in design, this meant importing huge quantities of closed mesh zinc gauze. There were a number of ways of combating mosquitos: to proof the whole house; to do one room only; to cover all – or part of – the verandah; to provide movable mosquito-proof cages; or simply, to put mosquito nets round the bed. Yet fitting wire gauze on the windows or verandahs prevented 'the perflation of the prevailing breeze' and hence, defeated the basic rationale for the bungalow – to keep cool. There was a need for an entirely mosquito-proof house: one cage or proofed room was insufficient: 'one cannot spend the early morning and evening after sundown in a small room'.

Keeping the compound clear of undergrowth and stagnant water was equally important. It was

> absolutely imperative that the site of a bungalow for non-native officers should be removed from the propinquity to native dwellings as it is not the bite of a mosquito per se which mattered but the bite of an infected mosquito. It is not segregation from natives as such but segregation from them as infective sources which is here emphasized.

Despite the much-emphasised sensitivity to economy, the cost of different types of bungalow varied between £1,000 and £2,000, more usually at the higher level. At Lagos, that of the general manager of railways cost £1,500; the principal medical officer, £1,775. The provision of punkas, mosquito cages, water tanks and other fittings brought the total to over £2,000.

Though different forms of bungalow developed in the ensuing decades, and governor's houses exhibited varying degrees of splendour, the basic concerns with ventilation, comfort, privacy, status, servants' quarters, specialised room space and family needs, were to govern colonial housing design until, and indeed, long after, the end of colonial rule.

The transition to capitalist urbanisation

The system of towns and cities was, with the introduction of the railway, the pre-requisite for the transformation of the rural economy. This transformation was broadly in three kinds of area: the established enclaves on the coast, the traditional towns and cities of West Africa, and in the new administrative towns or, in East Africa, settler towns, set up in previously rural areas. Whether for colonial official, missionary, merchant or teacher, the bungalow, variously modified but still a single family, Western house-type designed for European use in the tropics, and located in its compound, was the standard residential unit on all colonial settlements. These were based on a strict system of segregation.

For example, in the East African Protectorate in 1910, the governor, E.P.C. Girouard, issued a memorandum to his provincial and district commissioners in the Kenya Province.

> In native areas, the District Commissioner is responsible for the condition of the station and all matters connected with it. . . . Every DC should take a pride in keeping his station as clean and healthy as possible. . . . Gardens should be made . . . roads constructed . . . and the police and porter lines and other native locations should be laid out symmetrically. Regarding townships, when the Provincial Commissioner considered that the outlying township was likely to become permanent, he should communicate with the Land Office . . . and ask that the town be laid out on more permanent lines suitable for future development. In doing this, he should a) specify land required for government purposes b) nominate sites required for public buildings (markets, churches, hospitals, water-works, etc) and c) indicate the position of the following quarters
>> European business quarters
>> Indian business quarters
>> European residential quarters
>> Native location
>> Market garden site
>
>> (East Africa Protectorate, 1910:14-15).

In Nigeria, the foundations of the modern urban system were laid out by Lugard in his Townships Ordinance of 1917. As part of the system of 'indirect rule' – by which native institutions were preserved under the overall authority of the colonial power – the government provided for the creation, constitution and administration of all towns in Nigeria, categorised into first-, second- and third-class townships. These townships were areas *outside* centres of African population, set aside for colonial administration and commerce. 'The essential feature of a township is that it is an enclave outside the jurisdiction of the native authority and native courts which are relieved of the difficult task . . . of controlling alien natives, employees of government and Europeans.' The Non-European Reservation was for those African and Syrian migrant traders, labourers, police and others who were associated with the colonial regime but were not native to the local area (Home, 1976). In subsequent years, the two areas were to merge together.

The influence of Lugard on Nigerian urban development was so great, and his views so clearly spelt out, that it is worth examining them in some detail. When laying out townships, each compound in the European Reservation was to be 100 yards in depth, 70 to 100 yards wide (viz., from 1½ to 2 acres), and be enclosed by a live hedge, mud wall or substantial fence. Within this area, ornamental and shade trees and dhub grass were to be planted, though compounds were to be kept fairly clear; 'prisoners may be hired to clean up a compound from time to time.' Servants' quarters and stables would be at least 50 yards to the rear and near a backline, along which a sanitary lane was provided. The European Reservation was surrounded by a non-residential area 440 yards broad separating it from a non-European or Native Reservation. Apart from *bona fide* domestic servants, no Native might reside in the European Reservation and no European in the Native Reservation. Overcrowding should, for reasons of health, be prevented and not more than ten occupants should be on any plot. Houses were to be of burnt brick or mud walls and with non-inflammable roofing; angle iron for ridge poles and rafters was to be encouraged both to prevent fire hazards and decrease the cutting of trees which 'would soon denude the surrounding country of its timber and beauty' (Lugard, 1970:416 et seq.).

The object of the non-residential area was to segregate Europeans so that they were not exposed to attacks of mosquitoes infected with the germs of malaria or yellow fever 'by preying on Natives and especially Native children'. It was also seen as a safeguard against bush fires and those common in Native quarters. Finally, it also removed the inconvenience felt by Europeans 'whose rest was disturbed by drumming and other noises dear to the Native'.

On the other side of the European Reservation which did not face the Native Reservation, non-residential buildings such as a church or courthouse could be erected. The area could also be devoted to golf links, polo grounds, race course and other recreation purposes as well as railway shunting grounds and parade grounds of the army and police.

If not as avid an amateur architect-planner as his French contemporary in colonial North Africa, Maréchal Lyautey (Abu-Lughod, 1980), Lugard nevertheless had very developed views both on housing and planning. On the whole, he was in favour of two-storey houses with the upper floor kept for living and sleeping rooms.

The policy of segregation which he discussed on numerous occasions seems to have been the basic principle for his planning practice, despite the bitter controversy to which it gave rise both from British Indians and Africans that it was simply 'a manifestation of racial arrogance and prejudice'. Though he always justified it in terms of health, he also quoted Lord Milner who thought it desirable 'no less in the interests of social comfort and convenience'. Lugard believed that it should be made abundantly clear that what is aimed at is a segregation of social standards and not a segregation of races. The Indian or African gentleman who adopts the higher standard of civilisation and desires to partake in such immunity from infection as segregation may convey, should be as free and welcome to live in the civilised reservation as the European, provided, of course, that he does not bring with him a concourse of followers. The native peasant often shares his hut with his goat or sheep or fowls. He loves to drum . . . he is sceptical of mosquito theories (1965:149-50).

When Lugard amalgamated Northern and Southern Nigeria, moving the Northern capital from Zungeru to Kaduna in 1916, these principles were implemented on a wide scale. 'The strictest economy was practised in the move.' The 'temporary wooden houses' and old buildings at Zungeru were dismantled and 'every sound plank used for outhouses in the new capital'. The barracks, European and native hospitals and remaining bungalows became a training centre for troops. The only permanent brick structure of any value at Zungeru was the prison 'and this I propose to convert into a lunatic asylum for the whole of Nigeria which is most urgently required' (Kirk-Greene, 1968:94-6).

Given their political origins and rationale, the new European Reservations were to be greatly influenced by the bungalow idea and the assumptions on which it was based. Though the models described earlier were modified, both in scale and form, the model dwelling developed for Europeans retained its basic characteristics: generous dimensions, accommodation for single nuclear family but with separate provision for servants, imported 'tropical' design and materials (especially cement) and invariably in a large walled or fenced compound. A cluster of these, whether ten or two hundred, produced the characteristic lay-out of very low densities. To permit such a lay-out, extensive land area was required. Where this was near an existing town or village, for political, social, and cultural reasons, the European area was distanced from it.

To ensure the transfer of land from collective to individual ownership, legal, administrative and commercial rules were imported from England, even though, in the event, the transfer was not always successful. Likewise, to enforce and maintain the particular residential and commercial areas, bye-laws, environmental and building standards, and municipal legislation governing road widths, densities and construction standards were introduced, increasingly influenced by town planning and 'garden city' ideas from Britain (King, 1980c). In the traditional Yoruba city of Ibadan, the non-European Reservation or 'Sabon Gari' ('Strangers' Town') characteristically bore the name 'Gbagi', a Yoruba term for 'pegged out', reflecting the colonial surveyors' activities in 1904 (Mabogunje, 1968:194). Much of the modern form of West African towns, therefore, can be seen to derive from the bungalow-and-compound idea.

The bungalow as model

The change by some Africans to Western house forms seems to have taken place in a number of contexts. One was by the adoption of European lifestyles and housing models by African elites, in many cases, facilitated by the introduction of imported materials (plate 123); the second, was by the enforcement of colonial and European building standards in the new townships; the third, though this was a late development, was in the provision of housing for African government employees by the Public Works Department, or for African labour by some European firms. As, in many cases, Africans had no right to the permanent ownership of land or to buy property in urban areas, 'sanitary' housing was both required for labour and useful as an instrument of social control. All these contexts were part of much larger and complex economic, social and cultural changes. Though not the most important explanation, the easiest with which to begin is the introduction of imported materials and technology.

These, first evident in the coastal ports, with the introduction of the railway, were rapidly diffused inland. At different rates and in different areas they came to compete with the mud, grass, thatch, wattle and daub or baked brick traditionally used in various regions. An early change in Nigeria was the replacement of mud walls by baked brick. Two brick kilns were set up in Lagos in the 1860s, one of them by missionaries, a group to become increasingly influential in the introduction of European models and lifestyles, especially in relation to ideas of health. Later, cement was introduced, both for blocks and for plastering brick and mud houses. (Mabogunje, 1968:118) In the early twentieth century, Lugard had used reinforced concrete for European dwellings, and in French Senegal about the same time, the architect Auguste Perret had constructed concrete warehouses – a first priority for colonial nations exporting raw materials to the metropole. Cement became a major import, rivalled only perhaps by corrugated iron for roofs.

European missionaries had put up the first iron roofs in Ibadan in 1854; in the next fifty years it was to steadily replace thatch. In Lagos in 1862, European merchants requested the British governor that native houses be covered with a less combustible material than that in use; in 1877, a more specific proposal was made to cover, at the cost of the inhabitants, the houses of the poor with corrugated iron as a precaution against fire hazard. Though this was turned down, here too, by the end of the century, corrugated iron had become a popular roofing material (Mabogunje, 1968:118-9, 173).

Importing new materials had many and far-reaching consequences. For Africans to buy them meant accumulating capital and hence, further involvement in the wage economy. In the larger cities, traditional building skills began to be lost and, in different places and to different degrees, traditional housing models and materials downgraded in social esteem as foreign, imported models were adopted. Building became a specialised activity and metropolitan firms coming later in the twentieth century brought imported technology and new materials for large commercial and administrative buildings. The import of housing models and materials was increasingly stimulated by the growing numbers of Europeans in African towns; by 1960, the Congo, Kenya, Mozambique and Angola each had a population of over 50,000 Europeans.

Other glimpses can be gained into a process which remains largely uninvestigated. As Marx foretold about India, the railway system would become the forerunner of modern industry. Likewise in Africa, railway workshops and repair shops initiated, in many places, the onset of industrialisation. As far as imported technology is concerned, some illustrative data can be given. An early saw-milling plant was set up in Rhodesia in 1897 and a cement factory by the British South Africa Company in 1915. In Kenya, Portland Cement established the cement grinding of imported clinker in the early 1930s. With the Second World War cutting off imported supplies, domestic production was stimulated, again helped by increased European immigration once the war had ended, causing increased production of cement, asbestos tiles, pipes, metal doors and windows. A plywood factory was set up in 1948. As growing numbers of Africans entered wage labour, domestic consumption went up, with imported materials rising significantly from £20 million in 1946 to eight times this amount ten years later (Kilby, 1975).

The last decade of colonial rule gave British construction companies the opportunity to develop their multi-national connections. The United Africa Company brought Taylor Woodrow to Nigeria in 1953. One of colonial Africa's largest trading concerns, John Holt, founded in 1867, formed a partnership with Costains to participate in large-scale construction begun by the Ten Year Plan in 1947. By the mid century, a mass import of asbestos cement was taking place which, by the later 1970s, was to represent 80 per cent of all cement used in Nigeria.

The import of cement was to grow by astounding proportions. Though fairly static between 1925 and 1945, it grew from 100,000 tons in 1947 to eleven times that amount twenty years later until, with the collaboration of Associated Portland Cement, West African Portland Cement was set up in 1957. Other British firms, ICI, British Paints, Parmacem, established in the early 1960s, were to supply the materials for providing the finishing touches to increasingly European house-forms. Increasingly, Africans were consumers as well as producers (Hardoy and Satterthwaite, 1981; Kilby, 1969).

From hut to bungalow: the transition to the 'European' house

A detailed historical account of the transition to 'European' house forms has yet to be researched; the following provides only glimpses. Clearly, one of the pre-requisites is the change in ownership and development of a market in land; and subsequently, of a market in domestic property. This has been described for mid and later nineteenth century Lagos by Hopkins (1980). And even without a change in land ownership, new houses were built in traditional compounds.

In the Ahafo district of southern Ghana, British colonial administrators had introduced residential reorganisation and new ideas of housing and hygiene in 1915, by which time the shape of traditional Ashanti settlements and housing had begun to change. In the Goasco area, new towns had been set up on a grid pattern, the district commissioner responsible, 'embellishing his new bungalow with grass and rose bushes'; new sites were marked out with streets, avenues and town plots. By 1921, the census report referred to the tendency of old Ashanti houses to disappear and be replaced by square compound houses. Ten years later, the provincial commissioner noted that:

> in the large towns and villages along the motor roads, the old Ashanti compound – a rough quadrilateral built of swish or stick and roofed with thatch or leaves is gradually being replaced by well-constructed compound houses, 60-80 feet square, with verandahs, corrugated iron roofs, and with plenty of air space between the houses (Dunn and Robertson, 1973:96-8, 114-18).

Similar changes were taking place among the Bantu of north Kavirondo, Kenya, in the later 1930s. After a long discussion of traditional hut building techniques of timber-framed, circular, mud-walled and grass-roofed huts, German anthropologist Dr Gunther Wagner referred to recent changes: the use of nails instead of string for fastening parts, of petrol tins for doors. Under the influence of missionaries, separate huts had been introduced for cattle. A small group of economically advanced people, traders, teachers and a few chiefs and headmen, had

> altogether abandoned the traditional type of dwelling in favour of square houses of more or less European design, built of brick and with corrugated iron roofs. These had been

developed since 1935. They showed all kinds of individual designs, though some being very close copies of European bungalows with rooms furnished in semi-European fashion and surrounded by a lawn and flower garden.

Though their number was negligible in proportion to the entire population, and the various social and economic problems which they raised had not become vital issues, some were built by the paid labour of African masons and carpenters, trained by the industrial department of the Friends' African Mission or the Native Industrial Training Department at Nairobi (1956).

By the 1930s in Kampala, the typical conical hut of the Ganda was thought to be dying out, replaced by dwellings consisting of a mixture of burnt bricks and tiles, and with corrugated iron or flattened petrol tin roofs. In the 1950s, in inland East Africa, local hut-building techniques were being lost as a result of economic and cultural influences; craft skills were being lost and a shortage of traditional materials was developing as bush was cleared and swamps drained for further urban expansion (Atkinson, 1961).

In the early 1960s, a survey of Yoruba building in rural Nigeria described the development of a specialised building labour force, the breakdown of traditional ways of building, asbestos and galvanised iron replacing natural materials and a pronounced shift from local to non-local models with many new 'four cornered' buildings (Crook, 1966).

By the mid twentieth century, European social life and residential patterns had made a major impact on the emerging African city. In Ibadan, for example, the first European Reservation had been begun in 1901. Fifty years later, with the city as headquarters of the Western Province, there were over 2,000 European residents for whom three new Reservations had been established.

Up to 1952, these Reservations had been exclusively European but with the political changes of that year, an influx of Nigerians of similar status resulted in a further extension of the Reservations to five, now known as 'Government Reservations'. In the later 1960s, according to Mabogunje, they still preserved their 'high class character'. The new developments, laid out for government employees by the town planning authority, set up in colonial times, held to similar standards. In these areas, houses were set in the midst of extensive lawns, hedged with shrubs and flower gardens, the average density being two to four houses per acre and with some gardens over one acre. The campuses of Ibadan and Ife provided a similar standard. In Lagos, the highest grade residential areas had similar layouts (Mabogunje, 1968:231-3).

Writing in 1968, Mabogunje indicated that similar low-density house and garden lay-outs had been developed by government or government-sponsored agencies in recent post-Independence years. In these areas lived 'the most important members of the community in all spheres of activity in Lagos'. In the older residential areas, houses of the colonial type 'replicated as much as possible the English country house, including the fireplace'. Elsewhere in the city, Mabogunje identified other social areas, those with houses at twelve to sixteen to the acre catering for white-collar workers; the majority of such houses being modest, small size bungalows (ibid.:300-1). Accounts of Lagos in the 1970s show the persistence of vast differences in housing provision between industrial workers and the managers and senior government officials living in the Government Residential Areas (Peace, 1979).

Where these developments are characteristic of the expanding suburbs, other changes occurred in the traditional compounds of old-established Yoruba towns. Here, the compounds disintegrated by a process which Mabogunje describes as 'growth by fission'. This was due to the breakdown in the control-mechanism within the extended family system. This control mechanism resided, as it were, in the powers of the head of an extended family over the family land at a time when every member of the family depended in one way or other on agricultural land for his source of income. With modern developments, many members of a family can now turn to non-agricultural employment. . . . As a result the powers of the head of the extended family have been greatly weakened and the cohesiveness of the family considerably impaired. Add to this the disruptive influence of both Islam and Christianity in their preference for the nuclear family (polygamous or monogamous) and some of the factors contributing to the disintegration of the compound and the individualisation of housing units becomes clear.

   The result is that the traditional compound has been broken up into a number of separate housing units (1968:226).

According to Lloyd, the traditional compound houses were being replaced by two-storeyed houses and what he calls 'bungalows', though what is referred to is unclear (1974:115).

Conclusion: urbanisation and 'Westernisation'

Just what role the introduction of 'European' dwelling forms and colonial urban environments played in the process of social and cultural change in African cities, and how justified one is in describing such changes as 'Europeanisation', 'Westernisation' or 'bourgeoisification' are both highly controversial topics: the first, because it raises questions of physical or architectural determinism, the belief that particular physical forms determine or result in particular kinds of social behaviour; the second, because of its implicit cultural imperialism and the consequent failure to acknowledge the real impact, and present-day results, of both colonialism and neo-colonialism (Magubane, 1971).

   To begin with, it seems clear that much of the characteristic form of large parts of modern West African towns resulted from the patterns and policies of colonial urbanisation and the particular built environment which this introduced. Central to this was the idea of the European, later 'Government' Reservation, the basic unit of which, for the higher ranks, was the colonial bungalow – whether of one or two storeys.

   The concept of the bungalow required, as a pre-requisite, an extensive compound; the multiplication of bungalow-and-compound units necessarily led to a spacious, low-density lay-out for the neighbourhood. This lay-out – based as it also was on the political, social, cultural, 'sanitary' and racialist assumptions of the colonisers – required that it be separate from 'native' areas, both existing and future. In this context, even though such estates are only a small part of West African towns, the bungalow can be seen, if not as an independent determining factor in the nature of African urbanisation, as a major component in the inter-related social and physical process which brought this urbanisation about.

   In the second place, there is widespread agreement that the original colonial housing forms and residential areas, together with post-colonial developments, provide a physical and spatial setting for social segregation. The spatial lay-out of different housing types reflects the location of different social and economic groups within the urban area. In colonial times, residential segregation was on racial lines. Even though this was not always legally enacted, as under Lugard's regime, the laying down of high building and environmental standards and their enforcement by municipal authorities was sufficient to create racial segregation: the price mechanism did the rest (Elkan, 1975:661). With independence, African elites moved into European housing in exclusive residential areas. In the 1970s, an 'invariable feature of all major towns in East and Central Africa' was that 'the broad racial division into European, Asian and African residential areas is nowadays increasingly giving way to one based on status groups and classes'. The continued implementation of government and professionally prescribed standards ensures the use of such areas in maintaining social segregation (Mabogunje, et al., 1978:14; Parkin, 1975:41).

Thirdly, the modern, 'detached' European house, still often referred to as a 'bungalow', provides the setting for the 'modern' nuclear family, increasingly characteristic of elite and middle class urban Africa (Caldwell, 1968; Mariss, 1961). Most typical here are the university campuses which provide bungalows for both senior as well as junior staff. A recent study of the 'traditional' Nigerian city of Benin by an African scholar identified various house-types and related them to social and economic groups in the city. According to Onokerhoraya, 'bungalows in the Benin setting can be defined as houses designed for a single family, generally a high income one' (1977:37) (plate 130). Because of its design, the bungalow becomes another factor in separating nuclear families from their kin. Anthropologist Peter Lloyd writes of the Yoruba, 'the children probably live in the city, parents in the rural area or provincial town; the children's house is not designed to accommodate dependants, and cooking by gas or electricity is frightening to them' (1974:119). The design of the bungalow there made it more difficult for two or more families to share a dwelling. And in parts of Benin since the mid 1960s, the bungalow was the predominant form of house being built — of cement blocks, glazed windows and asbestos roofs. The high class housing region consisted of 95 per cent bungalows, with living rooms, three or four bedrooms, kitchen, bathroom and separate servants' accommodation some yards from the main house. These were built by public authorities and, in more recent times, by private individuals (Onokerhoraya, 1977:37). In other parts of Africa, however, the building of such bungalows has been opposed as uneconomic, as in Tanzania, principally because they cannot easily be separated into rooms and rented off.

Other studies have related changes in family behaviour to the introduction of new house forms and 'Westernisation'. According to Caldwell, the traditional practice was for parents to sleep in the same room as their children, but to eat apart from them. The values of 'Westernisation', however, improve the status of both women and children. In modern houses, therefore, parents and children sleep in separate bedrooms, enjoying more privacy and, among the Kumasi social elite, this was more favourable to family planning methods (1968:2). This observation, however, must be seen in the context of a variety of sleeping practices and the small number of such elites in Africa.

Finally, as the city itself becomes a centre for the accumulation of capital, so, on a smaller scale, does the house. From the early days of colonial penetration, property speculation and investment became a major new source of income for urban Africans. Investment in house property, with education, both giving a substantial return and considerable security, became typical forms of investment for Nigerian business elites, as well as for others at lower social levels with many landlords investing in multi-roomed tenements let to urban workers (Hopkins, 1980; Lloyd, 1974:59).

Yet inside the European-type bungalow, largely the product of public sector building, the spatial division into separate rooms encouraged the acquisition of goods to fill them. So, as housing estates mushroomed up in the post-war boom in Nigeria, the import of domestic consumer goods increased. Metropolitan firms, well established for European and African elites since the 1920s, opened up new department stores in the centre of cities: radiograms, television sets, refrigerators, clothes, imported settees and armchairs became standard equipment in Nigerian middle class homes, with local furniture manufacturers tending to copy imported styles. A local furniture industry was soon to develop.

As part of these processes, therefore, the bungalow – as a dwelling of European origins and style – becomes a major element in what many have seen as 'Westernisation' or 'Europeanisation' – the adoption of the language, dress, behaviour, family structure, values and tastes of Europe. In the 1950s and 1960s, Mitchell was one of a number of anthropologists who saw the adoption of a 'European way of life' – speaking English among themselves, using European furniture at home, eating European-type food – as an index of social prestige. Jahoda sought to demonstrate that the higher the education a person had received in Ghana, the more likely he or she was to be 'Westernised', i.e. living in a nuclear family household, eating three meals a day at regular times, reading newspapers regularly, belonging to non-traditional voluntary organisations. Higher education gave access to government jobs and government jobs entitled their occupants to government bungalows (1961; see also Magubane, 1971).

More recent studies have adopted a similar stance. In Blantyre City, Malawi, the typical ecological zones left behind by the colonial regime and now occupied by Africans were seen to be associated with different personality types. Higher-ranking government officials, company managers and ministers lived in the ex-European area of low-density, multi-roomed, large detached houses with large gardens, servants' quarters and telephones.

> In their mode and style of life they resemble the European middle class . . . wall to wall carpeting, one car or two, with a pool of domestic workers. The nuclear family is the norm. . . . Relations with kinsmen are selective and manipulative; poor relations are commonly shunned . . . accommodation is not readily given to kinsmen . . . the rural link has become relatively depersonalised.

For this group 'occupational position rather than tribal values is manifestly the chief basis of emerging social relations. . . . There is a de-emphasis on ethnicity, they are less religious and have literate wives.'

At the other end of the scale is the 'peri-urban area' with housing ranging from the well-built, to semi-shacks, untarred roads, pit latrines and scattered water taps. Here, occupants are labourers, the semi-skilled, messengers and market sellers. Here, ethnicity is a strong factor in residents' orientations, and urban-rural ties are strong (Chilivumbo, 1975). Similarly, Onokerhoraya shows a correlation between those with Western education and residence in European-style bungalows. And though Lloyd rightly distinguishes between 'Western' technology, cars and television common to all industrial societies, and family values, he concludes that 'with wealth and education the style of life within the home becomes more and more Western'. Along with dress, style of speech, including speaking English, and the car, the house and lifestyle is an important symbol of status. 'To some extent the Yoruba have inherited a material style of life created by the colonial administrators in moving physically into their homes'. There are qualitative differences among them in the styles of house furnishings which can be scaled from 'the more traditional to the more modern' (1974:118).

Yet 'Westernisation' and 'Europeanisation' are facile terms to describe the multiple and complex processes of change in urban Africa. One of the most radical African critics of the accounts of Western anthropologists has written:

Living in an urban setting . . . an African was unavoidably involved in a money economy. He had to buy his clothing, food, furniture, utensils; and the goods that came to be offered in the shops came from the factories that catered to an industrialised society. The acquisition of 'European' goods was not, therefore, in any sense 'imitative' or indicative of status, but a necessary consequence of being absorbed in a milieu dominated by factory-made goods. A similar compulsion dictated the acquisition of cultural values, such as Christianity. To obtain a school education Africans were obliged to embrace Christianity, since education was in the hands of the missionaries. The adoption of Christianity had many consequences, such as the acceptance of monogamous marriage, the wearing of European-style clothing and the abandonment of characteristic traditional pursuits such as beer-drinking, circumcision schools and traditional forms of worship. . . . Efforts at 'imitating' what is ethnocentrically called a 'European way of life' arise from the destruction of a previous way of life and the associational ties which that way provided (Magubane, 1971:425).

Whatever the situation, it is evident that the new residential environments and housing models provide a totally different set of symbols and indicators, both of status and behaviour, than those of pre-colonial Africa. As elsewhere in the world, the bungalow in Africa is a category of dwelling and as such, has a distinct social meaning which is evidently indicative of modernisation and associated with an emerging class structure. It is a class structure, however, where large, European-style houses form part of a system of inequality where salary differentials are as great as 50:1, and where there is 'a contrast between excellent living accommodation at nominal rents for a few and squalid accommodation at extortionate rents for the vast majority'. These are the words of an African observer who has called for a 're-examination of the historical . . . foundations of our habits of distribution . . . and condemnation of the gross inequalities between salaries, perquisites and services between a privileged class and a less privileged one' (Nduka, 1977:347). It has been this task which this chapter has attempted.

As for the general question of standards, housing design and the provision of shelter with which we began, it is clear from the discussion above that this is not simply a matter of changing physical phenomena such as design criteria and measurements. It is a question of changing lifestyles, consumption habits and ultimately, of the direction of the economy itself. It refers to questions of taste, standards of living and status symbols which derive ultimately not just from 'the West' but from a global system of capitalism which depends on accumulation and domestic consumption. The continuing cultural dependence in architecture and planning standards in Africa depends on continuing connections between the metropole and indigenous African elites. Reorienting construction to 'appropriate standards' is not simply a question of removing environments or even changing the standards on which they are based. It is a question of changing the values of an elite, or removing the elites themselves. And this, not only in African cities.

Chapter 7

Australia 1788-1980

The modest bungalow, occupying its own block of land, was a tribute essentially to the typical Australian drive for individual home ownership.

N.G. Butlin, *Investment in Australian Economic Development, 1861-1900*, 1964:223.

Introduction

In the earlier chapters of this book, some definite themes have been pursued; this one largely raises questions. The importance of Australia in the context of this study is that it provides us with what experimental science would call a 'control group', a population and set of circumstances with which some of the ideas advanced earlier can be tested.

All cases of overseas settlement provide a kind of laboratory situation where the influence of different forces shaping the built environment, whether geographic (climate, topography), social and cultural (kinship forms, values, world views) or economic and political, can be examined. The particular advantage of Australia is that, with its absence of indigenous urban development, the relative cultural homogeneity of its early settlers and the time and circumstances of its colonisation, a case study is provided which, even more so than in the cases of India and Africa, demonstrates the importance of political, economic and cultural factors in shaping the built environment. It is only by looking at Australia within the larger context of an emerging capitalist world economy on one hand, and a global colonial culture embracing Britain, India, North America, Africa and the Caribbean on the other, that an adequate understanding of her building – and other cultural – forms can be obtained.

How these forms are explained must obviously be of interest and importance to the Australians themselves. Yet in many ways, such forms are of equal significance to people in Britain. For what they demonstrate, and this might also be said for parts of Anglo-Saxon culture in North America or in British colonies elsewhere, are the forms of dwelling and property which British people have chosen when given the greatest economic and political freedom. It is a kind of experiment akin to testing people's values by giving them £1,000 and then watching how they spend it. Though native Australians may resent this, what their typical living patterns are – a suburban quarter-acre lot with every family owning its own detached, and generally single-storey, home – conceivably represent what a large majority of British people would like to have. It is a pattern which results from a combination of factors: a free market economy, the nuclear family, the symbolic expression of private property, and a cluster of social, cultural and historical preferences.

In an important sense, therefore, the bungalow, as we have discussed it so far, never went to Australia. It did not need to, as it was always there from the start. Despite the fact that today the *form* of the bungalow is more prominent as the model dwelling form in Australia than perhaps anywhere else in the world, the word itself is infrequently used. As the vast majority of houses are detached, single storey and located on their own lot, what use is there for the term 'bungalow'? Such dwellings are referred to as 'houses', 'homes' or 'homesteads'. In contemporary Australian parlance, 'bungalow' seems to have an ambiguous meaning. Depending on region or perhaps the person using the term, it might refer to a separate annex of a house, often just a flimsy shed of weatherboard, and sometimes used as a sleep-out. In Queensland, the Northern Territory and northern Western Australia, it might describe a distinctive form of 'tropical bungalow' (discussed below); in Sydney it is used occasionally to describe a particular type of luxurious suburban dwelling, or, in the special language of architectural history, to refer to the particular style of the 'California bungalow' of the 1920s, of which more anon.

Yet as far as existing evidence suggests, the term itself was, with perhaps the rare exception, not used to describe any particular type of Australian dwelling before 1876 when it was apparently introduced from England. The common names for dwellings in nineteenth-century Australia were, with the addition perhaps of 'cottage', as they are today. In the last quarter of the nineteenth century, 'bungalow' was occasionally used until, from about 1907-8, it became increasingly common with the importation of the California bungalow style. The use of the term to describe Australian dwelling-forms from the early nineteenth century would therefore seem to be not only anachronistic but, as we shall see below, also confusing (e.g. in Boyd, 1952; Freeland, 1968).

What this chapter is about, therefore, is – in broad terms – an explanation of the built environment: about the role of capital investment in relation to urban and architectural developments, about colonialism in relation to cultural forms. And where earlier chapters have discussed the development of the bungalow only if it was actually named as such, this one – for reasons which should become clear – will depart from that decision.

The chapter is in four parts. The first is concerned with the various historical forces, economic, cultural, social and political, which help to explain why the one-family, generally single-storey, detached dwelling became, as part of a particular type of urban development, the typical dwelling form of Australia. Though others have written on this theme before (Boyd, 1952; Freeland, 1968; Mullins, 1981; Neutze, 1977 and many more), I hope not simply to draw on their arguments but to add something as well.

The second part examines the form of early dwellings in Australia, especially where they approximate to the Anglo-Indian bungalow, and the influences which helped to produce it. Part three considers the circumstances behind the introduction of the *term* in the last quarter of the nineteenth century and its relation to architectural developments. In the final section, the forces leading to the introduction of the California bungalow as part of the vast proliferation of suburbs in the first half of the twentieth century, are discussed. Of particular relevance here are the assumptions behind the introduction of town planning and 'garden suburbs' introduced at this time. In some ways, therefore, the middle sections of this chapter approach closer to 'conventional' architectural history than what has gone before.

The shape of Australia's urban development

The attempt to see Australian history in terms of the evolution of a national character (distinct from British character) and the establishment of a culturally independent nation is a misleading and impossible historical exercise. Because of the nature and timing of its settlement, and the continuing importance of overseas connections, Australia – far from being or becoming a nation apart – was really one small part of an international urban, or suburban culture, created by Western civilisation. Metropolitanisation and the brief span of Australian history before 1900 gave the majority of the inhabitants . . . insufficient time, opportunity or inclination to develop a truly distinctive way of life. In fact, the major part of Australian effort was directed towards the precise opposite – an attempt to create provincial England in the Antipodes. This process was promoted by a continuous flow of people, capital, ideas and techniques from Britain (Glynn, 1975:79).

This comment is typical of a number of Australian scholars (e.g. Nadel, 1957; Sandercock, 1975; see also Denoon, 1979) who, by emphasising Australia's 'British origins', give precedence to what might be termed 'cultural factors' in explaining her architectural and urban development. The British and Irish who went to Australia, Glynn suggests, came from urban areas and brought their urban and domestic images with them. And though the early settlers in Australia were largely to live in towns, each brought with him an image of a rural ideal. Australian cities were established rapidly and from the beginning, they 'straggled across plentiful land, using the English country cottage as its model dwelling, creating suburbs well before other urban industrial societies'. They grew, according to Butlin, 'as a sprawl of detached cottages' (1964:213). For architectural historian Robin Boyd, this had something to do with 'the acquired English taste for privacy'. It was this taste which, he maintains, 'remained a prime motive through subsequent generations of home-building'. Other Australians have stressed the 'aggressive individuality' which characterised the culture of the early settlers, a 'searching for dignity and independence that had . . . first driven many of the "bloody emigrants" from the industrialised cities of the British Isles with dreams of a simple arcady that seemed, however mythically, to be their birthright' (McGregor, 1966:188; Mullins, 1981:72).

Had Australia been settled, as Glynn suggests, by the Spanish or the Chinese instead of the British and Irish, the pattern of urbanisation would have been different. One could also add that, if climatic or merely geographic factors had been paramount, and had Australia been settled by Arabs from the sixteenth century Middle East, for example, then the urban and architectural forms of central Australia might have been similar to those of comparable tropical and sub-tropical climes, such as Baghdad or Tunis. And as the aboriginal inhabitants of Australia had neither towns nor permanent dwellings, there was, as we have seen happened in India, no indigenous model or manpower to influence the immigrants' ideas.

British immigrants were as slow to adapt their housing to the climate as they were their clothes. Glynn quotes John Snodgrass writing on New South Wales in 1864:

How is it that Englishmen can be so stupid as to wear, in a climate where the glass is commonly at 90 in the shade, and sometimes even as high as 120, the black frock and dress coat of the home country, the heavy boots, the misshapen, unbecomming (sic) waistcoats and trowsers (sic).

A century or so later, another immigrant, this time a professor of architecture from India, was equally struck by the way that an established cultural practice, grounded, among other things, in notions of property, prevailed over what, in his view, were more logical arrangements:

In many settlements in central Australia . . . rows and rows of small houses with uninsulated roofs virtually sit in a dust bowl on plots which are far too large. Open spaces in relation to built-up areas are far too generous, and roads catering only for light traffic, far too wide (Saini, 1973:87).

In his own native north India, and in similar hot, dry tropical climes elsewhere, compact honeycombed clusters of multi-storey, courtyard houses were the norm. Yet the Australian settlement forms he described were as they had always been, the cottage ideal of a rural nineteenth century.

Similarly, the social forms for which the dwellings were built were those which prevailed in eighteenth- and nineteenth-century England. Though New South Wales was founded by a predominantly male immigrant population, many of whom were transported for life, their image of a family was of a two-generation unit, parents and children, and possibly grandparents, in one household, and it was this for which dwellings were generally built. It was a dwelling form where, in relation to land and property, types of tenure were relatively simple. One was either a tenant or a freeholder, without any of the complex tenure arrangements which we have seen in the peasant economies of Africa, or with the religious and social obligations characteristic of the countries of Islam.

Yet cultural and social explanations of dwelling forms are clearly not enough. Transplanting the image of a cottage-on-its-own-plot, the forms of the family, the notion of private, domestic property, are only partial explanations; the larger political economy must be discussed.

Australia was first and foremost a colony, founded in 1788. As such, it was financed, equipped and peopled from Britain, and was part of a British, European and largely Western capitalist economic system. The early, and much of the later, history of Australia was of an economy dependent on Britain, initially as a convict colony, and subsequently, as a supplier of raw materials and a consumer of Britain's processed goods. The first towns, Sydney (founded 1788), Newcastle (1804) and Brisbane (1824), were colonial port cities, despatching agricultural and pastoral produce and in turn importing supplies. Manufacturing was small, but warehouses, insurance and banking facilities made them rapidly into commercial cities. Because of the total absence of indigenous towns or villages, the foundation and growth of these colonial ports was a case of 'dependent urbanisation', to use Castells's (1977:43) phrase, in an even more quintessential sense than was the case, for example, in Lagos or Bombay. It was dependent urbanisation in the sense that it was the economic surplus created by Britain's industrialisation which made possible the towns and cities of Australia.

Within the colonial system as a whole, therefore, the functions of these cities were commercial and administrative: 'without the demand of commerce for bases and fishing grounds, and of English industry for wool and metals, the cities would hardly have grown as they did (Sandercock, 1975:8). Neither Australia, nor for that matter New Zealand, first settled by Europeans in the 1840s, ever had a peasant agriculture and hence never had any peasant settlements or peasant dwellings where people lived and produced solely for themselves. From the start, agriculture in Australia was commercial, producing for the market rather than for domestic consumption. Proportionally, therefore, rural farmhouses or 'homesteads' were few, though houses for the urban 'service' population were many. Thus, unlike certain cities in Britain, or the much later cities of Europe, those of Australia were never, by comparison, 'industrial'. They never had an inheritance of old, pre-industrial housing or newer rented 'industrial' housing built to accommodate labour close to factories. Or if they did, if we can allow the metaphor, it was left behind in Britain.

From the beginning, therefore, Australia developed as an urban nation. 'The British (convict and free) who settled the country came from a rapidly urbanising society and the majority of them came from urban areas. They introduced a technology and a set of values which, in Australian circumstances, gave rise to a high degree of urbanisation.' By 1891, two-thirds of the population lived in towns and cities, a proportion only matched by the United States in 1920, and by Canada in 1950. By 1971, 85 per cent of Australians lived in towns of over 1,000 inhabitants (Kilmartin and Thorns, 1978:40; Sandercock, 1975:7), and approaching half of all of them in the metropolitan centres of Sydney and Melbourne.

Yet paradoxically, it was a form of urbanisation which, within the dependent context outlined above, was a sort of distant suburb of Britain. In comparison with that country, there was never any shortage of land, even though the possibility of buying it was restricted by land laws not removed till the second half of the nineteenth century. Nevertheless, many people had their own plot. In an early despatch to Britain after landing with the 'First Fleet' in 1788, Governor Arthur Phillips proposed that 'the land be granted with a clause that will ever prevent more than one house being built on the allotment which will be of 60 feet in front and 150 feet in depth'. Whether Phillips was actually responsible, this lot size, though varying some feet either way in subsequent years was, according to Boyd, to become the norm in sub-divisions in the twentieth century. By this time, the population was spread 15 to the acre (1952:7). The cheapness, in relation to incomes, of urban and suburban land and building materials, and a commitment to the principles of the free market, permitted ever-increasing numbers of urban families to acquire their own houses on one-quarter and one-eighth blocks in outer urban areas.

By the end of the nineteenth century, therefore, each Australian capital had its collection of sprawling suburbs, in Glynn's words, 'sacrificing some of the economic and other advantages of high-density living in the interests of space and privacy'. Though row or terraced housing did, of course, exist, and occurred to a considerable extent both in the early colonial ports and also in Sydney, in comparison to British cities at the time, there were always far more detached, owner-occupied houses. As early as 1827, Cunningham wrote (*Two Years in New South Wales*) on visiting Sydney,

> Near the harbour, where ground is very valuable, the houses are usually contiguous, like those of the towns in England, but generally speaking, the better sorts of houses in
> Sydney are built in the detached cottage style . . . one or two storeys high . . . with
> verandahs in front and enclosed by a neat wooden paling.

Neutze (1977) makes the point that the shape of Australian cities was also heavily influenced by technology. Compared with most other colonial countries, Australia was settled very late, and much of its development took place after the introduction of mechanised transport, especially railways, which attracted immense investment from outside. Consequently, compared with the cities in many other countries, those of Australia were spread over large areas at very low density. As their major growth occurred in an era of mechanised transport, there was no reason to live within walking distance of shops, jobs and services.

Because of its colonial economy and the early development of rail and tramways, therefore, the majority of Australia's population were not just urban, but suburban. Australia in fact, was probably 'the first suburban nation' (Davison, 1979:100). In 1865, half of the population lived in municipalities with less than 20 people per acre. After 1880, the steam railway, electric tram and a huge building boom generated by British investment made for the further suburbanisation of the capital cities. The growth in population since then has meant that about 90 per cent of the increase in the capital cities has occurred between the 1880s and

1970s. Again, confirmation on the suburban developments of the late nineteenth century comes from an English visitor. According to Richard Twopeny, though the upper middle class often lived in two-storey houses, 'the most popular type of dwelling' was a single-storeyed house designed 'as an oblong block divided by a three to eight foot passage'. Terraces and attached houses were 'universally disliked and almost every class of suburban house is detached and stands in its own garden'. Nearly every house that could afford the space had a verandah which sometimes stretched the whole way round (*Town Life in Australia*, 1882). This preference for separate single-storey dwellings was to make late-nineteenth-century Melbourne, for example, so enormous, and to impress other visitors with its sheer physical extent (Davison, 1978:140).

Yet Australia's urban development was not only 'culturally British', colonial and, in a technological sense, 'post-industrial', her cities were 'pure' products of the expansion of capitalism; Australia itself was 'one of the purest manifestations that history had to offer of capitalistic societies' (McCarty, 1972). Fundamental to this was the concept of land and property ownership. The colonists brought with them attitudes to land as a source of wealth, power and security, and land speculation became a national hobby. Housing has always been an important component of investment, and between 1861 and 1938 dwellings accounted for not much less than half the total capital formation (Neutze, 1977:31). In this process, the connection with Britain was crucial. It was not just that the people, technology and image of the ideal dwelling came from Britain. So also did the finance. In the second half of the nineteenth century, the roots of Australia's prosperity lay in the expanding British world economy; in the three decades before 1890, the building industry absorbed one-third of total Australian investment. In the second half of the 1880s, £50 million of British capital poured into Victoria, fuelling a massive land boom in which speculators, who 'bought by the acre and sold by the foot', were instrumental in helping to extend Melbourne's suburbs at a time when plot values rose ten to twenty times in five years (Serle, 1972). After a struggle over land ownership in the 1860s and 1870s, freehold was established as the dominant form of tenure, by which time the land was largely settled. With labour shortages and high wages, home ownership was much more of a possibility than it had been in Britain. Thus, when the 1911 census first provided information on this question, it showed that about half of all housing in Australia was owner-occupied, a proportion not reached in Canada till 1920, the United States in 1950 and Great Britain in 1971. The percentage of owner-occupiers in Australia peaked at 74 per cent in 1966, and though it had fallen to 69 per cent in 1971, this was still, apart from Iceland, the highest percentage of home ownership in the world (Kilmartin and Thorns, 1978:22).

It was these developments which explain why, in the words of Max Neutze, 'the detached family house, instead of being exceptional, as in European cities, became the standard form of housing in Australia.' By the middle of the twentieth century, well over 70 per cent of Australians lived in what were effectively suburban areas; in the two major cities of Sydney and Melbourne, over 92 per cent of the inhabitants lived in suburbs outside the cities' boundaries.

If these factors provide some explanation for the predominance in Australia of the owner-occupied, single-family dwelling standing on its own plot, they are, none the less, only partial. After all, the 'cultural images' of British emigrants in the late eighteenth or early nineteenth centuries also included notions of the typical Georgian town with its squares, crescents and terraces. A comprehensive explanation of Australia's urban and architectural forms would need to provide a far more detailed account of the system of urban land-holding, the distribution of and access to capital, as well as the social, political and administrative institutions, or lack of them, which shaped the form of the built environment. The early settlements in New South Wales and Tasmania, for example, were run as 'military dictatorships', and this affected both legislation and the developments of institutions.

The single-family, generally single-storey, house on a quarter-acre block was, therefore, a product and symbol of many things – a colonial and capitalist economy and polity, basic cultural values such as privacy and domesticity, the concept of private property, and family structure amongst others. The multiplication of these single-family dwellings in the massive suburbanisation of the twentieth century was both a demonstration of, as well as a central element in, the overall accumulation of capital in Australia. These, then, seem to be the basic reasons for the characteristic dwelling type of Australia. What we may now examine is the existence of a bungalow form, in nature if not in name, in the early decades following the arrival of Captain Phillip in 1788.

The early Australian house

The early architectural history of domestic housing in Australia has been very well described by Freeland, Boyd, Cox and Lucas and others. It would serve little purpose, therefore, to repeat what others have done far better before. Yet digging around in Australia's history to trace the origins of the bungalow-in-form-if-not-in-name none the less raises questions which have more than an antiquarian interest, for example, about political and economic processes promoting cultural diffusion on a global scale or the question of housing in colonial settlement.

As the first settlers arrived in Australia a dozen years before the end of the eighteenth century, it seems fair to take the defining features of the bungalow as those existing in India at that time. As we have seen in Chapter 1, these essentially were of a single-storey detached dwelling, with a pyramidal, often thatched roof, of generally square or oblong plan and, most importantly, entirely or partly surrounded by a verandah. Bedrooms could be located in the enclosed four corners of the verandah; the dwelling occupied its own, generally enclosed and spacious plot.

The earliest shelter provided at Sydney Cove consisted of tents and marquees for the officers and guards of the first convicts. A prefabricated timber and canvas structure had also been brought for the use of Captain Phillip. The first solid dwelling to be built, other than the initial construction of slab and bark huts and others of clay-smeared walls and thatched roof, was the house for Governor Philip. This, put up in Sydney in 1788, naturally enough followed a contemporary English design. According to Freeland, it was 'an elegant brick house' and to Boyd, 'a two-storeyed, verandahless box with six rooms and the only staircase in the colony'. The glazed sash windows had been brought from England. However, as the convict-made bricks were poor and crumbled, all subsequent buildings other than the governor's house were single-storey, their roofs often covered with thatch or bark.

The dwelling forms which gradually developed in New South Wales over the next two or three decades were of various sizes, materials and forms. Whilst the model of the English cottage was often predominant, what is most relevant to our discussion is the existence of a bungalow type of dwelling with a verandah.

The first evidence of this already appeared in 1793-4 (if not earlier) at Paramatta, outside Sydney. Elizabeth Farm was (and still is) a single-storey building, rectangular in plan, with four rooms, two on either side of a large central hall, 68 by 8. A verandah with rooms at the corners ran along the east front, though apparently this seemed to be used as an external passage. The kitchen, laundry, meat house and servants' quarters were in another building at the back, a practice which, with its social, safety and sanitary advantages, was to continue for many houses well into the nineteenth century (Freeland, 1968:22).

Though this form was apparently atypical of domestic dwellings in the first three decades of Australia's settlement, it formed, according to Freeland, a 'primitive prototype of Australian country houses in New South Wales'. Where the typical forms before 1815 were 'verandahless, twin-windowed, hipped-roofed, cottage-type dwellings', from the 1820s, the homesteads of the new sheep stations tended to be 'large, spreading single storey houses with deep verandahs supported at their edges by thin wooden columns'. In the country areas the verandah was very popular before 1800 and by 1810, practically every country house had one. In Sydney itself, however, the town houses tended to be 'shadeless boxes' with less than half a dozen equipped with verandahs (Boyd, 1952).

Freeland is doubtless correct in suggesting that the verandah 'came second hand from the tropical countries of the East where it had been used from time immemorial in the tropics'. However, he also states, though provides no evidence to support it, that 'it had been taken back to the counties of Devon and Cornwall in England by the founders of empire. Thence it came to Australia.'

The cultural origins of the verandah on small cottage-like dwellings, either as an extended roofline, supported by pillars, or as an added structure built against the wall of the house is, for architectural historians, an important question. As far as Australia is concerned, however, it seems unlikely, or only marginally possible, that the main source was found in England. There is very little evidence of it having been used before the mid 1790s there, and considerable evidence that both the feature as well as the term were both gradually introduced from about that time. (See Appendix A.)

A more convincing account is that of Moffit who suggests that there were many British army officers in Sydney in 1788 who had served in colonies where verandahs were common and who were aware of their merits as a protection against sun and rain. For example, the earliest engravings of Sydney in 1788 show such a verandah on the house of Lieutenant Governor Ross who had served in the West Indies, Mediterranean and North America (1976:6).

In these developments, the key role was played by the army, and especially, by military engineers. Before 1825, all the governors of Australia were military officers, including Lachlan Macquarie, the Governor in Chief of New South Wales in 1810, who had spent part of his military service in India.

Just how influential Anglo-Indian dwelling models were on Australian domestic architecture, however, is a subject which has been little explored. Tanner and Cox (1975:20-1) state that, 'the first sources of Australian architectural design forms, the English Georgian farmhouse and the Indian bungalow as interpreted by the British, were translated into buildings by men who knew the models first hand,' and elsewhere that, 'the bungalow was introduced into Australia at an early stage by the officers of the army who had served in India, where Macquarie's regiment, for example, had been stationed. The typical Australian vernacular expanded from this model' (Cox, 1974:220). Yet no evidence is provided for these assertions. Moreover, no evidence has yet emerged that the term 'bungalow' was used in the first ten or fifteen years of Australia's settlement, which – because the term was not in use in Britain at that time – would provide more specific evidence of an 'Anglo-Indian' connection.

On the other hand, reference to 'a varando' in the *Sydney Gazette* in 1805 (Freeland, 1968:26) could imply familiarity with India, the Caribbean or anywhere else in the Iberian colonial empire where the term, and structure, were in use.

Yet there were certainly many connections between India and Australia, and it seems not unlikely that many East India Company officials retired there. In 1827, for example, 'A Retired Officer of the Honourable East India Company's Service' wrote *The Friend of Australia* in which he gave extensive advice on laying out the plans of towns including questions of architecture. Interestingly enough, the particular pyramidal type of Indian bungalow was not advocated. House roofs were better terraced (i.e. flat) in warm climates, permitting an evening lounge in hot weather. Only a slight declivity was advised to permit the rain to run off. 'All houses, whether of rich and poor, should have a piazza, alias verandah, round at least three sides' against the torrents of rain and in summer, against the glare. This, however, was literally a 'built-on piazza', as he continues, 'the roof of the verandah should serve as an open balcony for the upper rooms.' A year or so later, according to Moffit, another East Indian Company officer built 'a direct copy of an Anglo-Indian bungalow' near Liverpool, New South Wales. The house, 'Horsley' (1831), had 'typical Regency features of pavilion elements and pilaster, and shutters with adjustable louvres. Inside, the dining hall had large, Indian-style punkas'. This house, and another, 'Quamby' (1830s), at Hagley, Tasmania were 'by no means the first bungalow buildings in Australia but represent accurate reproductions of the Indian model' (Tanner and Cox, 1975).

The 'tropical bungalow' in Queensland[1]

Some of the most 'bungalow-looking' dwellings in Australia were built in Queensland in the later nineteenth century. Indeed, so similar are these to the Anglo-Indian variety that they deserve some special attention.

Boyd lists, as one of the five principal types of house plan in eighteenth- and nineteenth-century Australia, what he calls 'the bungalow'. This was 'based on the English cottage plan of the eighteenth century (and) had a central passage with two or three rooms on each side. Australia discarded England's upper floor, spread the house on the ground and added a verandah on every side. This plan survived in country districts for a full century from 1840.'

In the light of the earlier discussion, the suggestion that Australia 'added the verandah' needs to be questioned. There is, however, a tendency, for historians of 'new nations' to develop a notion of a 'national style'. In architecture, it finds expression, for example, in a search for 'the first Australian/New Zealand architect', or more specifically, in discovering that the 'tropical bungalow' (again an anachronistic use of the term) was 'the closest that Australia has ever come to producing an indigenous style' (Freeland, 1968:209).

The authority on the 'tropical bungalow' (we shall continue to use the term though there is no evidence that it was actually referred to as such when introduced) is Ray Sumner, on whose research the following is based. Within the time context of this study, Queensland was established relatively late in Australia's history. European settlers, attracted first by gold and subsequently by pastoral farming, moved into Queensland from the early 1860s. The earliest dwellings were largely built of local materials, mainly timber, and despite the prevalent tropical heat and seasonal extremes of humidity and drought, their design drew simply from the earlier ideas and models of housing which the settlers brought with them. The first dwellings were simply huts, often with a crude 'verandah' tacked on; subsequently, as settlement became permanent, two or four-roomed cottages developed, often with a verandah at the front.

The bungalow pattern seems to have been put up from the 1870s and 1880s. Sumner describes it as 'a low dwelling with an iron roof. It consisted of a square, occasionally rectangular, central core with four, sometimes six, internal rooms, ranged symmetrically along a central hallway, the whole being surrounded on three or all sides by verandahs between two and three metres wide.' (plates 132 and 133) Early bungalows were erected on wooden piles or stumps less than one metre above the ground. After about 1890, they were elevated about two metres above the ground. The reasons given are many: to overcome the problem of termites (white ants), to compensate levels in uneven sites, and to protect against flood hazards are the more common. The notion that ventilation was improved by elevation only seems to have been suggested after the style was firmly established. None the less, the practice continues in Queensland as the undercroft offers useful, cool, low-cost space.

Some of the early Queensland bungalows, all built at the earliest after 1860, adopted the common Anglo-Indian practice of enclosing the corners of the rear verandah to create additional room space, either for bathroom or kitchen. Others, for reasons of safety, privacy, or comfort, had separate kitchens at the rear. Corrugated iron seems to have been introduced for roofing and walls from the 1870s.

The question therefore arises as to how valid it is to describe what Professor Freeland calls 'the Australian bungalow' as 'Australian vernacular', if by this is meant, according to the *Oxford English Dictionary*, indigenous, or not of foreign origin? The spacious, single-storey dwelling, encircling verandah and room plan seem to have developed in Anglo-India from the mid eighteenth century, and probably also owe something to colonial practice in the Caribbean. The idea of the verandah also seems to have been well known to the French in Louisiana well before Europeans came to Australia. Just when Europeans adopted the widespread habit of the native inhabitants of tropical areas in raising houses on piers or stumps, whether as protection from insects, animals or other predators, or for reasons of defence, climate, privacy or other causes, is problematic, though it was suggested for Danish travellers to Africa in the 1790s (Kubler, 1944).

Though many improvements were certainly made to this house-type by its Australian inhabitants, and the particular combination of materials – especially corrugated iron, imported in vast quantities into Australia – produced some distinctive variations, it was perhaps less unique to Australia than some of her historians believe. Before these questions can be answered, however, more knowledge is needed about colonialism and architecture in the eighteenth century, and especially, of the activities and models of military engineers as they moved around the world.

'Bungalow' as Australian term

Looking for evidence of the term 'bungalow' in Australia's history can lead to a lot of interesting, if eventually misleading, diversions. For, whilst Australians may not commonly use the word to describe dwellings, no country in the world has so many 'bungalow-type' place names. According to the *Australia (1:250,000) Map Series Gazetteer* (Canberra, 1975), there is a suburb, Bungalow, in Cairns, Queensland (founded, 1878), a Bungalow homestead and Bungalow Flat in New South Wales, as well as two places called Bungalow Well in Western Australia. A slight alteration of the spelling, quite acceptable in the light of earlier chapters, gives us Bungaloo Bay (South Australia), Bungalo Well (W. Australia), as well as a town, Bangalow, a Bangalow Creek and a Mount Bangalore, all in New South Wales. This is not to mention Bungulla, Bungadoo and Bungalally, in other places on the continent.

Non-Australians, therefore, might be forgiven for thinking, particularly in the context of its actual housing stock, that the 'bungalow craze' of the early twentieth century had made a massive impact on Australia; until, that is, they discover that 'bungulla' is a New South Wales aboriginal term for the black bream tree common in different parts of the continent. . . . Whether any of these, especially suburban place names have anything to do with the bungalow as house form is a question only local topographers could discover.

The earliest identified reference to 'bungalow' applied to a dwelling in Australia occurs in 1876; and again, it provides an insight both into housing developments as well as the interpretation of architectural history. The first dwelling to be so called was a house named 'The Grange' built at Mount Victoria, New South Wales, in 1876, though the evidence emerges some years later. In *The Building and Engineering Journal* (Australia), 9, for the 13 December 1890 appeared a picture of a house captioned the 'Piddington Bungalow' with the following description

Figure 7.1   'Bungalow' reaches Australia: Piddington Bungalow, Mount Victoria, NSW, built 1876. Cultural links between Britain and Australia were a necessary extension and condition of a shared political economy. The idea and name were evidently picked up from the *Building News* in the early 1870s and adopted by Australian architect, J. Horbury Hunt (*The Building and Engineering Journal* (Australia) (13 December, 1890)

Bungaloo (sic) Residence

The page sketch of the bungaloo residence, Mount Victoria, represents the most substantially-built house on the Blue Mountains. It is now the residence of Mr. F.C. Jarrett, but was built for the late Hon. Mr. Piddington, at one time Colonial Treasurer of New South Wales, and was designed by Mr. Horbury Hunt, the President of the Institute of Architects of New South Wales.

According to two of Australia's leading architectural historians, Hunt is seen as one of the pioneers of 'modernism' in Australia. Freeland, for example, writes:

Hunt designed 'The Grange', Mount Victoria, as a long, low bungalow spreading along the side of a hill. Its unbroken brick walls were sheltered on all sides by the extension of the roof as a wide verandah. It had a low pitched roof with terra cotta cappings, and chimneys of a prototype used in future.

Freeland describes this as 'the first of Hunt's many houses which were to be pioneeringly modern in outlook and approach' (1974:92).

The fact that this house was built in 1876, and called a 'bungalow' was obviously not un-related to the appearance of the illustrations and descriptions of the Birchington variety in the *Building News* (available in Australia) between 1870 and 1874. Moreover, the architectural features selected by Freeland as being of particular interest in the establishment of 'modernism', 'the long, low bungalow' unbroken brick walls, low-pitched roof and prototype chimneys, bear a striking similarity to the designs illustrated in the magazine.

The significance of this data is not, however, to join a sterile debate about 'architectural origins' but rather to reinforce the earlier comments concerning a need in some areas of architectural history to identify 'leading figures'. Whatever the aesthetic or other merits of Hunt's 'bungaloo', what is perhaps of more importance is that 'The Grange' was also apparently constructed as a 'second home' in what became at first a sort of 'hill station' after the Indian model. It was eventually to become one of the major inland areas for Sydney owners of second, or vacation, homes. In the early twentieth century, what the *Building* magazine referred to as 'seaside week-end homes' (1918, 7:56) were to evolve from 'tents and shacks to cottages and bungalows' on the shore between Mordialloc and Frankston, outside Melbourne. The Australian vacation home is older than is generally believed (Murphy, 1977).

From the 1890s to the end of the century, it was, as Donald Johnson points out (1980), the *idea* of the bungalow that was more important than the number of storeys, or even style, which characterised the few bungalows which appeared in Australia. As earlier chapters have shown, there was enough literature on the Western bungalow idea and lifestyle in British and American journals from the 1880s, to say nothing of Briggs's book (1891), for the *named* bungalow to reach Australia. Not unimportant here were the many catalogues of 'portable buildings', a form of architecture which had a long and important history in Australia. And as the term at this time could refer to a house of either one or two storeys, it was not surprising that the same idea took hold in Australia.

What really generated the bungalow on a large scale, however, were developments in California rather than Britain. For these, we need to return to the larger economic and social scene.

The California bungalow as Australian suburban home

The second, and perhaps more genuine phase of the Australian bungalow movement began in the early twentieth century. Its source was firmly in the United States.

The popular American bungalow, it will be recalled, had first emerged in California about 1904-5, gathering momentum from 1906 and then turning into a flood with dozens of books, articles, and bungalows, produced in the next decade. It was this literature, together with the activities of builders and architects, which brought the California Bungalow to Australia.

The overall context of this development has been set out in earlier pages but there were more specific circumstances as well. In considering these, it is apparent that very similar trends were at work in both California and Australia.

By the 1890s, the prosperity of Australian cities and the building boom which had gone with it were over. 'Gone were the golden days of easy expansion, for the British world economy was constricted by competitors who had overtaken it technologically and carved out rival empires.' With the withdrawal of overseas capital and the collapse of speculative companies, profits fell, wages were forced down and severe unemployment continued for the next ten years (Sandercock, 1975:10).

Yet from about 1904, the volume of construction again began to grow until, by the First World War, it was greater than at any time since 1888. Imported materials were cheaper and new materials such as asbestos cement were lowering building costs: an average six-roomed house in 1912 cost £800 in brick, £550 in weatherboard and a little less in the new asbestos cement sheets (Boyd, 1952:72).

Just what caused this revival of building activity remains to be explained, but the growing provision of public transport was clearly an important factor. From the 'walking distance' cities of the 1880s, emerged the public transport cities of 1900. Then, with the introduction of the car and motorbus, a further revolution occurred. In each city, there were building as well as urban land booms, with massive suburban sub-divisions and enormous speculation in land. High wages and labour shortages were factors which enabled large numbers of Australians to buy their own property, however small. By 1911, one in two houses were owned by those who lived in them.

From then on, the commitment to single-family housing became total. After this, to quote Boyd, 'with the exception of a few pair houses, each new dwelling was now detached and isolated in its own ground. The gardenless town house . . . had gone with the new century.'

There were, however, other factors which help to explain this situation; in particular, the importation of town planning ideology from Britain and with it, the notion of the 'garden suburb'. The economic depression around the turn of the century had focussed Australian interest on questions of social welfare: between 1890 and 1914 it was to gain its reputation as a country of advanced social legislation. And it was in this period that the town planning movement emerged, closely allied with other movements for social reform (Freestone, 1981; Sandercock, 1975).

As the suburbs sprawled further from the centre, there was growing concern both to improve Sydney's slums as well as to check what was seen as the disorderly and wasteful manner in which, on the one hand, the sub-division of land, and on the other, the construction of houses (generally two separate processes in Australia), were taking place. The situation was made more serious by a dramatic increase in Sydney's population around 1910. The introduction of town planning measures was an attempt to bring order into the chaos.

The measures, along with the economic, social and political assumptions on which they were based, were imported wholesale from Britain, especially after the passing of the Housing and Town Planning Act of 1909. Some of the early protagonists of planning in Australia were, like architect John Sulman, British immigrants. But in addition, between 1912 and 1915, a steady procession of politicians and administrators came to Britain to study the rapidly growing town planning movement and especially, the notion of the garden city.

Yet as Sandercock and others have pointed out, this early commitment to planning had little to do with either eliminating poverty or changing the fundamentally capitalist system. On the contrary, it was seen as a way of maintaining social harmony by bringing order and a more rational approach to urban development. It was an approach which, by ensuring that all new areas were planned, would introduce zoning, and in this way, improve and maintain the value of land and property.

As the journal *Building* stated in its 'Town Planning Section' (12 January, 1914), 'Town planning is now regarded as a science.' What they did not add was that it was also good for business. For landowners, it meant increased land values; for employers, a healthy work force ('nothing could do more for the mental elevation of the workers and improve their stamina'); for architects, surveyors and the new profession of planners, it meant both work and power; and for the state, it meant increasing commitment to the idea of private property. For the assumptions on which planning was carried out were precisely those in keeping with Anglo-Saxon, 'garden city' traditions: very low density and, as expounded by one of the most active Australian supporters, C.C. Reade, one house, one family. And in Australia, what town planning meant was the setting up of garden suburbs. And as garden suburbs, by improving the 'house and garden' landscape, were a device to sell land, so 'architecture' and the idea of the 'artistic bungalow' were equally a device to sell property.

Australia's first Town Planning Association was formed in New South Wales in 1913, the prototype for others which followed in different states. Its early activists were a varied collection of people; apart from architects, engineers, reformers and politicians of varying hue, it also included real estate developer and company director, Richard Stanton, and the editors of the *Building and Real Estate Magazine*, (later, *Building*). By 1914, there was, among the many who could benefit from it, a wide interest in the aesthetic, social and political aspects of town planning, and especially the garden city and garden suburb ideas. What was largely, though not totally, absent, however, was Ebenezer Howard's original notion of the municipal, collective ownership of developed land. It was within this context, as well as the overall background of suburban expansion, that the California Bungalow (in both popular as well as 'architectural' form) arrived around 1907-8.

The same developments that we have seen elsewhere now took place in Australia. According to Freeland, in the first decade of this century, 'the idea of the bungalow was taken up and found its first popular use as a cheap, light summer camp or weekend house'; 'numbers of unlined low-pitched malthoid-roofed, wide verandahed weekenders' (in Australia, the term is actually used for a temporary dwelling), appeared on the harbourside hills of Balmoral in Sydney and Frankston in Port Phillip. In 1908, the first bungalow article appeared, 'The Building of a Bungalow', sub-titled, as if with prescience, 'A style that should prove popular in Australia'. The journal was *Building* (Australia), 15 June, 1908, issued monthly with a 'Property Owners' Section'.

For those acquainted with the earlier chapters of this study, the contents are, of course, now depressingly familiar. Accompanied by the pre-requisite picture of 'The rustic bungalow', the text, arriving in a roundabout way via Britain (1890s) and California (1904-8), trotted out the familiar phrases: 'to those long in cities pent . . . the sensation of drawing breaths of pure, country air ... far from crowds ... and the restraints of the city, brings one to a state of health, happy responsibility ... nomadic instinct ... solitary country'. At this point, a particular Australian angle was introduced. Australians were

> pleasure-loving people, to whom any respite from the daily task is an eagerly accepted excuse to get out into the splendid sun, and revel untramelled on yellow beaches, or in the sun-splashed shadows of the bush. On every favorite camping ground are dotted the shanties of the inveterate campers, in the bush the camp is more often a tent, testifying to the vagabond instinct. ... It is really to be wondered that more permanent huts are not erected in the bush. There is nothing more picturesque, comfortable and cheap than a log bungalow. ... [This] should always look as if it had grown from the ground, and was an integral part of the bush, equally as much as the trees and undergrowth.

From here followed the prescribed (male) bungalow ideology: wide fireplaces built of rubble, chimneys of rough, moss-stained stones, simple furniture, rugs and cushions; 'with a log fire blazing on the big hearth, and oneself stretched on a rug before it, well provided with good books and tobacco, it matters not how the wind blows nor what the world thinks.'

The adaptation from the 'vacation bungalow' to the suburban variety was simply a matter of time. Three months later in 'How to Build a Bungalow', the magazine again drew freely on American designs, especially from the *Western Architect*. There was 'a suggestiveness in the word bungalow that makes it interesting. Just now it is a popular catchword – all the more so because few of us have seen a real one. There is play for the imagination.' The bungalow offered the architect or builder an escape from 'the plan book designed and rule of thumb built cottage, the "ready made" house that is being advertised'. The accompanying plans and photographs provided a glimpse into what was going on in Californian suburbs – down to the leaded glass, oriental rugs and wall covered all over with vines.

The fact was that conditions in respect of transport, land speculation, investment and social aspirations, as well as climate, in parts of Australia were indeed very similar to those in southern California; hence, the relevance of the bungalow. Two early examples of the architect-designed variety, complete with 'sleep out', were built in Brisbane and Toorak, Victoria, in 1908 (plate 135). In 1909, *Building* was reproducing articles from the *Western Architect* and in 1910, the key word 'artistic' had crept in. As the bungalow books and articles sailed across the Pacific (in *House Beautiful, House and Garden, Architectural Record* or Saylor's *Bungalows*) other important developments took place (Johnson, 1980:48, 57).

Seeing the benefits, and profits, latent in the garden suburb idea, Richard Stanton, estate agent and developer, began the suburb of Haberfield, Sydney's first 'garden suburb'; here each resident owned his own house, and the bungalow idea seems to have been introduced into the later developments. More important as a setting was Daceyville, an early garden suburb which was the outcome of a Royal Commission on the Improvement of the City of Sydney and Suburbs in 1908. For this, an architectural competition was held and architect James Peddle, a British expatriate who had arrived in 1899 but had subsequently left for California, hurried back from Pasadena, keen to put into practice the bungalow models which by then were filling that town.

Bungalows, of the Californian variety, were becoming increasingly popular, and as Peddle wrote in a special 'Bungalow Number' of *Building* (December 1912), there were 'Some lessons we can learn from our American neighbours.' What impressed him was 'the new American thought of city planning', as evidenced in the comprehensively landscaped, commercial developments on the Oakley-Berkeley side of San Francisco. In particular, he admired the

111,112 Self-improvement, 1920-80: low-cost bungalows updated.
Hayes, outer London Suburb (*Author*)

113 Self-improvement, 1920-80: the pay-off.
Owners of early 20th century beach bungalows realise the value of their land, Hayling Island, Sussex
(*Author*)

An Old Whitewashed Cottage in North Wales and—

A Costly New Bungalow in the Same Neighbourhood—no Vulgarity
spared.

The "COTTABUNGA"
(Regd.)

THIS CHARMING BUNGALOW COTTAGE
delivered, carriage paid, to any goods station in
England or Wales, ready to
erect, for · · · **£245 : 10 nett.**
"COTTABUNGA" buildings may be seen dotted all over
the Countryside, North—South—East—West, and are
giving universal satisfaction. No better value at the
price is possible, and if you would enjoy the comforts
and luxury of this artistic residence this coming summer
place your order NOW.

Our illustrated Catalogue, No. 103, con-
taining full particulars and a full range of
other Bungalows, Pavilions, Motor Houses,
Chalets, etc., post free to any address.

BROWNE & LILLY, LTD.
THAMES SIDE, READING
Telegrams: Portable, Reading. *'Phone: Reading 587*

114, 115 The bungalow under attack: Wales, 1928 (original captions).
For the middle-class arbiters of taste, the bungalow symbolised an invasion of the 'countryside', a territory they had previously regarded their own. Both illustrations are from C. Williams-Ellis, *England and the Octopus*, 1928

This is the unfortunate shape that arises from a bungalow plan that is probably quite efficient in itself. The square box-like form and pyramid-shaped roof are the direct result of a square or wide-span plan.

116 Class conflict in the environment: popular culture versus professional elite.
Both illustrations, with original captions, are from publications of the Council for the Preservation of Rural England. The upper picture was frequently used by the Council, occasionally with stronger wording, i.e. 'this smug bungalow would be discordant in any rural area'. The box-like form was said to be 'squat' and 'ugly' (CPRE, *Building in Cheshire*, 1939)

A bungalow looks dwarfed and appears unhappy in a row of two-floored houses.

Varying the heights, designs or materials of adjacent houses is tantamount to varying the shape and colour of every pawn in a set of chessmen.

Photo by Van Ojen and Slokvis, The Hague

A new street in Holland in which every householder takes a pride in the orderliness, cleanliness and unity of the street as a whole.

117 The influence of professional control.
With increased authority given to state architect-planners, class-based visual criteria were to prevail over social or other considerations in shaping the built environment. 'Unhappy' bungalows were prohibited; the values of 'orderliness' and 'unity' favoured Corbusian tower blocks for dependent classes in the towns (CPRE, *Building in Cheshire*, 1939)

118 Living it up in the Hill Station: bungalows at Freetown, Sierra Leone, c.1906.
Increasing international competition led Britain to take a renewed interest in Africa at the end of the nineteenth century, sparking off a concern for the health of Europeans living there.

The value of the hill station had already been discovered in the West Indies and South East Asia in the eighteenth century and a large number had been established in India. In the early twentieth century, the idea, both in name and form, was transferred to Sierra Leone, 'Hill Station' established just outside Freetown (*Martin Banham*)

119 Hill Station bungalow. Photograph, 1982.
The bungalows were sent out from England. Local European folklore insists that they came from Harrod's of Knightsbridge (*Simon Banham*)

Zulu village, South Africa, before 1956.
By the mid-twentieth century economic and
political changes had led the Zulu to adopt
mixed farming, and this was reflected in a
reduction in the size of the cattle kraal in
their villages and atrophy of the outer heavy
timber stockade.

*Zulu homestead near
Mahlabatina–Ngoma road, South Africa,
1953.*

*Zulu house under construction, South
Africa, about 1902.*

120 African dwelling and settlement forms in rural South Africa: Zulu village and homestead, before 1956
(S. Denyer, *African Traditional Architecture*, 1978. Heinemann Educational Books and S. African State
Information Office) (original captions).

121 Housing and urban form in Kano, Northern Nigeria, c.1960 (S. Denyer, *African Traditional Architecture*,
1978. Heinemann Educational Books and Ministry of Information, Nigeria)

Four Kabakas of the Protectorate and their Katikiros.

CN 150   39 *House of Katikiro of Buganda.*

122, 123 Market penetration: the adoption of 'European' forms, Uganda, 1906 (original captions) (*Royal Commonwealth Society*)

3. Swahili-type houses, unimproved versions.

2. Types of semi-detached 'Quarters'.

4. A Swahili-type house; one of the improved versions.

124, 125, 126 Transformation of culture: 'modern', 'Western' or 'bourgeois' home? Dar-es-Salaam, 1950s. (original captions) (J. A. K. Leslie, *A Survey of Dar-es-Salaam*, 1963, Oxford University Press)

View of a township, showing old houses and mine surface operations in background.

The new bungalow type homes provided for Africans in the upper pay group.

127,128 Incorporated into the global economy: the bungalow as means, Northern Rhodesia (Zambia) c.1960. In the early stages, African labour was incorporated into the copper mines in company-provided dwellings, following traditional forms. Subsequently, 'new bungalow type homes' provide the transition to the urban economy (H. Powdermaker, *Copper Town*, 1962, Harper & Row, New York)

Plate 1. A colonial house style in Benin.

Plate 2. An example of a bungalow in Benin.

129, 130 Bungalow as 'house designed for a single (nuclear) family with high income' (Onokerhoraye, 1977), Benin, Nigeria (original captions).

The early 20th-century meaning of bungalow in Africa as 'a house suitable for European occupation' (a meaning derived from India) continues in use to describe a modern 'European', single family dwelling. The bungalow is occupied by senior African government officials (A. G. Onokerhoraye, 'The evolution and spatial structure of house types in the traditional Nigerian city: a Benin example', *Journal of Tropical Geography*, 45, 1977).

Housing in the slum clearance area

—and in the rehousing estate

131 Urban improvements: Lagos, Nigeria, c.1960 (P. Marris, *Family and Social Change in Africa*, 1961, Routledge & Kegan Paul) (original captions)

132 'Tropical bungalow' in Queensland: Rosebank, Townsville, built 1885 (*Ray Sumner*)

133 Chief Engineer's house, Queensland Meat Exporting Company, Townsville, built 1890.
Though the term 'bungalow' was probably not in use in Australia till the later 19th century, single-storey, single-family dwellings with a verandah were common from 1815 onwards. The links in this conception of a dwelling seem likely to have been provided by military personnel moving between the Caribbean, Britain, India and Australia. The 'tropical bungalow' shown here was a relatively late development (*Ray Sumner*)

134 California bungalow, Australian style: Kew, Victoria, 1923 (*D. L. Johnson*)

135 Suburban bungalow, architect's design: Victoria, 1908 (*D. L. Johnson*)

136 Privatised space: the one-person household, England, 1981 (*Author*)

137 Circulating the surplus: the bungalow and international tourism 1980s.
German brochure, Spanish resort, 'English beach', international bungalow.

138 Time-share bungalow, Caribbean: units 'available for exchange on a world-wide basis'.

139, 140 Half-way to the 'residence secondaire': the French bungalow as semi-permanent camp, St. Tropez, France, 1981.

141 The diffusion of concept and terms: camping stoves, South of France, 1981.
Cultural practice follows economic forms: the term 'week-end' was first recorded in French in 1906
(*Author*)

142, 143, 144 Creating needs: reinforcing the norms (*Author*)

The magazine that tells you what's on and where to go in London.
March 21-27 1980 No. 518 35p

Time Out

Northern Zone Control, Fife.

Sub Regional Headquarters 21, York.

Sub Regional Military Headquarters, Brentwood, Essex.

Home Office Radio Station, Brighton, Sussex.

RAF Wartling (now dismantled), Eastbourne, Sussex.

Beachy Head Coastguard Station. Eastbourne, Sussex.

The military's last outposts.

In the nuclear age civil defence is obsolete, survival of government is everything. Some of these innocent-looking bungalows hide the entrances to Britain's Regional Seats of Government.

145 The bungalow as sinister disguise: regional seats of government in the event of a nuclear attack (*Time Out*)

USA

Canada

Britain

146 The contemporary bungalow, 1980s: North America, Britain and Bangladesh
(*Author; Jim McIntosh*)

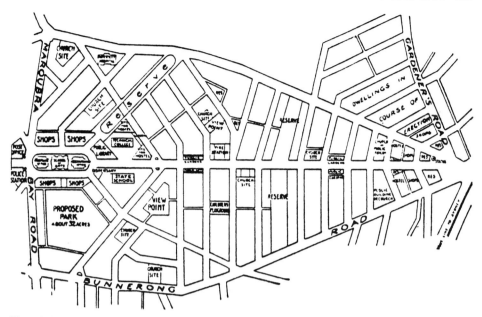

Figure 7.2 Importing the garden suburb: Daceyville, Australia, 1912.
As town and garden city planning ideas were imported from Britain, the California bungalow was brought in from the USA (*Rob Freestone*)

fenceless gardens. The problem in Australia was that 'we are too individualistic . . . we think of *my* piece of land, of *my* lot, of *my garden*, while our American neighbours think of *their* city.' His recommendation was 'to mingle a few communistic ideas with our natural individualism – remove some of our fences.' There was, however, as the magazine pointed out three years later, a need for 'Evolving the Australian type' of bungalow.

Yet apart from the Californian ideas, estate developer Richard Stanton went further. With the interest in garden cities accelerating in 1911-12, Stanton, operating under the seductively titled 'Town Planning Company of Australia' set up the garden suburb of Rosebery, a 'model and industrial development' 'some fifteen minutes out of Sydney central station' even though it was never actually on a railway. Here, his company was 'opening up 300 acres of magnificent building land, nicely subdivided, with 14 miles of road frontages upon which ARTISTIC HOMES are being erected with every known modern comfort and convenience, including electric light'. Bungalows in all but name, the 'ROSEBERY COTTAGES [were] the latest word in HOME COMFORT. Charming and dainty, both internally and externally with four, five or six rooms and kitchen'. Again, the major attraction was investment. As his advertisement in the Property Owner Section of *Building* (April 1913) indicated in block capitals: 'FOR AN INVESTMENT your decision should be IMMEDIATE' 'ROSEBERY PRICES MUST RISE'.

Not content with local products, Stanton imported a prefabricated timber bungalow from California. Erected in 1912 by the Redwood Export Company, of Castlereagh Street, Sydney, the local representatives of the California Redwood Association of San Francisco, the bungalow was the first and exhibition house of Rosebery, planned as a model working class suburb. According to Freeland, 'by introducing a full-blown, genuine and undiluted example of the Californian bungalow to the Australian scene, it acted as a stimulus, catalyst and model.' The large, prefabricated wall and roof units were assembled and set on brick footings and supplemented by a roughcast brick chimney. In every way the house was typical of its kind – large-spanning, low pitched gable, roof overhanging at the eaves and gables, low spreading verandah, carried on sturdy battened pylons, natural finish cedar panelling on the inside and complete with built-in cupboards. By 1917, the type of architecture that the Redwood bungalow epitomised was being everywhere accepted and enthusiastically embraced (Freeland, 1968:228).

As in California, the significance of the bungalow was not simply that it seemed the ideal dwelling for the suburbs; it also had three critical attributes: it was new, 'artistic' and hence, 'individual': it was described as – 'pretty', 'rustic', and 'different'. Architecture, or design, had a price tag: it could be used to raise prices, bring in high values. As one development company said of the first two (architect-designed) model cottages on a new garden suburb in 1914: they 'exercised a stimulating effect on the prices paid for adjacent land'. Hence, when Town

Figure 7.3 Design as commodity: the California bungalow used to sell land.
The California bungalow nominated as the Ideal Australian Home at the Town Planning Conference, Brisbane, 1918 (*D.L.Johnson*)

Planning Conferences were held at Adelaide (1917) and Brisbane (1918), of the designs shown at the accompanying Ideal Home Exhibition, it was the California bungalow variety which was actually built (Freestone, 1981).

The California bungalow brought changes to the suburbs. Broad-fronted rather than long and narrow, it forced sub-dividers to broaden their plots. With increasing ownership of cars from about 1915, access to a garage sited in a back corner of the site was needed, with an 8- to 10-foot driveway down one side of the house. The result was that the California bungalow primarily, but also the car, increased the normal width of a building block to 60 feet and as there was no reduction in the depth of the sites, by taking 25 to 50 per cent more land for each house, accelerated the physical spread of the suburbs (Freeland, 1968:231) (plate 134).

The character of the bungalow varied with different localities: Sydney, Melbourne, Adelaide, Queensland and Tasmania all had their various types. As adopted by builders, it was a style generally suitable for a small, single-storey or three-bedroomed house and partly for this reason it was restricted to lower and lower middle class areas. Yet as an architectural style it was also adopted for larger dwellings, for middle class clients and areas.

Though there were architect-designed bungalows, modelled perhaps on the work of Wright or the Californian designs of Greene and Greene, the majority were popular housing, built from builders' books and combining a mix of Californian, British and Australian elements. In addition to the mere attraction of investment, there were all the same social and economic influences at work which we have seen in Britain and the USA. As building costs increased after the First World War, architects became interested in the smaller house. With servants disappearing from the domestic scene, excess space became a burden. Labour-saving meant that a smaller kitchen became an asset and custom-built cupboards were fitted to every wall. The dining room disappeared, to be replaced by a 'common room' combining living and dining functions.

The selling points were as they had been in the USA: they were said to have 'cosy warmth, security, and quaint, roomy natural charm'. 'Even in winter this bungalow looks warm. . . This bungalow is sociable, agreeable – like the friend who is never cold.' 'The deep shadows invite one to lounge in languid disregard of passing time' – such were the meanings invested in the bungalow.

This 'genuine bungalow feeling' was conveyed in the newly opened suburbs of all the major capital cities, to be the dominant style from 1918 to the early 1930s.

As in the United States, the Australian bungalow reached its peak in the 1920s, boosted by a further boom in suburban development. In New South Wales, the new Local Government Act of 1919, again, derivative from Britain, brought with it further control of new roads, sub-divisions and building, and with this, the power to control the number of houses per acre in residential divisions.

By 1921, 43 per cent of the New South Wales population were living in the metropolis, 816,000 of them in the suburbs and just over one-eighth of that number in the City of Sydney itself. Since 1900, the suburbs had massively expanded while the inner city had correspondingly declined. The decades between 1911-21 and 1921-31 each added 300,000 to the suburban population of Sydney. The war had created shortages and this inspired the post-war boom within a 6- to 13-mile radius of public transport routes round the city. As one newspaper accurately predicted in 1920:

Now that the weather is warming up a resumption of subdivision sales is imminent. Agents are already arranging for what many believe will be a record season. . . . The

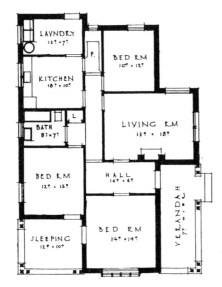

PLAN No. 27.

SUBURBAN HOME.

A Large Suburban Home with Three Large Bedrooms, Sleeping-out Verandah, Living-room, Kitchen and Offices. Cemented Brick Walls, Tile Roof.

Cost approximately £1350.

Figure 7.4 Global product, local style: Australian bungalow, 1923 (*Book of Australian Bungalows*, 1923). G.W. Phillips's *New Zealand Homes and Bungalows* appeared in 1912.

demand is here already. Whatever may be said of the improvidence of the Australian, he nevertheless has sufficient common sense to acquire his own home or at least strive hard for it (Sandercock, 1975:82-5).

The years to the mid 1930s were to represent the final fling of the bungalow style in Australia, by which time as elsewhere, she had her own collection of 'bungalow books'.[2] The bungalow phase had been a historical era where two key notions had come from outside: the garden suburb from Britain, the transformed bungalow from the USA. Both were ideologies of design, and both played an important role in reaffirming the long-established Australian tradition of private property, individually expressed. In the process, the capital market in housing and land was kept comfortably rolling along. It was a crucial era in a longer history during which the function of the Australian house was transformed from one of mere shelter to that of acting as a symbol of independence and social prestige.

FOR SALE — $112,000
Magnificent Bungalow

An exclusive residence architecturally designed for modern indoor-outdoor living.
The bungalow contains 4 bedrooms, en-suite/ dressing room, bathroom, main bathroom, sunken lounge, separate dining room, kitchen, breakfast nook, day room and laundry. Most of which open through floor to ceiling glass doors to outside areas.

OUTDOOR FEATURES
The main bungalow is set beneath a giant Jacaranda tree under which is a secluded outdoor entertaining area surrounded by palms and ferns with the landscaped inground pool a few metres beyond. Huge Porphyry rocks are a feature of the pool area. The entire driveway approach and pool side area is laid in brick into 2 car accommodation. Trees, rocks and shrubs are a feature of the front, giving complete privacy.
The block of land adjoining the property (under separate title) has been incorporated in the landscaping and is assimilated with the main bungalow and grounds by the total surround fence and double driveway gates. It contains a fully self contained retreat which houses the slashpine sauna. This area could double as guest or in-law accommodation.
The retreat has separate car entrance and accommodation. This delightful property is within 25 minutes of Brisbane G.P.O.

Contemporary bungalow: advert in Queensland daily paper, 1978 (Peter Newell).

Chapter 8

Speculations

> Migrants and shanty towns are part of a universal process which began only a few decades ago with the intensified penetration of the tropical world by financial capital and the rapidly advancing technology of the industrial nations. A world economy is being created in which most of the rich live in the latter, most of the poor in the former. . . .
>
> The shanty town house, built with the labour of family and friends . . . is designed to suit the whims and needs of its occupants. . . . The desirable little bungalow in the suburbs may be within their means – but it will not accommodate all the children.
>
> Peter Lloyd, *Slums of Hope. Shanty Towns of the Third World*. Harmondsworth, 1979, pp. 15, 169.

Introduction

Investigating the history of the bungalow has opened up a number of issues. This final chapter is devoted to speculating about some of them: suburbanisation and 'responses to urbanism', the relation of dwelling type to forms of tenure, type of economy and standards of living, the individual expression of private property, and some social changes represented by the bungalow, whether in Britain or elsewhere. In discussing these and a variety of other questions – the meaning of the bungalow as second home, 'tropical house' or merely as an irritant to British planners, and in examining its wider significance on a global scale – an attempt is made to draw some conclusions, and pose questions, for the present and future from what has largely been historical research.

'Counter-urbanisation': the bungalow as promoter and product

The previous chapters have shown that in Britain, the United States and, to a lesser extent, in Australia, the bungalow and the ideology behind it was produced by, and also helped to produce, the particular forms of suburban expansion characteristic of modern, industrial and capitalist societies with a free market in housing and land. The reasons why the British experience was somewhat different from that of the other two countries are discussed in more detail below. In this context, one framework in which to understand the bungalow is provided by what Berry calls 'counter-urbanisation', 'a process of population deconcentration [which] implies a movement from a state of more to a state of less concentration' (1976b:17).

One way to demonstrate this would be by using statistics, showing the change over time in the size of urban populations, their distribution in different sized cities and suburbs, the move to lower densities and then to correlate these figures with what is known about the introduction and development of the bungalow. A briefer way is given in the table below. What this suggests is the way in which people in these societies gradually became conscious of the changes affecting their environment and invented words to conceptualise, measure and name them. It gives the earliest identified use of various terms referring to aspects of urbanisation (and related phenomena) as well as facts concerning the bungalow referred to in the previous chapters. A glance shows how closely the two are inter-related.

Earliest identified use of selected terms referring to accelerated urbanisation, 1880-1930[a]	*Earliest identified reference outside Asia to:*[b]
	1869 bungalow (England: as seaside vacation house)
1874 'commuter' (USA)	1876 bungalow (Australia: as country vacation house)
	1879 'week-end'[d]
	1880 bungalow (USA: as seaside vacation house)
	1880 country cottage 'fitted up for summer use' (USA)
1884 'urbanised'	1884 evidence of early interest in 'week-end cottage' habit
1888 'urbanisation' (USA)	1887 bungalow (country)
1888 'suburbanism'	
1889 'urbanism'	1889 bungalow (South Africa)[e]
1890 'town planning'[c]	1891 bungalow: suitable for permanent country or suburban residence
	1891 bungalow defined as 'a little country house'
1893 'suburbia'	
1895 'motor car'	1895 discussion of bungalow for retirement in suburbs
1895 'motorist'	
1899 A.F. Weber, *The Growth of Cities in the 19thC.*	
	1903 'Craftsman bungalow' (USA)
1904 'urbanisation'	1904 'week-end bungalow'
	1904 suburban bungalow (South Africa)
	1905 'California bungalow' (USA)
	1908 suburban bungalow (Australia)
1910 'conurbation'	
1922 'suburbanisation'	
1926 'ribbon development'[b]	
	1927 'bungaloid growth'
1929 'urbanism' ('The newly-coined	

word 'urbanism' . . . denotes town-
planning' *The Times*; 16 July.)
1930   'urbanist' ('a specialist in or
advocate of, town planning')

[a]   From *Oxford English Dictionary*, 1978.
[b]   Sources given in text. Except where otherwise stated, terms refer to UK.
[c]   See L. Sandercock, *Cities for Sale*, Melbourne University Press, 1975, p. 16; also R. Freestone, 'John Sulman and the laying out of towns', *Planning History Bulletin*, 5, 1, 1983, p. 18.
[d]   The actual unit of 'holiday time' apparently existed in 1850 (Walton, 1983:30).
[e]   D. Radford, University of Witwatersrand.

As Berry points out, H.G. Wells had already suggested in 1902 that 'the railway begotten giant cities' he knew were,

> destined to such a process of dissection and diffusion as to amount almost to obliteration . . . within a measurable space of years. These coming cities . . . will present a new and entirely different phase of human distribution.

And then, almost as if he were referring to the bungalows beginning to rise around him,

> what will be the forces acting upon the prosperous household? The passion for nature . . . and that craving for a little private *imperium* are the chief centrifugal inducements. . . . The city will diffuse itself until it has taken up considerable areas and many of the characteristics of what is now the country. . . . We may call . . . these coming town provinces, 'urban regions' (1976:24).

Similarly, three years earlier Adna Ferrin Weber had suggested that the trend in urbanisation was towards the development of suburban towns (ibid.].

Yet reactions to the dense, highly concentrated, industrial cities of the nineteenth century have not been the same everywhere. Although all societies have developed policies of deliberate decentralisation as a solution to city ills, they have been strongly influenced by economic, social, political and cultural choices.

Berry suggests that three types of policy have emerged in the twentieth century as a response to industrial urbanisation around the world:

> *individualistic decentralisation* that has culminated in the decreasing size, decreasing density . . . and more ruralised life styles of the more liberal capitalist states;
>
> *planned new towns* as counterpoints to speculative private interest in the welfare states of Western Europe; and the
>
> Marxist search for a new settlement for mankind, the *city of socialist man* in which traditional antagonisms between city and country are no more (ibid.:10).

Yet Berry's categories apply only to the so-called 'developed world'; they comprehend neither the generally uncontrolled process of urbanisation in the 'third world' as these countries are incorporated into the capitalist world economy, nor the policies which attempt to control them. Nor does Berry examine the underlying forces behind 'counter-urbanisation' in free market societies: the reshaping of urban space by shifts in capital investment which have encouraged inner city decay and the expansion of the suburbs (see Fielding, 1982).

A more satisfactory framework for understanding the bungalow and the type of urban development it represents, whether suburbanisation or the second, vacation, home, is that provided by Fainstein and Fainstein (1979:392-3). They suggest that urbanism is connected by three elements to the substructure which produces it. First, there are the basic *processes* of economic activity; second, there are the *structures* by which economic processes are carried out or expressed; third, there are the *active agents* whose activities create and sustain the processes and structures. The examples indicated in their scheme would seem to apply to the circumstances responsible for the production of the bungalow as discussed in the preceding chapters, namely: the basic economic processes concern the production and circulation of value; the structures in which these processes are expressed are the spatial pattern of investment and the physical character of the built environment, including the specific character of urban form; the active agents who create and sustain these processes and structures are the industrialists, builders, bankers and state officials (in this case, local authority planners) whose activities have been discussed in the preceding pages.

However, as Fainstein and Fainstein point out, problems arise when an attempt is made to identify those aspects of urbanism arising directly from the system of economic organisation or mode of production, and those determined by the differing national and local socio-political systems. In this present study, this latter aspect has also included reference to cultural differences.

It is these national and cultural differences which Berry refers to when he suggests that the form of counter-urbanisation which he describes as 'individualistic decentralisation' results from the reassertion of 'fundamental predispositions of the American culture that . . . are antithetical to urban concentrations'. If this is so, then the history of the bungalow would seem to symbolise the typical reaction to urbanism in that society. For, according to Berry (drawing on an earlier source), the most important cultural traits are 'a love of newness', a desire to be 'near to nature', the 'freedom to move' and 'individualism', the major features with which the bungalow was marketed in the United States.

Yet as was pointed out in the Introduction, such all-inclusive or 'cultural' explanations ignore other facts about questions of supply and demand, the ownership of land, the right to private property, and the principles behind the organisation of the state. Other factors are needed to explain why the separate, single-family house is so characteristic and widespread in some societies, such as Australia and the United States, whereas multi-household forms (flats and apartments) are more common in others. Is the relationship to be explained solely in political and economic terms or, in those societies with a private market in dwellings and land, by the extent of home ownership? And what are the larger economic, social and spatial implications raised by changes in the types of dwelling in a nation's housing stock and the relation of these to changes in tenure?

It is in the context of these questions that the significance of the bungalow is appreciated. Here it is understood in its most accepted sense as a physically separate, single-storey, single-family (or single-household) dwelling, as distinguished from separate houses of more than one storey and non-separate, multi-family accommodation: flats (apartments), terrace (row) housing, or semi-detached (duplex). In comparison to the separate or detached house containing equal accommodation, it is also clear that the bungalow generally takes up more land.

Tenure and dwelling type: the significance of the bungalow

The question of why certain types of housing prevail in particular societies is both interesting and more complex than it might seem. Fortunately, it is one which has recently been carefully explored, on a cross-cultural basis in different industrial capitalist societies by three different scholars (Agnew, 1981; N. Duncan, 1981; Kemeny, 1981). Certain conclusions are worth stating.

Although it might be easily assumed that the higher the *per capita* income in a society, the higher the proportion of households owning their own dwelling, with two of the wealthiest nations, the United States and Australia, having ownership rates of almost 63 and 69 per cent respectively, Sweden and Switzerland, both with much higher per capita incomes than Australia, have only 35 and 28 per cent home ownership respectively (Kemeny, 1981:8). In contrast, some relatively poor 'developing' countries such as India and Indonesia have very high rates of home ownership. In Asia as a whole, about 80 per cent of households own their homes compared to about 70 per cent in Australia, 69 per cent in North America and Canada, 62 per cent in Latin America, 50 per cent in Europe and 40 per cent in Africa (Nationwide Building Society, *World Housing*, 1980) (Kemeny's figures are for different years).

Comparing Australia, Sweden and Britain, Kemeny suggests that detached and semi-detached houses constitute 87, 43 and 49 per cent respectively of all dwellings in these societies, the remainder constituted by 'other' dwellings. Taking the three major cities of Sydney, Stockholm and London, roughly three-quarters, one-third and one-half of dwellings respectively were 'houses', the remainder being flats or 'other dwellings'. He concludes that the percentage of 'houses' in each of these cities was 'strikingly similar' to the percentage of home ownership (ibid.:43-4).

Agnew also suggests that in other free-market societies, there is a relationship between rates of ownership and separate single-family housing. In the United States, where 66 per cent of all dwellings are detached single-family houses, 83 per cent are privately owned (1980). At the other end of the scale, 28 per cent of dwellings are of multi-family design (apartments), but only 17 per cent of these are owned. In Britain, the figures are similar, if not so large: more than 54 per cent of households in terraced, detached and semi-detached housing (84 per cent in the case of the latter) owned or were buying their property. These three categories were said to make up almost 80 per cent of the total housing stock. On the other hand, only 7 per cent or less of the households living in flats or maisonettes (comprising 19 per cent of the housing stock) owned or were buying their dwellings (1981:69-70). In Britain, however, the terraced and semi-detached houses are more common and it is obvious that, as Agnew points out, access to a specific type of house varies according to what is available. In different countries, the availability of land, construction methods and styles, building codes and preferences of people for different types of housing differ.

Kemeny concludes, though not with any sense of defeat, that the reasons responsible for different housing stocks are 'historical, cultural and ideological' (1981:44). It is at all these three levels that the history of the bungalow adds to our understanding of these issues.

The bungalow and de-industrialised urbanisation

What evidence is there to suggest that a gradual move is taking place in Britain, not only to higher rates of owner-occupation, but for this to be expressed over time, say from 1920 onwards, in a move to detached houses and bungalows?

Until relatively recently in Britain, the bungalow has generally been a 'private sector' dwelling, owned by its occupants. And though many inter-war bungalows were small, often low-cost housing, others, especially since 1950, have been substantial, and relatively expensive. For the last few years, for example, Building Societies Association figures from all regions suggest that the average price of bungalows is second only to that of detached houses among six standard types of dwelling (bungalow, detached, semi-detached, terraced, purpose-built and converted flat).

Insufficient data exists to show the various proportions of dwelling types being constructed in Britain, but a study in 1959 concluded that there had been 'a remarkable growth in the popularity of the bungalow since the war'. In nine of sixteen towns sampled with populations between 29,000 and 250,000 (excluding London and very large cities), bungalows constituted over 50 per cent of all dwellings built in 1957. Bungalow development was seen to be equal to private house development outside large cities and though especially, and expectedly, popular in coastal resorts such as Bournemouth, where almost 88 per cent of all dwellings built were bungalows, it was also over 72 per cent in typical industrial towns of Lancashire and Yorkshire. In rural districts, between two and five times as many bungalows as houses were being built (Cheer, 1959).

In a later study on the north-west coast, Cowburn (1966) found bungalows to be the most popular type of new housing. In the last few years, some 30 per cent of all new building-society loans have been for detached houses of which 10 per cent have been for bungalows, mainly built since 1960. However, the distribution of these loans has varied greatly according to region. Only 1 per cent of the loans on bungalows were granted in the Greater London region compared to 32 per cent in Northern Ireland and between 10 and 15 per cent in other areas in England (BSA Bulletin April 1981). (Ample evidence for the popularity of the Irish bungalow can be found in the nine editions or reprints of Jack Fitzsimons, *Bungalow Bliss*, containing eighty designs 'approved for all grants', published in Eire between 1971 and 1977.)

Yet this data must be viewed in the light of evidence on de-centralisation and the steady fall in the population of all large cities, and especially London, in the last three decades. This has been paralleled by a proportionate rise in suburban populations, in country areas, and in small towns and large villages. Preliminary reports from the 1981 census indicate that between 1971 and 1981, all large cities suffered substantial population losses, ranging from Glasgow (22 per cent) to Manchester (17 per cent), Liverpool (16 per cent) and Birmingham (8 per cent). In contrast, remoter districts of Cornwall, Suffolk and Humberside experienced growth rates of 10 per cent. The three English regions lacking a large industrial conurbation showed the biggest population gains. The largest was in East Anglia (11.7 per cent) which amongst all English regions incidentally also had the largest percentage of building-society loans granted for bungalows (15 per cent) during 1980. The next largest population gains were in the south-west (6 per cent) and east Midlands. With Yorkshire and Humberside, both these regions had the next highest proportion of loans granted for bungalows (11 per cent). In these cases, loans granted to all types of detached housing were greater than or equal to those given to semi-detached or terraced housing (BSA Bulletin, April 1981).

Part of the explanation for these data can be attributed to the growing trend of 'retirement migration' which is predicted to increase (Law and Warnes, 1980). Yet longer-term explanations can be pursued.

Many nineteenth-century British cities were primarily concerned with industrial production. The cheapest, least space-consuming dwelling was the terrace, and especially, the

Figure 8.1 Contemporary culture: the bungalow, for and after work, 1980s.
Both models are for Britain's expanding 'sun belt': the commuter's two car 'ranch bungalow' in the south-east, the 'retirement bungalow' in the south-west (*SNW Homes*) (See also plate 93)

minimal back-to-back house. In today's increasingly global economy, industry disappears or is transferred to low-wage areas of the 'Third World'. For the capitalist industrial system which produced it, the concentrated labour of terraced streets no longer has any logic. Instead, today's 'high tech', often transnationally-owned industry seeks out unspoilt 'green field' sites in regions without an industrial past. These developments, and an increasingly professional and 'tertiarised' workforce are also behind the growth of the commuter belt 'executive ranch house'. And where nineteenth-century, inner city back-to-backs were an outcome of industrial production, two-car, split-level bungalows are designed for increasing consumption. In 1961, 29 per cent of 16 million British households had cars; in 1981, it was 45 per cent of 20 million. Within the same period, two- or more-car households rose from 2 to 15 per cent (Department of Transport, 1982).

What this evidence suggests is that since mid-century or before, people have not only been moving out of larger cities into suburbs, smaller towns and rural areas, but also out of (rented) flats, terraces and 'semis' into (owned) detached houses and bungalows; what the larger economic, social, political or spatial implications are provides scope for speculation and research. If such a move is happening, the implications are many, whether for land and energy use, the balance between privatisation and public provision (Kemeny, 1981), or the much larger issue concerning the relationship between political economy and the production and reproduction of everyday ways of life.

The bungalow in continental Europe

The introduction of the term 'bungalow' into other European languages can, with other data, be taken as sufficient evidence of its existence either as permanent country and suburban dwelling or, in smaller or prefabricated form, as temporary 'weekend' or summer house. In either case, it is a 'response to urbanism' in certain capitalist societies and, if in permanent form, may also imply a move to higher rates of owner-occupation as expressed in the individual, suburban house.

In Germany, the term seems to have been in use in both senses from about the 1940s, and with the same ideological connotations. Discussing bungalows in Germany, Italy, Holland, Belgium, Denmark and England, in 1958, the authors state (in German),

> Bungalow, though a word often derided by professionals as inappropriate and merely fashionable, has come to represent for many of our contemporaries, the concept of a distinct longing. It is an expression of the need for rest, of a return to Nature, of protection from the wearing side-effects of modern technology. And finally, of the fulfilment of the desire to live, undisturbed, as an individual. . . . Today, everyone understands the word to mean the one storey, detached house of modern conception which allows man, through the utilisation of modern technology, to live in comfort, protected from cold, heat, rain, storm and noise, close to nature (Betting and Vriend, 1958).

In addition, however, the bungalow was being increasingly introduced for outer suburban dwellings, and modifying traditional forms of German design. In the words of an architectural critic, it was 'the pitiful, stunted form of the earlier free-standing villa: a too short and too high building draped with all the attributes of a single family house . . . the irresolvable conflict between owning a small house and wishing for a pompous country seat (freisitz)' (Nestler-Bode, 1976:25). For some German architects, however, the bungalow expressed other ideas as in 'Der Bungalow', built for the Federal Chancellor, for official functions, in Bonn in the early 1960s. It was

> an expression of a political idea . . . in an age of vanishing social differences, it is not fitting for the head of government to be exalted and glorified by a kind of rhetorically embellished classicism in concrete. Politics today needs not formality and ceremoniousness, but contacts, discussion and understanding between people . . . modern art stands for the importance of man as a free individual . . . this is reflected in the bungalow (Steingraber, 1967:54-5).

In the contemporary German press there are advertisements for the komfort winkelbungalow (comfortable, L-shaped), luxusbungalow (luxury), doppelbungalow (semi-detached), spitzenbungalow (with pyramid roof), atrium bungalow and others. What they all have in common is their spacious suburban or commuter's rural setting. In France too, and elsewhere, the term and phenomenon have similarly been in use since the 1930s both for vacation use (see below) as well as for permanent living. P. Vanneau's *Soixante Bungalows*, Brussels and Paris (about 1960) includes, for example, designs for a 'bungalow économique pour deux personnes' and a 'chalet de weekend'. Suburban bungalows are equally common in Belgium and Holland.

Whilst this data is slender evidence on which to suggest that a similar move towards 'owner-occupied' single-family, suburban bungalow homes is taking place on any scale in these countries, more concrete information is available on Switzerland. Here, accommodation has traditionally been rented: in 1970 under 28 per cent of households lived in their own privately owned accommodation, and in many urban areas, the multi-family housing unit was common. In the last ten years, however, there has been a rapid move to owner-occupation, much of it expressed in the detached outer suburban villa (Garnier, 1981). It is also in this context that the single-storey bungalow, both in word and form, is beginning to be found in Switzerland; it is part of 'counter-urbanisation' in capitalist Europe (Fielding, 1982).

The proliferation of households and dwellings

Some further speculations can be pursued. In some pre-industrial, pre-capitalist past, dwellings provided shelter and, with a parcel of land, as well as animals and tools, were places of work, residence and recreation. There was not in such societies, the clear distinction between work and life, or as today, between work and leisure. Also in the dwelling, sick members were nursed, children learnt their adult roles and, when there was one, the surplus product was stored. Here, different members and generations of a family produced and consumed their livelihood.

The impact of industrial capitalism was not only to separate work from residence but to drain away from the dwellings all functions of production (except for the reproduction of labour) and make it principally a place of consumption. Other institutions (and buildings) developed to take on specialised tasks: the factory, bank, hospital, school, brewery and, as economy and society were transformed, more agencies were created or modified to control and classify the emerging working population – the prison, workhouse, or asylum.

With economic and technological change, and as the scale of the market increased, the size of the surplus capital grew, to be reinvested and kept in circulation in specialised places, and buildings for leisure. The most obvious expression of this was the holiday resort or, closer to the main dwelling and workplace, the various places and buildings for urban recreation.

With these developments, there occurred in the basic dwelling – though varying according to divisions of class and wealth – an increase in the number and divisions of rooms, such that each had its specialised function, and could accommodate consumer goods. As population and economic growth increased, the more separate, self-contained and single-family dwellings there were, the greater was the demand to fuel the growing economy.

As part of this process, where the aim of producers is to maximise profit by constantly creating and then satisfying 'needs', to commoditise requirements, kinship relations have also been fragmented. Though this is seen most clearly in India or the countries of Africa, where the impact of capitalist forms of production and urbanisation on the extended family and lineage system of peasant economies at least partly accounts for the emergence of nuclear families, it can also be seen in the 'developed' industrialised market economies of the West.

Here, over time, as demographic change has taken place, and especially changes in the expectation of life, individual units of accommodation have been created for different generations or for individuals at various stages of the life course. This is most obviously demonstrated by the emergence of the 'retirement resorts' with their tens of thousands of purpose-built bungalows, each with its individually-owned complement of consumer goods, from the washing-machine to the lawn-mower. A pre-requisite for these relatively recent developments (they have, in effect, occurred mainly during the last hundred years) has been the social production, or 'invention' of state-supported 'retirement'. As technology has developed to lower production costs and increase profits in the conditions of late capitalism, labour has become increasingly dispensable, to be dumped, irrespective of choice, at an increasingly lower age. Yet with increased life expectancy and state-supported retirement, the retired still perform the function of consumers. The history of the bungalow provides further fuel to these speculations.

Some of the most perceptive insights can be derived from the lyrics of popular 'bungalow songs', some ten of which have been written since 1920. Shorter has argued that, with the rise of the market economy, material considerations were gradually replaced by romantic love in bringing couples together: the role of the family and community as socialising agents for the young was replaced by that of the market, which also required that people were more mobile. As romantic love demands seclusion, couples distanced themselves from the community, as enforcer of tradition.

> The romantic revolution which began late in the eighteenth century, sweeping across vast
> reaches of class and territory in the nineteenth, to become – in the twentieth – the
> unassailable norm of courtship behaviour, carried two components: a new relationship
> of the couple to each other; and a new relationship, for them, as a unit, to the
> surrounding social order (1976:149).

The rise in romantic love which Shorter associates with the rise of the market economy has in the twentieth century been fused with the growing commitment to the concept of property ownership. The rise in marriage rates (at lower ages), coupled with the rise in home ownership, has been accompanied by the emergence of an ideology promoted especially by building societies and house builders, linking together romantic love, family building and home ownership: one of the most important social categories targeted by advertisements for new housing are 'the newly weds'.

In this context it is worth noting the words of popular 'bungalow songs' of the 1920s and 30s, in which four themes predominate:

1   The lyrics all centre round two people, a couple ('a home just built for two', 'a bungalow for two', 'two love birds' 'love seat for two', 'where two hearts entwine').

2   The association of the bungalow with romantic love ('our little love nest' 'the joy of a girl and boy' 'a bungalow, a piccolo and you').

3   The emphasis on the social and spatial distancing of both the couple and the bungalow ('far from the city' 'in the country far away' 'free from care and strife').

4   The emphasis on domesticity and affection by the use of the diminutive ('our little love nest' 'to own a little bungalow' 'three little things are all I desire – a bungalow, a piccolo and you' 'to build a little bungalow' 'it does not take much money to own a little bungalow').

With this notion of domesticity are other 'homely' images – 'a picture window', 'a fireplace that shines', 'a portrait on the wall'. This powerful combination of love, domesticity, and idyllic rustic seclusion in the bungalow prompts a very fundamental question: has there ever been, at any other conjunction in history, a purpose-built dwelling produced, not for a family of at least parents and children, but simply as 'a home just built for two'? (Appendix B; also Johnston, 1980:180; King, 1981).

This also seems to be the only plausible explanation for the third social category, after the 'retirement bungalow' and 'bungalow for two', for which, in its early days of Britain, the bungalow was designed – the 'bachelor's bungalow' of architect R.A. Briggs in 1891. Though 'bachelor flats' and 'hostels for single women' have been built in different cities and settlements and clearly relate to the social and sexual organisation of work, the creation of a 'bachelor's bungalow' in the country can only be explained by reference to the workings of the market economy. In which societies up to that time were spacious dwellings built simply for the occasional unmarried males? The need is to keep capital in circulation by constantly creating new needs. The long-term effects of this have apparently been to assist in the fragmentation of household units by creating an ideology where those who can afford it are housed in their separate, individual space, whether this is the specially adapted 'granny flat' in Britain or the specially designed apartment building for the 'swinging singles' in the United States (Hancock, 1980:179). The most recent American census drew attention to the fact that more people were living alone in American cities than at any previous time in her history. In England and Wales, with a gradually rising population, 55 per cent of a more rapidly growing number of separate households (some 22 million by 1985) consist of either one or two persons compared to 21.5 per cent in 1911 (*Social Trends*, 1981; Halsey, 1972). A recent study of one hundred old people's homes in Britain concluded that it was not the design of facilities to which residents objected but the fact that they did not have exclusive (property) rights over their use (Peace, 1982). The individualism and privatisation characteristic of modern capitalist societies is clearly very much bound up with the private ownership of dwellings and land, nowhere better expressed than in the bungalow, and more recently, the growth of owned 'studio apartments'.

Such speculations raise more fundamental questions. What is the relation between cultural values and economic process, or between ideology and the conditions that produce it? And in relation to the built environment, is it that the economic system produces the ideology, the ideology produces the environment and the environment helps to reproduce both ideology and the economic system?

Bungalow as name

Much has been made in this study of the name 'bungalow'. It might, for example, be asked why a new name was necessary to describe a type of dwelling introduced into England in 1869 which, though new in many respects, was old in others, and part of a continuing cultural tradition. Why was the first bungalow not simply labelled 'cottage'?

Cottage has its original referents in feudalism, just as bungalow has its referents in capitalism.* It was a term (and building) introduced into England during the third quarter of

---

* Cottage was originally defined according to the economic and social status of its occupants, being the dwelling of a 'cottar', a peasant who held, under the feudal system, a given amount of land in return for

the nineteenth century, which Hobsbawm suggests was 'the first world wide era of urban real estate and a constructional boom for the bourgeoisie' (1975:212). 'As the basic needs of families for food, clothing and shelter are met, at least for a majority of the population, so the demand for these tails off and capitalists must seek to produce other types of goods. . . . In particular, the goods and services which have expanded under, if not been invented by, late capitalism, involve those especially concerned with recreation and leisure' (Johnston, 1980:180,118; also Harvey, 1973:311).

The introduction of both the reality *and* name was a classic case of the creation of needs, of the emphasis on change and fashion associated with the consumer society. It is not surprising that popular poets, playing on words, have described the one who lives there as the 'bungalowner' or 'bungaloner'. In the conditions of late capitalism, the ownership of a bungalow, indeed, any type of dwelling, has more to do with storing capital than providing shelter.

'Suburban sprawl': the cause and consequences of the British exception

The introduction and spread in the popularity of the bungalow seem to confirm Tabb and Sawer's point that 'urban cultural forms and architectural structures manifest a consumerist orientation' (1978:4).

In this context, the experience of Britain, in comparison with the United States and Australia, is different. In Britain, the relative absence of the spreading suburb ('sprawl' in the terms of its critics) characteristic of these other Anglo-Saxon societies is the major feature distinguishing British patterns of urbanisation in the twentieth century. The reason for this is that the distinctively British style of planning has, in the well-chosen phrase of Hall, resulted in 'The Containment of Urban England' (1973).

The particular aim of this planning policy, developing gradually from the ideas of Howard and others in the late nineteenth century, and especially embodied in the Town and Country Planning Act of 1932 and other legislation since, has been to make a clear distinction between 'town' and 'country'. In maintaining this division, it is remarkable – to say the least – how explicit the planning profession has been in defining its role as a dialectic response to both the bungalow and its lesser version, the chalet. Gilg, for example, writing on 'Countryside planning. The first three decades, 1945-75', in the context of second homes, concludes that the effect of planning 'has been to prevent the sprawl of cheap chalets and bungalows that would undoubtedly spread without planning control' (1978:94).

Yet this compartmentalised treatment of 'countryside planning' does not consider other implications. The fundamental distinction between 'town' and 'country' which, with the rare exception (Banham et al., 1969), is the most inherent assumption of British planning, is essentially a cultural distinction sustained by particular economic and class interests as has been discussed in Chapters 3 and 5. It provides a useful example of how the distribution of power embodied in particular relations between classes under-pins or sustains ideologies which, in turn, reinforce the way in which the environment is shaped. To complete the circle, the environment then helps to uphold and 'prove' the ideology. Societies reproduce themselves. That this distinction, economic, social, cultural and environmental, between

---

labour (*OED*). 'Bungalow' also has origins and associations in colonialism, second homes, suburban development and the fragmentation of households.

'town' and 'country', represents a particular distribution of power, and is a particularly 'English' distinction, is apparent especially in comparison to North America and Australia where other initially Anglo-Saxon societies have been established. There, however, the forces of popular democracy and free-market principles have operated without the constraints of either more limited land supplies, as in Britain, or especially, a strong class hierarchy, headed by a landed aristocracy, in which the interests of the most powerful have been articulated by a bourgeois intelligentsia.

That it is such an English 'cultural attitude', embodied within a particular distribution of power, is also confirmed by the way in which 'town and country' ideas, including even the unlikely concept of the 'Green Belt', were transplanted to India, Africa and elsewhere in the Empire, along with other institutions and ideologies of British planning (King, 1980c). It is clear that the initial criteria for choosing the term 'Green Belt' were visual and aesthetic; had they been economic it would presumably have been called the 'Rural' or 'Agricultural Belt'.

Two comments, the first by way of an 'aside', can be made in relation to the outcome of the planning system in Britain. And both grossly simplify the situations described. Firstly, history has demonstrated that many of the self-built or cheaply built bungalows constructed fifty, or in some cases, eighty, years ago have been transformed into substantial dwellings and may also form part of established settlements. And where once such self-built aspirations were universally condemned by an intellectual establishment, today attitudes towards housing, planning and architectural issues are, after a fifty-year interval (1930-80), arguably more liberal and pluralistic (though see also Figure 5.7).

More important is the second point. The effect of reproducing the environment in this 'town and country' image of the upper and middle class, by preventing inexpensive and often self-built housing, and by curtailing the supply of land, helped to exclude a large proportion of the population from home ownership and to create an artificial shortage of land. As working people were deprived of the opportunity of buying or building inexpensive houses at prices, and with standards, which they could afford (rather than, in many cases, with those satisfying the aesthetic criteria of those in power), a housing class was created dependent on the state. This class, relatively small before 1914, was subsequently to reach massive proportions and to become a captive market for municipal housing, and especially, for municipal architects and planners.

Never in the realm of public housing, to modify a famous phrase, was so much owed by so many to so few. Equally committed to 'preserving the countryside' and the cultural values of a ruling establishment, the 'environmental professions' – architects and planners – were, for some two or three decades, given free rein to experiment and build as they chose, whether in the Corbusian idiom of 'high-rise' or in the collectivist pseudo-socialism of multi-family flats. In either case, it was not simply 'urban England' which was contained but also a dependent, renting working class which was encapsulated in the segregated council estate.

The connection, therefore, between controlling 'bungaloid growth' ('suburban sprawl' in others' terms) and the emergence of the large-scale, multi-unit tower block or urban 'cliff dwelling' is direct. In this way, the 'town and country' distinction and the relative absence of 'sprawl' was upheld – at the cost of one-third of all households denied access to the prevailing form of tenure in the society, private property ownership. Nor is this to ignore the existence of opposing views committed to the state ownership of housing and land or, as Kemeny persuasively argues, to a pluralism of tenures.

Where, for a variety of historical, geographical and social reasons, suburban spread was allowed, it was especially in the traditional 'working class' region (in cultural if not necessarily economic or political terms) of the Lancashire coastal plain. Here, as Cowburn (1966) has incisively shown, the bungalow was to become the most favoured form of popular housing. It was, like the car or fridge, a consumer object with which people could identify and, like these, it could be 'embraced' – unlike a unit in the block of flats. Not only was 'the Englishman's house his castle': it was also, by its location on the plot, surrounded by a moat. It rejected the standard architectural assumption that, when a number of dwelling units were to be built, there had to be 'a massive architectural expression'. 'When houses are to be built together, the designer seems unable to resist the urge to "communise" the individual houses.' Yet the interest of the bungalow-owner was, not least with regard to re-sale, to have a universal standard product which none the less demonstrated his and her own personal possession.

The bungalow as second home

A further major issue prompted by investigating the historical development of the bungalow is the phenomenon of the 'second' or 'vacation' home which, depending on how it is conceptualised, can be related to the questions of 'dual residence', social equity, 'seasonal suburbanisation' or consumerism.

To date, much research on second homes has been oriented to applied questions concerning recreational or countryside planning, or, in relation to the housing shortage, to those of social justice. With some exceptions (Clout, 1974; King, 1980a), studies within a larger theoretical and historical context have been rare. There is, however, a need for further research on both a historical and cross-cultural basis which takes account of two- or more-home ownership in Asia, Africa and Latin America.

Following on Berry's (1976a) work, Martinotti (1980) established a framework in which to examine 'responses to urbanism', across a variety of societies and at different times, including Britain in the nineteenth, Italy in the early twentieth and Vietnam in the late twentieth centuries. The aim was to identify the way in which different cultural, economic, technological, political and policy variables, at different times and in different places, responded to or 'controlled' the urbanism generated by industrialisation in the 'developed' societies. In the British case, the individualistic, 'non public' response represented by the 'country' or 'weekend cottage' as second home of the turn of the century was seen as a much more important process than is usually assumed (ibid.:xii; King, 1980c).

According to Lichtenberger, 'the future significance of this process, initiated by the metropolitan leisure society, cannot be over-estimated,' and it will 'undoubtedly constitute the most important process of urbanisation in the years to come.' In some parts of the Tyrol (Austria) over 50 per cent of homes were second homes in the mid 1970s and ownership of property by non-nationals was becoming a major political issue (1976:87).

More weight is lent to Lichtenberger's prediction, not only by the evidence presented here which indicates that the mass purpose-built vacation house has been well-established for at least a century, but also by the growth of second homes, not only in capitalist but also socialist economies. In Czechoslovakia, outside Prague, there are some 100,000 second homes, with every fifth family owning one. Many owners live in state-owned dilapidated flats in the city and prefer to spend their money on a privately owned 'second home' outside. Although Soviet law does not permit families to own more than one unit of housing, second homes flourish in Poland and Bulgaria (French and Hamilton, 1979:444-5 and passim). In many cases, it is evident that socialist tower blocks in the city give rise to weekend cottages outside it (Shaw, 1979).

In France where, like Sweden, some 20 per cent of households own second homes, the annual movement of millions of people towards the south coast each year is in a large part generated by the growing ownership of the 'résidence secondaire'. Those not yet in a position to afford them none the less make the same journey, staying for two months in semi-permanent camping sites. Here, for some, accommodation is provided in 'bungalows' (plates 139, 140).

The question of second homes represented by what are appropriately called 'rental investment bungalows' in Spain, the Canary Islands or the Caribbean has, in recent years, been given accelerated impetus by the rapidly growing industry of time-sharing, or multi-ownership. Following the first developments in the French Alps in 1967, the time-sharing industry has grown immensely, especially from the mid 1970s. In the United States, it was estimated in 1981 that time-share sales, at 1.5 billion dollars, represent some 3 per cent of the total value of completed residential property. In Britain, where the first development was introduced in 1975, sales had amounted to £40 million by 1982. Although this represents only $1^{1}2$ per cent of the total amount spent on holiday tourism by British residents, and about the same percentage of the total value of new private sector house construction in 1980, the introduction of time-sharing could have very considerable impact on the ownership – through the introduction of part-ownership – as well as the construction of second homes and holiday developments on a global scale (O'Neill, 1982). The political implications of these developments raise other questions. Allowing for cycles of boom and recession, it is possible that with increasing real wages, the phenomenon of two-salary households as an increasing proportion of women have paid employment, and extended transport facilities, two-home ownership (either in whole or in part) will increase, if only for a minority. Overall in Britain there were in 1981 some 2 million more houses than households, and by the end of the century, the number of cars is predicted to double. The main limits to two-home ownership are likely to be the price and availability of fuel and policies of the state.

In the early 1980s, in a modest British east-coast resort, estate agents were advertising equally modest properties as suitable 'for first time second home buyers'; in Germany, *Die Welt* (31 July 1982) was advertising bungalows in Spain, with private swimming pools, 'in bewachten, exklusiven Clubgelände' (in guarded, exclusive Clubland). The local, national and international implications of two-house ownership need considerable further research.

The bungalow as 'tropical house'

Another important research area is the history of 'tropical architecture and planning'. The introduction into tropical societies, as part of the process of colonial exploitation, of the architectural and urban forms of industrial, capitalist Europe, raises issues of fundamental empirical and theoretical importance. The built environment of colonialism, of which the bungalow is perhaps the most representative element, was first and foremost an economic and political fact; it was also part of a larger process by which goods and labour were incorporated into the metropolitan economy. It was equally a social and cultural phenomenon: the colonial settlers formed a particular social organisation and their dwellings, lay-outs and settlements, including the incorporation of indigenous peoples, were a product of this organisation.

Yet whilst all modern colonisers were from Europe, and as such shared many cultural outlooks and beliefs, they were also markedly different, bringing to their settlements, and especially the houses in which they lived, their own cultural traditions, whether from Spain, Portugal, France, Britain, the Netherlands, Scandinavia or Germany. Moreover, such traditions changed and developed over time: theories and experience of construction, expectations and knowledge about health, notions about the organisation of labour as well as religious and political ideas concerning the people over whom they ruled. Equally important were the vast range of cultures colonised and the particular junctures in history when the colonisation occurred.

The anodyne phrase 'tropical architecture' masks a cluster of controversial facts. Its emergence as a sphere of (European) knowledge marks the expansion of Europe into areas where Europeans had not previously lived. It elides or skims over the fact that 'tropical architecture' was for people of alien cultures exercising colonial power. The application of its principles, whether concerning design, construction, materials, sanitation, lay-out or technology, first to colonial and then to 'native' populations was inseparable from the total economic, social and political restructuring of the culture being controlled.

A detailed historical account of the emergence of consensual ideas about 'tropical architecture and planning' among the colonial powers and the way in which the domestic culture and environment as well as the larger physical and spatial environment of local peoples was transformed would provide one of the most important insights into the penetration of this world by the capitalist world economy. It would also greatly further understanding not only of how societies produce their environments but how environments help to produce societies themselves.

The bungalow as global phenomenon

What this study has assumed, though not systematically explored, is the emergence of a capitalist world economy *and* culture which has been responsible, at different times and in different places, for the development of the bungalow in its various guises. It has been concerned with the conditions which have produced the bungalow as a cultural phenomenon – as a term, as a form of dwelling and as a particular kind of urban settlement, economy and way of life.

Many American scholars, most recently, Downing and Fleming (1981:269), have suggested that, in relation to the USA, 'bungalows represent one of the first common house types to break regional boundaries and gain national popularity'. Though the term bungalow is no longer in everyday use there, the single-storey ranch house developed from it (as also in Canada, though there the term persists) is now one of the most characteristic forms of suburban dwelling. What this study has suggested is that the bungalow, with variations in form, was one of the, if not *the*, first common house-types (particularly in terms of function as suburban and temporary, vacation house dwelling) to break national boundaries and become part of an international, though capitalist urban culture. As with the high-rise, city-centre office block, what its global diffusion represents is the transfer of institutions, images, of ways and models of living, of a particular kind of material and non-material culture which is produced by the modern, industrial free market economy. As Harvey pointed out a decade ago, if the capitalist economy is to be maintained, it is *necessary* for urbanism to generate expanding consumption. And much of the expansion in the Gross National Product in capitalist societies is bound up in the whole process of suburbanisation (1973:271) and the automobile industry with which it is associated. Introduced as a mass phenomenon, the bungalow was based on a bourgeois image of the world – a separate, privatised environment. As part of the reaction to the city, the move to single-family, mainly single-storey suburban homes, or temporarily, to vacation bungalows in resorts, is what the development of the bungalow means in the rich, industrial capitalist countries of 'the North'.

Simultaneously, in the so-called developing world of 'the South', in Asia, Africa and Latin America, the introduction of the 'modern' bungalow has resulted from the penetration of those countries by free market institutions and 'Western' or 'bourgeois' tastes, styles and standards of living (Lloyd, 1979:prologue). The modern housing form of which the 'European bungalow' was an early prototype, and the suburbs to which it gives rise, provide the physical and spatial setting for the consumer goods of an expanding economy: it contrasts with the traditional environment it gradually replaces (e.g. Schwerdtfeger, 1982:312)

A pre-requisite for the understanding of these domestic life-styles is the need to trace the historical emergence, in the regions of the capitalist world economy, of a 'global urban culture' which has led to the situation described by Harvey (pp. 2-3) or Murphy (1970:25): 'With the creation of a global commercial network, the spread of industrialisation and the technological revolution in transport and transferability, cities everywhere are becoming more like one another.' The origins of this culture are in the emergence of a global system of production and the beginnings of an international division of labour in the nineteenth century. At the end of that century, for example, British capital and trade were the major sources of foreign investment in Latin America: the predominantly commercial orientation of Latin American cities at that time can be understood primarily by reference to the high degree of manufacturing characteristic of Britain's industrial cities. Metropolitan growth in Britain was based on external economic relationships (Browning and Roberts, 1980). The growth of ports like Glasgow and Liverpool was inextricably and interdependently linked to the rise of the capitalist world economy just as their decline results from the restructuring of capital within that system. Likewise, the development of Lancashire 'cotton towns' can obviously only be fully understood in relation to the overseas markets which absorbed four-fifths of the cotton goods exported, mainly in the 'underdeveloped world' (Hobsbawm, 1969:146).

In contemporary discussions of inter-dependent development, Sunkel and Fuenzalida (1979) have drawn attention to the impact of transnational capitalism on national development, a phenomenon which is not only a way of organising labour and capital but which is also 'a set of ideas about the world and a global community of people who subscribe to them'. This transnational community they see as being made up of people who, though belonging to different nations, nevertheless have similar values, beliefs and ideas 'as well as similar patterns of behaviour as regards . . . housing, dress, consumption patterns and cultural orientations in general'. It is also represented in cities by a distinctive spatial organisation with local elite communities concentrating in suburban residential areas and reproducing (in so-called developing countries) the urban structure, housing style and architectural lay-out of the core countries. Similarly, Kumar (1980) has discussed how transnational enterprises have transformed societies and cultures, whether through book publishing, educational systems or consumption patterns in general; their role has been to create 'culturally relevant markets for Western goods'. Third world elites have learnt 'to define development in terms of capitalist criteria rather than with reference to those standards which are rooted in their own cultural system' (Kumar, 1980:166, 248).

The historical restructuring of the physical environment, including the transformation of architecture, dwelling forms, and urban space, is crucial to the process which Kumar describes and ranges from changing patterns of land-ownership to the use of new, often imported, materials. The transplantation of urban planning ideas between the core countries of industrial capitalism (Sutcliffe, 1981) must be seen not only in relation to the international and colonial system on which the prosperity of those cities was considerably based (not least in the early twentieth century when much formal planning was introduced) but also, in relation to the transfer of that ideology for the laying out of colonial, and ultimately 'Third World' cities as they were incorporated into the world economy (King, 1980c). The physical, spatial and technological transformation of the domestic as well as the larger urban environment is, after the transfer of land ownership rights, the most fundamental pre-requisite for creating the city as a place for consumption. The export of capital in the nineteenth and early twentieth centuries was, in many cases, accompanied by the export of 'intellectual technology' of British expertise, whether in regard to railway systems, urban planning or municipal administration. The capital, ideas and people which helped to set up the road and railway systems, the municipal water and electricity supplies created the infrastructure for further production and consumption.*

Evidence suggests that the main developments in the creation of this 'urban culture' were well under way in the three decades preceding 1914: all round the world, Western transport and other technology was being introduced, institutions established and increasing numbers of people were moving from place to place. Ideas about cities, sanitation, housing, planning and health were being transplanted, part of the rapid extension of a growing international professionalism represented by 'international' exhibitions and over 2,000 'international' congresses which took place in the ten or so years before the First World War (Sutcliffe, 1981:166). Though it should be made clear in this context that 'international' refers to the system of states as it existed at the turn of the century, including imperial powers with their colonial possessions.

A world system of cities was being created which was being used for transferring labour, capital, technology and ideas around the world. Between 1870 and 1900, tourism was organised on a world scale: Thomas Cook and Sons was 'an institution of the British Empire' by the 1880s, extending the privileges of the upper class to the bourgeoisie and petit bourgeoisie of the industrialised nations (Turner and Ash, 1975). It was at this time that the standards of the 'global urban culture' were being established. It was a culture expressed not only in economic, social, political and linguistic terms but also in physical, spatial and architectural ones.

In discussing the new international division of labour which has emerged in the modern world, Cohen (1981) outlines the rise of the 'global cities'. Whilst centres of production have emerged in the developing nations, centres for the formulation of corporate strategy and international finance have not. Instead, new 'global cities' have emerged such as New York, London, Frankfurt and Zurich, the centres of international finance and the headquarters of multi-national corporations operating on a world-wide scale. It is these whose presence is manifest in the so-called 'international style' of architecture, whether in the Western headquarters or in the subsidiary offices in the capitals of developing countries.

In a different sense, the modern bungalow is also part of this 'international style' and is equally bound up with colonialism and the international division of labour. Yet where the district commissioner's or planter's bungalow overseas was symbolic of the process by which a surplus was extracted from the colonial economy, at home, as 'second home' or as spacious

---

* This and the previous page are largely drawn from King (1983a).

dwelling in the country or suburbs, it was part of the process by which the capital surplus in the domestic economy was consumed.

It is now generally accepted that the processes of 'development' and 'under-development' are one; they are both part of one world history. The development of the industrial nations at the core was also part and parcel of the 'under-development' of the agrarian or now industrialising nations at the periphery. What is less clear are the particular implications of this process for the growth of towns, cities and suburbs at the core.

The need to view the cities of a country as a unified system where growth or decline in one region has repercussions in a number of towns is now taken for granted. What is even more necessary is to see these processes as part of a global urban system where developments in one sector of the world economy are ultimately, if not always so obviously, connected to urban developments in another.

The bungalow, and the phenomena it represents – the consumption of surplus wealth in the second home, the expansion of leisure resorts and outer suburbanisation – 'took off' in Britain between 1870 and 1914, at the 'height of empire'. Whether as holiday or suburban home, the bungalow phenomenon occurred at a time of immense urbanisation and suburbanisation associated with the massive accumulation of capital in Britain as a result of industrialisation and colonialism. In the last years of the nineteenth century, the rise in the overall standard of living with its increased devotion to leisure was as much the outcome of a global imperial economy and investments overseas (Mathias, 1978; chapter 11) as were Briggs's bungalows and country houses in Surrey. In these years, the Lancashire seaside holiday was to become 'a mass experience', the high levels of working-class participation being unique to what a recent study innocently calls 'the cotton district' (Walton, 1983:30-3). The phenomenon was greatly to expand the northern seaside resorts. Though the same study gives five conditions for the rapid growth of this holiday demand, it omits the most fundamental: the supply of cotton and the fact that over half of cotton exports at this time went to a dependent India whose own spinning capacity had been 'completely wiped out' (Bayly, 1983:432; Hobsbawm, 1969:147) by colonialism. In the 1930s, the shift from declining 'cotton town' terraces to southern 'semis' or, after 1950, to local bungalow suburbs and retirement bungalows at the seaside (see pages 249, 257) was equally associated with a global restructuring of production. That these same 'cotton town' terraces are now occupied by labour from Bangladesh, India or Pakistan is also not coincidental. If part of inner-city decay results from expansion at the outer suburbs, another part results from the forces promoting third-world urbanisation on the periphery and their effect on cities at the core (see also Fielding, 1982:31).

In the late nineteenth century, whilst the empire was taking most of Britain's exports, India was supplying much of her tea, rice and wheat. Between 1871 and 1900, as larger areas of northern India were turned over to grain, wheat exports to Britain increased thirteenfold (Bayly, 1983:432), changes which Barrat Brown connects to an increasing frequency of famine (1978:105-9). 'As our empire has grown larger', wrote J.A. Hobson in *Imperialism* (1902), 'a larger and larger number of (officials) have returned to this country . . . many of them wealthy . . . devoted to luxury and material display . . . Could the incomes expended in the Home Counties and other large districts of Southern Britain be traced to their sources, it would be found that they were in large measure wrung from the enforced toil of vast multitudes of black, brown or yellow natives'. Though the connections may not always be direct, these data are equally necessary to explain the bungalow. As (another) Walton has put it (1976:309), 'much of what is often crucial in explaining local phenomena is extra-local in origin'.

During the course of the last century, as *per capita* incomes in the industrial nations have gone up, the gap between these and those of the developing nations of Asia has increased (Kuznets, 1966:393); where the difference in *per capita* income between rich and poor countries was in the ratio of 2:1 in 1800, it is about 20:1 today (Hay, 1977:85). Bangladesh, one of the poorest countries in the world, with a gross national product per head less than 1 per cent that of the United States, one of the richest, and about 1½ per cent that of the United Kingdom (World Bank, 1981:134), was the starting point for this study. What the history of the bungalow has shown is that these facts are not unrelated. The bungalow is both a product, and symbol, of a complex yet inter-related world.

Appendix A

An architectural note on the term 'verandah'

Veranda, verandah: 'an open portico or light roofed gallery
extending along the front (and occasionally, other sides) of a
dwelling or other building, frequently having a front of lattice work,
and erected chiefly as a protection or shelter from the sun or rain'

(*Oxford English Dictionary*, 1980).

The concept of the verandah, whether understood as a semi-enclosed space created (on a single-storey house) by the extension of the roof down and outwards, and supported by pillars, or by an 'additional' structure incorporated on to the side of the building, is an essential feature of the 'colonial' bungalow for much of its history. In some respects, it could be seen as a defining one which distinguishes the bungalow from other single-storey dwellings.

Both geographers as well as architectural historians have seen it as an important subject, demanding 'detailed investigation in the East, as well as in England, the West Indies and the United States'.[1] Its importance is not simply a matter of 'style'; it is a feature which has frequently characterised the dwellings of people who have moved from their normal habitat in temperate zones to hotter climates where the houses which they constructed have been adapted to meet cultural expectations established in their countries of origin. Though features similar to the verandah, and with comparable functions, naturally exist in the vernacular architecture of many 'hot climate' countries, the verandah is not a universal 'tropical' feature. For example, many dwelling forms of traditional African cultures do not have this feature, which underlines the view that different peoples have different perceptions about climate, the 'need for shade' outdoors, and the different functions which dwellings perform.

The reasons for the existence of the verandah, therefore, are complex, and require far more discussion than space here permits. For example, consideration would need to be given to structural or geographical factors, such as the availability of materials permitting such a feature; to cultural considerations, regarding the perception and tolerance of climatic conditions; to social factors, regarding the social organisation of communities and whether shelter was provided in terms of clustered or 'collective' units which simultaneously provided climatic protection. Other economic, political or behavioural factors govern what space is available for use in a dwelling, or what time is available to utilise this space. The questions are endless. Whatever the earlier history of the verandah, however, it often became, either in itself or as an integral part of the bungalow, particularly symbolic of 'tropical' and especially colonial lifestyles.[2] In comparison to the dwellings of native peoples, whether in India, Africa or Australia, it was a sign of European 'adjustment' to the climate, a feature made necessary by the social as well as spatial separation of one dwelling from another and, as a space to spend one's spare time, it was a symbol of economic and political status. Whilst geographers and others may trace evidence of the feature itself, the following notes provide some insight into the introduction of the term.

It is generally accepted that the term 'verandah', as used in England and France, and later in the British colonial world, came into the English language from India, the origins being either Persian or, more likely, Spanish or Portuguese.[3] For example, the first recorded use is in 1498 in Portuguese and is in an account of the voyage of Vasco da Gama to India. Numerous other instances of its use in Portuguese and Spanish, without definition, occur in the seventeenth century. The verandah was native to the folk and medieval vernacular houses of northern Portugal and Spain,[4] was introduced to Brazil and possibly reached the West Indies,[5] although so far there is no record of the term being in use there in the eighteenth century.

The first recorded use of the term in English is in 1711 when, in an Indian context, reference is made to a building having 'a paved court, and two large verandas or piazzas'.[6] It is worth noting that, until about 1800, the term 'piazza' is frequently used in English not only to explain the meaning of 'verandah' but also, whether in the West Indies or in colonial and post-colonial North America, to refer to what subsequently was often called 'verandah'. 'Piazza', like the other terms used to explain the 'new' term 'verandah' such as 'portico', 'colonnade', or 'arcade', had been imported into English from the Mediterranean (Italian). Literally meaning a square or market place in Italian, 'piazza' had in English been erroneously applied to a colonnade or covered gallery or walk surrounding a 'piazza proper', and hence to a single colonnade in front of a building. This practice 'appears to have begun with the vulgar misapplication of the name to the arcades built after the designs of Inigo Jones on the north and east side of Covent Garden instead of the open market place' and was being used in this way in England in the mid seventeenth century.[7]

From the mid eighteenth century, an increasing number of references to 'verandah' are recorded in English, all of them from an Indian context, though with a variety of spellings (e.g. feerandah, virander): 'small ranges of pillars that support a pent-house or shed, forming what is called in the Portuguese lingua franca, veranda',[8] or in 1787, when the orientalist Sir William Jones, living in rural Krishnagar, outside Calcutta, referred to his 'pastoral mansion' as 'a thatched cottage with an upper storey and a covered verome or veranda, as they call it here, all round, well boarded and ten or twelve feet broad'.[9] In the earliest definition of the bungalow (1793), Hodges refers to 'the whole [being] covered with one general thatch, which comes low to each side, the spaces between are *viranders* or open porticoes.'[10]

The first recorded use of the term in English, in England, is in 1800 when architect John Plaw published a cottage design 'with a viranda, in the manner of an Indian bungalow',[11] though the feature itself had appeared at least some years earlier.[12] Evidence suggests that it is from perhaps the second or third decades of the nineteenth century that the type of verandah characteristic of the Anglo-Indian bungalow and hence the form (if not with the name) of the bungalow itself was introduced into Britain. In North America, however, and no doubt elsewhere, the feature had existed at least from the late seventeenth century, where it was generally termed a 'piazza'.[13] French colonial architecture in Mississippi in the late eighteenth century also produced a one-storey house on piers, the whole surrounded by a 'galerie' which, though not a continuation of the roof, was none the less functionally similar to the verandah.[14] Similar forms were known in the West Indies.[15] The term verandah, however, does not seem to have been applied to any of these features.

That the next known reference outside India to a 'varando' occurs in Sydney, in 1805,[16] suggests a positive Indian or Anglo-Indian link to Australia, via the British. Its newness in

England is confirmed by Southey who, in 1807, wrote, 'Here is a fashion lately introduced from better climates, of making verandas, verandas in a country where physicians recommend double doors, and double windows as a precaution against intolerable cold.'[17] In the United States, the word had arrived at least by 1819 when an advertisement in the South Carolina newspaper, the *Courier*, referred to 'A Marine Villa . . . on Sullivan's Island . . . with two verandas'.[18] From about this time, the term seems to have been used as an alternative for 'piazza'.[19]

In England, as an 'added' rather than integral form, the verandah became increasingly common as a fashionable architectural feature from this period. Apparently referring to its recent introduction, architect J.B. Papworth wrote in 1818, 'no decoration has so successfully varied the dull sameness of modern structures in the metropolis as the verandah.'[20] In this form, and often using wrought iron, it had become primarily a decorative, rather than functional, feature, as is confirmed by a more detailed description of 1843: it was

> a sort of light external gallery with a sloping roof of awning-like character, supported on slender pillars and frequently partly enclosed in front with lattice work. The verandah is both of Eastern name and Eastern origin, and appears to have been first introduced into this country towards the end of the eighteenth century. As here applied, however, it is a mere excrescence in design, assimilating with no one style practised by us and so far tolerable only for small villas and cottage residences where no style is attempted and where it affords a cheap substitute for a colonnade providing shelter against rain and sun, and a dry walk or seat *al fresco*, attached to sitting rooms on the ground floor.[21]

Though no systematic research has been undertaken on this, the 'genuine' verandah, as in the Indian bungalow, formed from the projecting roof, seems to have been adopted into country house lodges and early cricket pavilions in Britain from the second or third decades of the century.

Come down to Bungalow Town (c.1910-12)

There's a cute little spot on the map
Not far from London Town . . .
Won't you come down to Bungalow Town
Bungalow Town with me?
There are lots of things there
Besides the fresh air
To keep you company.

There's fun and there's laughter
And lots of things after
So, if you feel a bit run down . . .
The worse you are the more the ladies love you
So come down to Bungalow Town!

(Recalled from memory of 'Zonophone' record,
courtesy, Fred Challenger. See plates 56-58)

Appendix B

The bungalow in song

The following help to convey the nature of imagery associated with the bungalow. Some reference is made to the lyrics of popular songs in Chapter Eight.

A Bungalow of Dreams (1928?)
Bix Beiderbecke

Our little love nest
Beside a stream
Where red, red roses grow
Our bungalow
Of dreams

Far from the city
Somehow it seems
We're sitting pretty in
Our bungalow
Of dreams

Just like two love birds
We'll bill and coo
I'll whisper love words
For only you

A bit of heaven
Beside a stream
I know you'll love it so
Our bungalow
Of dreams

In the Land of the Bungalow (1929)
George F. Devereux

I just got off the sunset train
I'm from the Angel Town
The Golden West Los Angeles
Where the sun shines all year round
I left a girlie back there
She's the sweetest girl I know
She said 'Goodbye'
I'll wait for you
In the Land of the Bungalow

Chorus
In the Land of the Bungalow
Away from the ice and snow
Away from the cold
To the Land of Gold
Away where the poppies grow

I just can't keep my tho'ts away
From California's shore
The Land of Flow'rs & Winter Show'rs
How I miss you more and more
As soon as I can get away
I know that I will go
Back to the girl
I love the best
In the Land of the Bungalow

Away to the setting sun
To the home of the orange blossom
To the land of fruit & honey
Where it does not take much money
To own a little Bungalow

(from R. Winter, *The California Bungalow*, Los Angeles, 1980)

A Bungalow, a Piccolo and You (1933)
Lewis, Sherman & Campbell; Henry Hall
& BBC Dance Orchestra

Underneath your window
Every night I stand
Pleading for your wonderful caress
Listen at your window
And you'll understand
What it takes to bring me happiness

Chorus
Three little things are all I desire, dear
A bungalow, a piccolo and you

Three little things set my heart on fire, dear
A bungalow, a piccolo and you

Life will be complete
When my songs I tweet
On a love seat
Built for two

Chorus

A Bungalow for Two
Dorothy Evans; Oz Hill, with orchestra
(1950s?-1960s?)

A home just built for two
A picture window too
A door that opens with thanksgiving
A fireplace that shines
Where two hearts entwine
In a bungalow
For two

A terrace on the hill
A nesting whippoorwill
The music of our love resounding
Echoing the joy
Of a girl and boy
In a bungalow
For two

There'll be silvery laughter
Sometimes purple tears
But we'll have something to remember
In our golden years

A portrait on a wall
And friends will come to call
To share with us
Our peaceful living
Later we will see
Maybe there'll be three
In a bungalow
For two

Bungalow in Quogue 1977(?)
(Jerome Kern; P.G. Wodehouse, from
musical *Very Good, Eddie*, Lynn
Crigler DRG)

O let us fly without delay
Into the country far away
Where free from all this care & strife
We'll go and live the simple life

Out here the voice of nature calls
I'll go and get some overalls
Get the last year's almanac
To read at night when things go slack

Chorus

Let's build a little bungalow in Quogue
In Jappa? or in Taxilo (?) that's all (?)

Where we can sniff the scented breeze
And pluck tomatoes from the trees
Where there is room to exercise the dog

How pleasant it will be to life, the jog (?)
To fill the bowl and feed the bran the hog
Each morn' we'll waken from our doze
When Reginald the rooster crows
Down in our little bungalow in Quogue

Let's build a little bungalow in Quogue
In Jappa?, in Taxilo (?) that's all (?)
If life should tend to be a bore
We'll call on Farmer Brown next door
And get an earful of his dialogue

When Nature comes and brings us snow
    and fog
We'll fortify our systems with hot grog
And listen when the lights are still
To Wilberforce the Whippoorwill
Down in our little bungalow in Quogue

Bungalow Love 1974
(Rik Kenton, vocal with inst. accomp.
Island)

Bungalow love
Such slow love
Lovely girl
. . . Sugar
Love to me now
Come . . .
Close your eyes, girl
So you can't see

Chorus
Let me give you love
Let me give a little love
Let me give a little love
To your heart (Babe) (4)

She makes the boys laugh
She makes the girls cry
She makes the birds sing in the wind.

Tangerine night (?)
Should be nice
Thank . . .
Jumble street . . .
. . . girl's heart

Chorus (4)

Gimme, gimme, gimme, gimme,
    gimme, gimme, etc etc
Love from your heart, babe
    gimme, gimme, etc etc
C'mon, baby, C'mon, baby
    etc etc
Let me lay, let me lay,
Let me lay you down.

Notes

Chapter 2 Britain 1750-1890

1 Much information on early Kent resorts is by courtesy of John Whyman; my thanks for other items are also due to R.S. Holmes and John K. Walton, whose valuable *English Seaside Resort*, appearing at proof stage of this book, enabled only minor adjustments in Chapter 8.

2 Evidence that these were the first bungalows to be built and named as such in England comes from three independent sources: 'to Mr John Taylor' (the architect) 'must be awarded the credit of the introduction of these modified Indian country houses into England' (H. Mayhew, *Birchington and its Bungalows*, Canterbury, 1881:18); 'by a bungalow, Mr (R.A.) Briggs does not mean a house for a special locality, like those near Margate to which the title was first applied in England' (*The Architect*, 1891:215); 'The first English bungalow was built at Westgate on Sea by Mr John Taylor, the architect, and this, duplicated, forms the nucleus of the present town' (*Building News*, 7 July 1905:3); and also 'Taylor was the first architect who built and popularised bungalows in England and these were distinguished from ordinary houses by being generally of one storey only and covered with a roof of one span from back to front' (ibid, 29 June 1906:904).

At Westgate, the first was built between August and October 1869 and a second in 1870 on a plot facing the Esplanade, east of Sussex Square. Both are demolished, although one of the other four houses constructed by Taylor ('Sea Tower') remains. Also in 1870, two bungalows, on a square plan, were built at Westcliff, Birchington; one of these, east of 'Coleman's stairs', was still occupied in 1980 and therefore had the distinction of being the oldest surviving named bungalow built in Britain and probably in the Western hemisphere. About 1872-3, three more were built close by on a rectangular plan; one of these ('Fair Outlook') was still occupied in the early 1980s. A two-storey 'bungalow' (now 'Skyross') followed in 1873. The first wooden pre-fabricated bungalow built in England and named as such was put up about 1877 in Beach (later Rossetti) Avenue; it was auctioned in 1952 and subsequently demolished. The Bungalow Hotel, still flourishing, was built about the same time, with the same system. These eight bungalows were designed by Taylor. In 1881-2, four 'Tower Bungalows' (still remaining) were designed and built by J.P. Seddon and a further one, by the builder, W.E. Martin. Information comes from Mayhew (1881) Ordnance Survey maps, 1872-1898, various guides and directories and especially from the *Building News*, between 1870 and 1874, 1895 and a series of 27 articles in 1905-6 giving comprehensive details and drawings. These articles were written by someone intimately connected with the construction, possibly the builder, W.E. Martin, or, less likely, Seddon. Taylor, having taken out various patents for improvements to 'portable buildings', died between 1879 and 1895.

I am grateful to various residents and others for information, especially Mr A.G. Stevenson, Wing Commander Presland, Messrs Benefield and Cornford, Estate Agents, the late F.J. Cornford JP, Mr J.C. Shaffer, Mr H. Hambidge, Dr W.E. Houghton-Evans and Mr M. Darby.

Chapter 3 Britain 1890-1914

1 For information on 'Bellagio' I am grateful to various local residents including Messrs R.H. and P.D. Wood, R.W. Kidner, Mrs I.P. Margary, and Mrs D. Leman.

Other information is from the County Records Office, East Sussex County Council, C.G. Harper, *Motoring in the South of England*, RAC Guide, London, n.d. but about 1914: 140, and J.D. Kornwolf, *M.H. Baillie Scott and the Arts and Crafts Movement*, Johns Hopkins Press, Baltimore, 1972.

Chapter 5 Britain 1918-1980 – Bungaloid growth

1 For this section see *Parliamentary Debates*. Official Reports (Hansard) 8 December, 1919: 24 April, 1923; 21 and 25 July, 1923; see also Burnett, 1978, chapter 8; Richardson and Aldcroft, 1968.

2 Peggy Pollard c. 1928. I am grateful to the late Clough Williams-Ellis for this poem.

3 See, for example, CPRE Reports, *The Thames Valley from Cricklade to Staines*, 1929; W. Harding Thompson, *Cornwall*, for CPRE, 1930; *The Threat to the Peak*, 1932; *Ryedale*, 1934; *The Penn Country of Buckinghamshire*, 1933; *Wirral Countryside*, 1933; see also Design and Industries Association, *The Face of the Land*, 1930.

4 For this section see *Hansard*, 2 February, 1932; 3, 7, 25 June 1932; 25 June, 1935; also *Town and Country Planning Act*, 1932; *Restriction of Ribbon Development Act*, 1935. See also Cherry, 1972:150-1; 1974, 103-8.

Chapter 7 Australia 1788-1980

1 Ray Sumner kindly sent the material on which the Queensland section is based, and Rob Freestone, his paper on the introduction of garden-city ideas into Australia.

2 Don Johnson suggests that there were perhaps ten to fifteen bungalow books produced in Australia in the 1920s apart from many imported from the United States and Britain.

Appendix A

1 H.R. Hitchcock, 'American influences abroad', in E. Kaufmann, ed., *The Rise of American Architecture*, Pall Mall Press, London, 1970, pp. 3-50, p. 9, note 9; J.D. Edwards, 'The evolution of vernacular architecture in the Western Caribbean', in K. Wilkerson, ed., *Cultural Traditions and Caribbean Identity: The Question of Patrimony*, University of Florida, Gainsville, 1980, pp. 291-346; R.L. Lewcock, *Early Nineteenth*

Century Architecture in South Africa. A Study of the Interaction of Two Cultures, 1795-1837, Balkema, Cape Town, 1963. 'Verandah' was used in South Africa, c. 1805.

2 For example, the title of J. Pope Hennesey, *Verandah. Some Episodes in the Crown Colonies, 1867-89*, Allen & Unwin, London, 1964, and numerous similar essays, 'From my Veranda', etc.

3 Yule and Burnell, 1903, under 'veranda'.

4 Edwards, 1980, quoting Lewcock, p. 125.

5 Edwards, 1980.

6 Yule and Burnell, 1903.

7 *Oxford English Dictionary*, Clarendon Press, Oxford, 1980, 'piazza'.

8 Yule and Burnell, 1903.

9 S.N. Muckherjee, *Sir William Jones. A study in eighteenth century British attitudes to India*. Cambridge University Press, 1968, p. 113.

10 Yule and Burnell, 1903.

11 J. Plaw, *Sketches for Country Houses, Villas and Rural Dwellings*, Taylor, London, 1800.

12 C. Middleton, *Picturesque and architectural views for cottages, farmhouses, and country villas*. Published by E. Jeffrey, London, 1793.

13 H. Morrison, *Early American Architecture*. Oxford University Press, New York, 1952, pp. 132, 495.

14 Ibid., p. 258. See also M. Macrae, *The Ancestral Roof. Domestic Architecture of Upper Canada*, Clarke Irwin, Toronto, 1967 for its widespread use in Canada from c. 1830.

15 Edwards, 1980.

16 J.M. Freeland, *Architecture in Australia. A History*. Cheshire, Melbourne, Canberra & Sydney, 1968, p. 26.

17 In C.A.M. Fennel, *The Stanford Dictionary of Anglicized Words and Phrases*. Cambridge University Press, 1892. Under 'verandah'.

18 B. St J. Ravenel, *Architects of Charleston*, Carolina Art Association Charleston, SC, 1945, p. 107. The architect of the house, arriving in the American South in 1817, came from Bath, Somerset and probably brought the term from England. I am indebted to Clay Lancaster for this information.

19 Morrison, p. 495; also Clay Lancaster, personal communication.

20 J.B. Papworth, *Penny Cyclopaedia*, etc. J. Taylor, London, 1818. Preface.

21 C. Knight, ed., *Rural Residences*, Knight, London, 1906b, vol. 26, p. 251.

Select bibliography

Whilst the book attempts a (lightly) theorised history, it would be impossible to list all the theoretical works drawn on. Hence, only those items referred to in the text, together with some other key titles, are included below. As for empirical material, there are hundreds of books and articles referring to the bungalow; though most books and many articles have been consulted, it would be impossible to list them all. Much of the primary, empirical material has come from titles listed at A, B and C. The main bibliography includes both general reference works as well as primary sources.

A Architectural, building and planning journals and periodicals
(except where otherwise stated, these refer to titles published in the United Kingdom)

American Architect and Building News (USA)
The Architect
Architectural Review
British Architect
The Builder
The Builders Journal
Building (Australia)
Building News
Building World
Country Life in America (USA)
The Craftsman (USA)
Garden Cities and Town Planning
The Illustrated Carpenter and Builder
Indoors and Out (USA)
Journal of the Royal Institute of British Architects

B Other periodicals, journals

BSA Bulletin (Building Societies Association) London
The Bungalow
Ladies Home Journal (USA)
The Studio
The World's Work and Leisure

C Catalogues of manufacturers of portable buildings (these are generally undated. An approximate date has been added where this is not given).

Boulton & Paul *Bungalow Cottages for Small Holdings*, Norwich, c. 1907 (dates in text
    refer to dated drawings).
Boulton & Paul *Homesteads for Small Holdings*, Norwich. n.d.
Boulton & Paul *Catalogue of Horticultural Buildings*, 1889.
Braby, Frederick *Catalogues*, various, 1889-1914.
Cooper, W. *Illustrated Catalogue of Goods*, Old Kent Road, London, c. 1900, 1910.
Morton, Francis Catalogue, etc., 1873 (Liverpool City Library)
Rowell, David *Catalogue*, etc., c. 1890 (RIBA Library)
Smith, Harrison *Bungalows, Residences, Cottages*, c. 1906? Birmingham.

Abercrombie, P. (1926), *The Preservation of Rural England*, University of Liverpool Press and
    Hodder & Stoughton, London.
Abercrombie, P. (1933), *Town and Country Planning*, Oxford University Press, London.
Abrams, P. and Wrigley, E. (1978), *Towns in Societies*, Cambridge University Press.
Abu-Lughod, J.L. (1980), *Rabat. Urban Apartheid in Morocco*, Princeton University Press,
    New Jersey.
Abu-Lughod, J. and Hay, R. (eds.) (1977), *Third World Urbanisation*, Maaroufa Press,
    Chicago.
Acquah, I. (1958), *Accra Survey*, University of London, London.
Adams, H.L. (1910-15), 'Railway carriages as houses', *The Harmsworth Magazine*, Brighton
    Public Library.
Adshead, S.D. (1923), *Town Planning and Town Development*, Methuen, London.
Agnew, J. (1981), 'Home ownership and identity in capitalist societies', in Duncan, J.S. (ed.)
    (1981), pp. 60-97.
Aiken, M. and Castells, M. (1977), 'New trends in urban studies', *Comparative Urban
    Research*, 4, 2 and 3, pp. 7-10.
Aitken, E.H. (1889), *Behind the Bungalow*, Thacker, London (also, 1897, 1904, 1907).
Alavi, H. (1980), 'India. Transition from feudalism to colonial capitalism', *Journal of
    Contemporary Asia*, vol. 10.
Alldridge, T.A. (1910), *A Transformed Colony, Sierra Leone*, Seeley & Sons, London.
Allen, G. (1919), *The Cheap Cottage and Small House*, Batsford, London.
Allison, L. (1975), *Environmental Planning. A Political and Philosophical Analysis*, Allen &
    Unwin, London.
Amin, S. (1977), 'Urbanisation and dependence in Black Africa. Origins and contemporary
    forms', in Abu-Lughod & Hay (eds) (1977), pp. 140-54.
Amory, C. (1952), *The Last Resorts*, Harper, New York.
An Old Bohemian (1881), 'A health resort on the Kentish coast, in and out of season',
    Tinsley's Magazine, 28 March, pp. 259-68.
Angeli, H.R. (1949), *Dante Gabriel Rossetti. His Friends and Enemies*, Hamish Hamilton,
    London.
Anon. (1887), 'Bungalow at Paterson, New Jersey', *Building* (USA), vol. 6, no. 11 (plate).
Anon. (1904), 'The comfortable bungalow in California', *Ladies Home Journal*, January.
Anon. (1905), 'Some California bungalows', *Architectural Record*, vol. 18, September, pp.
    217-23.
Anon. (1906a), 'The bungalow at its best', *Architectural Record*, vol. 19, May, pp. 394-5.
Anon. (1906b), 'The California bungalow', *Architectural Record*, vol. 20, October, pp. 297-
    305.

Anon. (1911), 'What is a bungalow?' *Arts and Decoration*, vol. 1, no. 12, October, p. 487.

Anon. (1925), *Book of Australian Bungalows*, Sydney.

Archer, M. (1960), 'The Daniells in India and their influence on British Architecture', *RIBA Journal*, vol. 67, no. 11.

Archer, M. (1966), 'Aspects of classicism in India; Georgian buildings in Calcutta', *Country Life*, vol. 132.

Archer, M. (1962a), 'Sir Charles D'Oyly and his drawings in India', *Apollo*, November, pp. 173-81.

Archer, M. (1962b), 'India revealed. Sketches by the Daniells', *Apollo*, November.

Archer, M. (1964), 'Georgian splendours in South India', *Country Life*, vol. 130, pp. 728-31.

Archer, M. and W.G. (1955), *Indian Painting for the British, 1770-1880*, Oxford University Press, London.

Armstrong, W. (1979), 'New Zealand: imperialism, class and uneven development', *Australian and New Zealand Journal of Sociology*, vol. 14, no. 2, pp. 297-303.

Ashworth, W. (1972), *The Genesis of Modern Town Planning*, Routledge & Kegan Paul, London.

Atkinson, G.A. (1961), 'Jobbing builders or self help for African housing', *Journal of African Administration*, vol. 3, no. 1, pp. 46-9.

Atkinson, G.F. (1859), *Curry and Rice (on forty plates) or The Ingredients of Social Life at 'Our' Station in India*, Day & Son, London.

Audsley, G.A. (1912), 'The American bungalow', *Building News*, 24 May, pp. 725-6.

Australian Council of National Trusts (1971), *The Historic Buildings of Norfolk Island*, ACNT, Sydney.

Baker, P. (1974), *Urbanisation and Political Change. The Politics of Lagos, 1917-67*, University of California Press, London.

Ballhatchet, K. and Harrison, J. (1980), *The City in South Asia. Pre-modern and Modern*, Curzon Press, London.

Banham, R., Barker, P., Hall, P. and Price, C. (1969), 'Non-plan. An experiment in freedom', *New Society*, 20 March.

Barrat Brown, M. (1978), *The Economics of Imperialism*, Penguin, Harmondsworth.

Bartell, W. (1804), *Hints for Picturesque Improvements in Ornamental Cottages*, London.

Bayly, C.A. (1975), *The Local Roots of Indian Politics. Allahabad, 1880-1920*, Clarendon Press, Oxford.

Bayly, C.A. (1983), *Rulers, Townsmen and Bazaars. North Indian society in the age of British expansion, 1770-1870*, Cambridge University Press.

Berry, B.J.L. (ed.) (1976a), *Urbanisation and Counter-urbanisation*, Sage, London.

Berry, B.J.L. (1976b), 'The counter-urbanisation process: urban America since 1970', in Berry, 1976a, pp. 17-30.

Best, G. (1973), *Mid-Victorian Britain, 1851-75*, Panther, London.

Betting, W. and Vriend, J.J. (1958), *Bungalows, Deutschland, England, Italien, Holland, Belgien, Danemark*, Die Planung Verlag, Muller-Wellborn, Darmstadt.

Binstead, A.M. (1899), *Gal's Gossip*, T. Werner Laurie, London.

Blakiston, J. (1829), *Twelve Years' Military Adventures in Threequarters of the Globe*, 2 vols, Henry Colbourn, London.

Blanchard, S.L. (1867), *Yesterday and Today in India*, W.H. Allen, London.

Boddy, M. (1980), *The Building Societies*, Longman, London.

Booth, J.D. (ed.) (1927), *The Works of A.M. Binstead*, T. Werner Laurie, London.

Boumphrey, G. (1938), 'Shall the towns kill or save the country?', in Williams-Ellis (1938).

Boumphrey, G. (1940), *Town and Country Tomorrow*, Nelson, London.

Bourne, G. (1912), *Change in the Village*, Nelson, London.

Bowley, M. (1960), *Innovations in Building Materials*, Cambridge University Press.

Bowley, M. (1966), *The British Building Industry*, Cambridge University Press, Cambridge.

Boyd, R. (1952), *Australia's Home*, Melbourne University Press, Melbourne.

Briggs, M. (1937), *How to Plan Your House*, English University Press, London.

Briggs, R.A. (1891), *Bungalows and Country Residences*, Batsford, London (later editions, 1894, 1895, 1897, 1901).

Briggs, R.A. (1894), 'Bungalows', *The Studio*, vol. 3, pp. 20-6.

Brockway, L. (1979), *Science and Colonial Expansion*, Academic Press, London.

Brooks, H.A. (1972), *The Prairie School. Frank Lloyd Wright and his Mid-West Contemporaries*, Toronto University Press, Toronto.

Brown, H. (1948), *The Sahibs. The Life and Ways of the British in India*, Hodge, London.

Browning, H. and Roberts, B. (1980), 'Urbanisation, sectoral transformation and the utilisation of labour in Latin America', *Comparative Urban Research*, 8, 1, pp. 86-104.

Brunner, A.W. (1884), *Cottages, or Hints on Economical Building*, Comstock, New York.

Buchanan, F. (1838), *The History, Antiquities, Topography and Statistics of East India*, 3 vols, W.H. Allen, London (journals of 1814).

Burnett, J. (1978), *A Social History of Housing, 1815-1970*, David & Charles, Newton Abbot.

Butlin, N.G. (1964), *Investment in Australian Economic Development, 1861-1900*, Cambridge University Press, Cambridge.

Cain, P.J. and Hopkins, A.G. (1980), 'The political economy of British expansion overseas, 1750-1914', *Economic History Review*, vol. 33, no. 4, pp. 463-90.

Caldwell, J.C. (1968), *Population Growth and Family Change in Africa*. Australian National Press, Canberra.

Carpenter, E. (1905), *The Simplification of Life*, Treherne, London.

Carter, H. (1981), *The Study of Urban Geography*, Edward Arnold, London (3rd edition).

Castells, M. (1977), *The Urban Question*, Edward Arnold, London.

Chambers, W.I. (1924), *Bungalows*, Crypt House Press, Gloucester.

Chase, L. (1981), 'Eden in the orange groves. Bungalows and court houses of Los Angeles', *Landscape*, vol. 25, no. 3, pp. 29-36.

Chaudhuri, K.N. (1978), *The Trading World of Asia and the East India Company, 1660-1760*, Cambridge University Press, Cambridge.

Cheal, H. (1921), *The Story of Shoreham*, Ginbridges, Hove.

Checkoway, B. (1980), 'Large builders, federal housing programmes and postwar suburbanisation', *International Journal of Urban and Regional Research*, vol. 4, no. 1, pp. 21-45.

Cheer, J.S. (1959), 'Bungalow development', *Journal of the Town Planning Institute*, vol. 25, 2 January, pp. 43-6.

Cherry, G.E. (1972), *Urban Change and Planning*, Foulis, Henley-on-Thames.

Cherry, G.E. (1974), *The Evolution of British Town Planning*, Leonard Hill, Leighton Buzzard.

Chilivumbo, A.B. (1975), 'The ecology of social types in Blantyre', in Parkin (ed.) (1975), pp. 309-18.

Church, R.A. (1975), *The Great Victorian Boom, 1850-73*, Macmillan, London.

Clark, R.J. (1972), *The Arts and Crafts in America, 1876-1916*, Princeton University Press, Princeton.

Cloher, D.U. (1975), 'A perspective on Australian urbanisation', in Powell, J.M. and Williams, M., *Australian Space: Australian Time. Geographic Perspectives*, Oxford University Press, London, pp. 104-49.

Clout, H.D. (1974), 'The growth of second home ownership: an example of seasonal suburbanisation', in J.H. Johnson (ed.) (1974).

Cohen, R.B. (1981), 'The new international division of labour', in Dear and Scott (eds) (1981), pp. 287-318.

Cohn, B.S. (1971), *India. The Social Anthropology of a Civilisation*, Prentice Hall, New Jersey.

Colonial Office, Africa (West) (1909), *Correspondence respecting the design of Bungalows provided for Government officials in West Africa (April 1906-January 1909)*, Colonial Office, London.

Comstock, W.T. (1908), *Bungalows, Camps and Mountain Homes*, Comstock, New York.

Connor, P. (1979), *Oriental Architecture in the West*, Thames & Hudson, London.

Cooney, E.W. (1949), 'Capital exports and investment in Britain and the USA, 1856-1914', *Economica*, NS, vol. 16, pp. 346-56.

Coppock, J.T. (1973), 'The changing face of England, 1850-1900', in H.C. Darby (ed.) (1973).

Coppock, J.T. (1977), *Second Homes. Curse or Blessing?* Pergamon Press, Oxford.

Cottrell, P.L. (1975), *British Overseas Investment in the Nineteenth Century*, Macmillan, London.

Coulson, E. (1971), 'The impact of the colonial period on the definition of land rights', in V. Turner (ed.) (1971), pp. 193-215.

Council for the Preservation of Rural England (CPRE) (1929), *The Thames Valley from Cricklade to Staines*, University of London Press, London.

CPRE (1932), *The Peak District. Its Scenery, Disfigurement and Preservation*, CPRE, Sheffield.

CPRE (1933), *The Penn Country of Buckinghamshire*, CPRE, London.

CPRE (1934), *Ryedale. A Report*, CPRE, London.

CPRE (1934), *Wirral Countryside*, University of Liverpool Press, Liverpool.

The Country Gentleman (1905), *The Book of the Cheap Cottages Exhibition*, Country Gentleman and Land & Water Co., London.

Country Gentleman's Association (c. 1912), *Artistic Country Buildings*, CGA, London.

Country Houses (1912), *Country Houses and Bungalows*, Northwestern Properties, London.

Cowburn, W. (1966), 'Popular housing', *Arena. Journal of the Architectural Association*, Sept.-Oct.

Cox, K.R. (ed.) (1978), *Urbanisation and Conflict in Market Societies*, Maaroufa Press, Chicago.

Crook, P. (1966), 'Sample survey of Yoruba rural building', *Odu*, vol. 2, no. 2, pp. 41-71.

Current, W.R. and K. (1974), *Greene and Greene*, Fort Worth, Amos Carter Museum of Western Art.

Dahrendorf, R. (1970), 'On the origin of inequality among men', in A. Beteille, (ed.), *Social Inequality, Selected Readings*. Penguin, Harmondsworth, pp. 30-42.

Daily Mail (1922), *Daily Mail Bungalow Book*, Daily Mail, London (continued, with intervals, up to the mid 1970s).

Dani, A.H. (1961), *Muslim Architecture in Bengal*, Asiatic Society of Pakistan, Dacca.

Darby, H.C. (1973), *A New Historical Geography of England*, Cambridge University Press, Cambridge.

Darby, M. (1978), 'The first bungalows', *Country Life*, 3 August, pp. 306-9.

Davey, P. (1981), *Arts and Crafts Architecture*, Architectural Press, London.

David, A.C. (1906), 'An architect of bungalows in California', *Architectural Record*, vol. 20, pp. 307-15.

Davison, G. (1979), 'Australian urban history: a progress report', *Urban History Yearbook*, Leicester University Press, Leicester, pp. 100-9.

Dear, M. and Scott, A.J. (1981), *Urbanisation and Urban Planning in Capitalist Society*, Methuen, London.

Denoon, D. (1979), 'Understanding settler societies', *Historical Studies*, vol. 18, pp. 511-27.

Denyer, S. (1978), *African Traditional Architecture*, Heinemann, London.

Department of Transport (1982), *Transport Statistics, 1971-81*, HMSO, London.

Design and Industries Association (1930), *The Face of the Land. Year book of the DIA*, Allen & Unwin, London.

Desmond, R. (1976), 'Photography in India during the nineteenth century', in India Office Library, *Report for the Year 1974*, HMSO, London.

Dickens, P. (1975), 'A disgusting blot on the landscape', *New Society*, 17 July, pp. 127-9.

Dingle, A.E. and Merret, D.T. (1972), 'Home owners and tenants in Melbourne, 1891-1911', *Australian Economic History Review*, vol, 12, no. 1.

Dodwell, H.H. (ed.) (1929), *Cambridge History of India*, 5 vols, Cambridge University Press, Cambridge.

Downing, A.F. and Scully, V.J. (1952), *The Architectural Heritage of Newport, R.I., 1640-1915*, Harvard University Press, Cambridge, Mass.

Downing, F. (1982), 'The common bungalow planning tradition', *Little Journal*, Society of Architectural Historians, Buffalo, N.Y.

Downing, F. and Fleming, U. (1981), 'The bungalows of Buffalo', *Environment and Planning B*, vol. 8, pp. 269-93.

Dougill, W. (1936), *The English Coast. Its Development and Preservation*, CPRE, London.

Duncan, N.G. (1981), 'Home ownership and social theory', in J.S. Duncan (ed.) (1981), pp. 98-134.

Duncan, J.S. (ed.) (1981), *Housing and Identity. Cross-Cultural Perspectives*, Croom Helm, London.

Dunn, J. and Robertson, A.F. (1973), *Dependence and Opportunity, Political Change in Agafo*, Cambridge University Press, Cambridge.

Dyos, H.J. and Aldcroft, D. (1974), *British Transport. An Economic Survey*, Penguin Books, Harmondsworth.

East Africa Protectorate, Kenya Province (1910), *Memoranda for Provincial and District Commissioners*, Nairobi, Government Printer.

'Economist' (1927), *An Ideal Bungalow. How to build it well and at lowest cost and pay for it in a few years as rent. Eligible for the Government subsidy*, Simpkin Marshall, London.

Edelstein, M. (1981), 'Foreign investment and empire, 1860-1914', in Floud and McCloskey (1981), pp. 70-98.

Edwards, A.E. (1981), *The Design of Suburbia. A Critical Study in Environmental History*, Pembridge Press, London.

Edwards, J. (1980)·, 'The evolution of vernacular architecture in the Western Caribbean', in K. Wilkerson (ed.), *Cultural Traditions and Caribbean Identity. The Question of Patrimony*, University of Florida, Gainsville, pp. 291-346.

Edwardes, M. (1967), *A History of India*, Mentor, London.

Elkan, W. (1975), 'How people came to live in towns', in Duignan, P., Gann, L.H. (eds), *Colonialism in Africa, 1870-1960*, vol. 4, Cambridge University Press, Cambridge.

Elsam, R. (1804), *An Essay on Architecture*. Published for the author, London.

Evans, R. (1982), *The Fabrication of Virtue. English Prison Architecture 1750-1840*, Cambridge University Press, Cambridge.

Fainstein, N.I. and Fainstein, S.F. (1979), 'New debates in urban planning', *International Journal of Urban and Regional Research*, vol. 3, no. 3, pp. 381-403.

Fennel, C.A.M. (1892), *The Stanford Dictionary of Anglicised Words & Phrases*, Cambridge University Press, Cambridge.

Fielding, A.J. (1982), 'Counter urbanisation in Western Europe', *Progress in Planning*, vol. 17, pp. 1-52.

Flemming, U. (1982), 'Structure in bungalow plans', *Environment and Planning B*, vol. 8, pp. 87-96.

Floud, R. and McCloskey, D. (1981), *The Economic History of Britain since 1700*, vol. 2, 1860-1970s, Cambridge University Press, Cambridge.

Fogelson, R.M. (1967), *The Fragmented Metropolis. Los Angeles, 1850-1930*, Harvard University Press, Cambridge, Mass.

Foster, W. (1921), *The English Factors in India, 1655-60*, Clarendon Press, Oxford.

Frank, A.G. (1978), *Dependent Accumulation and Underdevelopment*, Macmillan, London.

Fraser, W.H. (1981), *The Coming of the Mass Market, 1850-1914*, Macmillan, London.

Freeland, J.M. (1968), *Architecture in Australia. A History*, F.W. Cheshire, Canberra.

Freeland, J.M. (1974), *Architect Extraordinary. The Life and Work of John H. Hunt, 1838-1904*, Cassel, Australia.

Freestone, R. (1981), 'Australian responses to the Garden City idea', Paper presented to Section 21 (Geographical Sciences) 51st ANZAA's Congress, Brisbane, mimeo.

French, R.A. and Hamilton, F. (eds) (1979), *The Socialist City. Spatial Structure and Urban Policy*, Wiley, Chichester.

Friedlander, D. (1966), 'Internal Migration in England and Wales', *Population Studies*, vol. 19.

Fryer, J. (1909), *A New Account of East India and Persia, 1672-81*, Hakluyt Society, London.

Fuller, B. (1913), *The Empire of India*, Pitman, London.

Furedy, C. (1979), 'The development of modern elite retailing in Calcutta, 1890-1920', *Indian Economic and Social History Review*, vol. 16, no. 4.

Gann, L.H. and Duignan, P. (eds) (1978), *The Rulers of British Africa, 1870-1914*, Croom Helm, London.

Garnier, A. (1981), 'La maison individuelle en Suisse et dans la canton de Vaud', *Ingenieurs et Architectes Suisses*, 20 August, pp. 273-9.

Gebhard, D. (1975), *Charles F.A. Voysey. Architect*, Hennesy and Ingalls, Los Angeles.

Ghosh, S.C. (1970), *The Social Condition of the British Community in Bengal, 1757-1800*, E.J. Brill, Leiden.

Gilg, A. (1978), *Countryside Planning. The First Thirty Years, 1945-75*, David and Charles, Newton Abbot.

Girouard, M. (1971a), 'Days of Victorian glory. Cromer', *Country Life*, 26 August, p. 502.

Girouard, M. (1971b), *The Victorian Country House*, Country Life, London.

Glaab, T.N. and Brown, A.T. (1976), *A History of Urban America*, London, Collier Macmillan.

Gloag, J. (1938), 'The suburban scene', in Williams-Ellis (ed.) (1938), pp. 187-99.

Glynn, S. (1975), *Urbanisation in Australian History, 1788-1900*, Nelson, Australia.

Glynn, J. and Oxborrow, J. (1976), *Inter-war Britain. A Social and Economic History*, Allen & Unwin, London.

Gottdiener, M. (1977), *Planned Sprawl. Private and Public Interests in Suburbia*, Sage, London.

Grant, C. (1849), *Anglo-Indian Domestic Life*, Thacker & Spink, Calcutta.

Grant, C. (1859), *Rural Life in Bengal*, Thacker & Spink, Calcutta.

Granville, A.B. (1841), *The Spas of England and Principal Sea-bathing Places*, 3 vols, Henry Colbourn, London.

Gubler, J. (1980), 'Architecture and colonialism', *Lotus International*, vol. 26, pp. 5-19.

Gutkind, P.C.W. and Waterman, P. (eds) (1977), *African Social Studies, A radical reader*, Monthly Review Press, New York.

Hall, P. et al. (1973), *The Containment of Urban England*, Allen & Unwin, London, 2 vols.

Halsey, A.H. (ed.) (1972), *Trends in British Society since 1900*, Macmillan, London.

Hambidge, H. 'Westgate-on-Sea, 1909-69', H. Hambidge, Westgate-on-Sea. n.d.

Hamilton, A. (1744), *A New Account of the East Indies*, 2 vols, London.

Hancock, J. (1980), 'The apartment house in urban America' in A.D. King, (ed.) (1980), pp. 151-92.

'Hansard' *Parliamentary Debates: Official Reports*, House of Commons.

Hardoy, J.E. and Satterthwaite, D. (1981), *Shelter: Need and Response. Housing, Land and Settlement in Seventeen Third World Nations*, Wiley, Chichester.

Hardy, D. (1979), *Alternative Communities in Nineteenth Century England*, Longman, London.

Harley, C.K. and McCloskey (1981), 'Foreign trade and the expanding international economy', in Floud and McCloskey (1981), pp. 50-69.

Harmon, R.B. (1983), *The Bungalow Style in American Domestic Architecture*, Vance, Monticello.

Harper, R. (1977), 'The conflict between English building regulations and architectural design', *Journal of Architectural Research*, vol. 6, no. 1, pp. 24-33.

Harrison, P.T. (1909), *Bungalow Residences*, Crosby Lockwood, London.

Harvey, D. (1973), *Social Justice and the City*, Edward Arnold, London.

Harvey, D. (1977), 'The urban process under capitalism: a framework for analysis', *International Journal of Urban and Regional Research*, vol. 6, no. 1, pp. 24-33.

Hay, R. (1977), 'Patterns of urbanisation . . . in the Third World', in Abu-Lughod and Hay (eds) (1977).

Hayden, D. (1976), *Seven American Utopias. The Architecture of Communitarian Socialism, 1790-1975*, MIT Press, Cambridge, Mass.

Hayden, D. (1981), *The Grand Domestic Revolution. A History of Feminist Designs for American Homes, Neighborhoods and Cities*, MIT Press, Cambridge, Mass.

Headrick, D. (1981), *Tools of Empire. Technology and European Imperialism in the Nineteenth Century*, Oxford University Press, London.

Hebdige, D. (1981), 'Towards a cartography of taste, 1935-62', in Waites, B. et al., *Popular Culture. Past and Present*, Croom Helm, London, pp. 194-218.

Heber, R. (1828), *Narrative of a Journey*, 1824-5, 2 vols, J. Murray, London.

Herbert, G. (1978), *Pioneers of Prefabrication*, Princeton University Press, Princeton.

Hobsbawm, E.J. (1969), *Industry and Empire*, Penguin, Harmondsworth.

Hobsbawm, E.J. (1975), *The Age of Capital*, Weidenfeld & Nicolson, London.

Hodges, W. (1793), *Travels in India during the Years 1780-3*, J. Edwards, London.

Hodson, F.T. (1906a), *Practical Bungalows for Town and Country*, Chicago (later editions 1912, 1916).

Hodson, F.T. (1906b), 'The California bungalow', *Architectural Record*, vol. 19, pp. 394-5.

Holdsworth, D.W. (1977), 'House and home in Vancouver', in Stelter, G.A. and Artibise, A.F.J. (eds), *The Canadian City*, McClelland & Stewart, Toronto, pp. 186-211.

Holdsworth, D.W. (1981), 'House and home in Vancouver: the evolution of a West coast urban landscape, 1886-1929', PhD thesis, University of British Columbia.

Holdsworth, D.W (1982), 'Regional distinctiveness in an industrial age: some Californian influences on British Columbia housing', *The American Review of Canadian Studies*, 12, 2, pp. 64-81.

Hole, V.W. and Pountney, M. (1971), *Trends in Population, Housing and Occupancy Rates, 1861-1961*, HMSO, London.

Holzman, J.M. (1926), *The Nabobs in England. A Study of the Returned Anglo-Indian, 1760-85*, Columbia University Press, New York.

Home, R.K. (1976), 'Urban growth and urban government', in Williams (ed.) (1976), pp. 54-75.

'Home Counties' (1905), *Country Cottages. How to Build, Buy and Fit them up*, Heinemann, London (later edition, 1910).

Hopkins, A.G. (1980), 'Property rights and empire building. Britain's annexation of Lagos, 1861', *Journal of Economic History*, vol. 40, no. 4, pp. 777-98.

Howell, S. (1974), *The Seaside*, Studio Vista, London.

Hull, R.W. (1976), *African Cities and Towns before the European Conquest*, Horton, New York.

Hunter, W.W. (1899-1900), *A History of British India*, 2 vols, London.

Hutchins, F.G. (1967), *The Illusion of Permanence: British Imperialism in India*, Princeton University Press, New Jersey.

Illich, I. (1978), *The Right to Useful Employment*, Marion Boyars, London.

India, Government of (Consulting Architect) (1910-16), *Annual Reports on Architectural Work in India for the Years, 1909-1916*, Calcutta.

Jackson, A.A. (1973), *Semi-detached London*, Allen & Unwin, London.

Jahoda, G. (1961), 'Aspects of westernisation. A study of adult class students in Ghana', *British Journal of Sociology*, vol. 12, no. 4, pp. 375-86.

James, L.H. (1935), *The Modern Bungalow*, Practical Building Company, London.

Jeffreys, J. (1858), *The British Army in India. Its preservation by an appropriate clothing, housing, location, recreative employment and hopeful encouragement of the troops*, Longman, Brown, Green, London.

Jennings, A.S. (1908), *The House Beautiful. A practical guide to the artistic decoration and furnishing of moderate-sized homes, etc.*, Greening, London.

Jensen, R.G. (1976), 'Urban environments in the United States and the Soviet Union: some contrasts and comparisons', in B.J.L. Berry (ed.) (1976), pp. 31-42.

Joad, C.E.M. (1931), *The Horrors of the Countryside*, Hogarth Press, London.

Johnson, D.L. (1980), *Australian Architecture, 1901-51. Sources of Modernism*, Sydney University Press, Sydney.

Johnson, J.H. (ed.) (1974), *Suburban Growth. Geographical Processes at the Edge of the Western City*, Wiley, London.

Johnston, R.J. (1980), *City and Society. An Outline for Urban Geography*, Penguin Books, Harmondsworth.

Karn, V. (1977), *Retiring to the Seaside*, Routledge & Kegan Paul, London.

Kaufmann, E. (1975), 'The Arts and Crafts. Reactionary or progressive', in *Record* of the Art Museum, Princeton University, vol. 34, no. 2, pp. 6-12.

Kaye, B. (1960), *The Development of the Architectural Profession in Britain*, Allen & Unwin, London.

Keeley, C.J.H. (1928), *Bungalows and Modern Homes*, Batsford, London.

Kemeny, J. (1981), *The Myth of Home Ownership*, Routledge & Kegan Paul, London.

Kemp, T. (1978), *Historical Patterns of Industrialisation*, Longmans, London.

Kilby, P. (1969), *Industrialisation in an Open Economy*, Cambridge University Press, Cambridge.

Kilby, P. (1975), 'Manufacturing in colonial Africa', in Duignan, P. and Gann, L.H. (eds), *Colonialism in Africa, 1870-1960*, vol. 4, Cambridge University Press, Cambridge.

Kilmartin, L. and Thorns, D.C. (1978), *Cities Unlimited*, Allen & Unwin, London.

King, A.D. (1973a), 'The bungalow: the development and diffusion of a house-type', *Architectural Association Quarterly*, vol. 5, no. 3, pp. 5-26.

King, A.D. (1973b) 'Social process and urban form: the bungalow as an indicator of social trends', *Architectural Association Quarterly*, vol. 5, no. 4, pp. 4-21.

King, A.D. (1974), 'The language of colonial urbanisation', *Sociology*, vol. 8, no. 1, pp. 81-110.

King, A.D. (1976), *Colonial Urban Development. Culture, Social Power and Environment*, Routledge & Kegan Paul, London.

King, A.D. (1977a) 'The westernisation of domestic architecture in India', *Art and Archaeology Research Papers*, vol. 11, pp. 32-41.

King, A.D. (1977b), 'The Bengali peasant hut: some nineteenth century accounts', *Art and Archaeology Research Papers*, vol. 12, pp. 70-8.

King, A.D. (ed.) (1980a), *Buildings and Society. Essays on the Social Development of the Built Environment*, Routledge & Kegan Paul, London.

King, A.D. (1980b), 'A space for time and a time for space: the social production of the vacation house', in King, A.D. (1980a), pp. 193-227.

King, A.D. (1980c), 'Exporting planning: the colonial and neo-colonial experience', in Cherry, G.E. (ed.) (1980), *Shaping an Urban World*, Mansell, London, pp. 203-26.

King, A.D. (1980d), 'Historical patterns of reaction to urbanism: the case of Britain, 1880-1939', *International Journal of Urban and Regional Research*, vol. 4, no. 4, pp. 453-69.

King, A.D. (1980e), 'Colonialism and the development of the modern south Asian city: some theoretical considerations', in K. Ballhatchet and J. Harrison (eds) *The City in South Asia. Pre-modern and modern*. Curzon Press, London, pp. 1-19.

King, A.D. (1981), 'Bungalow bliss: domestic imagery and the ideology of romance in the lyrics of popular songs, 1920-75', Paper for Annual Conference, Social History Society (*Popular Culture*), mimeo.

King, A.D. (1982a), 'Words, dwellings and the property market: notes towards a folk taxonomy of building form'; paper given to the Welsh School of Architecture, Staff seminar, Cardiff. Mimeo.

King, A.D. (1982b), 'Colonial architecture and urban development: the reconversion of colonial typologies', *Lotus International*, vol. 34, pp. 46-59.

King, A.D. (1983a), 'Colonial cities: global pivots of change', in Ross and Telkamp (eds), (1984).

King, A.D. (1983b), ' "The world economy is everywhere": urban history and the world system', *Urban History Yearbook*, (1983), Leicester University Press.

King, A.D. (1983c), 'Culture and the political economy of building form', *Habitat International*, vol. 7, nos 5/6, pp. 237-48.

King, A.D. (1983d), 'The social production of building form: theory and research', NSAV congress, 'Sociologie, Bouwen en Wonen', University of Amsterdam (forthcoming, *Society and Space*).

King, A.D. (1984a), 'Colonial architecture re-visited: some issues for further debate', in K. Ballhatchet, (ed.), *Changing South Asia: City and Culture*, Asian Research Service, (in press).

King, A.D. (1984b), 'Capital city: physical and social aspects of London's role in the world economy', in J. Friedmann and G. Wolff (eds) (1984), *World Cities in Formation. Development and Change* (in press).

Kipling, J.L. (1911), 'The origin of the bungalow', *Country Life in America*, vol. 19, no. 8, pp. 308-10.

Kira, A. (1976), *The Bathroom*, Penguin Books, Harmondsworth.

Kirk-Greene, A.H.M. (1968), *Lugard and the Amalgamation of Nigeria*, Frank Cass, London.

Koch, R.J. (1918), 'In search of bungalows: what we found', *House and Garden*, vol. 13, pp. 9-11.

Kornwolf, J.D. (1972), *M.H. Baillie Scott and the Arts and Crafts Movement*, Johns Hopkins Press, London.

Kubler, G. (1944), 'The machine for living in eighteenth century West Africa', *Journal of the American Society of Architectural Historians*, vol. 4, no. 1, pp. 30-2.

Kumar, K. (ed) (1980), *Transnational Enterprises, Their Impact on Third World Societies and Cultures*, Westview, Boulder, Co.

Kuznets, S. (1966), *Modern Economic Growth*, Yale University Press, New Haven and London.

Lakeman, A. (1918), *Concrete Cottages, Bungalows and Garages*, Concrete Association, London (later editions, 1924, 1932, 1949).

Lancaster, C. (1958), 'The American bungalow', *The Art Bulletin*, vol. 40, no. 3, pp. 239-53.

Lancaster, C. (1960), *Architectural Follies in America*, Tuttle, Rutland & Tokyo.

Lancaster, C. (1963), *The Japanese Influence in America*, Walton H. Rawls, New York.

Lancaster, C. (1984), *The American Bungalow*, Abbeville Press, New York (in press).

Laslett, P. (1974), *Household and Family in Past Time*, Cambridge University Press, Cambridge.

Latham, A.J.H. (1978), *The International Economy and the Underdeveloped World, 1865-1914*, Croom Helm, London.

Law, C.M. and Warnes, A.M. (1980), 'The characteristics of retired migrants', in Herbert, D.T. and Johnston, R.J. *Geography and the Urban Environment*, vol. 3, Wiley, Chichester, pp. 175-222.

Lawrence, E. (1982), *Annual Abstract of Statistics*, HMSO, London.

Lazear, M.H. (1907), 'The evolution of the bungalow in California', *Indoors and Out*, vol. 4, no. 1, pp. 7-12.

Leavis, F.R. and Thompson, D. (1933), *Culture and Environment. The Training of Critical Awareness*, Chatto & Windus, London.

Lent, F.T. (1899), *Summer Homes and Camps*, Boston, F.T. Lent.

Lewcock, R. (1963), *Early Nineteenth Century Architecture in South Africa: A Study of the Interaction of Two Cultures, 1785-1837*, Balkema, Cape Town.

Lewin, T.H. (ed.) (1909), *The Lewin Letters, A Selection from the Correspondence and Diaries of an English Family*, Constable, London.

Lichtenberger, E. (1976), 'The Changing Nature of European Urbanisation', in Berry, B.J.L. (ed.) (1976), pp. 81-108.

Llewellyn-Jones, R. (1980), 'The city of Lucknow before 1856' in Ballhatchet and Harrison (1980), pp. 88-128.

Lloyd, B. (1981), 'Women, home and status' in Duncan, J. (ed.) (1981), pp. 181-97.

Lloyd, P.C. (1974), *Power and Independence. Urban Africans' Perceptions of Social Inequality*, Routledge & Kegan Paul, London.

Lloyd, P.C. (1979), *Slums of Hope? Shanty Towns of the Third World*, Penguin Books, Harmondsworth.

Lockyer, C. (1711), *An Account of the Trade in India*, S. Crouch, London.

Lubeck, P. and Walton, J. (1979), 'Urban class conflict in Africa and Latin America', *International Journal of Urban and Regional Research*, vol. 3, pp. 2-29.

Lugard, F.D. (1970), *Political Memoranda. Revision of Instructions to Political Officers on Subjects Chiefly Political and Administrative, 1913-18*, Frank Cass, London (earlier editions, 1906, 1909).

Lugard, F. (1965), *The Dual Mandate in Tropical Africa*, Frank Cass, London.

Mabogunje, A.L. (1968), *Urbanization in Nigeria*, University of London Press, London.

Mabogunje, A.L. (1979) Review of A.B. Anderson, *African Traditional Architecture* (1977), in *Journal of the Society of Architectural Historians*, 38, 3, p. 291.

Mabogunje, A.L. (1980), *The Development Process. A Spatial Perspective*, Hutchinson, London.

Mabogunje, A.L. Hardoy, J. and Misra, R.P. (1978), *Shelter Provision in Developing Countries. The Influence of Standards and Criteria*, Wiley, Chichester.

McGregor, C. (1966), *Profile of Australia*, Hodder & Stoughton, London.

Magubane, B. (1971), 'A critical look at indices used in the study of social change in colonial Africa', *Current Anthropology*, vol. 12, no. 4, pp. 419-44.

Makinson, R.L. (1977), *Greene and Greene. Architecture as a Fine Art*, Peregrine Smith, Salt Lake City & Santa Barbara.

Marris, P. (1961), *Family and Social Change in Africa*, Routledge & Kegan Paul, London.

Marsh, J. (1978), *Edward Thomas. A Poet for his Country*, Elek, London.

Martinotti, G. (1980), 'Deurbanisation and villagisation: Introduction', *International Journal of Urban and Regional Research*, vol. 4, no. 4, p. xii.

Masterman, C.F.G. (1918), *The Condition of England*, Methuen, London.

Massey, D. (1979), 'In what sense a regional problem?' *Regional Studies*, 13, pp. 233-43.

Massey, D. and Catalano, A. (1978), *Capital and Land*, Edward Arnold, London.

Matthias, P. (1978), *The First Industrial Nation. An Economic History of Britain, 1700-1914*, Methuen, London.

Mayhew, A. (1881), *Birchington and its Bungalows*, Canterbury, Kent.

Mayhew, A. (1882), *The Chronicles of Westgate-on-Sea*, Canterbury, Kent.

McCarty, J.W. (1972), 'Australian capital cities in the nineteenth century', in Schedvin and McCarty, eds (1972), pp. 104-20.

Meller, H. (1976), *Leisure and the Changing City*, Routledge & Kegan Paul, London.

Mellossi, D. and Pavarini, M. (1982), *The Prison and the Factory*, Hutchinson, London.

Miller, F. (1901), *The Training of a Craftsman*, Virtue, London.

Misra, B.B. (1961), *The Indian Middle Classes. Their Growth in Modern Times.* Oxford

University Press, London.

Moffit, P. (1976), *The Australian Verandah*, Ure Smith, Sydney.

Morris, A.E. (1978), *Pre-cast Concrete in Architecture*, George Godwin, London.

Morrison, P. (1905), *Rambling Recollections*, Swan Sonnenschein, London.

Morton, F.A. (1906), *The Simple Life on Four Acres*, Werner Laurie, London.

Mullins, P. (1981), 'Theoretical perspectives on Australian urbanisation. Material components in the reproduction of Australian labour power'. *Australian and New Zealand Journal of Sociology*, vol. 17, no. 1, pp. 65-76.

Murie, A., Niner, P and Watson, C. (1976), *Housing Policy and the Housing System*, Allen & Unwin, London.

Murphy, P.A. (1977), 'Second homes in New South Wales', *Australian Geographer*, vol. 13, pp. 310-17.

Murphy, R. (1970), 'Historical and comparative urban studies', in Putnam, R.G. et al. (eds), *A Geography of Urban Places. Selected Readings*, Toronto, pp. 25-32.

Murray, J. (1895), *How to Live in Tropical Africa*, John Murray, London.

Murray, J.A.H. (1888), *A New English Dictionary on Historical Principles*, Clarendon Press, Oxford (subsequently, *Oxford English Dictionary*, all later editions and supplements).

Nadel, G.J. (1957), *Australia's Colonial Culture*, Melbourne.

Nanda, B.R. (1962), *The Nehrus*, Allen and Unwin.

Naylor, G. (1972), *The Arts and Crafts*, Thames & Hudson, London.

Nduka, O.(1977), 'The rationality of the rich in Nigeria' in Gutkind and Waterman (eds) (1977).

Neild, S. (1979), 'Colonial urbanism: the development of Madras City in the eighteenth and nineteenth centuries', *Modern Asian Studies*, vol. 13, no. 2, pp. 217-46.

Nestler-Bode, H. (1975), *Deutsche Kunst seit 1960*, Architektur, Munich.

Neutze, M. (1977), *Urban Development in Australia*, Allen & Unwin, London.

Nicoll, J. (1975), *D.G. Rossetti*, Studio Vista, London.

Nilsson, S. (1969), *European Architecture in India, 1750-1850*, Faber, London.

Noble, J. (1973), 'Contingency housing', *Architects Journal*, 24 October, pp. 976-99.

Oliver, P. (ed.) (1970), *Shelter and Society*, Barrie & Jenkins, London.

Oliver, P. (ed.) (1975), *Shelter in Africa*, Barrie & Jenkins, London.

Oliver, P., Davis, I. and Bentley, I. (1981), *Dunroamin. The Suburban Semi and its Enemies*, Barrie & Jenkins, London.

O'Donnell, P. (1978), 'The beginning of the modern home in the 1920s', Childhood and Government Project, Working Paper, 19, University of California, Berkeley.

O'Neill, S. (1982), *Time-sharing. Its Implications for Building Development*, Final Year Project, Department of Building Technology, Brunel University.

Onokerhoraya, A.G. (1977), 'The evolution and spatial structure of house types in the traditional Nigerian city: a Benin example', *Journal of Tropical Geography*, vol. 45, no. 2, pp. 118-26.

Padfield, J.E. (1896), *The Hindu at Home*, Simpkin, Marshall, London.

Pahl, R.E. (1975), *Whose City?* Penguin, Harmondsworth.

Paris, C. (1982), *Critical Readings in Planning Theory*, Pergamon, Oxford.

Parkes, F. (1850), *Wanderings of a Pilgrim in Search of the Picturesque*, Pelham Richardson, London.

Parkin, D. (ed.) (1975), *Town and Country in East and Central Africa*, Oxford University Press, London.

Patmore, J.A. (1970), 'The spa towns of Britain', in R.P. Beckinsale (ed), *Urbanisation and its Problems*, Blackwell, Oxford, pp. 47-69.

Peace, A. (1979), *Choice, Class and Conflict*, Harvester, Brighton.

Peace, S. (1982), 'The balance of residential life: a study of 100 old people's homes', paper given to the British Sociology Association Study Group on Sociology and Environment, February, 1982. mimeo.

Peacehaven Estates (c. 1927), *Peacehaven. The Land of Sunshine and Health*, London.

Peel, J.D.Y. (1980), 'Urbanisation and urban history in West Africa', *Journal of African History*, 21, 2, pp. 272-80.

Phillips, G.W. (1912), *New Zealand Homes and Bungalows*, Christchurch.

Phillips, R.R. (1920), *The Book of Bungalows*, Country Life, London (later editions, 1922, 1926).

Pickvance, C.G. (1976), *Urban Sociology. Critical Essays*, Tavistock, London.

Pimlott, J.A.R. (1976), *The Englishman's Holiday*, Faber & Faber, London.

Platt, K. (1923), *The Home and Health in India and the Tropical Colonies*, Bailliere, Tindall & Cox, London.

Pollard, S. (1979), *The Development of the British Economy, 1914-1967*, Edward Arnold, London.

Porter, B. (1975), *The Lion's Share. A Short History of British Imperialism, 1850-1970*, Longman, London.

Pott, J. (1977), *Old Bungalows in Bangalore*, privately printed, London.

Potter, T. (1909), *Buildings for Small Holdings*, Batsford, London.

Price, C.M. (1916), *The Practical Book of Architecture*, Lippincott, Philadelphia and London.

Radford, W. (1908), *Radford's Artistic Bungalows*, The Radford Architectural Bungalow Company, Chicago & New York.

Ragatz, R. (1970), 'Vacation housing. A missing component in urban and regional theory, *Land Economics*, vol. 46, no. 2, pp. 118-26.

Raghuvanshi, V.P.S. (1969), *Indian Society in the Eighteenth Century*, Associated Publishing House, New Delhi.

Rao, G. Subha (1969), *Indian Words in English. A Study in Indo-British Cultural Life and Linguistic Relations*, Clarendon Press, Oxford.

Rapoport, A. (1977), *Human Aspects of Urban Form*, Pergamon, Oxford.

Renbourn, E.T. (1963), 'Seasonal fluxes and fevers of acclimatisation. An introduction to the history of tropical adaptation', *Journal of Tropical Medicine and Hygiene*, vol. 66, no. 8, pp. 193-203.

Retired Officer of the Hon. East India Company (1830), *The Friend of Australia*, Hurst Chance, London.

Ricci, J.M. (1979), 'The bungalow. A history of the most predominant style of Tampa Bay', *Tampa Bay History*, 1, pp. 6-13.

Rice, A. (1973), 'The Heyday of Bungalow Town', *Country Life*, 19 April, pp. 1099-100.

Richardson, H.W. and Aldcroft, D. (1968), *Building in the British Economy between the Wars*, Allen and Unwin, London.

Roberts, B. (1978), *Cities of Peasants*, Edward Arnold, London.

Robertson, P. (1978), *Shell Book of Firsts*, Ebury Press, London.

Robinson, R.M. (1929), *Coutts: The History of a Banking House*, London.

Rodenweldt, E. (1938), *Tropenhygiene*, Enke, Stuttgart.

Ross, R. and Telkamp, G. (eds) (1984), *Colonial Cities*, University of Leiden Press.

Rossetti, W.M. (1895), *Dante Gabriel Rossetti. His Family Letters*, Ellis & Elvey, London.

Rossetti, W.M. (1906), *Some Reminiscences*, Brown Langham, London.

Rowbotham, S. and Weeks, J. (1977), *Socialism and the New Life*, Pluto Press, London.

Roxborough, I. (1979), *Theories of Underdevelopment*, Macmillan, London.

Russell, W.H. (1860), *My Diary in India in the Year 1859-60*, 2 vols. Routledge, Warne & Routledge, London.

Saini, B.S. (1973), *Building Environments*, Angus and Robertson, London.

Saint, A. (1976), *Richard Norman Shaw*, Yale University Press, New Haven.

Samson, G.C. (1910), *Houses, Cottages and Bungalows for Britishers and Americans Abroad*, Crosby Lockwood, London.

Sandercock, L. (1975), *Cities for Sale*, Melbourne University Press, Melbourne.

Saul, S.B. (1962), 'House building in England, 1890-1914', *Economic History Review*, vol. 15, no. 1, pp. 119-37.

Saunders, P. (1981), *Social Theory and the Urban Question*, Hutchinson, London.

Sauvant, K.P. (1981), 'From economic to socio-cultural emancipation', *Third World Quarterly*, vol. 3, no. 1, pp. 48-61.

Saylor, H.H. (1911), *Bungalows. Their Design, Construction and Furnishing*, Grant Richards, New York.

Schedvin, C.B. and McCarthy, J.W. (1976), *Urbanisation in Australia. The Nineteenth Century*, Sydney University Press, Sydney.

Schmitt, P.J. (1969), *Back to Nature. The Arcadian Myth in Urban America*, Oxford University Press, New York.

Schwartz, B. (ed.) (1976), *The Changing Face of the Suburbs*, University of Chicago Press, Chicago & London.

Schwerdtfeger, F. (1982), *Traditional Housing in African Cities*, Wiley, Chichester.

Scott, L. (1936), 'Preservation of the countryside', in Betham, E. (ed.), *House Building, 1934-6*, Federated Employers Press, London.

Serle, G. (1972), *The Rush to be Rich. A History of the Colony of Victoria, 1883-89*, Melbourne University Press, Melbourne.

Shah, A.M. (1974), *The Household Dimension of the Family in India*, University of California Press, London.

Sharar, Abdul H. (1974), *Lucknow: The Last Phase of an Oriental Culture*. Paul Elek, London.

Sharp, T. (1932), *Town and Countryside. Some Aspects of Urban and Rural Development*, Oxford University Press, London.

Shaw, D.J.B. (1979), 'Recreation and the Soviet City' in French and Hamilton (eds) (1979), pp. 119-44.

Shaw, R.N. (1878), *Sketches for Cottages and other Buildings*, W.H. Lascelles, London.

Sheail, J. (1981), *Rural Conservation in Inter-war Britain*, Oxford University Press, London.

Shorter, E. (1976), *The Making of the Modern Family*, Collins, London.

Singleton, G.J. (1973), 'The genesis of suburbia. A complex of historical trends', in Massotti, L.H. and Hadden, J.K. (eds), *The Urbanisation of the Suburbs*, Sage, London, pp. 29-50.

Sinha, P. (1978), *Calcutta in Urban History*, Firma K.M. Private Ltd, Calcutta.

Slater, T.R. (1978), 'Family, society and the ornamental villa on the fringes of English country towns', *Journal of Historical Geography*, vol. 4, no. 2, pp. 119-37.

Sloane, J.V.N. (1978), 'The development of the urban and social structure of Bournemouth, 1840-1940', PhD thesis, University of Surrey.

Smith, M.P. (1980), *The City and Social Theory*, Blackwell, Oxford.

Smith, T.R. (1868-9), 'On buildings for European occupation in tropical climates, especially India', *Proceedings of the Royal Institute of British Architects*, 1st series, p. 18.

Social Trends (1975-1981), HMSO, London.

Southall, A. (1971), 'The impact of imperialism on urban development in Africa' in V. Turner (ed.) (1971).

Spate, O.H. and Learmonth, A.T.A. (1965), *India and Pakistan. A General and Regional Geography*, Methuen, London.

Spear, P. (1963), *The Nabobs*, Oxford University Press, London.

Spear, P. (1965), *A History of India*, vol. 2. Penguin Books, Harmondsworth.

Spitzer, L. (1968), 'The mosquito and segregation in Sierra Leone', *Canadian Journal of African Studies*, 2, 1. pp. 49-61.

Srinivas, M.N. (1976), *Social Change in Modern India*, Cambridge University Press, Cambridge.

Steingraber, E. (1967), *Der Bungalow*, Gunther Neske, Bullingen.

Street-Porter, T. (1975), 'A chalet by the sea', *Observer Magazine*, 15 June.

Sumner, R. (1978), 'The tropical bungalow: the search for an indigenous Australian architecture', *Australian Journal of Art*, vol. 1, pp. 27-40.

Sumner, R. and Oliver, J. (1978), 'Early North Queensland housing as a response to environment', *Australian Geographer*, vol. 14, pp. 14-20.

Sutcliffe, A. (1981), *Towards the Planned City. Germany, Britain, the United States and France, 1780-1914*, Blackwell, Oxford.

Sutcliffe, G. (ed.) (1898), *The Principles and Practice of Modern House Construction*, Blackie, London.

Sunkel, O. and E.F. Fuenzalida (1979), 'Transnationalisation and its national consequences', in J.J. Villamil (ed.) (1979), *Transnational Capitalism and National Development*, Harvester Press, Brighton.

Swenarton, M. (1980), *Homes fit for Heroes*, Heinemann, London.

Tabb, W. and Sawers, L. (eds) (1978), *Marxism and the Metropolis*, Oxford University Press, New York.

Tandon, P. (1961), *Punjabi Century, 1857-1947*, Chatto & Windus, London.

Tanner, H. and Cox. P. (1975), *Restoring Old Australian Houses and Buildings*, Macmillan of Australia.

Tarapor, M. (1981), 'Art education in Imperial India: The Indian Schools of Art', Paper presented to the Seventh European Conference on South Asian Studies, SOAS, University of London.

Taylor, N. (1973), *The Village in the City*, Maurice Temple Smith, London.

Temple, R.C. (ed.) (1911), *The Diaries of Streynsham Master, 1675-80*, 2 vols, John Murray, London.

Tennant, W. (1803-4), *Indian Recreations; consisting chiefly of structures of the domestic and rural economy of the Mahomedans and Hindoos*, 2 vols, C. Stewart, Edinburgh.

Thomas, B. (1973), *Migration and Economic Growth*, Cambridge University Press, Cambridge.

Thompson, F.M.L. (1963), *English Landed Society in the Nineteenth Century*, Routledge & Kegan Paul, London.

Thompson, F.M.L. (ed.) (1982), *The Rise of Suburbia*, Leicester University Press.

Thompson, L.D. (1912), 'The Rampant Craze for the Bungle-Oh', *Country Life in America*, vol. 22, no. 6, p. 20-1.

Thompson, S. (1860), *Health Resorts and How to Profit from Them*, Warner, London.

Thompson, W.H. (1930), *Cornwall. Survey of its coast, etc. for CPRE*, University of London Press, London.

Thorne, D.C. (1972), *Suburbia*, MacGibbon & Kee, London.

Tobin, G.A. (1876), 'Suburbanisation and the development of motor transportation' in Schwartz, B., pp. 95-111.

Trajer, J. (1980), *The People's Chronology*, Heinemann, London.

Trevelyan, G. (1894), *Cawnpore*, Macmillan, London.

Turner, J.F.C. (1976), *Housing by People*, Marion Boyars, London.

Turner, L. and Ash, J. (1975), *The Golden Hordes. International Tourism and the Pleasure Periphery*, Constable, London.

Turner, V. (ed.) (1971), *Colonialism in Africa, 1870-1960*, vol. 3, Cambridge University Press, Cambridge.

Vant, S. (1929), *Bungalows, Pavilions and Cottages. How to Build and Adapt Them*, Frederick Warne, London.

Villamil, J.J. (ed.), (1979), *Transnational Capitalism and National Development*. Harvester Press, Sussex.

Wade, R.C. (1969), 'Introduction' to Schmitt, (1969), pp. vii-x.

Wagner, G. (1956), *The Bantu of North Kavironds*, Oxford University Press, London, 2 vols.

Walker, R.A. (1978), 'The transformation of urban structure in the nineteenth century and the beginnings of suburbanisation' in Cox, K. (ed.) (1978), pp. 165-212.

Walker, R.A. (1981), 'A theory of suburbanisation: capitalism and the construction of urban space in the United States' in Dear, M. and Scott, A.J. (eds.) (1981), pp. 383-430.

Wallerstein, I. (1974), *The Modern World System*, Academic Press, London & New York.

Wallerstein, I. (1976), 'The three stages of African involvement in the world economy' in Gutkind, P.C.W. and Wallerstein, I. (eds), *The Political Economy of Contemporary Africa*, Sage, London, pp. 30-52.

Wallerstein, I. (1979), *The Capitalist World-Economy*, Cambridge University Press, Cambridge.

Walton, J. and Massotti, L.H. (eds), (1976), *The City in Comparative Perspective. Cross-national Research and New Directions in Theory*, Sage, London.

Walton, J. (1976), 'Political economy of world urban systems: directions for comparative research', in Walton and Massotti (1976), pp. 301-13.

Walton, J. (1979), 'Urban political economy', *Comparative Urban Research*, vol. 7, no. 1.

Walton, J. and Portes, A. (1981), *Labour, Class and the International System*, Academic Press, London.

Walton, J.K. (1983), *The English Seaside Resort. A Social History, 1750-1914*, Leicester University Press.

Walvin, J. (1977), *Beside the Sea*, Allen Lane, London.

Ward, C. (1976), *Housing. An Anarchist Approach*, Freedom Press, London.

Ward, C. (1977), 'Lost freedoms in housing,' *New Society*, 12 May, pp. 271-4.

Ward, C. (1980), 'The Essex plotlands', Fourteenth Burrows Lecture, University of Essex, February. Typescript.

Weber, A.F. (1899), *The Growth of Cities in the Nineteenth Century*, reprinted Cornell University Press, New York.

Weaver, L. (1926), *Cottages. Their Planning, Design and Materials*, Country Life, London.

West Pakistan, Government of (1956), *Design of 'A' Class Bungalows and Houses for Satellite Towns*, Punjab Public Works Department, Government Printing, Lahore.

Whiffen, M. (1969), *American Architecture since 1780*, MIT Press, Cambridge, Mass.

White, C.E. (1923), *The Bungalow Book*, Macmillan, New York.

White, P. (1980), 'Urban planning in Britain and the Soviet Union', *Town Planning Review*, vol. 51, no. 2, pp. 211-26.

White, R.B. (1965), *Prefabrication. A History of its Development in Britain*, HMSO, London.

Whyman, J. (1970), 'Kentish resorts before 1900', University of Kent, Department of History, mimeo.

Williams, E. (1944), *Capitalism and Slavery*, University of North Carolina Press, Chapel Hill.

Williams, G. (ed.) (1976), *Nigeria. Economy and Society*, Tavistock, London.

Williams, R. (1973), *The Country and the City*, Chatto & Windus, London.

Williams, R. (1976), *Keywords*, Fontana, London.

Williams-Ellis, C. (ed.) (1928), *England and the Octopus*, G. Bles, London.

Williams-Ellis, C. (ed.) (1938), *Britain and the Beast*, Readers' Union, London.

Williamson, T. (1810), *The East India Vade Mecum*, 2 vols, Black, Parry, London.

Willmott, P. (1982), 'Support for suburbia', *Times Higher Education Supplement*, 12 March, p. 13.

Wilson, E. (1876), *Healthy Skin*, J. Churchill, London.

Wilson, H.L. (1910), *The Bungalow Book. A short sketch of the evolution of the bungalow from its primitive crudeness to its present state of artistic beauty and cozy convenience, etc.*, Wilson, Chicago.

Winter, R. (1975), 'The Arts and Crafts as a Social Movement', *Record* of the Art Museum, Princeton Universtiy, vol. 34, no. 2, pp. 36-40.

Winter, R. (1980), *The California Bungalow*, Hennessey & Ingalls, Los Angeles.

Wolf, R. (1956), 'Recreational land use in Ontario', PhD thesis, University of Toronto.

Woodruff, P. (1965), *The Men who Ruled India*, 2 vols, Jonathan Cape, London.

Woodruff, W. (1973), 'The emergence of an international economy, 1700-1914', in C.M. Cipolla (ed.), *The Fontana Economic History of Europe*, Fontana, London, pp. 656-737.

World Bank (1981), *World Development Report, 1981*, World Bank, Washington, D.C.

Wright, G.W. (1980), *Moralism and the Model Home. Domestic Architecture and Culture Conflict in Chicago, 1873-1913*, University of Chicago Press.

Wright, G.W. (1981), *Building the Dream. A Social History of Housing in America*, Pantheon, New York, esp. ch. 9, 'The progressive housewife and the bungalow'.

Wright, H. Myles (ed.) (1948), *The Planners' Notebook*, Architectural Press, London.

Wrightson, P. (1965), *The Small English House*, Catalogue 5, Weinreb, London.

Wrightson, P. (ed), (1973), *The English Picturesque Villa and Cottage, 1760-1860*, Indianapolis Museum of Art, Indianapolis.

Yoho, J. (1913), *The Craftsman Bungalow Book*, Puget Sound News, Seattle.

Yule, H. and Burnell, A.C. (1903), *Hobson-Jobson. A Glossary of Colloquial Anglo-Indian Words and Phrases*, John Murray, London.

Name index

Subject index